WHEN SCOTLAND
WAS JEWISH

WHEN SCOTLAND WAS JEWISH

DNA Evidence, Archeology, Analysis of
Migrations, and Public and Family Records
Show Twelfth Century Semitic Roots

Elizabeth Caldwell Hirschman
and Donald N. Yates

McFarland & Company, Inc., Publishers
Jefferson, North Carolina, and London

The present work is a reprint of the illustrated case bound edition of When Scotland Was Jewish: DNA Evidence, Archeology, Analysis of Migrations, and Public and Family Records Show Twelfth Century Semitic Roots, *first published in 2007 by McFarland.*

LIBRARY OF CONGRESS CATALOGUING-IN-PUBLICATION DATA

Hirschman, Elizabeth Caldwell, 1949–
When Scotland was Jewish : DNA evidence, archeology, analysis of migrations, and public and family records show twelfth century Semitic roots / Elizabeth Caldwell Hirschman and Donald N. Yates.
p.   cm.
Includes bibliographical references and index.

ISBN-978-0-7864-7709-8
softcover : acid free paper ∞

1. Jews—Scotland—History.   2. Jews—Scotland—Genealogy.   3. Scotland—History.
4. Scots—History.   5. Scots—Genealogy.   I. Title.   II. Yates, Donald N.
DS135.E5H57   2013   941.1'004924—dc22   2007006397

BRITISH LIBRARY CATALOGUING DATA ARE AVAILABLE

On the cover: Scotland Highlands © 2013 Photodisc

Manufactured in the United States of America

McFarland & Company, Inc., Publishers
Box 611, Jefferson, North Carolina 28640
www.mcfarlandpub.com

Contents

Preface

All research inquiries worthy of the name are voyages of discovery. Initial ventures set sail for terra incognito, while those which follow usually must be content to map more precisely the exact dimensions of the intellectual locale, noting minute details of mental flora, fauna, minerals and climate. Along these latter explorations exacting measurements are taken, objects and phenomena carefully categorized and labels affixed according to the earlier theoretical structures already in place. Gradually an imposing edifice of agreed-upon understanding is constructed; overlaying topographical interpretations become concretized into dogma and no one bothers to re-examine the underlying structure itself.

Very commonly, these accreted Received Views are zealously guarded by their creators, because they serve important social, political and ideological agendas. Such theoretical edifices have become naturalized features of the cultural landscape and serve to support and perpetuate the prevailing world-view. To challenge this knowledge structure, in whole or in part, is seen as a threat to the larger ideological narrative of "This is the way the world is" in which it is embedded. Received views, therefore, are defended vigorously and those challenging them do so with full awareness that they will likely be attacked by those stakeholders vested in maintaining the status quo.

The present work, brazenly titled *When Scotland Was Jewish*, is a privateering journey into heavily traveled waters. We propose that much of the traditional historical account of Scotland rests on fundamental interpretive errors. Further, we believe that these errors have been perpetuated in order to manufacture and maintain an origin story for Scotland that affirms its identity as a Celtic, Christian society. While pursuing Scottish nationalism is likely a noble goal, the equation of Scotland with Celtic culture in the popular (and academic) imagination has obfuscated, indeed buried, a more accurate and profound understanding of its history.

As the title suggests, we believe that much of Scotland's history and culture from the 1100s forward is Jewish. We believe that much of her population, including several national heroes, villains, rulers, nobles, traders, merchants, bishops, guild members, burgesses, and ministers were of Jewish decent. We describe how the ancestors of these persons originated

1

in France and Spain and then made their way to Scotland's shores, moors, burgs and castles from the reign of Malcolm Canmore to the after-throes of the Spanish Inquisition.

We anticipate that our claims will be vigorously disputed, especially by those who hold most dear the notion of Scotland as a Celtic heartland. We expect that anti–Semites will be incensed that we have dared to co-opt one of the principal archetypes of WASP iconography and graft it to Judaism. We expect also that Jews and philo–Semites will be bemused and confused — does this mean that they should stop by to reconnoiter Edinburgh on their next trip to Jerusalem? We hope that Muslims will be pleased to learn that we have also identified remnants of Islamic culture in Scotland.

Our research proposals, as unlikely as they may seem, are founded upon documentation available to scholars for centuries—census records, archeological artifacts, castle carvings, cemetery inscriptions, religious seals, coinage, burgess and guild member rolls, noble genealogies, family crests, geographic place names and oil portraits. Indeed, the blatancy and bulk of the evidence was so overwhelming that we were amazed no one had presented the thesis before we did.

How — or perhaps why — were surnames such as Izatt, Hyatt, Abell, Oliphant, Elphinstone, Isaac, Sharon, Lyon, Mamluke and Yuell not recognized as Judaic and Islamic by prior investigators? How could the presence of the Tetragrammaton — emblazoned on the title page of a Glasgow psalter dating from 1623 — be overlooked for almost 400 years? Why did no one question the presence of Islamic crescents and stars engraved throughout Fyvie Castle? Why was the presence of Stars of David on Scottish coins dating from the 1200s not commented upon previously? Did the fact that the Marquis of Argylle's castle is located in the village of Succoth (a major Jewish holiday) not seem odd to prior historians? Were not other onlookers puzzled by the dark, Semitic and Mediterranean appearances of the royal Stewart family — especially the Earl of Moray, James Stewart — or of John Knox, Archibald Campbell or Allen Ramsey as their portraits hung in the National Portrait Gallery of Scotland? Put bluntly, why were these marked inconsistencies with a presumed Celtic past not interrogated forcefully, or indeed at all?

Despite our drawing attention to these uncomfortable pieces of the historical record, however, we knew that advocates of the traditional story of Scotland would remain unconvinced. Thus, we also made use of an evidentiary source not available to prior scholars: DNA testing. Beginning in 1998 commercial testing of paternal and maternal DNA haplotypes became publicly available. In 2000, we availed ourselves of this new technology and began examining the lineages of some of the major "clans" in Scotland which we believed, based on historical evidence, were of Jewish descent. As is discussed in detail in the present work, all of the lines we examined do show evidence of Mediterranean origins and do have matches to present-day practicing Jews. Further, independent DNA testing conducted by other researchers on Scottish populations has confirmed the presence of Mediterranean and Middle Eastern genes in Scotland's population.

It is our great hope that readers will embark on this journey with an open mind and a willingness to entertain the possibility that Scotland's origins may indeed require revision. We believe that you will find, as we did, that there is ample evidence of a strong Jewish presence in Scotland and that you will never again view Scotland — her people or her history — as you once did.

Chapter 1

The Origins of Scotland

Scotland today is a country smaller than the state of South Carolina, with about 5 million inhabitants, two-thirds of whom live in Edinburgh, Glasgow, Dundee, Aberdeen, Inverness and Stirling, its Six Cities. Half the size of England, it has a higher standard of literacy and education, and as many urban centers and universities, as its southern neighbor. Scotland is located on the same northern latitude as Labrador, Norway and Moscow; the average summer temperature registers a brisk 57 degrees. It has been said, "There are two seasons in Scotland, June and winter."

Although Scotland is home to one of the oldest continuous kingdoms and parliaments in existence, its political standing as a part of the United Kingdom remains ambiguous. "The sense of national identity seems to have emerged much earlier here than elsewhere in Europe," according to a leading authority (Cunliffe 2001, p. 546). The national tourism board captures this distinction very delicately when it says that Scotland's civic culture and nationhood are "not readily defined, but readily identifiable." So the question arises of why the influence of this rather small, inclement and remote nation should loom so large.

Significantly, the pursuit of its native history was long prohibited in Scotland. Elitist English authorities excluded Scottish history from the national curriculum as a matter of educational policy. In 1949, Lord Cooper complained to the Scottish Historical Society that it was possible for a Scottish student to take a degree in history *without any knowledge of Scottish history.* "There was a subject called British History," he said, "which proved on examination to be English history with occasional side glances at Scotland through English spectacles whenever Scotland crossed England's path" (L. Kennedy 1995, pp. 7–8).[1]

If the modern history of Scotland is unsettled, there is even less agreement about the medieval period that preceded it. As one American historian comments, "Scottish history suffers from a profusion of very general surveys, a multitude of specialized studies and monographs, and not enough good books in between" (Herman 2001, p. 431). This appraisal applies with particular aptness to the early period of Scottish history, where both specialists and generalists find it difficult to come to terms with the emergence of

Modern Scotland and its major cities. Map by Donald N. Yates.

Scotland against the backdrop of European history. The Stewart dynasty remains particularly mystifying. Until the appearance of an "official" genealogical compilation in the 1990s (and some would say even after it), the origins of the Scottish royal family were simply not known.

The authors of an *Encyclopaedia Britannica* article on Scotland (1911 edition) suggest that the historical causes which kept England and Scotland separate for 700 years were mainly racial, though they then somewhat contradictorily go on to state that "from a very early period, the majority of the people of Scotland were, if not purely English by blood, anglicized in language and, to a great extent, in institutions." More riddles occur as we delve into Scotland's earlier periods of development:

> In A.D. 78–82 Agricola, carrying the Eagles of Rome beyond the line of the historical border, encountered tribes and confederations of tribes which, *probably* [emphasis added], spoke ... varieties of the Celtic language. That the language had been imposed, in a remote age, by Celtic-speaking invaders, on a prior non–Celtic speaking population, is probable enough, but is not demonstrated. There exist in Scotland a few inscriptions on stones, in Ogam, which yield *no sense in any known Indo-European language*. There are also traces of the persistence of descent in the female line, especially in the case of the Pictish royal family, but such survivals of savage institutions, or such a modification of male descent for the purpose of ensuring the purity of the royal blood, yield no firm ground for a decision as to whether the Picts were Aryans or non–Aryans.

The authors conclude that it is "unnecessary here to discuss the Pictish problem," about which, as we shall see, no satisfactory solution has gained acceptance even to this day.[2]

Curiously, we also are informed that European scholarship, centered around the revival of letters in the reign of Charlemagne (768–814), was, in large part, inspired by an international elite of Irish and Scottish scholars (Moss 1998, pp. 249–50, 288; Laistner 1957). It was Irish and Scottish monks who rescued the flame of civilization from the collapse of Rome and carried arts and sciences to the Continent during the Dark Ages. The Celtic Church was responsible for founding Luxeuil, Fontenelle and Corbey in France; Bobbio and Susa in Italy; St. Gall, Fulda, Salzburg and Würzburg in Germany, and most of the other seats of learning that, in turn, generated the efflorescence of culture of the Carolingian age and, later, the twelfth-century renaissance, with its "discovery of the individual" (Southern 1961; Haskins 1957). The Scottish mathematician Michael Scot (? 1175–1234) was regarded as the most brilliant mind of his era. He studied philosophy and science at Oxford, Paris, Bologna and Rome, acquired knowledge of Arabic in Spain and Italy, and produced a fresh translation and commentary on the philosophy of Aristotle, as well as influential works on science and medicine (J. W. Brown 1897). His countryman John Duns Scotus, who died in 1308, was the founder and leader of the famous Scotist School (T. Williams 2003). Who were these Scottish culture-bearers?

Into this scholarly and historical breach arrive two researchers with purportedly Scottish ancestry and a thesis that seems, on the face of it, absurd: Scotland was Jewish. This assertion not only flies in the face of "received" history (what little of it there is), but also assaults two longstanding cultural stereotypes of what Scots are like and what Jews are like. In the popular imagination, Scots are large, red- or blond-haired persons of fierce demeanor, who wear plaid wool kilts, brandish swords and war axes, drink copious amounts of ale and whiskey, and eagerly seek out forums in which to exhibit their prowess as warriors. They are unschooled, wild marauders, loyal to clan, kith, and kin.

Jews, on the other hand, are seen commonly as originating in *shtetls* in Eastern

Europe, timid, bookish, dark-haired, clad in dark apparel, and usually hunkered down over ancient Hebrew manuscripts. Except for the juxtaposition of, let us say, Eskimos and Parisians, it is hard to conjure up two more opposite ethnic stereotypes.[3]

So why are we proposing that many of Scotland's people were Jewish? For the simple reason that is true. In the chapters that follow, we present evidence from several empirical sources—DNA, public records, anthropological observations, architecture, archeological excavations, family and clan genealogical records, censuses, cemetery inscriptions, burgess and guild membership rolls, ethnographic reports, and synagogue membership rolls. These document the seemingly incredible claim that Scotland was, and remains, a country populated largely by persons of Jewish descent.

The evidence presented does not suggest some ancient Jewish visitation based on a "lost tribes" theory, in other words, that a Jewish tribe dispersed from Judea/Palestine in antiquity and somehow wandered its way to Scotland, morphing over time into a population of Gaelic warriors. No; our argument is grounded upon documented historical migrations into Scotland from various European countries, primarily France, the Low Countries, Hungary, and Germany. These migrants, we propose, were persons of Jewish ethnicity whose descendants now comprise the majority of the present population of Scotland. Further, we also argue that the greater part of the estimated 4 million Scots and Scots-Irish who immigrated to the New World were drawn from this same ethnic ancestry.

The Melungeons

Our story begins with an ethnic group to which both authors belong. The Melungeons are a people who have been dwelling in the Appalachian Mountains of the southeastern United States for between 300 and 500 years. Their origins have been the subject of intense speculation for at least three centuries (Ball 1984; Bible 1975; Elder 1999; Gallegos 1997, 1998; Mira 1998).[4] Typically, they are described as having dark skin, black or dark-brown straight hair, brown or blue eyes and European features (Ball 1984; Bible 1975). A popular culture book written by a self-identifying Melungeon (N. B. Kennedy 1996) renewed interest in investigation of the group's origins and stimulated an abundance of scholarly research. A detailed biogenetics study undertaken by the present authors supported what Kennedy had earlier proposed: The Melungeons were, in large part, a Sephardic Jewish and Moorish community that began as early as 1540 with the De Soto Expedition to the southeastern United States (Hirschman 2005). The composition of this community was augmented over the intervening centuries by incoming Sephardic Jews and Moors who found refuge in such way stations as the Low Countries, Germany, France, Italy, Greece, and England after fleeing the Iberian Peninsula due to religious persecution (Hirschman 2005).

One of the factors delaying accurate ethnic identification of Melungeons was that several carried Scottish or Scots-Irish surnames, such as Caldwell and Kennedy, and had immigrated to the American colonies from Scotland or Northern Ireland during the 1600s and 1700s. Since the conventional view was that there were extremely few Jews living in either Scotland or Ireland prior to the early 1800s (Smout 1998), this seemed to be an anomaly. Had their original surnames been altered or Anglicized to help the Melungeons blend in with surrounding Scots-Irish and English settlers? This was what many Melungeons, as well as Melungeon researchers, believed (e.g., Elder 1999).

We arrived at an alternative, though seemingly preposterous, hypothesis: What if the Scots-Irish, Scottish and English surnames carried by Melungeons had *not* been altered? What if their ancestral surnames really *were* Caldwell and Kennedy and Fraser and Bruce and Campbell and Skene? What if these purportedly Scottish and Scots-Irish and English settlers were *technically* from those countries of origin, but were *ethnically* of Sephardic Jewish and Moorish ancestry?[5] Eliyahu Skean was a "Scots-Irish" Appalachian pioneer, whose family is intertwined multiply with others of Melungeon background in eastern Kentucky. His Semitic features were a point of pride with Skean, according to children and grandchildren, and he fondly recounted memories of the family's Scottish homeland and clan.

Given limited funds, we decided to initiate a series of tests on our thesis by obtaining Y-chromosome DNA samples from (1) persons of known Melungeon roots in our own ancestry (who may or may not have actually emigrated from Scotland) and (2) nine Scottish clans whose surnames are found among Melungeon populations. To do this, we contacted a set of Melungeon relatives and posted requests on Internet genealogical forums for male persons in a direct line of patrilineal descent from the nine Scottish clans of interest. These were Alexander (a sept, or sub-clan, associated with MacAlister and MacDonald), Bruce, Campbell, Douglas, Forbes, Fraser, Gordon, Leslie, and Stewart/Stuart. We asked for and received genealogical documentation and selected two donors from each clan.

The results stunned us. In every case where exact 12-marker matches could be obtained for the individual, the DNA locus was found to be centered in Spain and Portugal. Further, some of the Melungeon and Scottish clan donors had exact matches to living Jews; and *all* of the donors had one-off or two-off matches to present-day Jews. We became concerned that our speculations might actually be correct. Yet if it were, why is Scotland not currently viewed as a country with a significant Jewish patrimony? How could so many persons of ethnically Jewish descent be living there and no one, including them, be aware of it?

The answers to these enigmas, put very simply, appear to be that, first, early Jews who did live in Scotland practiced an underground or secret form of their religion (called Crypto-Judaism); second, a minority of the descendants of these early Crypto-Jews *did* in some cases revert to the open practice of their faith upon arriving in the American colonies; and third, the majority of the descendants of these Jews are now unaware of their ancestors' religious practices, because their faith was so well dissembled, and because of conversion to Protestantism and assimilation over the intervening centuries.

Over the course of this book, we chart a possible path of development for these events. We also provide documentation suggesting that perhaps the majority of the Scots people, especially those in the southwest and northeast of Scotland, are of Sephardic Jewish descent. And we argue that many of these same Scots today continue to practice a "Reform" type of Judaism. It is called Presbyterianism.

A Major Revision of Scots History

Most Americans, and certainly most Scots, probably believe they know "a lot" about the history of Scotland. But as the author of the recent book *In Bed with an Elephant* notes, "the worst features of anglicization were the exclusion of Scottish history and literature in the school syllabuses" (L. Kennedy 1995, p. 7). In the absence of official versions written and approved by Scots, most of us draw our notions of Scottish history from motion pictures like *Braveheart* and *Rob Roy*— never mind that the former may have been a "a wildly crude Hollywood distortion of the Wallace story" (Ascherson 2002, p. 41) and the latter is based on the work of Sir Walter Scott, the romantic inventor of the historical novel and (largely discredited) promoter of the "great Highland revival" of the early 1800s (Herman 2001, pp. 291–319).

Seven famous Scotsmen are pictured here: Presbyterian reformer John Knox; scholar George Buchanan; Marquis of Argyle Archibald Campbell; the Earl of Ancram, Robert Kerr; poet Allen Ramsay; Earl of Southesk, James Carnegie; and physician William Gordon. As cursory inspection will affirm, none of these prominent Scotsmen looks typically Scottish; in fact, they appear rather dark and Semitic; yet, here they are — Scottish aristocrats. The Scottish royal Stewarts were equally dark and Semitic in appearance. Of Charles II's dusky appearance his mother, Queen Henrietta Maria, "had been half mortified, writing after her confinement that the child was so dark she was ashamed of him ... he was quickly dubbed the 'Black Boy.'" Enemies made out that he was a "black bastard" begotten by a "black Scotsman" (MacLeod 1999, p. 219).

This woodcarving of Presbyterian reformer John Knox (1512–1572) depicts him as having a full beard, covered head and Semitic facial features. We will propose that Knox was the son or grandson of Sephardic Jewish émigrés to Scotland. Courtesy Scottish National Portrait Gallery.

We propose that many, perhaps most, present-day Scots are descended from the same types of ancestors who produced these personages. Further, we suggest that their forbears were Mediterranean Jews from France, Spain, and Portugal. If we are to be believed, however, we must provide much sounder documentation than a series of portraits. So we turn now to a discussion of some important facts missing from most people's knowledge of Scottish history. We will review five well-known books. As we shall show, Scotland was not, and is not, predominantly Celtic, nor is its ethnic history even known with accuracy.

The Lords of the Isles, Ronald Williams (1984/1997)

In his historical narrative of Clan Donald and the early kingdom of the Scots, Williams (1997) recounts what is termed the *origin myth* of the Dalriadic settlers of Scotland and Ireland. Remarkably, this story does not begin in northern or western Europe, but rather tells about a people who came from Scythia, east of the Baltic Sea in Central Asia, and migrated through what is now northern

This portrait of George Buchanan (1506–1582) depicts him as having Semitic features, a beard and head covering. Buschanan was a renowned classical scholar and historian. Courtesy Scottish National Portrait Gallery.

Greece (Thrace), northern Africa (Egypt), Spain, and Gothland (present-day Germany, the Low Countries, and England) before finally reaching their "Island of Destiny," which we now call Ireland. The leader of this migrating people, who called themselves Gaels, was first Goidal Glas, and later Miled. According to legend, while in Spain, Miled married an Egyptian princess, Scota, who brought with her to Ireland a black marble rock, the Stone of Destiny, upon which were carved runes or hieroglyphics.

Williams then goes on to dismiss this romantic tale and firmly locate the origin of the Gaels/Celts near the Danube River in central Europe, although he claims that the Celts then expanded their domain from that center eastward to the Baltic and southward to Italy and Spain. (Thus, the romantic origin myth and Williams's account are not actually so far apart geographically.) What Williams seems to want to dismiss, perhaps unconsciously, is the notion that the early Scots and Irish settlers may have been something other than "pure" western European, that is, fair haired, blue-eyed, and light skinned. There were to be no Spaniards, Italians, Greeks, or North Africans included among the noble race claiming Ireland and Scotland. This subtle yet pervasive effort at whitewashing Scottish history has colored (or more properly, "uncolored," as it were) a more valid and inclusive accounting of its origins. For our present purposes, however, we do not care whether Queen Scota and her Stone of Destiny from Egypt and Spain really existed.[6] That is not the origin story that we will be putting forward.

Williams's discussion of Scottish history continues through the gradual giving way of pagan Druidic ritual to the arrival of St. Columba (560 C.E.?) and the establishment of the Celtic Church. Several points need to be clarified here, since we will return to them in the reviews of other historians' work. First, the Scottish (and Irish) churches at this time were *not* directed by, or even in contact with, the Catholic pontiff in Rome. They were not Roman Catholic. They may not even have been fully Christian, but syncretistic, like many early medieval religions. That modern observers look back after a lapse of 1,500 years and identify the early Scottish church as "Roman Catholic" during the era following 500 C.E. is false, tendentious, and very misleading. Indeed, except for the existence of Christian artifacts such as the Book of Kells and carved Celtic crosses, there is little evidence to suggest a strong early Christian presence in Scotland. As we will investigate later, the so-called Scottish saints (e.g., St. Machar of Aberdeen) are not even proven to be Christian per se. Contemporaries describe them as unspecified "holy men" or "religious teachers." No written accounts of their teachings or religious doctrines survive. It was only centuries later that they were labeled as Christian.

According to Williams, "the Celtic Church of St. Columba ... developed a number of independent characteristics of its own. It boasted no central authority and its leaders were the individual 'saints' and abbots who founded monastic communities and sanctuaries after the pattern of Iona. Many clergy retained a secular mode of life and fathered sons who succeeded them.... The Celtic Church also had its fanatics—a sect called the Culdees[7] who referred to themselves as 'the friends of God' and chose to live apart as 'anchorites'" (pp. 50–51).

Archibald Campbell (1598–1661) was 8th Earl and 1st Marquis of Argyll. Clan Campbell DNA samples indicate an Iberian origin for this family. Campbell's facial features and headcovering appear distinctly Jewish. Campbell was a strong supporter of the Protestant Reformation. Courtesy Scottish National Portrait Gallery.

Williams describes the subsequent arrival from Hungary of Queen Margaret, the wife of Scots king Malcolm Canmore, in the mid–1000s. And now something very important happens for our thesis.

> [Margaret's] story ... had its beginning in the earlier dynastic wars of England. On the death of Edmund Ironside in 1016, his two sons ... fled to Sweden and from thence to Hungary, where the elder, Edward, married Agota, a daughter of King Stephen of Hungary.... Edward and Agota had three children — Edgar, Margaret, and Christina. Years later, Edward the Confessor [king of England] ... sent Ailred, Bishop of York, to fetch back the refugees from Hungary.
>
> Edgar and his sisters ... in 1068 escaped to Scotland where Margaret became the second wife of Malcolm Canmore. A deeply pious lady, she found Scottish society crude and uncivilised, and conceived a mission to convert the Scots from their northern barbarism and Celtic custom.... [Malcolm Canmore] forsook Gaelic for her language, substituted wine for mead, and welcomed to his court the strangers of her choice. These included a number of Hungarians who had accompanied the family to Britain and to whom Malcolm now gave lands in Scotland.... After the conquest, the influx of foreigners was further augmented by Norman adventurers ... not least among them a hopeful Breton called Walter Fitzalan ... who later became Steward of Scotland and ancestor of the Stewart Kings....
>
> Donald Bane [ca. 1033–1099] was the last Celtic [monarch] worthy of the name. Those who followed, though by blood half–Celt, were by disposition Anglo-Norman, and the gradual Normanisation of Scotland proceeded through successive reigns. The now familiar names emerged — de Bruce, Soulis, de Morville, Cunningham, Hay, Mowbray, Sinclair, Menzies, Fraser, Grant — and others of Norman or Breton origin.
>
> By the middle of the ninth century, the Hebrides and the coastlands of ancient Dalriada had been effectively lost [by the Celts] to the emerging kingdom of central Scotland, [and] another, more terrible race of incomers had reached the Isles and now dominated the Celtic Sea. The western Gaels were engulfed by the Viking tide from Scandinavia [pp. 60–61].

Thus perished the Celtic substratum of Scotland: With Vikings to the north, Hungarians and French to the south, the Celtic Gaels were swept away.

Williams provides us with some information on what the new Scottish population looked like after 1100 C.E. One Viking invader, Thorfinn II the Black (died ca. 1060), was reputed to be

Robert Kerr (1578–1654), the First Earl of Ancram. Note his head covering and facial physiognomy. Courtesy Scottish National Portrait Gallery.

extremely large and tall, "ugly of aspect, black-haired, sharp featured and somewhat tawny" (p. 102). Except for his enormous size, Thorfinn is not exactly the handsome, blonde Viking warrior one might envisage.

Two additional points made by Williams require attention. The first concerns the Beatons,[8] a hereditary family of medical doctors (p. 216). We learn that they were the traditional physicians to the Lord of the Isles. The family had come to the Isles from Ireland in the rule of Angus Og (1299–1330) and were famous for their exceptional learning and knowledge. "They reportedly followed the teachings of Avicenna the Persian, whose canon was the basis of European medical practice for over five hundred years. In a period when it was becoming fashionable to think of the Islands as unlettered and barbaric, the Beatons possessed a copy of Avicenna's eleventh-century work long before it was translated into English, or faculties of medicine were established in the universities of Scotland and England. Members of the family also became seannachies (landed nobility) in Mull and the Outer Hebrides. Their library was known to include the earliest translation into any European language of an account of *The Fall of Troy*." Notably, the primary centers of medical science at that time were Persia and Iberia, countries ruled by Muslims and populated extensively by Jews. As will be discussed later, it is likely that Judeo-Islamic civilization was the origin of the Beaton family and its medical knowledge. Their presence in Scotland is an indication of important intellectual currents at work.

In this portrait, Allan Ramsay (1686–1758), the poet, is shown to have a Mediterranean complexion. He wears an orange silk turban and brown Middle-Eastern or Moroccan style coat and shirt. Courtesy Scottish National Portrait Gallery.

Second, Williams remarks that bagpipes—the musical instruments most associated in the popular imagination with Celts and Scotland—first gained popularity in Scotland at the outset of the 1500s. This was an age when Celtic culture was in eclipse, but it was a time that saw the mass expulsion of Jews and Moors from Spain due to the Spanish Inquisition. Significantly, the bagpipe originated in ancient Mesopotamia and Greece and was popular in Spain and southern France before it entered or re-entered

Ireland and Scotland. It is a Middle Eastern and Central Asian musical instrument, not one indigenous to the British Isles.[9]

The Canmores, Richard Oram (2002)

From Williams' account, we now turn to a shorter work by Oram (2002), focused on the Scottish ruling family of primary importance to our thesis. The Canmore Dynasty began in 1058 with the ascension of Malcolm Canmore to the Scots throne and lasted until the end of Alexander III's reign in 1286. The connections are depicted in Figure 1 on page 13.

Examining the genealogy in Figure 1 provides some indication of just how European and Mediterranean the Scottish royal family became. Malcolm and Margaret's son Alexander I not only carried a Greek given name previously unused by Scotland's nobility, but he also married Sybilla, the illegitimate daughter of England's King Henry I. Alexander's brother, David I, who ruled from 1124 to 1153, married a French noblewoman, Matilda de St. Liz (Senlis, a town in Normandy), granddaughter of William the Conqueror. This king's given name, David, was also previously unknown among the Scots lairds. In fact, he was only the second King David in world history—the first, of course, being King David of Jerusalem (ca. 1000 B.C.E.).[10] As we shall argue, this did not come about randomly, but resulted from the Scots royal family's belief that they did, in fact, descend from the Jewish King David. We will argue that the family *was* of Jewish patrilineal ancestry and faith, but of western (Sephardic), rather than Semitic and Middle Eastern, genetic descent.

Traveling farther down the

James Carnegie (1692–1750), the 5th Earl of Southesk, was a staunch Jacobite supporter of the Royal Stewart family. This caricature shows him to have an extremely prominent nose. Courtesy Scottish National Portrait Gallery.

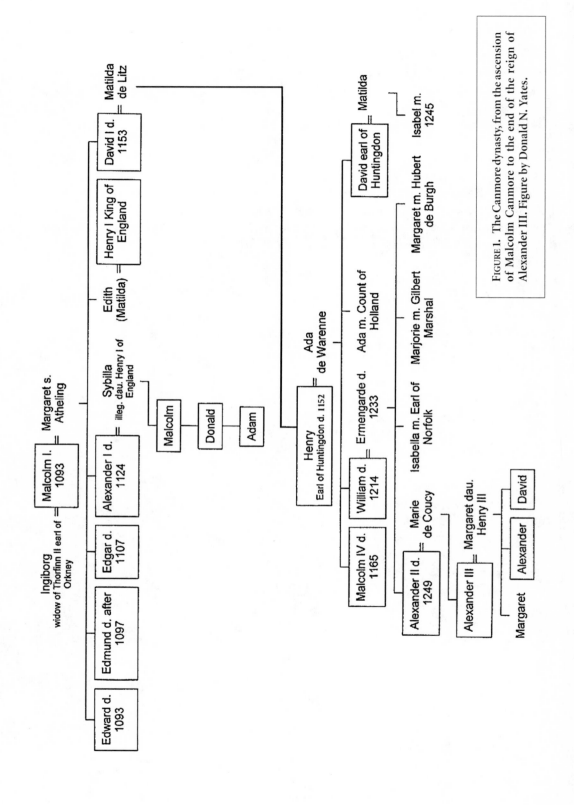

FIGURE 1. The Canmore dynasty, from the ascension of Malcolm Canmore to the end of the reign of Alexander III. Figure by Donald N. Yates.

Canmore genealogy, we find additional Flemish, Dutch, and French wives entering the royal household, along with Hebrew and Mediterranean names such as Ada, Isabel, and Yolande joining with the continued use of Alexander and David. The last descendant of King Alexander and Queen Sybilla was Adam, a rebel who died in 1186. Oram comments on the Judaic tenor of the latter Canmores:

> David projected an image of the king as lawgiver. Law codes attributed by tradition to David form the basis of medieval Scots law and the foundations of a system of sheriffdoms for the local administration of law were laid down by the king. But David was no remote figure.... Elred wrote of the king sitting at the door of his hall to receive petitions from the humblest of folk.... To an extent it was a cultivated image, to be seen most clearly in the portrayal of David in the initial letter of his grandson's great charter to Kelso Abbey. There sits David, long-haired and bearded, presented as Solomon alongside the youthful and beardless Malcolm IV....
>
> Although he continued to patronize the established [religious] orders, such as the Benedictines and Tironensians, and founded one further Augustinian monastery at Cambuskenneth, most of his favour was targeted towards the new and even more austere Cistercian monks.... In 1136 ... he brought a colony of Cistercians from Rievaulx in Yorkshire to Melrose in Tweeddale [p. 46].

As will be discussed subsequently, the Cistercian order in many ways appears to be modeled on Judaic religious precepts.[11] The entry of Jewish religious imagery into Scotland's culture is further indicated by the six-pointed Star of David marking the coinage of King Alexander III (1249–1286).

The Borders, Alistair Moffat (2002)

Moffat's work focuses on the part of southern Scotland lying directly above the English border. Because this part of the country was frequently a point of contention between England and Scotland, it was often marred by violence. Yet it also served as a haven for persons of marginalized status

William Gordon, physician at King's College, Aberdeen (1632–1640), was educated at Padua University. We propose that Gordon was of Sephardic Jewish descent. Courtesy of Aberdeen University.

seeking to escape persecution for religious or political reasons. Quick dashes from one side to the other could be made by those seeking to avoid arrest for any variety of offenses. And as Moffat notes, the area was also one that early on was well acquainted with the Mediterranean. In 687 C.E., monks at Lindisfarne raised up a shrine to one of their bishops, Cuthbert. To commemorate him, a special text of the four gospels was created:

> A gospel book of such richness was no small undertaking.... Eadfrith's palette for the illustrations sometimes traveled immense distances; lapis lazuli came from Afghanistan, indigo from the Mediterranean, kermes (carmine red) from North Africa and folium (pink) from the south of France.... Though the other famous gospels of the period from Kells and Durrow in Ireland are profoundly Celtic in their look, Lindisfarne is much more influenced by the Mediterranean; Roman lettering, Byzantine painting, and a Near-Eastern [Middle Eastern] style of decoration [p. 125].

Obviously, Scotland of the 600s was not an isolated outpost; it had trading ties across the Mediterranean and the Middle East.[12] There is strong archeological evidence for a lively Atlantic and Mediterranean trade in Scotland between the fall of Rome and birth of the Holy Roman Empire under Charlemagne, though historians are hard put to explain it. The annals of Iona, the Holy Island, are full of references to contact with Gaul. The widespread distribution of Mediterranean pottery from the fifth and sixth centuries throughout the British Isles is a puzzle. "It is not possible, from the archaeological evidence, to estimate the intensity and duration of this 'trade' with the Mediterranean," writes an expert on the pre-history of Europe. "The question is incapable of resolution." The earliest group of imports appears to have come from North Africa, the coasts of Turkey and Egypt, via Carthage, the Straits of Gibraltar and the Portuguese ports in the Tagus and Mondego estuaries (Cunliffe, pp. 477–79).

This connection was enhanced greatly by the entry from 1100 C.E. onward of traders, merchants, and nobles from France, Hungary, and the Low Countries during the reign of King David I. At Selkirk in southern Scotland, David granted lands to a group of French monks. Signing the charter were the following noblemen: "Robert De Bevis, Robert de Unfraville, Walter de Belebec, Robert de Painton, Cospatric brother of Dalfin, Hugh de Moreville, Pagano de Braiosa, Robert Corbet, Reginald de Muscamp, Walter de Lindsey, Robert de Burneville, Cospatric the Sheriff, Cospatric son of Aldeve, Uchtred son of Scot, Macchus, Colbanus, Gillemichael, Odardo Sheriff of Bamburgh, Lyulf son of Uchtred, Radulph the Englishman, Aimar the Gallovidian, Roger de Leceister and Adam the Chamberlain" (p. 147)—a mixed bag indeed!

Other noble families residing along the Borders at this time had also come from mainland Europe. They included the Avenels, de Soules, Riddells, Baliols, and the progenitor of the Stewart family. It was a nobility, as Moffat observes, that was multilingual, sophisticated, well traveled, and intensely endogamous. And additionally, we propose, of Jewish religious affiliation.

Although Scotland is often depicted as being a primitive and rural country during medieval times, this assessment rests on an inaccurate perception. As Moffat writes:

> It is highly likely that there was a market at Roxburgh [Scotland] for some considerable time before 1113.... What converted a local market ... into an international trading center was the dynamic trade in wool and hides. The stimulus for this change came from *Flanders* and

Northern Italy where cloth and leather goods began to be produced in industrial quantities for re-export as well as domestic consumption. What created this demand for raw wool and hides was not new technology, but the first effective deployment of merchant capital....

The sequence was simple. Merchants from the cities of Bruges, Ghent and elsewhere had sufficient capital to buy bulk quantities of wool and hides at the summer and autumn markets at Roxburgh, and the abbeys of Melrose and Kelso could guarantee that these raw materials would be available.... With 5% of the total Scottish wool clip..., the Cistercians at Melrose could act like a corporation and wield considerable power in the marketplace.... The Melrose monks were urbane and experienced negotiators with access to information on prices and conditions of trade in other wool-producing areas of Europe.... No one crossed the North Sea in an empty ship.... Cargoes from Europe included sugar, pepper, cumin, onions, garlic, currants, ginger, almonds, rice, basil, alum, dyestuffs, metal pans, cauldrons, locks, timber and iron.

Across the North Sea, back in Flanders and Northern Italy, merchants fed the wool into their cloth production network.... Production went on in hundreds of workshops in the towns and cities. Numbers employed could be very large and, for example, at Douai in the 13th century there were 150 merchant drapers each employing 100 people....

Fifteen religious houses, all of them producers of wool and hides, held properties in Berwick, and there the foreign merchants maintained places of business. These resembled the "factories" of English traders in colonial India, where a sort of diplomatic immunity was allowed, and where outsiders could live in communal safety. "The Red Hall" was the name of the Flemish trading center at Berwick and as many as 30 merchants operated out of it at one time. German merchants were to be found at "The White Hall," and in Roxburgh a place called "The Black Hall" is listed but no particular nationality attached. Perhaps all foreigners used it [pp. 169–71].

By 1212 C.E., Berwick's lucrative trade had moved into private hands. Provosts and registered guild burgesses regulated the commercial operations of the town, the guild hall being built on land purchased from one *Simon Maunsel* (p. 17). That same decade a man we have already mentioned, Michael the Scot, likely from Melrose, was at the University of Toledo in northern Spain translating Aristotelian manuscripts *written in Arabic into Latin*. Michael served as a multilingual translator in Sicily and Palermo, as well. In 1378, a master mason, John *Lewyn*, was hired to refurbish the walls of Roxburgh Castle. Around 1400, a Parisian master mason, Jean *Moreau* ("Moor"), was commissioned to enlarge Melrose Abbey (p. 224).

These trade patterns, capabilities, and names were most common to two ethnic groups at the time: Spanish Moors and Sephardic Jews. Not only did Islamic mercantilism far surpass that of western Europe and Christendom, but Jews were well represented in all branches of European business and industry, with the possible exception of agriculture and foodstuffs preparation. Jews and Muslims came to dominate such fields as banking, shipping, chemicals and pharmaceuticals, glass, silk and paper manufacture, the book trade, and jewelry and precious stones during this time period.

History of the Scottish People: 1560–1830, T.C. Smout (1969/1985)

Smout's encyclopedic account of Scotland focuses primarily on the post–Reformation period. Of interest to us, however, is his discussion of the reasons leading to the overthrow of Catholicism by Protestantism. Foremost among these was the remarkable corruption of the Roman Church in Scotland:

> From the middle of the fourteenth century onwards it [the Catholic Church] suffered from the increasing decay of its corporate spiritual life, as it did everywhere else in Europe. This was greatly accelerated in Scotland by the erosion of its own freedom: kings gained the right to nominate bishops and abbots and abused it by appointing their own bastards to high clerical office when they were still only children; nobles came to control monasteries and cathedrals, and took over church lands as though they were their own. By 1560 ... the church was very largely at the mercy of unspiritual laymen, its foundations corrupt and worldly, its parish churches empty and ruined, its bishops a byword for immorality, and its congregations often contemptuous of its services.
>
> But to this black generalization there were several bright exceptions. Throughout the fifteenth century there had been great clerics, like Bishop Wardlaw, who founded Scotland's first university at St. Andrews in 1410, Bishop Turnbull, who founded Glasgow University in 1451, and Bishop Elphinstone, who founded King's College, Aberdeen, in 1496 and was the first patron of printing in Scotland.

As will be described shortly, these three churchmen were likely of Jewish ancestry and governed parishes with largely crypto–Jewish populations. None of Scotland's "Big Three" universities ever required students to take a religious oath, a factor that rendered them attractive to Jews from as far away as South Carolina. Non-Christians were excluded from studying at Oxford or Cambridge, and most English and American universities of the period mandated an oath on the New Testament naming Jesus Christ (Collins 1990, p. 15). Smout continues his description:

> [T]he Scottish monasteries had by 1559 long since ceased to be vehicles for spirituality. They had become nothing more than property-owning corporations. Control over the property was frequently in the hands of laymen, or sometimes of secular clerics who by hook or by crook had secured the title of abbot or "commendator" (literally "protector") in order to divert the income of the monastic lands into their own pockets. The crown itself had been the worst offender in this respect. James V, for example ... had wrung permission from the Pope ... to appoint three baby sons, all illegitimate, to be titular abbots of Kelso and Melrose, priors of St. Andrews and Pittenweem, and abbot of Holyrood respectively; a fourth was later made prior of Coldingham and a fifth abbot of the Charterhouse....
>
> The nuns, though few in number, were more scandalous than the monks. They were normally too illiterate even to write their own names.... They were frequently so undisciplined that they no longer even bothered to live within the nunnery precincts.... If this was the state of monks, friars and nuns, what was to be expected of the secular clergy in the parishes? They took their tone from a hierarchy where appointments had for many years been made on purely political grounds.... James IV had set the pace by making his illegitimate son *Archbishop of St. Andrews* at the age of eleven [p. 50].

Smout then notes that the Protestant Reformation was embraced readily by the merchants, burgesses and educated members of Scottish society; he attributes this to the emphasis the new doctrine placed on a direct relationship to God. He alludes also to the presence of a "secret church" among this segment of the population:

> Protestant numbers snowballed.... By 1559 there was already an alternative church existing in many parts of Scotland, awaiting some revolutionary stroke to bring it to power. [Protestantism] succeeded by taking the right strategic bastions in society. It succeeded in the burghs, where ... the traditions of secrecy and co-operation among members of craft guilds and merchant guilds, and of co-operation between the burgesses of different towns acting in

their common interest, made towns the ideal environment to sustain a secret and cellular church organisation [p. 55].

Contrary to Smout's arguments, however, it would *not* have been in the *financial* or *political* interests of this very same group to support the overthrow of the prevailing, corrupt Catholic Church as a social institution. Indeed, it was these very people who were benefiting already from the Roman church as it was currently operating. What Smout overlooks, as do virtually all other observers, is that the crypto–Jewish society we propose was present in Scotland since 1100 had been strengthened enormously during the previous five decades by the arrival of thousands of *converso* Jews fleeing the Spanish Inquisition.[13] As we will argue in chapter 10, crypto–Jewish practice was now poised to transform itself into Protestantism.

Smout describes the robustness of the burgh-based Scots economy in the post–Reformation period. With each burgh acting as a self-governing unit, electing its own burgesses and monitoring apprenticeships for both merchants and craftsmen, Scotland became an active international trade center. And in each burgh, a small set of families governed the town both politically and financially. From Aberdeen, Scotland traded as far eastward as Russia, Poland and the Baltic, while from Glasgow and Edinburgh, she traded south and west to England, France, Spain, the Americas, and the Caribbean. Primary export products were wool, hides, fish, paper, coal, salt, and linen. And in each of these industries, specific families came to dominate the trade, often forming oligopolistic partnerships with family members residing in ports such as Bordeaux, Rouen, Cadiz, Lisbon, Warsaw, Rotterdam, London, Barbados, Danzig, Stockholm, Bergen, the Canary Islands, and Riga.

Judaic scholars have often pointed to the phenomenon of "Court Jews," figures primarily located in central Europe, serving kings and princes as bankers, tax collectors, and army provisioners, but it was not until the 1980s and '90s that historians began to revisit this subject and focus attention on the Jews who settled on the Atlantic seaboard (Cesarini 2004, pp. 1–11). The designation of "Port Jews" was born. In cities ranging from Trieste to Glasgow, from Salonika to Hamburg, the social type of the previously overlooked Sephardim of Spain and Portugal was thrown into high relief. Of them, we learn, for instance, that "they eschewed the traditional autonomous Jewish community and enjoyed improved legal status which permitted voluntary affiliation to the Jewish collectivity.... They questioned Jewish religious tradition, having been estranged from it for so long, and displayed a form of ethnic Jewish identity" (pp. 2–3). And: "The distinctive role of Sephardim as precursors [of the Enlightenment], who experienced emancipation as a gradual development, has been [relatively speaking] ignored" (p. 4).

The Scottish burgess system in many ways combined the roles of court Jews and port Jews. Smout describes it in the following terms:

In each burgh there was one basic division into burgesses and non-burgesses, and another within the burgess groups between merchants and craftsmen, organised into a merchant guild and craft guild respectively. To the burgesses alone belonged the privileges of being members of a burgh: the rest of the inhabitants were mere indwellers with no more right to elect the magistrates, to trade or to belong to a craft than a country bumpkin from the landward parts.

A man could become a burgess in several ways: normally he had to pay some money to the corporation and to prove that his name was upon the apprenticeship books of the town.

In the sixteenth and seventeenth centuries most new burgesses were either the sons or the sons-in-law of existing burgesses. Sons could follow their fathers paying a smaller entry fine and serving a shorter apprenticeship than strangers. Those who married the daughter of a burgess ... gained the same concession: it was a way of making certain that the daughters of merchants and craftsmen were at a premium in the marriage market.

Others, not so lucky in birth or love, had to pay a slightly higher entry-fee and wait for a period after they had finished their apprenticeship.... Strangers and "outland men," however, no matter how well qualified they might already be as merchants or craftsmen in other burghs, had to pay quite heavily for admission....

The first purpose of the merchant guild was to maintain a monopoly within a monopoly, to preserve from ambitious craftsmen and unfreemen both within and without the burgh the community's right of foreign trade that only a free merchant burgess could enjoy....

The second purpose of the guild was to provide the organization by which the merchants could dominate the town council: ... When ... the old council gained the right of electing the new one, an even smaller elite was able to emerge from within the merchant guild and consolidate themselves in positions of power. Thus Dundee in the early seventeenth century was dominated by the Wedderburnes, the Goodmans, the Haliburtons, the Clayhills and half a dozen other families united by bonds of marriage and mutual interest [pp. 148–149].

We have included this passage from Smout to show in detail exactly how the burgh system operated and to draw attention to the potential it offered for collaborative efforts among the patrician families in any given Scottish city. By a pattern of endogamous marriage across several generations, an economically and socially cohesive infrastructure was established in each burgh. Religion, political office, financial capital, credit, and trade outlets could all be controlled securely and perpetuated in this fashion, with virtually no supervision from outside. These conditions were ideal for the presence of crypto–Judaism.

As Smout further reports, Scotland's young men from these leading families were not schooled in a parochial Protestant enclave, but rather sent abroad for their education — usually to centers where *converso* Jews were present and prominent on university faculties. Many affluent Scots were educated in Rouen, Marseilles, Bordeaux, Amsterdam, Lyon, and London, and in Venice, Padua, Rome, and Livorno (Leghorn) in Italy. Brilliant Scots minds, such as that of John Napier (1550–1617), the inventor of logarithms, and James Gregory (1638–1675), an astronomer and mathematician who developed the first reflecting telescope, sprang from these sources. Gold and silver smithing, two Jewish skills of long standing, were practiced brilliantly "in the second half of the sixteenth century" by Edinburgh artisans— exactly the time period one would anticipate for *converso* immigrants incoming from France, Holland, Italy and England.

On the southern Scottish border at Falkirk, the Carron iron works were established in 1759, Carron being a French *converso* surname. By 1801 immense deposits of black-band iron ore had been identified by David Mushet (Moshe), which would provide the resource for Scotland's great steelmaking industry of the nineteenth century. And as we shall see in chapter 3, Glasgow merchants became rich from a triangular tobacco trade with the American colonies and the Caribbean. By the late 1700s Scotland ran a lucrative import-export trading network that reached from Virginia and South Carolina to Jamaica and Barbados, to France, Germany, and Holland, onward to Sweden, Poland, and Russia — all locales where *converso* Jews had settled and opened up banks, shipping firms and manufactories. As Smout wonderingly writes about these Scottish entrepreneurs, "It would be interesting to know as much about their *religious affiliations* and their childhood upbringing as we do about their parentage" (p. 364). It would indeed, and so we turn now to a review of the last historical monograph examined in this introductory chapter.

The Forgotten Monarchy of Scotland, Prince Michael Stewart (2000)

The author of this Scottish history is HRH Prince Michael Stewart of Albany, head of the Scottish Royal House of Stewart, a descendant of the Stuart Pretenders. The word "pretender" did not originally have a pejorative meaning. These royals are *de jure* (legal) successors of the last Stuart monarch Queen Anne, with whose death in 1714 the throne passed to the Hanoverians.[14] An immediate giveaway to Prince Michael's storyline is his listing as "Honorary President of the Association of Jewish Students of Glasgow University" (other titles of his include, for example, Titular Prince of France and Poland, and Duke of Normandy and Aquitaine). Why is the current heir of the Stewart dynasty of Scotland also head of the Glasgow University Jewish student association? Because he is of Jewish ancestry.

HRH Michael Stewart puts the circumstances in a rather straightforward manner in his narrative: The Stewart family maternal line in France was descended "from the Tribe of Judah"; he believes his family is of Davidic ancestry (that is, from the Jewish King David); and he is therefore a Jew by descent. The Stewarts were among that set of French families that came to England with William the Conqueror and his Norman army in 1066. Originally named FitzAlan, the family took the name of Stewart after serving as royal stewards to the Bruce dynasty of Scotland. By marrying the female heir of King Robert Bruce in 1315, Walter Stewart (who by this time served also as regent) ensured that his son Robert II eventually advanced to the throne of Scotland.[15]

HRH Michael Stewart, it should also be noted, *does* give credence to the Stone of Destiny origin story, believing that an Egyptian princess named Scota did come to Ireland and that the Picts and Gaels both originated near the Black Sea (Scythia) in southeastern Europe. As he states, "From Tamar and Eochaid (Echad) were descended most of the royal lines of Ireland ... through which all Kings of Scots traced their succession from the Biblical Kings of Judah" (p. 70). While HRH Michael Stewart may believe this explanation for the ancient Jewish lineage of the Scottish kings, we do not. We could be wrong; he could be correct; but the story is too far-fetched to support serious historical argument. Further, we do not require these remote origins, for France in 1050 is a more proximate — and provable — source for Judaic ancestry.

What HRH Michael Stewart's narrative *does* offer us, however, is a more detailed and nuanced version of Scottish history than we have seen previously; one with several significant clues about a Jewish presence there. First, he notes (p. 19) that the Celtic Church retained several Jewish practices, while deliberately resisting conformation to Roman Catholicism. From 906 C.E. onward, the Last Supper ritual was celebrated only at Passover/Pesach; infant baptisms were not practiced, and no crucifixion imagery or icons were used.

Stewart also writes that the Old and New Testaments were weighted equally within the Celtic Church, and further:

> Unlike their Catholic counterparts, the priests of the Celtic Church were allowed to be married, and their hereditary offices were passed from father to son....[16] Given that Jesus' own teachings formed the basis of the faith, the Mosaic structure from the Old Testament was duly incorporated. Judaic marriage laws were observed, together with the celebrations of the Sabbath and Passover, while Easter was correctly held as the traditional feast-day of the Spring goddess, Eostre... [p. 30].

He also describes accurately, if a bit patronizingly, the merging of Constantine's brand of Christianity with preexisting pagan cults in the Middle East:

> Contrary to traditional belief, Emperor Constantine the Great (A.D. 274–337) did not embrace Christianity as the religion of Rome; [rather,] he adapted Christianity into a new form that was ... actually related to the Syrian Sol Invictus cult of sun worship. [Constantine] redefined Jesus' birthday to comply with the Sun Festival on 25 December, and substituted the sacred Sabbath (Saturday) with the Sun-day ... the high-points of Judaic Christianity were conveniently merged with the pagan tradition, and the Persian cult of Mithras, which stressed the concept of final judgment ... [p. 31].

Stewart provides us with a different perspective on the arrival of the "outsiders" into Scotland during the 1100s, noting that many of these immigrants were Flemish, rather than French per se: "Although some Normans ventured into Scotland at the time of Malcolm III ... there was no effective penetration until the reign of King David I (1124–53).... The resultant settlement was far more Flemish than Norman, even though some of the noble families of Flanders..." (p. 32).

Stewart argues that these Flemish newcomers were attractive to King David because of their skill in administration, international trade and business. They were also good farmers and weavers. Once the Flemish and Normans arrived, King David established them in a series of Sheriffdoms[17] and incorporated them into the Scottish judicial system.

The wife of Scottish Kind David was Maud de Lens of Boulogne, Flanders, the widow of Simon de Senlis (St. Liz) (bearing a Jewish given name) and the wealthiest woman in Britain. Stewart states, "Maud was not only a cousin of the Count of Flanders, she was also a cousin of Godefroi de Bouillon, Guardian of the newly created kingdom of Jerusalem. David's policy had been to implement a mercantile strategy that would link Scotland to a trading empire centred upon Bruges and managed by Flemish families throughout Eastern and Western Christendom" (p. 43).

Accompanying Maud to Scotland was a host of Boulogne kinsmen: Walter Fleming (now Seton), Gilbert de Ghent (now Lindsay), Robert de Commines (now Comyn and Buchan), Arnulf de Hesdin (now Graham), the Advocate of Bethune (now Beaton). Stewart also states that Flemish ancestry characterized the Scottish families of Abernethy, Anstruther, Baird, Balliol, Boswell, Brodie, Cameron, Campbell, Crawford, Douglas, Erskine, Fleming, Fraser, Hamilton, Hay, Innes, Leith, Leslie, Murray and Oliphant (p. 34).

Thus, many of the surnames we think of as typically Scottish are in fact Flemish and French — as were the people carrying them. In chapters 3 and 4, we will document the intermarriage and consanguinity among the Norman nobles, both in Scotland and in families related to them in France and Flanders. The cohesiveness of these bonds of kinship provided a unified political and economic network that spanned Western Europe and the Holy Land.

The royal house of Bruce came to an end in 1371, when Robert's son David (age 47) died after a sudden illness in Edinburgh Castle without a male heir. Robert the Bruce's daughter, Marjorie, however, had married Walter, the 6th High Stewart of Scotland (ca. 1292–1326). She died giving birth to a son, Robert II, who served as regent during David's frequent absences and was crowned in Scone Abbey on March 26, 1371, initiating the Royal Stewart dynasty. Stewart describes his installation procedure, which was that of a priest-king, modeled after those of Israel.[18]

> Firstly, the King-to-be was passed through a ritual of purification to become an ordained people's priest. He would then appear at the Church Abbey of Scone, dressed in white as a symbol of integrity.... With his hand upon the Stone [of Destiny], the King would swear his Oath of Fealty as the people's champion. He was duly anointed, and then sat upon the separate and much larger Coronation Stone.... In the early days the crown was no more than a circlet of gold, and its symbolic concept was to catch the eye of God ... [A]t that stage would the religious ceremony begin, led by the Bishop and the seven priests. There were readings from Old Testament scriptures, along with prayers... [pp. 75–76].

Also according to Stewart, it is frequently presumed that Robert de Brus was a Norman, but this is not true. The de Brus had held lands in Normandy, but Robert carried the azure Flemish lion of Louvain when he came to Britain.

Conclusions

So where does this discussion and review of Scottish history leave us? First, we have found one Scot of aristocratic descent who claims Jewish ancestry. Admittedly, this is not an overwhelming showing in a country of five million persons, but at least it is a start.[19]

Second, we hope we have convinced the reader that Scotland after 1100 C.E. was no longer peopled exclusively or even predominately by Celts. With Vikings to the north and French, Flemings, and Hungarians to the south and center, there were few Celts left in possession of land or titles at the turn of the millennium-plus-one-century mark. A dialect of Anglo-Norman Middle English replaced the older Gaelic language at the court and other local seats of government as early as 1100. Indeed, the view of most historians today is that the clans were not so much a holdover from Scotland's dim tribal past as a creation of her feudal period of development. As we are reminded repeatedly, "the bonds that held the clan together were land and landholding," while the origins of Scotland "had as much to do with French-speaking Normans as with ancient Celts" (Herman 2001, pp. 121–22).

Chapter 2

DNA and Population Studies:
"But Why Do You Think
They Were Jewish?"

It is very hard to *prove* someone is Jewish. To begin with, even living, present-day Jews may disagree about who and what a Jew is. The broadest definition, that adopted by most Reform Jews today, describes Judaism as an international community of persons who share the same monotheistic faith and are guided by the same commandments and Torah. In this view, Jews may come from many ethnic backgrounds, some of them converts, others Jews by birth, all of them equal: there is no possibility of one person being "more Jewish" than another.

Many Orthodox Jews, however, disagree with this view and consider only other Orthodox Jews to be "really" Jewish; they can even quibble among themselves about which Orthodox group is the *most* Jewish. Further, persons whose mother or father was born Jewish may be considered Jewish by some Jews, but not by others. Persons whose mother or father converted to Judaism or who themselves converted may not be accepted as Jewish by all Jews. Even persons whose parents were both born Jews and are now practicing Jews, but who do not belong to a temple, may not be pronounced Jewish by all Jews. Thus, Jewish identity is a complex and controversial issue, which we will not attempt to resolve here.[1]

To complicate matters further, Jews who were born of two practicing Jewish parents, and who themselves belong to an Orthodox synagogue, may not necessarily be of Semitic ancestry. That is, they may not carry the genes of the ancient Hebrews. Instead, some time between 3,000 years ago and the present, their ancestors decided to *become* Jews, and the family has continued to practice that faith ever since. Most Jews now living do not have predominantly Semitic ancestry in their genetic makeup. This is particularly the case for the maternal line. As geneticist Steve Olson puts it in *Mapping Human History* (2002, pp. 109–110), "The mitochondrial DNA sequences of Jewish females are even more diverse than the Y chromosomes of males, suggesting that non–Jewish women converted or married into the faith even more often than men." Importantly for our purposes, descendants of medieval Spanish, French and Italian Jews— that is, the Western or Mediterranean Jews of Sefarad — are *not* primarily of Semitic ancestry. Rather, most belong to what is called the R1b Y chromosomal DNA haplogroup, the most common paternal lineage in Europe and in countries of the New World founded by Europeans.[2]

What about simply regarding as Jewish any person who now publicly "self-identifies" as such? While seemingly reasonable, this solution will not work in the case of Crypto-Jews (secret Jews). Though a term normally reserved for Jewish Iberian exiles after the pogroms of 1391 and especially after the Edict of Expulsion in 1492, it can also be applied to ancestrally Jewish Scots, ancestrally Jewish Germans, ancestrally Jewish Melungeons, and in fact to any ancestrally Jewish persons whose forebears feared identification or detection, chose to hide their true identity, and practiced that religion in secret. For up to 600 years, Crypto-Jews had to survive without rabbis, yeshivas, torahs, or synagogues, isolated from openly Jewish communities in Eastern Europe, Islam and the Mediterranean, and subject to a kind of "double hostility" from their surrounding societies (Santos 2000). The religious status of these Marranos,[3] *conversos, Anusim* ("the Forced Ones") and New Christians challenged some of the best rabbinical minds of the day (Netanyahu 1999).

And so, to determine if the Scottish families in question were of Jewish descent, we used a process of inductive reasoning. We relied on clues from several different types of evidence — historical, genealogical, linguistic, archeological, geographic and genetic. By considering these different sources, we can argue that a given family had a *very high probability* of being Jewish upon their arrival in Scotland. In some cases this is no problem: certain of these families still *are* Jewish and can document lineal descent from Scots forebears. But in most cases we are going to have to finesse this conclusion by looking at the overall pattern of evidence for that family, including their associated lines and marriage preferences. The formal term for this branch of science is the statistical inference of demography from DNA sequence data.

In this chapter, we focus on DNA samples collected from descendants bearing the surnames of prominent Scots in the "early/first wave" and "later/second wave" migrations from the Continent. The first set of families included Alexander, Bruce, Campbell, Douglas, Forbes, Fraser, Gordon, Leslie and Stewart. The second set of surnames included Caldwell, Christie, Cowan and Kennedy. We selected these families because we believed, a priori, they had a high likelihood of being Jewish. Why did we believe this? Because these are all Scots surnames found in high numbers among the Melungeon population of Appalachia. As noted at the outset, we are of Melungeon descent; we have learned that some of our ancestors (perhaps all) *were* practicing Jews at some time in their past and in some instances still are. We have corresponded with many cousins in our various lines who have come to the same conclusion, namely, that their Scots (and French, German, Dutch, Portuguese, German, Swiss, Italian, Welsh, Irish and English) ancestors practiced the Jewish faith. This fact was hidden from most of us until just recently. But it need not remain hidden from you.

DNA and Surnames

Before describing the DNA results, let us review the emergence of this new tool in genealogical and anthropological studies. The investigation of surnames in genetics can be said to go back to George Darwin, son of the founder of evolutionary science. In 1875, Darwin *fils* used surnames to estimate the frequency of first-cousin marriages and calculated the expected incidence of marriage between people of the same surname. He arrived at a figure between 2.25 percent and 4.5 percent for cousin-marriage in the population of Great Britain (Jobling, June 2001, p. 353), with the upper classes being on the high end and the general rural population on the low end. (Admittedly, this was a pretty crude effort by modern scientific standards, but quite innovative for its era.) The next stimulus toward using genetics to study family history had to wait until the 1990s, when certain locations on the Y chromosome were identified as being useful for tracing male-to-male inheritance.

It all began when a Canadian nephrologist of Ashkenazi parentage attended synagogue one morning and noticed that a Sephardi congregant with the same surname as his—Cohen—seemed to have completely different physical features (Kleiman 2001; Thomas et al. 1998; Skorecki et al. 1997). According to Jewish tradition, Cohens are descended from the same male ancestor, the priest Aaron, brother of Moses, and as such are regarded as the hereditary Jewish priestly caste, called upon first to come forth and read Torah in temple services. The nephrologist reasoned that if Kohanim (plural of Cohen) were indeed the descendants of only one man, they should have a common set of genetic markers and should perhaps preserve some family resemblance to each other.

To test that hypothesis, he made contact with Professor Michael Hammer of the University of Arizona, a leading researcher in molecular genetics and pioneer in Y chromosome research. The publication of their study in the prestigious British science journal *Nature* in 1997 sent shock waves through the worlds of science and religion. A particular marker (now known as the Cohen Modal Haplotype, or CMH) did indeed appear in 98.5 percent of men bearing the surname Cohen (or a variation thereof such as Cone). It was apparently true that knowledge of their priestly calling and descent from the Biblical Aaron had been strictly preserved for thousands of years (Skorecki et al. 1997; Thomas et al. 1998). Moreover, the data showed that there were very few "non-paternity events," testimony, as one Jewish scholar put it, to the faithfulness of thousands of Mrs. Cohens down through the ages (Kleiman 2001).[4]

The first to test the new methodology in general surname research was Bryan Sykes, a molecular biologist at Oxford University (Sykes and Irven 2000). His study of the Sykes surname obtained valid results by looking at only four markers on the male chromosome. It pointed the way to genetics becoming a valuable assistant in the service of genealogy and history. Sykes went on to found the first home DNA testing firm, Oxford Ancestors, and write the popular book *The Seven Daughters of Eve* (2002).

To conduct our research we identified two persons for each surname who could document, genealogically, their exclusive male-line descent from a Scots-born male forebear carrying that surname. Our first lab results arrived in September 2000. The laboratory looked at twelve markers on the Y chromosome prone to genetic mutation (polymorphism). Taken together, the resulting scores, called short tandem repeats (STRs), or alleles, make up a haplotype, a unique genetic profile shared by males of the same paternal descent. Each test result was then compared with the Y-STR Haplotype Reference Database (YHRD), a collection of over 28,000 samples taken from 249 world populations

(Willuweit et al. 2005). Nearly 23,000 distinct haplotypes are identified within the European section of YHRD; there are also Asian, African and North American sections. This extremely informative gene bank, though it has a few underrepresented areas such as France, serves as the final word for forensic scientists and courts of law the world over, as well as for professional genealogical casework. Matches in the FTDNA database, Ybase, and other available concordances were also used.[5] The raw scores for these analyses are shown in appendix A.

Alexander: Surname from the Ancient World

Let us begin our discussion of haplotypes with *Alexander*, a surname commonly found in both Melungeon and Scots genealogies. An Alexander donor with ancestry in the Southern Appalachians took our test.[6] There were two exact (12/12) matches found at FTDNA, both of unknown ancestral origin. An extended comparison produced 22 one-step (11/12) mutational matches (in other words, the same scores on all markers but one).

On the basis of a predictive model, the Alexander haplotype was assigned to haplogroup (common lineage, gene type) R1b. Interestingly, in addition to four Scottish matches and twelve English matches, its one-step mutation had a match also with a Jewish donor in Poland, a French male and four Belgian males. Could the Continental distribution of the haplotype be an indication of its "deep history"? In the much larger YHRD (22,970 haplotypes), on a nine-marker basis, it elicited a single full match in Limburg, Netherlands (1/50), while haplotype neighbors (one-step mutations, related farther back in time) included the following:

Antioquia, Colombia (European)	2 / 407	Latin America
Argentina (European)	1 / 301	Latin America
Asturias, Spain	1 / 90	Europe
Barcelona, Spain	1 / 224	Europe
Bern, Switzerland	1 / 91	Europe
Birmingham, UK	1 / 97	Europe
Budapest, Hungary	1 / 194	Europe
Cantabria, Spain	2 / 101	Europe
Connecticut, USA (Hispanic American)	1 / 52	North America
Damascus, Syria	1 / 100	Asia
England-Wales, UK (Afro-Caribbean)	1 / 107	Europe
Greifswald, Germany	1 / 208	Europe
Madrid, Spain	1 / 152	Europe
Marche, Italy	1 /108	Europe
Missouri, USA (European American)	1 / 59	North America
New York City, USA (European American)	1 / 155	North America
Rio de Janeiro, Brazil (European)	1 / 126	Latin America
Rostock, Germany	1 / 203	Europe
São Paulo, Brazil (European)	1 / 447	Latin America

Texas, USA (European American)	2 / 78	North America
Virginia, USA (African American)	1 / 47	North America
Sicily, Italy	1 / 199	Europe
Southern Portugal	1 / 112	Europe
Stuttgart, Germany	2 / 453	Europe
Switzerland	1 / 149	Europe
Tyrol, Austria	2 / 230	Europe
Zaragoza, Spain	2 / 120	Europe

The astounding news was that of 72 near-matches in the YHRD, 22 (nearly one-third) were in Spain, Portugal or countries once ruled by these colonial powers, including Antioquia (Colombia) and Madeira (Spain), both places known to have large populations of Sephardim. There was even a Scottish Alexander genetic cousin in Damascus, Syria. The modal score (most frequent response) was central eastern Spain, the original homeland of innumerable Crypto-Jews now living in Mexico and the American Southwest (Santos 2000).[7]

Forbes

Let us examine *Forbes* next. In the Forbes DNA surname project of Kenneth Forbes, Forbes I matched a David Forbes *circa* 1785, of Montrose, Scotland, and Forbes II a William Forbes of South Carolina.[8] Forbes I had 40 exact matches in the Recent Ethnic

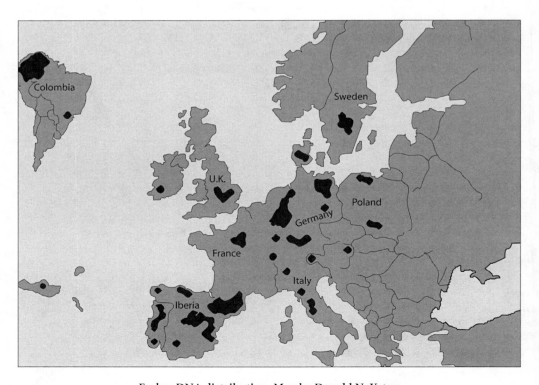

Forbes DNA distribution. Map by Donald N. Yates.

Origins section of the FTDNA database. Comparison of the scores with the extended database of Dr. Hammer at FTDNA showed only one exact match (Ireland — probably our donor), but 34 one-step and two-step mutations, including England, France, the Shetland Islands, Polynesia (European admixture), Ukraine (Ashkenazi), Portugal, Italy, Philippines (European admixture), Poland and Spain (Basque), illustrating the wide dissemination of this genetic pattern. The presence of Polynesian and Filipino matches underscores the fact that the bearers of this haplotype sometimes traveled by ship to distant countries. Admixture was also suspected in matches with an Inuit from Greenland, an Indonesian, a Japanese, a Micronesian, an Arab from Israel, some native Siberians and a Chinese Muslim of Central Asian descent on the historic trading route known as the Silk Road.

In the YHRD, Forbes I elicited 167 matches throughout the world, weighted toward southern Europe and the Mediterranean. The modal center was in northern Spain (Basques), with noteworthy peaks in Colombia, the Pyrennes, Brazil, northern Portugal, Paris (France), Valencia, Madrid and Barcelona (Spain), Poland, London, Argentina, Texas and New York City (European and Hispanic descent). More than 50 percent of the matches were in Iberia or Hispanic populations in the New World. If we were to project the sample size onto the country of Colombia, 2 percent of the population, or 400,000 Colombians, could be said to be carrying the "Forbes" haplotype (even though they would likely have different surnames). Further, it can be inferred with a high degree of confidence that these Colombian males would all have a common ancestor who lived, according to estimates of average mutation rates, about a thousand years ago, when the first surnames were being established. Eight out of 224 Barcelonans also matched: in other words 3.6 percent of that population. By these measures, then, this Forbes haplotype appears to be Iberian.[9]

Forbes II differed from Forbes I on five markers, suggesting different original ancestors for these two donors, despite their having the same surname. Both were assigned to haplogroup R1b. The pattern of matches for Forbes II yielded a worldwide distribution.[10] Results included multiple matches with three other surnames (Arnold, Toole, and McQuiston).[11] We believe that both branches of Forbes came to Scotland from France or the Spanish Peninsula sometime in the not-so-distant past. Significantly, there *are* Jews by the name of Forbes buried in the Sephardic communities of Brazil (Whiznitzer 1960), and several generations of Forbeses (along with Alexanders) were partners in the important Pensacola-based trading house of Panton, Leslie and Co., later called John Forbes and Co. (Sutton 1991).

Bruce

Next, let us consider the surname *Bruce*. Our Bruce donor[12] proved also to be R1b and matched with the surnames Fookes (German *Fuchs*, English *Fox*, both common Jewish surnames), Kent, Ferguson and Harris (2). Harris was the name of 1 in 84 patrons of Anglo-Jewish charities in an 1884 study compiled by Jacobs, making it 13th in rank among British Jewish surnames. Bruce had exact matches in the FTDNA Recent Ethnic Origins database in Bohemia (1 out of 15) and England, with an additional 14 of "unknown" origin. One-step (11/12) matches included Scotland (8 out of 500, or 1.6 percent), U.K. (26 out of 2406, or about 1 percent), Germany (10 out of 576, or 1.7 percent), and France (3 out of 165, or 1.8 percent, with Keskastel, a town in Alsace that had a noted medieval Jewry, being 2 of those, plus an additional 1 classified as of unknown country origin). There were also matches with a Russian Ashkenazi donor, Mexico, Denmark and the Netherlands (2 out of 13).

A search of the YHRD database produced 38 matches. These were fairly well concentrated along the Rhine River between France and Germany, with Freiburg (Germany) being the modal response (5 out of 433, or 1.2 percent), followed by London (3 out of 247, or 1.2 percent). There were also scattered matches in Brussels (Belgium), Finland, Sicily, Norway, Sweden, Gotland, northern Poland and southern Portugal, as well as Brazil. The sole French hit (Paris) was striking in view of the small sample set in the database, only 109 total, all from Paris and Strasbourg. The Scots Bruce line, of course, claims to come from France, and the etymology of the name (de Brousse, Lat. *bruscia* "brush, brushwood") leads to Normandy and Flanders.

Campbell

The DNA of our *Campbell* donors emerged as a relatively uncommon haplotype and though fairly pan–European, was, again, concentrated in Iberia. Our participants matched two donors in the later-forming Campbell Surname DNA Project. Campbell matches in the FTDNA database were in Ireland and of unknown origin, with one-step matches in Sweden (1 out of 69), England (18 out of 2039), Germany (4 out 576), Ireland (3 out of 617), Scotland (11 out of 500) and "unknown" (23). Two-step matches were found in Belarus (Russia, 1 out of 86), Denmark (1 out of 49), France (2 out of 165), Holland (1 Ashkenazi-Levite and 1 Dutch-Mennonite out of 40), Sicily (1 out of 103), Germany (7 out 576), Iceland (3 out of 119), Shetland Islands (5 out of 45, or 11 percent), Poland (1 out 102), Wales (3 out of 76) and Iberian locations (including Andalusia and Mexico: 4 out of 254 total for these countries, or 1.6 percent).

Notable two-step Campbell matches from Hammer's database at FTDNA included several Ashkenazi Jews (Belarus, Holland, and Russia), plus matches in Spain, Italy, Greece and Syria. The Ashkenazi match from the Netherlands was noted as Levite. Matches in the YHRD database (25) yielded Colombia, Birmingham (England), London and New York City (Latino) in a tie as modal scores and included Cantabria (in northern Spain), central eastern Spain, central Portugal, Moscow, Paris, Southern Ireland, Belgium, Holland, Sweden, Russia, and Hungary.

The bulk of the participants (12 out of 17) in the Campbell Surname Project fell into the R1b haplogroup and had genealogies traced back to a large Campbell colony in Rockbridge/Augusta County, Virginia, coming from Northern Ireland via Pennsylvania. There were numerous marriages between Campbells and Davidsons (a common Jewish surname), McKees (Mackey, Mackie, etc., Jewish surname), Hays (Jewish surname), and Alexanders.

In American history, Campbell County, Tennessee/Kentucky, is a rocky and inaccessible area of the southern Appalachians near the Melungeon heartland. It was named after one of Daniel Boone's right-hand men and long harbored an important Crypto-Jewish community that was evidently gathered around Richard Muse (born 1752, died after 1840),[13] a land agent. Also settling there were two branches of the Cooper family, relatives of the scout for Boone, William Cooper (about 1725–1782).

The Campbellite denomination, loosely Primitive Baptist, was a network of circuit meetings strong in the early years of the nineteenth century in Tennessee. It was characterized by absence of belief in the Christian trinity, worship without icons, avoidance of all writing, adherence to orally transmitted law, the wearing of kippot (Jewish skull caps), reading of the Old Testament only, use of Jewish wedding ceremonies, and Saturday religious meetings, with designation of the primary house of worship as a "temple" and temporary meeting places as "tabernacles."[14] One Dinana Campbell is buried with a death date of 1821 and the familiar Jewish symbol of a hand pointing to a star in Purrysburgh Cemetery in South Carolina, an early Crypto-Jewish religious colony on the Savannah River.

Campbells were among the leading Jewish families in Jamaica,[15] and there are 14 persons surnamed Campbell listed in Rabbi Malcolm Stern's American Jewish genealogies (1991). It is also a leading name researched by the Jewish Genealogical Society of Great Britain. Campbells, including Isaac and Israel, were among the first settlers of the Republic of Texas, and they were among founders of the Watauga Country experiment in republicanism in Tennessee.[16] We hypothesize that Campbell as a surname may be related to Campanal, a Marrano surname (see chapter 3).

Our two Douglas samples did not match each other exactly, but were very close. It would appear we are likely dealing with branches of the same family, a Scottish clan of royal descent first attested as lords of the South Isles as early as the 9th century C.E. In the FTDNA database, on a two-step basis, Douglas I produced an Ashkenazi match in Belarus (White Russia), 3 matches in the Shetland Islands (out of 45, or 6.7 percent of the population), 45 matches total from the U.K. (one-third of all matches), and notable matches in Switzerland (2/69) and Spain (3/103), besides a scattering of Scandinavian matches. In the YHRD database there were two matches for Douglas I: Albania and Cologne.

Douglas II had 6 matches in the YHRD database: Colombia, Freiburg, Liguria (northern Italy), Limburg (Netherlands), Lombardy (the region around Milan), and London. With Colombia, we are seeing more of the Iberian pattern witnessed with Forbes and our previous Scots surnames. Douglas I with its 12, 14 values on DYS 385 may be the parent haplotype. A simulation in the YHRD, inputting these scores for DYS 385 and allowing the other two sites to vary between the values for Douglas I and II, produced a "generic Douglas" of 80 hits, widely distributed, over one-third (28) of them in Iberian-settled places, including Argentina, Brazil, Madeira, Colombia and all Portuguese populations. Significantly, Douglas II exactly matched three Jewish males with Ashkenazi surnames at FTDNA.

Gordon

We obtained three *Gordon* DNA donors from two different sources. The first, labeled Gordon III, came from a Clan Gordon descendant from Scotland. The second two were

Jewish Gordons from Russia, labeled Gordon I and II. We wanted to learn if these two Gordon populations were related genetically.

The Gordon III donor from Scotland carried haplotype R1b and matched individuals with the following surnames: Cowell, Kendrick, Nichols, Wingo, French, Day, Beckendorf, Brown, Sisson (11), George (2), Picklo, Hill, Mock, Shelton, Radcliffe, and Clark. The several matches with Sisson, a version of Sasson, Sosa, Sassoon, Shushan and Ibn Shoshan, are notable as this is the post-exilic Hebrew name for "happiness," associated with the *fleur de lis* or lily that served as a symbol of the House of David during the Middle Ages (Jacobs 1901–1906). Gordon III is one step away from the extremely widespread Lavender haplotype, which has been traced to French Jewry (Lavender 2003).

Gordon III's exact matches in the REO database were either in the British Isles or of unknown origin: Ireland (2), Scotland (2), United Kingdom (1), unknown origin (3), and Wales (2). One-step mutations showed a thin, but consistent, distribution throughout Europe, including Austria (2/42), Switzerland (6/69), Germany, Holland (6/40), France (3/165), Italy, Slovakia, Sweden, Iceland, Denmark, Jamaica, and Ashkenazi matches in Poland and Russia. There were also matches by admixture with native Siberians, Inuits, Polynesians, Filipinos, Micronesians, Indonesians, Japanese, Africans, Arabs, Chinese Muslims and Uyghurs (a Turkic people in Central Asia). In the YHRD database, there were 73 matches. Every population in present-day Germany was covered, with the capital, Berlin, being the modal response (6/548 or 1.1 percent). The Iberian picture was uneven, however, with high numbers for Colombia/Antioquia (5), and 2 hits in central Portugal, but none in the northern or southern parts of that country.

The donors we have labeled Gordon I and II (and which are Russian Jewish Gordons) fit the Cohen Modal Haplotype (CMH) and are haplotype J2. In the words of FTDNA, "Haplogroup J is found at highest frequencies in Middle Eastern and North African populations where it most likely evolved. This marker has been carried by Middle Eastern traders into Europe, Central Asia, India, and Pakistan." Moreover, the J2 sub-haplogroup "originated in the northern portion of the Fertile Crescent where it later spread throughout central Asia, the Mediterranean, and south into India. As with other populations with Mediterranean ancestry, this lineage is found within Jewish populations."

Gordon I had two exact surname matches at FTDNA: Norwalk and Horn (a relatively common Jewish surname, derived from Hebrew *shofar*). An exact match was found in the Hammer worldwide Jewry database with an Ashkenazi Jew from the land of Radzivil (Radziwill, Belarussia). One-step matches included Ashkenazim from Austria-Hungary, Hungary, Romania and Uzbekistan. Of the two-step matches, there were Ashkenazis from Lithuania, Russia (3, one of whom self-identified as a Cohen), Austria-Hungary, Belarus, Czechoslovakia, and Poland (Makov). In addition, there was one each of the following: India (tribal), Iran (Mazandarani) and Arab. Thus, the CMH is not restricted to Jews, but is also found among Arabs, Persians and other Middle Eastern peoples. Three-step matches included a Greek from Australia and a Samaritan from Israel. (Extended near-matches such as these are pertinent because we are dealing with an ancient genetic pattern, said to go back three to four thousand years.) In the YHRD database, Gordon I elicited three matches: Argentina, Netherlands and Latium (the area around Rome).

Gordon II matches and near-matches at FTDNA echoed the Gordon I results, and a one-step match from Czechoslovakia listed as a self-identifying "Sephardi." Gordon II exactly matched persons with the last names of Kaplan (a Hebrew name formed from K P L N—כפלנ—meaning "descendant of Cohen")[17] and Jordan (2). These Jordans comprise Group JG5 in the Jordan Surname DNA Project.[18] (The surnames Jordan and Gordon are likely permutations of one another.)

The corresponding matches in the YHRD with Gordon II also are revealing. They include Barcelona, Bulgaria, Bogota (Colombia), Lausanne, Ostergoëtland/Joënkoëping (Sweden), and Sicily, in addition to matches in Egypt, Syria and Turkey. It is known that people descended from the ancient Biblical Hebrews settled in all these places—in Spain from Roman times (and thence to South America after 1492), in Bulgaria and Sicily during Hellenic and Byzantine times, in Switzerland during the High Middle Ages and early modern period, and in Gothland, joining, respectively, the Iberian, Bulgarian, Greek, Swiss and Gothic indigenous populations. Lausanne, for instance, in addition to being a haven for Protestant reformers, was a favorite refuge for French, Italian and Iberian Jews.

The history of the early settlement of Jews among the Scandinavian peoples is little investigated, but a substantial early Jewish population is suggested by the fact that in 1751 a group of Norwegians arrived in London and petitioned the Spanish and Portuguese Jews' Synagogue of Bevis-Marks to admit a large number of their countrymen who wanted to return to the open practice of Judaism (Endelman 1979, p. 283). As we shall discuss in a later chapter, Scottish Gordons established trading stations and manufactories throughout the Baltic, traveled to Russia in the service of the Tsar (*and* in the Appalachians with the Melungeons), and even married into the English nobility, where the poet Byron, Lord George Gordon (1788–1824), became their greatest ironic hero.[19]

Stewart and Caldwell

The *Stewart* donor scores match those of the *Caldwell* donors in the second wave of immigration, so we now move to a discussion those Jews or Crypto-Jews who joined their coreligionists in Scotland after 1300. What we term the Caldwell-Stewart haplotype is the most frequent male haplotype on record. It is widely distributed throughout Europe. In America, it occurs in most ethnic populations, including African-American and Hispanic (due to admixture). Stewart and Caldwell surname matches at FTDNA included: Agin, Arnold (one of the most common Colonial American Jewish surnames),[20] Bell ("good looking" in French), Brown,[21] Canterbury, Carter, Cordova (Sephardic), Castano (Sephardic), Chamberlain and Chambers (from Latin *Camerae* and cognate with Cameron, "of the chamber"), Cooper, Cullen, Davenport (Welsh "David's port"), Elliston, Etheridge/Everidge (likely formed from *Österreicher* "from Austria"), Franklin (from France), French (from France), Hooper (cognate with Cooper), Jacobs (a leading English Jewish surname whose meaning in Hebrew is "merchant"),[22] Lovett/Lovitt (= Levite), German/Jarman (from Germany), Gibbs (often Jewish, a shortened form of Gabriel),[23] Goheen (Yiddish for "impure," *goyim*), Harry (French Harré, related to Harrison),[24] Hutchinson, Kuchinsky (Polish form of the preceding), Mallett (French Sephardic surname), Maxwell (Scottish clan name), May (often German Jewish), Mordecai (Hebrew), Noe (a common Portuguese Jewish surname), Ramey (French Jewish), Rodriguez (a common *converso* surname), Rose (an example of a Jewish "purchased" name, formed from Hebrew Rosh, "head"), Rosenboom (German Jewish "rose tree"), Saylor (German), Schmidt (German), Schoch (meaning "chess," "exchequer," or "accounts" in German), Shelton (English landed gentry),[25] Smothers, South, Stewart, Wall (compare Wahl, Walling), Walter (Norman), Warner (Norman *Guarnier*), Waters, West, White, and Woods (Sylvan).

In the YHRD there were 594 matches representing about three percent of all samples in the database. This haplotype has been labeled — falsely, in our opinion — the (Western) Atlantic Modal Haplotype (AMH), a description going back to Wilson et al. (2001). We believe it is much more accurately labeled a Mediterranean or Iberian modal haplotype. AMH, along with its close mutational neighbors, is the genetic type of one-third of the population of Portugal (Gusmao et al. 2003). Nearly 40 percent of the AMH matches come from Iberian populations (Spain, Portugal, Madeira, Canary Islands, Latin America). Further, the AMH/Caldwell-Stewart progenitor appears to have been responsible for siring 8 percent of the population of the city of Barcelona, 8.3 percent of Zaragoza, 6 percent of Cantabria, and 12 percent of the Pyrenees; altogether about 6 percent of the modern population of Spain and Portugal! Matches also occur in Turkey, Egypt, Syria and the Philippines, as well as Polynesia and Indonesia.

Of the 5 or 6 haplotypes identified by the Stewart/Stuart DNA Project,[26] the Caldwell-Stewart haplotype corresponds to the most common, S4235. One Stewart matched Caldwell exactly, and the other was only a slight variation, perhaps an Irish branch to judge from the 14 matches found in Ireland. Clearly, the Caldwell-Stewart pattern represents a prolific lineage, one favored by historical circumstances.

Caldwell

As the distribution map shows, the Caldwell haplotype left descendants in areas ranging from Scandinavia through central Europe and Germany, down to Italy, across to France and Spain, and over to the British Isles. One match was also found in Turkey. As we will see in chapter 4, according to their origin story the family actually claims to have lived in most of these places. Their motive for migration is remembered as having been a desire to escape religious persecution.

A glance at the distribution of the AMH Caldwell-Stewart haplotype, combined with a knowledge of European history, suggests that the major population segment in today's Spain and Germany — leaving aside France for the moment — likely did not come from Roman or Celtic DNA, two obvious candidates. Neither hypothesis would be a sufficient causal argument for the Scandinavian matches. Both these origins would be hard pressed to account for the Polish matches, as well as for the population density geared toward the North and Baltic seas. The history of Europe is the history of its biggest conquerors. The chronicling of the most frequently-occurring Y chromosomes should correspond to the fortunes of ancient fathers who begat large numbers of sons over the generations.

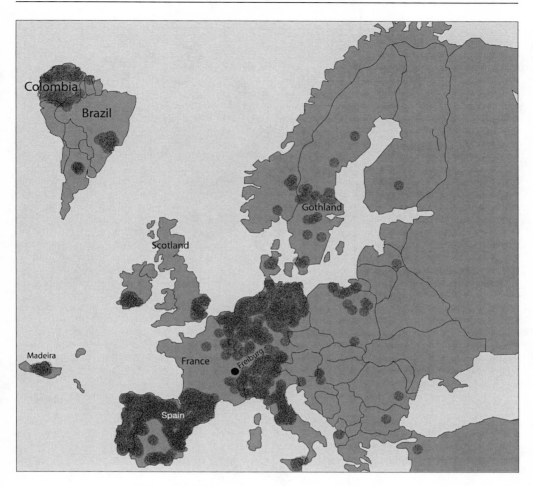

Caldwell DNA distribution. Map by Donald N. Yates.

Let us attempt to solve the origins of this haplotype by gauging the era in which this prolific R1b father lived. Male haplotypes are believed to mutate at a constant rate. This "genetic clock" was chosen for kinship determinations because it "ticks" about once every thousand years and can thus be compared with written records, genealogy and historical sources of information. Usually, heteronymic matches (those between persons of different surnames) reveal a common ancestor who lived between 1,000 and 2,000 years ago, prior to the use of surnames. The Caldwell-Stewart allele configuration, then, likely arose during in the Middle Ages (500–1500 C.E.) or the late Roman period (1–500 C.E.). Since 500 C.E., some of the descendants would have moved from their ancestral home, while some remained behind.

We believe the only people who had contact with all these relevant populations within the appropriate time period were the Germanic tribes that originated in the far north of Western Europe and overran the Roman Empire from the fourth to sixth centuries of the Common Era. They came from the Baltic and harried the borders of the empire in Thrace, Hungary and Pannonia; they are called the Goths. We pick up the Caldwell-Stewart hap-

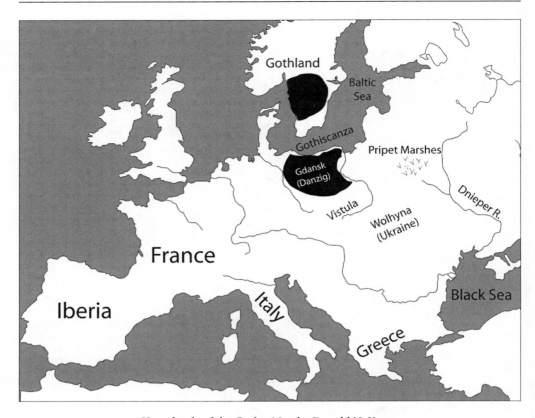

Homelands of the Goths. Map by Donald N. Yates.

lotype trail in Wolhynia (Ukraine), the ancestral home of the Goths before their division into Visigoths and Ostrogoths. Gothic legends tell of a migration from the mouth of the Vistula to the Sea of Azov that took them through a vast swamp. In crossing a river, probably the Dnieper, some of their people became separated from the main group and were left behind. In the words of one historian:

> Old songs tell the story of the trek of the Goths from Gothiscandza to Scythia.... Modern archeology assumes a slow shift of the East Pomeranian-Masovian Wielbark culture into the archaeological region that has been named, since the turn of the century, after the village of Cherniakhov near Kiev. The advance of the Polish culture into the Ukrainian area thus presents itself as a process that lasted from the end of the second until far into the third century.... To this stage belongs also the early phase of the Cherniakhov culture in Wolhynia [Wolfram 1988, p. 42].

The left-behinds stayed in an area that eventually became the medieval state of the Ukraine. The largest group of Goths continued to travel over a thousand miles to the "Greutungian heartland in southern Russia," where "the peoples of the Cherniakhov [Wolhynian] culture certainly had the military and logistical capability to enforce their authority in the vast expanses of Russia" (p. 87). There, the Gothic king "ruled over all peoples of Scythia and Germannia as if they were his own" (p. 88). From this farthest eastward point, they turned west (now being termed Visigoths) and began to prey on the

Roman provinces of Greece, Turkey and the Balkans. Eventually, they joined the Ostrogoths, their ancestral cousins, and descended on Italy. Still later, they established the kingdom of Toulouse in southern France around 418 C.E. and the Visigothic kingdom of Toledo in Spain in 568–711 (Wolfram 1988, appendix 2). There they virtually replaced the resident Romano-Celtic-Punic population, already decimated by wars with their kindred tribes, the Suevi, Vandals, Alani and Silingi.

We read from another authority (Hodgkin 2000, pp. 15–17):

> It was reserved for the Goths ... to deal the first mortal blow at the Roman state [the sack of Rome by Alaric in 410].... The Gothic nation, or rather cluster of nations, belonged to the great Aryan family of peoples, and to the Low German branch of that family.... The information which Jordanes [flourished about 550 C.E.] gives us as to the earliest home and first migration of the Goths is as follows: "The island of Scanzia [peninsula of Norway and Sweden] lies in the Northern Ocean, opposite the mouth of the Vistula, in the shape like a cedar-leaf. In this island [peninsula], this manufactory of nations, dwelt the Goths with other tribes...."
>
> The migration from Sweden to east Prussia [is supported by] Pytheas of Marseilles ... who lived about the time of Alexander the Great [and who] speaks of a people called Guttones, who lived by an estuary of the Ocean named Mentonomon, and who apparently traded in amber (Pliny, *Natural History,* xxxvii.2) ... and who must therefore have been settled on the south-east coast of the Baltic at least as early as 330 before Christ.

Why do we identify the Visigoths, though, as the source of the AMH Caldwell-Stewart haplotype and not one of the numerous other Germanic tribes—for example, the Franks, Burgundians, Saxons, Siling or Asding Vandals, Suebi, Alamanni, Juthungi,

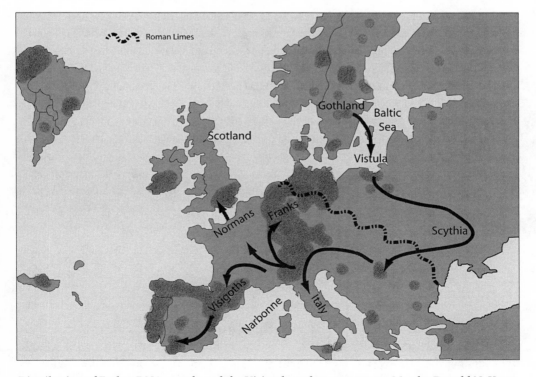

Distribution of Forbes DNA sample and the Visigoth settlement pattern. Map by Donald N. Yates.

Iazyges, Carp, Taifali, Gepids, Heruli, Alans, or even the Visigoths' cousins, the Ostrogoths? Suspicion might fall instead on the Suebi, who crossed the frozen Rhine in the winter of 406–7 C.E. with the Vandal and Alan hordes and two years later were said to number 80,000 as they crossed the Pyrenees into Iberia (Cunliffe 2001, pp. 428, 449).

With the Visigoths' second conquest of the peninsula beginning in 455 under Theoderic I and the end of the kingdom of Toulouse in France (507), however, the Suebi "merged imperceptibly with the indigenous population" in the northwest, "making the last significant contribution to the gene pool of the region" (p. 449). This left the Visigoths as masters of Iberia until the arrival of the Arabs two centuries later. A map of Germanic settlement in the fifth and sixth centuries shows their densest concentration is a fan-shaped crescent between Toledo and Barcelona, *the exact center of the modal scores for the AMH Caldwell-Stewart haplotype* and homeland of the Sephardic Jewish population in the cities on the Ebro and in "northeast central Spain" targeted by the Spanish Inquisition in later centuries (p. 449). The map gives the broad picture and shows the origin and travels of the Visigoths superimposed on the distribution map of one of our Scottish clans, Forbes.

Kennedy

Our *Kennedy* donor is a one-step mutation from the AMH Caldwell-Stewart pattern. He has an allele value of 15 instead of 14 at DYS 385b, the same as Gordon IV. Surname matches included Broom, Cothron, Harris, Irving, Mitchell (2), Sanches, Moore, Briley, Grant, Stewart, Slavin, Gordon, Mock (3), Mauk (3), Elliston, Alford, Rea, Garvey, Bannon, Robinson, Edstrom, Kraywinkel, Beal (2), Devine, and Dyas (Dias, Diaz)—a mixture of names emanating from Scotland, England, Germany, Portugal, Spain, Hungary, Wales, France, Poland and Denmark. Exact haplotype matches in the FTDNA and Hammer databases were England (2, one from the Isle of Man), France, Iceland, Polynesia (European admixture), Portugal and one of unknown origin. One-step mutations were found in Cuba, Denmark, England (2), Finland, France, Germany, Holland (Ashkenzi-Levite), Hungary, Iceland, Ireland, Italy (Apulia), Norway, Poland, Polynesia (2, European admixture), Portugal, Russia (Native Siberian), Shetland Islands, Spain (Andalusia and Basque), and one unknown. Matches in the YHRD database closely replicated the AMH Caldwell-Stewart pattern, only on a smaller scale, with the significant difference that Kennedy had fewer Scandinavian matches.

Leslie and Christie

The *Leslie* haplotype is a two-step mutation from the AMH Caldwell-Stewart pattern. (It has a repeat of 14 instead of 12 at microsatellite 439.) Clan Leslie has a reliable tradition that the name was brought to Scotland from Hungary by one Bartolomaeus Ladslau (Latin *Ladislaus*) around 1120. Supporting this traditional story, we found numerous near-matches with persons tested from the Ukraine, Hungary and Russia, as well as some from Scandinavia and a high number of matches in the Mediterranean.

The *Christie* haplotype had 18 matches in YHRD, the modal response being northern Portugal. One-third of the Christie matches were Portuguese (6/18), with 2 from Belgium, 1 from Caceres (in Spain on the Portuguese border), 1 from Cologne, 1 from Croatia, 1 from Düsseldorf, 1 from Freiburg, 1 from London, 1 from Magdeburg, 1 from Sao Paulo (Brazil), 1 from Sicily and 1 from Zeeland (Netherlands).

The name Christie ostensibly refers to the bearer's status as a follower of Christianity, but such a designation would only make sense if acquired in a land where Christians were the minority (such as Arab Palestine), or else bestowed on a convert. Sometimes *converso* Jews purposely adopted explicitly Christian surnames such as Cruz (cross), Santa Maria, or Santa Cruz (Saint Cross!): in 1389 Solomon Halevi, the chief rabbi of Burgos in Spain, took the name Pablo de Santa María when he converted, or pretended to convert, to Christianity (Gitlitz 2002, pp. 5, 10–11, 201–2).

Fraser

Our *Fraser* results come from the Fraser DNA Project.[27] This appears to be a haplotype with a great deal of variability centering around what can perhaps be hypothesized as the ancestral type. Let us explore the matches:

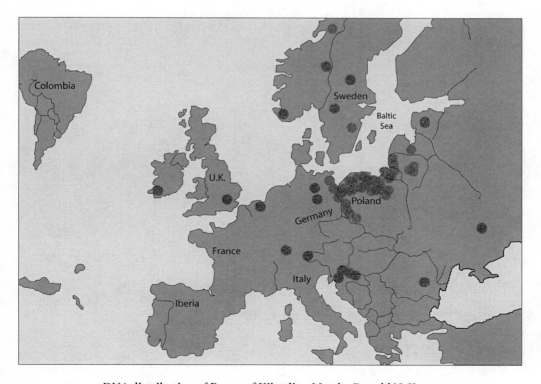

DNA distribution of Fraser of Kiltarlity. Map by Donald N. Yates.

The Fraser donor from Kiltarlity in Inverness-shire (northern Scotland) produced no French or Iberic matches, but yielded a strong Polish and Baltic resonance. Northern Poland, with 8 matches out of 47, or 17 percent of the total, proved the modal score. If we add up all matches for Polish cities, we arrive at a figure of 19, or 40 percent of all matches. Lithuania had 4 matches, and in fact all the Baltic states were represented. This Scottish Fraser also has numerous Swedish, Polish, Russian and Ukrainian cousins—not the places one would expect to find Gaelic stock if Fraser were Celtic or Pictic.

With the second Fraser donor (Aberdeen) scores, the Polish genetic matches drop away. We have 6 matches only: in Colombia (Antioquia), Freiburg, Liguria, Limburg, Lombardy, and London. The closely related Richmond, Virginia, Fraser donor has a single match, in the Pyrenees, the borderland between Spain and France.

With the Edinburgh Fraser donor we get a broader picture. Its 53 matches reveal a wide distribution. French connections emerge, with 3 matches in Strasbourg and 1 in Paris. Northern Poland, with 5 matches, is the modal score. At the same time, we have heavy coverage of northern and east central Spain and all regions of Portugal, including 2 matches (out of 133) from the Pyrenees, a location that was the sole match for Richmond, Virginia, Fraser donor. During the anti–Jewish riots in northern Spain in 1391, and again after the 1492 Edict of Expulsion, Jews crossed and recrossed this mountain chain many times, finding temporary refuge in southern French cities.

The Hastings Fraser donor is only one marker different from the Edinburgh Fraser

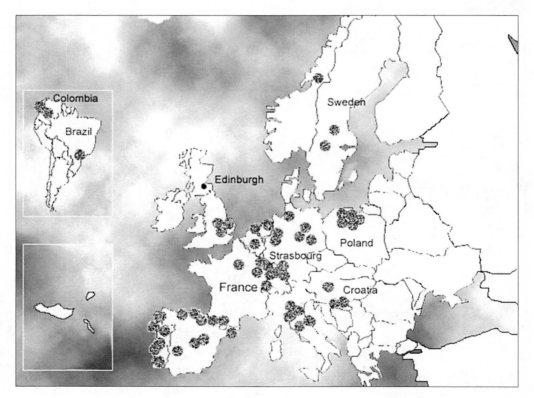

DNA distribution of Fraser of Edinburgh. Map by Donald N. Yates.

and, in fact, is identical to the AMH Caldwell-Stewart haplotype. The Alexandria, Virginia, Fraser donor is a two-step mutation away from it, evidently a unique haplotype, and thus not able to be investigated.

Based on this analysis, we propose that the Edinburgh donor represents the main Fraser ancestral line, which was originally French and Iberian. By contrast, the Inverness Fraser line, which differs on three markers, seems to be predominantly Polish in origin. Thus there seem to be two ancestral clans of Frasers in Scotland, the Frasers who probably came from Anjou in southern France around the time of David I, and the Frasers of Lovat, who arrived later, during the reign of Robert the Bruce.[28]

Cowan

It remains to examine the *Cowan* data. Here we are confronted with a Scottish "clan," some members of which carried knowledge of their Jewishness from Scotland and Ireland to the Appalachians, where they dwelled alongside the Melungeons. While strictly not part of the Melungeon project, the Cowan Surname Project[29] participants were kind enough to make available their results. To date, twenty-five Cowan surname bearers have been tested. They may be divided into 5 haplotypes, of which Cowan IVa (R1b) is the modal haplotype, representing 8 out of 25 of the donors (see fig. 2).[30]

Cowan IVa had the following surname matches (aside from other Cowans): Allison, Berry, Blakely, Blanchard, Bussanich, Csalpinski (Polish), Doherty (and variants Dougherty, Dohty, Dowtertie, etc.), Dalton/Dolton, Dorsey, Harrison, Jones (2), Kennedy, Kenny, Knowles, Leisner, MacKlin, McLaughlin, MacQueen,[31] MacTiernan (2)/McTernan, Milligan, Parvin, Perryman (Sephardic, "pear man"), Reed, Rodgers, Shanahan, Sinor (2, Spanish *Señor*, Seneor),[32] Soakell (Jewish), Stidham, Walker, Ward, and Wilson. It is one marker distant from four other Cowans. In the Hammer/FTDNA haplotype database, Cowan IVa had four exact matches: 2 in Iceland, 1 Anglo-Celt, and 1 of unknown origin. In the YHRD database, the 9 matches were London-modal (4, nearly half), with 3 from Southern Ireland, and 1 each from Berlin and Madeira.

With the exception of France (which is not well represented in the database), these matches corresponded to the English, Scots, Irish, Spanish and German (Polish) surnames we noted above. Keeping in mind the Icelandic matches mentioned already, we propose that this rather geographically restricted haplotype is a later formation from the same Visigothic ancestor whose distribution we have seen in AMH Caldwell-Stewart. Though it spread primarily in the British Isles, it is part and parcel with the same familiar pattern.

Cowan III, a two-step match with Cohen IVa, matched 6 persons with the last name Maxwell, another Scottish clan. It also matched a Stone, Koontz (Hebrew "righteous priest"),[33] Aboy, Avery, Bell, Pope, McCarthy, and Chenault. Exact matches in the FTDNA database included England (4), France, Ireland, Polynesia (European admixture), Scotland (15/520, or 2.8 percent), Spain, and unknown origin (9). From the English and Scottish matches, it is again apparent that this is a family with numerous descendants in the British Isles.

	Control No.	Name	393	390	19 I 394	391	385 a	385 b	426	388	439	389 I 389 I	392	389 II
1.	13583	Cowan I	13	24	13	9	13	14	11	12	10	14	11	30
2.	7388	Cowan II	13	24	14	10	11	14	12	12	12	13	13	30
3.	11152	Cowan IIIa	13	24	14	11	11	14	12	12	12	12	13	28
4.	7375	Cowan IIIa	13	24	14	11	11	14	12	12	12	12	13	28
5.	10883	Cowan IIIb	13	25	14	11	11	13	12	12	12	13	13	29
6.	11081	Cowan IV	13	25	14	11	11	13	12	12	12	13	14	29
7.	7382	Cowan IV	13	25	14	11	11	13	12	12	12	13	14	29
8.	7384	Cowan IV	13	25	14	11	11	13	12	12	12	13	14	29
9.	11178	Cowan IV	13	25	14	11	11	13	12	12	12	13	14	29
10.	7376	Cowan IV	13	25	14	11	11	13	12	12	12	13	14	29
11.	7381	Cowan IV	13	25	14	11	11	13	12	12	12	13	14	29
12.	12443	Cowan IV	13	25	14	11	12	13	12	12	12	13	14	29
13.	7377	Cowan IV	13	25	14	12	11	13	12	12	12	13	14	29
14.	7379	Cowan V	13	26	16	10	11	14	12	12	10	13	11	30
15.	9142	Cowen V	13	26	16	10	11	14	12	12	10	13	11	30
16.	7758	Cowan V	13	26	16	10	11	14	12	12	10	13	11	30
17.	9970	Cowan V	13	26	16	10	11	14	12	12	10	13	11	30
18.	7386	Cowan V	14	25	14	11	11	13	12	12	12	13	14	29
19.	13547	Cowan V	14	25	14	11	12	13	12	12	12	13	14	29

"Cowan haplotype chart." Figure by Donald N. Yates.

However, in the YHRD European database half of the 36 matches were in greater Iberia, and there were 2 (out of 99) in Strasbourg, France, as well as matches in Poland, Sweden and Italy. Projecting the Cowan III data on the total population of Scotland (estimated at 8 million), we can infer that there are about 180,000 males on its sod, moors or sidewalks carrying the Cowan III haplotype. They all likely descend from a single common ancestor who lived about 1,500 years ago, circa 500 C.E.[34] And if our hypothesis is correct, he was a Visigoth who lived in southern France.

Cowan V is an R1a haplotype and shows an Eastern European ancestry common to Ashkenazi Levites. There was an exact match at FTDNA with an Ashkenazic Jew from the village of Komi in Russia. The YHRD European matches are in Finland (2), Leipzig, Ljubljana, London, Stuttgart, Ukraine, Warsaw and Wroclaw. This branch's DNA matches that of a Polish Ashkenazi Jew named Bennett Greenspan (the founder of FTDNA), and its one-step mutations consist of 16 matches, 13 of which are identified as Ashkenazi-Levite, from Germany (2), Austria (2), Belarus (3), Hungary, Lithuania (2), Poland (2), Russia (3), and France.

Conclusions

It is time to summarize our arguments. If Scottish clan surname research and genetic haplotype history take us back to the early centuries of the Common Era and imply common ancestors in France and Spain that were primarily R1b, what makes us think that the Scots who paternally inherited these genes were, by religion, Jewish? For one, certain of these lines have continued to be Jewish down to the present, either in a cultural or religious sense. Our presumption is that the Jews carrying R1b haplotypes converted to Judaism sometime during the past 1,000 to 1,500 years. We will develop this thesis in depth in chapter 5.

Further, the abundance of matches between these Scotsmen and Ashkenazi and Sephardi Jews, in Diasporic locales as far flung as Colombia and Lithuania, suggests they were cut from the same cloth. In the case of the AMH Caldwell-Stewart haplotype, we have seen that it corresponds to a Visigothic prototype situated today in the exact population center of Europe (Freiburg-modal).[35] The two Fraser clans, on the other hand, exhibit a "butterfly" pattern of distribution, with possible Sephardic and Ashkenazic wings. In the case of Clan Cowan, we will later suggest that R1b and R1a males adopted the Cowan/Coen surname indicative of the Jewish priestly caste when they converted to Judaism around 750–900 C.E. Even though these Scots were not Semitic descendants of Aaron or the priest-kings of ancient Judea, they thought of themselves as such. As we shall show in later chapters, the Stewarts began very early to style themselves as Davidic in their ancestry. They became honorary Levites, affiliates of the tribe that traditionally provided the soldiers and craftsmen, defenders and sextons for the Jerusalem Temple.

Chapter 3

Genealogies of the First Wave of Jewish Families, 1100–1350 C.E.

In this chapter we focus on a set of noble families entering Scotland from 1050 to 1350 which we propose were Jewish. They are Bruce, Campbell, Forbes, Leslie, Douglas, Gordon and Stewart. We present genealogical and historical evidence to document the Jewish ancestry of these families.

Bruce

The de Brusse family of Flanders and Normandy entered England in 1050 as part of the entourage of Duke Richard I; the family remained in Britain subsequent to the conquest of England by Richard's son, William the Conqueror, in 1066. Robert de Bruce (d. 1094) married a Norman woman, Agnes St. Clair,[1] and was the son of a Norman woman, Emma of Brittany. Other members of the de Brusse/Brousse family in France emigrated not only to England, but also to what are now Hungary, Germany, the Netherlands and Poland. Some members of this family were and are practicing Jews (M. Stern 1991).

Our research question is whether the de Brusse family in England, and later Scotland, were practicing Jews, as well. As their genealogy shows, several Hebrew and Mediterranean given names are found among the early Bruces; among these are Adam, Emma, Isabel, Agnes, Agatha, Euphemia, David, Matilda, and Eleanor. By the early 1300s, the Bruce family in Scotland had produced Robert I (the Bruce), King of Scotland, who reigned from 1306 to 1329. Robert I, King of the Scots, married Isobel of Mar (1295), producing a child, Marjory de Bruce. The de Mar family (i.e., "from the sea/ocean") was also French Mediterranean in origin.[2] Robert subsequently married Elizabeth de Burgh (also of French origin), having a daughter with her as well, Matilda (Maud). Robert I also had a son, David (b. 1325), by either Elizabeth or a mistress, and two additional children, Elizabeth and Robert, by mistresses.

What should draw our attention at this point are the spouses of Robert I's children.

Matilda/Maud married *Thomas Isaac*, a man with an undeniably Hebrew surname which Jacobs (1902–1911) found to be the most common among British Jews during this time period. From this union came Joanna, who married John de Ergardia (of French origin), producing a daughter, Isabel, who married Sir John Stewart: from this union sprang the Stewarts of Cardney. Further, Robert I's daughter, Elizabeth, by an unknown mistress, married Sir Walter Oliphant, a family surname also known to be Sephardic.

This lineage, together with the DNA evidence of a Southern French or Spanish Jewish origin for the Bruces (chapter 2), strongly suggests that this family was aware of its Judaic heritage and chose marital partners and given names designed to perpetuate this heritage. When Bruces from Scotland arrived in the American colonies during the 1600s and 1700s, the marital patterns of at least some members suggest that the Crypto-Judaic practice had been carried forward to the New World (Stern 1991). We compiled the following genealogical chart from information available online at http://www.scotlandroyalty.com.

Fig. 3: Genealogical Chart of the Bruce Family

Robert de Brusse

Robert de Brusse aka Brusi, birth date unknown, was the first to use the name "Robert the Brus" or some variation. He married Emma of Brittany (ca. 1020) in Normandy. They had one son:
1. Robert de Bruce (d. ca. 1084)

Robert de Brus

Robert de Bruce, birth date unknown, came over to England with William the Conqueror. He married Agnes St. Clair (d. 1080) and they had one son:
1. Adam de Bruce

Adam de Brus

Adam de Brus, birth unknown, went to England in 1050 as attendant to Queen Emma, daughter of Richard I of Normandy. Adam de Brus married Emma Ramsay and had a child:
1. Robert de Bruce

Robert de Bruce

Robert de Bruce (d. 1141), born ca. 1078, married Agnes Paynell (aka Agnes Bruce, a distant cousin) and had three known children:
1. Adam I (d. 1164; m. Ivelta de Arches) had a son:
   a. Adam II (d. 1196; m. 1 Joanna de Mescines; m. 2 Agnes of Aumale)
2. Robert de Bruce III
3. Agatha (m. Ralph Talybois)

Robert de Bruce

Robert de Bruce (d. 1194), aka Robert le Meschin, was Lord of Annandale. He married Euphemia and had a son:
1. William de Bruce

William de Bruce

William de Bruce (d. 1215), 4th Baron of Annandale, was born ca. 1178 and married Christina or Christine. They had one known son:
1. Robert de Bruce

Robert de Bruce

Robert de Bruce, 4th Baron of Annandale, was born ca. 1195. He married Isabella/Isobel Huntington. They had two sons:
1. Robert Bruce
2. Edward le Bruce of Ireland

Robert Bruce

Robert Bruce, Lord of Annandale, was born in 1210. His first marriage was on (or possibly before) 12 May 1240 to Isabel (Isabella de Clare, b. 2 Nov. 1226). Sometime prior to 10 May 1275 he married Christian d'Irby.

Child by Isabel
1. Robert de Brus

Sir Robert de Brus

Sir Robert de Brus, Lord of Annandale, was born in July of 1243. He first married in Turnberry in 1271, to Marjorie of Carrick (Countess of Carrick, wife of Adam de Kolconquhar). Through this marriage he also became Earl of Carrick. After her death in 1292, he resigned the title of Earl of Carrick to his (unknown) son, and married Eleanor who, after Robert's death, married Richard de Waleys.

Children by Marjorie
1. Robert I, Bruce, of Scots
2. Unknown (Earl of Carrick)
3. Christian (d. 1357; m. Gratney of Mar)
4. Mary (m. 1316 Sir Alexander Fraser [d. 1332])
5. Maud (m. Hugh Ross [ca. 1275–19 Jul 1333])

Child by Eleanor
1. Isabel (m. Thomas Randolph, Chamberlain of Scotland)

Robert I Bruce, of Scotland

Robert I, epic hero, was commonly known as "Robert the Bruce," King of Scotland. Robert I was born 11 July 1274 in Turnbury (Turnberry), Essex. In ca. 1295 he married Isobel of Mar (aka Matilda; ca. 1278–ca. 1320). They had one child prior to her death, after which he married Elizabeth de Burgh (1280/1–26 Oct 1327). He also had children from (an) unknown concubine(s).

Child by Isobel
1. Marjory de Bruce

Child by Elizabeth
2. Matilda or Maud (ca. 1310–20 July 1353; m. Thomas Isaac b. ca. 1300) had daughter:
a. Joanna (b. ca. 1377; m. John de Ergardia b. ca. 1317) who had daughter:
1. Isobel (ca. 1362–21 Dec 1439; m. Sir John Stewart)

Child by Elizabeth or concubine
3. David II (boy King of Scotland; b. ca. 1325; m. as infant to Princess Joan, young sister of King Edward II of England)

Children by unknown concubine
4. Elizabeth (m. by 1329 Sir Walter Oliphant [d. after 20 Oct 1378])
5. Robert (d. 12 Aug 1332)

Robert the Bruce died (rumored from leprosy) in Cardross Castle, Firth of Clyde, Scotland, on 7 June 1329. He is buried at Dunfermline Abbey, Fife, Scotland.

Marjory de Bruce

Marjory de Bruce, Princess of Scotland, was born ca. 1297. She married 1314/15 Walter Stewart, 6th High Steward of Scotland. Princess Marjory died 2 March 1315/6. She is buried at Paisley Abbey, Renfrewshire, Scotland. They had one child:

1. Robert II Stewart of Scotland, later King of Scotland

The bronze bust of Robert the Bruce's skull on display at Dumfermline Abbey. The bones around the right side of the mouth are deformed, likely as a result of leprosy. Photograph by Elizabeth Caldwell Hirschman.

We visited several of the sites in Scotland associated with Robert I. At Bannockburn, the Scottish Cultural Center shows a reconstructed model of Bruce's head. Apparently Bruce did suffer from leprosy and the disease had disfigured his mouth and nose. Bruce lies buried at Dunfermline Abbey. Reportedly his skeleton, uncovered in 1819, shows a split sternum, where his heart was removed at death to be transported to Jerusalem by a Douglas. Unfortunately, Douglas was slain by the Moors in Spain on his way to Jerusalem; Bruce's heart was recovered from the battle and is interred either at Dunfermline Cathedral or at Rosslin Chapel.[3]

As will be discussed in chapter 5, Bruce was very likely a Templar, through his marriage to a St. Clair. Freemason symbols are present on some stones at Dunfermline Abbey churchyard. The Templars were largely transmuted into the Freemason order after 1306.

The Royal Bruce coat of arms depicts a central lion rampant (lion of Judah), a widely recognized symbol of the Judaic royal line of David. The arms of Robert I's brother, Edward, not only shows a lion rampant, but also places an Islamic crescent over the lion's heart, suggesting perhaps Muslim or Arab ancestry in addition to Jewish. Notably, the arms of the de Mowbray, Plantagenet, Bohun and Beaumont families also prominently carry the Lion of Judah symbol. All these families originated in France and (we propose) believed themselves to be of Davidic descent. Notably, arms of the Beaton/Bethune family discussed in chapter 1 also bear the Islamic crescent.

The Scottish Saltire flag hangs in Dumfermline Abbey; we propose that the symbol is derived from the Cabalistic Tau/Tough image. Photograph by Elizabeth Caldwell Hirschman.

Dunfermline Abbey Churchyard photographs show a Tau/Tough symbol marking a Freemason or Templar grave and a skull and crossbones marking a Templar or Freemason grave. Photographs by Elizabeth Caldwell Hirschman.

Campbell

The Campbell surname seems to have originated in the mid–to late 1300s (Smout 1969). We believe that the first members of this family arrived in Scotland as a result of anti–Jewish pogroms in France and Spain in the middle of the fourteenth century (Benbassa 1999). Below we have excerpted material taken from the Clan Campbell Web site at http://www.tartans.com/clans/Campbell/Campbell.html to demonstrate how a process of "Gaelicization" naturalized this family, which originated outside Scotland (Smout 1969), disguised its French and Semitic roots. As noted in chapter 2, some Scottish Campbell families in Latin America considered themselves to have "always been Jewish."

> The surname **Campbell**, most probably derived from the Gaelic cambeul (twisted mouth), is one of the oldest in the Highlands, and a crown charter of 1368 acknowledges Duncan Mac-Duihbne as founder of the Campbells who were established as Lords of Loch Awe. The founder of the Argyll line was Cailean Mor (d. 1294), whose descendent, Colin Campbell (d. 1493), 1st Earl of Argyll, married Isabel Stewart of Lorne....
>
> Sir John Campbell (1635–1716), 11th Laird of Glenorchy, was created Earl of Breadalbane in 1681. Described as being "cunning as a fox, wise as a serpent, and supple as an eel ... [he] knew neither honor nor religion, but where they are mixed with interest...." His line was founded by the colourful crusader "black" Colin Campbell (d. 1498), who received Glenorchy in 1432 from his father, Sir Duncan Campbell. The Campbells of Loudoun are descended from Sir Duncan Campbell, second son of the first MacCailean Mor, who married a Crauford of Loudoun.

The Campbell septs include several with an apparent Hebrew connection (*italicized*)[4]:

> **Septs:** Arthur, Bannatyne, Burnes, Burness, *Burnett*, Burns, Connochie, Conochie, Denoon, Denune, Gibbon, *Gibson, Harres, Harris*, Hawes, Haws, Hawson, *Isaac, Isaacs*, Iverson, *Kellar, Keller, Kissack, Kissock*, Lorne, MacArtair, MacArthur, MacColm, MacColmbe, MacConachie, MacConchie, MacEller, MacElvie, MacGibbon, MacEver, MacGlasrich, MacGubbin, MacGure, *MacIsaac*, MacIver, MacIvor, *MacKellar*, MacKelvie, MacKerlie, MacKerlich, *MacKessack, MacKessock, MacKissoch*, MacLaws, MacLehose, MacNochol, MacNocaird, *MacOran*, MacOwen, MacPhedran, MacPhun, *MacTause, MacTavish*, MacThomas, *MacUre*, *Moore, Muir*, Ochiltree, *Orr*, Pinkerton, *Taweson, Tawesson*, Thomas, Thomason, Thompson, Thomson, *Ure*.

The Gaelic word *duibne* means "black" or "dark." Such a designation probably referred to a dark skin or complexion, as early portraits of the Campbells show them to have olive or tawny skin and dark hair and eyes. Material gathered from Melungeon genealogies illustrates that several Campbell lines in the American colonies had Hebrew naming patterns, for example, using Israel, Orra, and Tabitha as given names.

An ancestor of the Marquise of Argyll Archibald Campbell (chapter 1) was closely allied to the Royal Stewart house, even marrying a Stewart. Yet in the late 1500s he dramatically broke with the Stewarts, who had become ardent Catholics (despite believing themselves Jewish by descent), and supported the Protestant Reformation. The Protestants' principal spokesman in Scotland, John Knox (chapter 10), came to Castle Campbell and preached to the Campbells and other supporters. The Campbellite denomination mentioned in chapter 2 seems to have been the fruit of the Campbells' abhorrence of Catholicism and partial embrace of Knox's Presbyterianism. We believe their early and strong support for Knox was founded on a Crypto-Judaic orientation, which found Protestantism more congenial than Catholicism.

The Campbell coat of arms does *not* bear a lion rampant. Thus they do not see themselves as having Davidic ancestry. It *does* carry an oared sailing ship with furled sails, not a Viking or Celtic type of vessel, but a Mediterranean-style merchantman. The iconography suggests they arrived in Scotland from the Mediterranean and chose to settle there.

Forbes

The surnames Forbush, Fawbush and Fawbus all appear to be alternate spellings of Forbes.[5] We believe that the family name originally was derived from the Moroccan Sephardic surname Farrabas, which is related to Phoebus. Several colonial members of the Forbes family living in Charleston, S.C., and Savannah, Ga., were openly Jewish, belonging to the Spanish-Portuguese synagogues there and being buried in Sephardic cemeteries (M. Stern 1991). Given below is an informative GenForum posting from a Forbes/Forbush/Farrabas descendent.

Daniel Forbes/Forbush

By Michael Forbush

(From "Forbes and Forbush Genealogy: The Descendents of Daniel Forbush" by Frederick Clifton Pierce)

The first record of Daniel Forbes, or Forbush, or Farrabas, that I can find in this country is in Cambridge, Mass. He married, March 26, 1660, Rebecca Perriman, who is supposed to be the sister of Thomas Perriman, Weymouth, 1652.... Their son, Isaac b. 1656, m. Jane Rutter and resided in Marlborough.... February 27, 1664 and March 27, 1665 Daniel Farrabas was granted by the town of Cambridge these several lots....

Daniel's wife, Rebecca, died May 3, 1677 and he married second May 23, 1679 Deborah Rediat[6] of Concord, who was the daughter of John Rediat of Sudbury, who was a freeman in 1645. By his wife Ann ... he had John b. April 19, 1644; Samuel b. October 22, 1653; Eliza b. 12 Aug. 1657; Deborah, b. 1652; Mehitable, who m. Nathaniel Oaks and d.s.p. Nov. 25, 1702.

John Rediat was probably born in England in 1612 and came to America in the good ship "Confidence" of London, of which John Jobson was master; Daniel Farrabas was a resident of Cambridge, Concord, and Marlborough, Mass. He had the following children with Rebecca (Perriman):

i.	Daniel, born Cambridge, March 20, 1664; married Dorothy Pray
ii.	Thomas, born Cambridge, March 6, 1667; married Dorcas Rice
iii.	Elizabeth, born Cambridge, March 16, 1669
iv.	Rebecca, born Concord, Feb. 15, 1672; married Joseph Byles
v.	Samuel, born about 1674; married Abigail Rice
	Daniel had the following children with Deborah (Rediat):
vi.	Jon born 1681; married Martha Bowker
vii.	Isaac born Oct. 30, 1682;
viii.	Jonathan born March 12, 1684; married Hanna Farrar Holloway

Note in the description above the intertwining of several Mediterranean-Sephardic surnames: Rediat, Jobson, Perriman, Rice (Reiss), Farrar; as well as a preponderance of

Hebrew and Mediterranean given names, e.g., Hannah, Jonathan, Dorcas, Daniel, and Deborah.

Septs allied with Clan Forbes are listed below. Notice the several permutations of the surname and also its linkage with the Berry (Sephardic), Walters and Watts names.

Bannerman	Fordice	Meldrum
Berrie/Berry	Fordyce	Michie
Boyce	Furbush	Middleton
Boyes	Lumsden	Walter
Faubus	Macouat	Walters
Fobes	Macowatt	Watson
Forbess	MacQuattie	Watt
Forbis	MacWatt	Watters
Forbus	Mechie	Wattie[7]
Forbush	Mekie	Watts

Fraser

The Frasers of Scotland acknowledge their medieval ancestral origins in France, the Lady Saltoun recently clarifying that the name "probably came from Anjou" (Fraser 1997, p. 1). Their associated septs, as listed below, include several Sephardic Jewish surnames. Among these are Bissett, Frizell, Frew, Olivier, Sim, Simon, Simpson and variations thereof.

Bissett	Mackim	Simon
Brewster	Mackimmie	Simpson
Cowie	Macsimon	Sims
Frizell	Mactavish	Syme
Frew	Oliver	Twaddle
Macgruer	Sim	Tweedie

The Clan Fraser Web site (http://www.fraserchief.co.uk) states:

It is generally believed that the name Fraser traces its origins to the French provinces of Anjou and Normandy. The French word for strawberry is *fraise* and growers are called *fraisiers*. The Fraser arms are silver strawberry flowers on a field of blue. The Frasers first appear in Scotland around 1160 when Simon Fraser made a gift of a church at Keith in East Lothian to the monks at Kelso Abbey. The Frasers moved into Tweeddale in the 12th and 13th centuries and from there into the counties of Stirling, Angus, Inverness and Aberdeen. About five generations later, Sir Simon Fraser was captured fighting for Robert the Bruce and executed with great cruelty by Edward I in 1306....

Frasers of Philorth [Lord Saltoun]. The senior line is descended from Sir Alexander Fraser, who married Robert the Bruce's widowed sister, Lady Mary. His grandson, Sir Alexander Fraser of Cowie, acquired the castle and lands of Philorth by marriage with Lady Joanna, younger daughter and co-heiress of the Earl of Ross in 1375. Eight generations later, Sir Alexander Fraser, 8th laird of Philorth, founded Fraser's Burgh by royal charters obtained in 1592 and also built Fraserburgh Castle. His son, the 9th laird, married the heiress of the Abernethies, becoming Lord Saltoun,[8] and in 1669 their son, Alexander Fraser, became the 10th Lord Saltoun. The present Chief of the Name of Fraser is Flora Marjory Fraser, 20th Lady Saltoun, who is an active member of the House of Lords. The family seat is Fraserburgh, Aberdeenshire.

Frasers of Lovat [Lords Lovat]. The Frasers of Lovat[9] descend from Sir Simon Fraser who married Lady Margaret Sinclair. Documents dated 12th September 1367, connect a Fraser with the lands of Lovat and the Aird.... Beauly was founded in about 1320 by John Bisset, who also built Lovat Castle. About 1460 Hugh Fraser, 6th Laird of Lovat, became the 1st Lord Lovat.

The seal of William Fraser, bishop of St. Andrews (1279), shows a man in a central Tau position flanked by an Islamic crescent and six-pointed star. The line of bishops of St. Andrews included some persons we believe are likely of Judaic descent, including, besides Fraser, William Malvoesin (1202–1230), David de Bernham (1239–1253), Abel de Golin (1254), Gamelin (1255–1253), James Ben (1328–1332), and William Scheves (1478–1497). The St. Andrews cemetery has several graves with Freemason symbolism. Additionally, on display at the cathedral museum are several very early sarcophagi marked with Templar images. Perhaps most remarkable of the artifacts at St. Andrews, however, is a large carved stone sarcophagus dating from the late 700s depicting the Jewish king David battling lions. We will argue in chapter 5 that it was during this time period that a Jewish holy man, Machir of Narbonne (France), either in person or through representatives, visited Scotland and proselytized its inhabitants for the Jewish faith.

Leslie

The Leslies are one of the very few Scottish landed families to acknowledge an ancestry other than Celtic or French. According to both clan history records and our DNA results, their ancestor was a man named Bartholomew Ladslau from Hungary who ventured to Scotland with Queen Margaret's entourage (Klieforth 1993). Bartholomew later became chamberlain to Queen Margaret (Smout 1969). The role of chamberlain or steward was one performed often by Sephardic Jews in England, France, Portugal and Spain, as they were well educated, multi-lingual and traveled internationally (Benbassa 1999; Benbassa and Rodrique 1995; Stern 1950). Historically, the origins of "chamberlain," like many courtly titles of European royalty, lie in Persian, or "Oriental," ideas of high rank and luxurious palace life, notably continued by the caliphs and other rulers of Islam. The Leslies became the Earls of Leven and Rothes, both of which are Jewish/Hebrew appellations.

As is the case with our other families, Scottish-originating Leslies exhibited Judaic naming practices in the American colonies, and members of the Scottish-based family group openly practiced Judaism in Charleston, S.C. and Savannah, Ga., where males were also leading figures in the Freemasons' temples (Stern 1991). Charleston was the port of

Above and opposite: Tombs with Templar symbols in St. Andrews churchyard cemetery. Photographs by Elizabeth Caldwell Hirschman.

Top: Grave marker with Cabalist symbols, St. Andrews churchyard. *Bottom:* Freemason tomb, St. Andrews churchyard. Both photographs by Elizabeth Caldwell Hirschman.

Top: Judaic "Book of Life" motif gravemarker, St. Andrews cemetery. *Bottom:* David sarcophagus at St. Andrews Cathedral Museum, ca. 900 C.E. Note the presence of leopards, gazelles and lions—all symbols of Israel. Both photographs by Elizabeth Caldwell Hirschman.

Templar sarcophagus, St. Andrews Cathedral Museum. Photograph by Elizabeth Caldwell Hirschman.

entry for what was called Scottish Rite Masonry, and Savannah's chapter was established as Solomon's Lodge #1 (Roberts 1985).

Panton, Leslie and Company in Pensacola, Fla., was at one time the largest trading firm in the Western Hemisphere. It was founded by Sephardic Scotsmen who had all been active as traders in Charleston and Savannah and whose families were multiply entwined, both by marriage and by business ties. Through contacts with Basil Cowper and John Gordon of Charleston, William Panton, John Forbes and several junior Leslie partners took over the Scots-run Spalding and Kelsall establishment based at Frederica on St. Simon's Island, Georgia (Braund 1993, p. 56). There was also a shifting alliance with the various subsidiaries and affiliates of Clark and company, centered in Augusta, Georgia. The new partners developed Pensacola in Spanish West Florida as their entrepôt. From here, Panton, Leslie and Co. traded with the world. It had energetic "factors" in every major Creek Indian town throughout Choctaw territory and as far west as Arkansas and Texas. Its ships sailed without interference between Spanish harbors in the Caribbean to and from Cadiz, Lisbon, Glasgow, London, Amsterdam, Hamburg, Le Havre, and even Turkish, Moroccan and Barbary ports. Indian chiefs placed orders for French wine and Scots whiskey; hatters and furriers in Hamburg and London received skins and pelts; flour and other staples poured into Cadiz and Havana.

With the death of the senior partner in 1805, Panton, Leslie and Co. was reorganized as John Forbes and Company. The Creek War and American annexation of Florida in 1813 began the firm's long decline. It was dissolved in decades-long proceedings conducted under Spanish, Napoleonic, American, British equity, admiralty, and international law (Coker 1986).[10]

Douglas

This noble Scots family first appeared in Britain around 1300 and settled on the Scottish border (Brown 1998). One standard reference book observes that the "Douglases were one of Scotland's most powerful families [and] it is therefore remarkable that their origins remain obscure" (Way and Squire 1998, p. 384). We have seen in chapter 2 that the Douglases have many branches, but all seem to agree in being originally Gothic, with the majority of DNA matches turning up in the Iberian peninsula. The name Douglas means "dark stranger" in Gaelic and may have originated from the Mediterranean complexions of the family's founders (M. Brown 1998).[11] The Black Douglases (so named for their dark coloring) were the dominant force on the borders between England and Scotland from 1300 to 1455 (M. Brown 1998). Family portraits attest to their ancestral Mediterranean physiognomy.

Septs associated with the Douglas clan include Blackstock, Blalock, Brown, Drysdale, Forrest, Inglis, Kilgore, Kirkpatrick, Lockerbie, McGuiffie, Morton, Sandilands, Soule, Symington, Troup and Young. The following genealogy is based on *The Black Douglases* (1998):

William of Douglas is the "first of [the Douglas name] for which any certain record has been found." He is thought to have been born in or before 1174. "William was surely related to [probably brother-in-law of] Freskin the Fleming, who came to Scotland before the end of the reign of David I." It is believed that both William of Douglas and Freskin the Fleming came with their families from Flanders, "perhaps connected with the House of Boulogne."

Other than the possible connection with the Fleming, the wife of William of Douglas is unknown. He did however have one known son:

1.   Archibald of Douglass, who was given lands at Hermiston in Lothian.

Archibald of Douglas was born sometime prior to 1198 and died ca. 1240. While his marriages are unknown, he had two known sons:

1.   Sir William of Douglas
2.   Sir Andrew of Douglas, ancestor of the Douglases of Morton

Sir William of Douglas, known as "Longleg," was born ca. 1200 and died sometime after 1274. He had two sons:

1.   William "le Hardi" Douglas
2.   Hugh of Douglas

Sir William "le Hardi" Douglas was born ca. 1240.

While governor of Berwick he was captured when the town was besieged by the English and spent time in an English prison. He was released later only after agreeing to accept English King Edward I as overlord of Scotland. However, he later fought alongside William Wallace. He first married *Elizabeth Stewart*, and later married *Eleanor de Louvaine*. He had one child by each, and one of uncertain maternity:

1.   Sir James Douglas, "the Good," by Elizabeth Stewart. James was a lifelong friend and supporter of Robert the Bruce, King of Scots. After the Bruce's death, Sir James was the Black Douglas charged to take the heart of Robert the Bruce to Jerusalem. Sir James died in battle in Spain during the crusade against the Moors. He had one known (illegitimate) son:
a.   Archibald Douglas, "the Grim," who fought in the defense of Edinburgh castle against English King Henry IV in 1400, and achieved the rank of Lieutenant General of Scotland. Was killed in action along with his son while fighting the English in France.
2.   Sir Archibald of Douglas, child by Eleanor de Louvaine
3.   Hugh Douglas (Lord of Douglas)

Sir Archibald of Douglas was born ca. 1297. He married ca. 1328 Beatrice Lindsay, and they had two known children:

1.   Eleanor Douglas
2.   William of Douglas

Sir Archibald of Douglas defeated Edward de Baliol, King of Scotland, in 1332 and was appointed Regent of Scotland during the minority of King David II. He was killed on 19 July 1333.

William of Douglas, 1st Earl of Douglas, was born ca. 1323. His first marriage was to Margaret, Countess of Mar (daughter of Donald, 8th Earl of Mar). Whether through death, affair, or divorce, either before or after Margaret of Mar, he was also associated with and possibly married to *Margaret Stewart*. He also had at least one other child by marriage or affair. Children by Margaret of Mar:

1. James Douglas of Drumlanring
2. unknown (m. Alexander Montgomerie)

Child by Margaret Stewart:

3. George Douglas

Child by unknown:

4. Margaret Douglas (m. Sir Herbert Herries)

George Douglas, 1st Earl of Angus, and born ca. 1376, is credited with being the found of the "Red Douglas" branch of the Douglas family. He married on 24 May 1387 *Lady Mary Stewart* (daughter of King Robert III of Scotland). They had three children:

1. Elizabeth Douglas (b. ca. 1397; m. Alexander Forbes)
2. William Douglas
3. Mary Douglas, m. Sir David Hay (1421/34 — before 1 Mar. 1478); son:
a. John Hay (1st Lord Hay of Yester)

Sir William Douglas, 2nd Earl of Angus, was born ca. 1399. In 1425 he married Margaret Hay and had two children:

1. George Douglas
2. Helen Douglas, m. by 1460 William Graham (ca. 1448–1472)

George Douglas, 4th Earl of Angus, was born after 1425. He was married to Isabel Sibbald, and they had two known children:

1. Archibald Douglas
2. Jane Douglas, m. David "the Younger" Scott, who d. 1492

Archibald Douglas was born ca. 1454, and was the 5th Earl of Angus. He married on 4 Mar. 1467/8 Elizabeth Boyd and had three children:

1. George Douglas
2. Sir William Douglas
3. Lady Marjory Douglas (b. after 1467/8, m. Cuthbert Cunningham)

George Douglas, Master of Angus, was born ca. 1469. He was married by March of 1487/8 to Elizabeth Drummond (b. ca. 1460) and had five children:

1. Alison Douglas
2. Archibald Douglas, 6th Earl of Angus, b. after 1488, m. 1. Margaret Hepburn, affair with Stewart (first name unknown), m. 2. Princess Margaret Tudor, m. 3. Margaret Maxwell
3. Elizabeth Douglas, b. ca. 1489, m. John Hay
4. George Douglas, ca. 1490–Aug. 1522, m. Elizabeth (Isabella) Douglas
5. Janet Douglas, ca. 1495–17 Jul. 1537, m. John Lyon

Notable in this genealogy are the relatively frequent marriages with the Royal Stewart family (which regarded itself as being of Jewish ancestry), marriage to cousins of the same name (Douglas), and alliances with other families believed to be of Jewish descent (for instance, Forbes, Hay and Lyon). We might also draw attention to the perpetuation of the Greek name George, a name drawn from the orbit of late antiquity and the Byzantine world.

Gordon

The Gordons first distinguished themselves in south central Scotland during the 1300s; the family then moved to Aberdeen on the northeast coast of Scotland (Smout 1969). Here they entered several guilds normally occupied by persons of Jewish ancestry, e.g., gold and silver smithing, banking, international trading, tin working and leather tanning (McDonnell 1998). The Gordons seem to have originated in France, where the name was probably Jardine, meaning "garden" or "gardener," which was perhaps later conflated with the name Jordan.[12]

However, there is a strong family tradition of origination in Macedonia (northern Greece), a sojourn in Spain and subsequent immigration to southern France. If this is the case, then the family probably came to Britain with William the Conqueror in 1066. Their clan septs include the surnames Jardine, Gardner, and Gardener in addition to Gordon. Additional surnames associated with this clan are given below. Several of these are common to Sephardic and Ashkenazic Jews (e.g., Blair, Davidson, Hay, Lyon, Napier, Hebron, Pollack).

Aiken	Henderson
Bisset	Hepburn/Hebron
Blair	Jardine
Broun/Brown	Lyon/Leon
Burnett	MacBean/Bean
Carnegie	Mhoir
Chisholm	Moubray
Davidson	Muir
Eaken	Napier
Fleming	Oliphant
Gardyne	Pollock/Pollack
Glass	Wemyss
Hay	Wier/Weir

As with the other families we have studied, Gordon portraits show them to be dark-skinned with Mediterranean features. Moreover, we have remarked on the fact that poet Lord (George Gordon) Byron's uncle openly practiced Judaism in England during the 1700s (see chapter 2, note 18).

Stewart

We have already discussed the Stewart family in some detail in chapter 1. The Clan Stewart (Stuart) Web site states the following[13]:

The Stewarts descend from the seneschals of Dol in Brittany (France). They came to England with William the Conquerer; Walter the Steward came to Scotland with King David I. Walter was created Steward of Scotland and given estates in Renfrewshire and East Lothian.... James, 5th High Steward, swore fealty to Edward I of England, but later joined William Wallace in his quest for Scottish Independence. On Wallace's death, he joined the cause of The Bruce. Walter Steward married the Bruce's daughter, Marjorie, thus securing the Kingship for his son on the death of Bruce's only son, David II. Sir Walter's son and Bruce's grandson, Robert Stewart, became King Robert II.... The Royal line continued with male heirs until Mary, Queen of Scots. The Stewarts held the Scottish (and later the English) throne from Robert II until 1714.

Among the septs allied with the Stewarts are several having Sephardic ties; these include Lombard/Lumbard, Lyle, DonLevy, Leay, Levack, Lay, Lea, Lew, Lewis, Robb, Mitchell, Glass, Jameson, and Jamieson. The Lev surnames derive from the Hebrew tribe of Levi, Robb from Rueben, Mitchell from Michal, Jameson from Chaim, and Glass from glass-production, a Sephardic skill. Lombard/Lumbard (from Langobardi, the 6th century invaders of Italy) was an early medieval name for money-changers from Italy, many, if not most of them, Jewish; in England, it became synonymous with "banker" and left its heritage in the name of the main street in the City of London where the stock exchange took shape (Adler 1939, pp. 211–12). In medieval Oxford, Lombard Hall was named after its Jewish proprietor (Tovey, p. 8).[14]

As we explored in chapter 1, HRH Prince Michael Stewart (2000) claims to be of Davidic Jewish descent.[15] In chapter 5 we will present documentation concerning Jewish communities dwelling in France prior to the arrival of the Normans. To complete the picture of Scots-Jewish families, however, it is probably most appropriate to include in this chapter several Stewart-connected genealogies which suggest a strong Jewish ancestry feeding into those Norman, Frankish, French, Hungarian and Flemish families that made their way to England — and onward to Scotland — during the 1050–1150 time period.

Figure 4, Hungarian Descent of the Kings of the Scots, shows the descent to Margaret, the wife of Malcolm Canmore (1058–1093), who became King of Scots at the time of the Norman conquest of England. Notably, Margaret descends from several persons who would appear to be Jews: among them Zoltan, his consort, the daughter of Maroth, Prince of Bihar, Geza, Prince of the Magyars, whose first daughter was named Judith (= female form of Judah) and whose second daughter married a king of Hungary named Samuel Aba (Fig. 5).

The genealogy of Maud (Matilda) de Lens shows that Malcolm and Margaret's son, David I of Scots, also appeared to marry a woman of Jewish descent, Maud de Lens. Her ancestors included Louis the Pious, King of the Franks (d. 840), who was married to a Judith. The same genealogy also indicates that the grandmother of William the Conqueror was a French woman named Judith — and further, that Maud de Lens' mother was also named Judith. Although it may seem odd to place so much emphasis on the female given name *Judith*, keep in mind that this was the Middle Ages, a time when the ethnic identity of given names was of critical importance. It is very unlikely that a woman of noble birth would be named Yehudah unless she was, indeed, a Jewess, and it was wished by her parents that she be recognized as such.

The degree of consanguinity in the family of the Conqueror also becomes apparent from this genealogy. The Vatican tried to prevent his marriage to Matilda of Flanders, his 8th cousin twice removed, related to him within a forbidden eleven degrees of canon

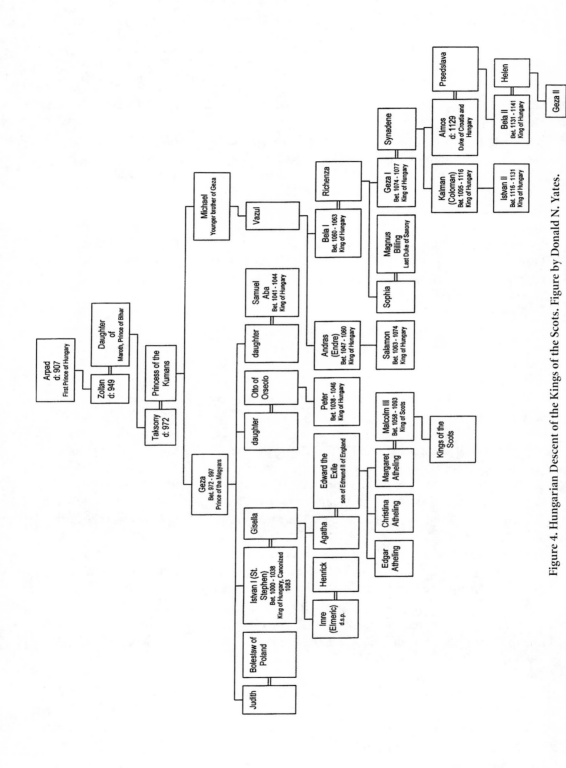

Figure 4. Hungarian Descent of the Kings of the Scots. Figure by Donald N. Yates.

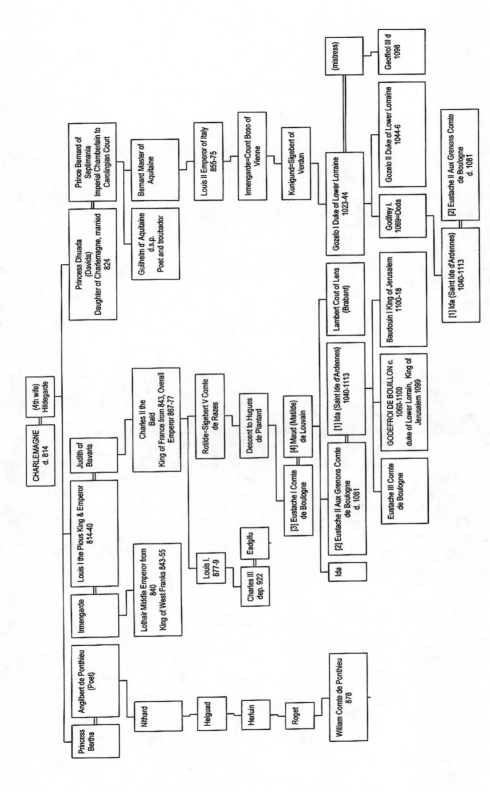

Figure 5. Davidic Descent from Charlemagne to the Kings of Jerusalem. Figure by Donald N. Yates.

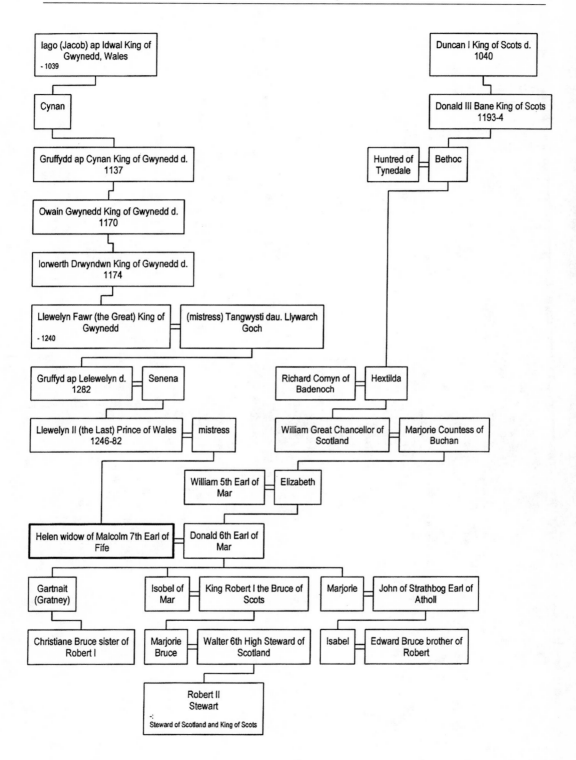

Figure 6. Descent from Iago (Jacob), King of Wales, to Isobel of Mar. Figure by Donald N. Yates.

law. Maud de Lens was also his cousin, within the same degree. His children went even farther: Henry Beauclerc's second wife was Adelicia, daughter of Ida and Geoffrey of Brabant. She was a 3rd cousin through one parent and a 4th cousin through the other.[16] Albert II of Namur and his wife Princess Regulinde were 4th cousins, clearly illegal (having a 7th degree of consanguinity).

Figure 6 shows the descent path to Isobel of Mar, who married Robert I Bruce and was the mother of Marjorie Bruce and grandmother of Robert II, the first Stewart monarch. Through Isobel's mother, Helen, her lineage continues back to Iago (Jacob) ap Idwal, king of Gwynedd (Wales). By the same reasoning used with Judith, we can infer, given the historical context, that the name Jacob marked one as a Jew.

Figure 7 shows the ancestry of Mary of Guise, wife of James V of Scotland. Here we see the extensive entry of Middle Eastern and Mediterranean ancestry into the Royal Stewart lineage. Persons such as Isaac Angelos, Hasan Artsume, Stephen of Armenia, John (Isaac) Comnenos, Isabella of Cyprus, Esther, Judith Bonne of Bohemia, and Louis the Duke of Saxony are certain to have contributed not only Judaic, but also Central Asian and Mediterranean heritage to the Scottish Royal Family.

And finally we arrive at figure 8, the *pièce de resistance.* It shows the ancestry of the House of Boulogne and kings of Jerusalem, to which many of our Scottish clans are linked. We start out with Dagobert I, King of the Franks and a Merovingian (rumored by various Biblical conspiracy theorists to be of Jewish ancestry, possibly Davidic). We follow this line down to Theodoric, named Makir Theodoric, whom we will discuss presently when we turn to St. Machar of Scotland in chapter 5. In the same line, just below him, we find William de Toulouse de Gellone, the Davidic-descended head of the Jewish state of Septimania in southern France and founder of the Judaic Academy at Gellone (791–828 C.E.). We will also discuss him at some length, in a future chapter.

Significantly we see Judaic naming patterns among the Merovingians and Carolingians. Charlemagne names one of his daughters Dhuada (= Davida, feminine form of David),[17] and one of his sons, Louis the Pious (d. 840), as we have already noticed, married Judith of Bavaria. Poignantly, these lineages continue onward until they reach the Bouillons and Baudouins (Baldwins) who served as the kings of Jerusalem during the Crusades.

Figure 7. Ancestry of Mary of Guise

Descent to Marie de Guise-Lorraine, wife of James V of Scots

Khachi'k Artsruni Prince of T'ornavan	Manuel Comnenos
Hasan Artsruni	John Comnenon d 1067 = Anna Dalassena
Abulgharin Artsruni Governor of Tarsus	
↓	Alexis I Comnenos Eastern (Byzantine) Emperor 1081–1118 = Irene, dau of Andronikus Dukas

daughter
= Oshin I
Prince of Lambron

John (Ioannes) II Comnenos   Isaac Comnenos
Eastern Emperor 1118–43
Hetum II   = Prisca (Irene), dau of
Prince of Lambron   King Ladislaus I of Hungary
& Tarsus

Smbat I   John (Isaac) Comnenos
Prince of Paperon d 1153   d 1174

Rita
dc 1210   Maria   Theodora = Andronikus I Comnenos
= Stephen of Armenia   = Amuary I (Amalric)   Eastern Emperor
son of King Leo I   King of Jerusalem d 1174   1183–5

                                                   Amalric I
                                  Isabella I   of Cyprus
                                  of Jerusalem dc 1208   Amuary II
Doleta   = Henri I   of Jerusalem
= Bertrand I   Count of Champagne   d 1205
Lord of Giblet,   King of Jerusalem 1191–7
Cyprus   Irene
                                                               = Isaac II Angelos
                                                               Eastern Emperor 1203–4
Hugh de Giblet   Alice of Champagne —=— Hugues I   Irene
Baliff of Cyprus d 1233   of Cyprus d 1219   = Philip
                                                           of Swabia
                                                           d 1208

Bertrand II de Giblet   Isabella of Cyprus   Henry I   Kunigunde
d 1258   d 1264   of Cyprus   = Wenzel III (Vaclav)
                        = Henry of Antioch   d 1253   King of Bohemia
                                                               1230–53

Margaret   Hugues II   Premsyl Otakar II
= Baudouin d'Ibelin   of Cyprus   King of Bohemia
of Vitzada   d 1267   1253–78
                        Hugues III of Cyprus   = Kunigunde
                        King of Jerusalem   dau of Rostislav
                        d 1284   Prince of Halitch

Isabel
= Guy d'Ilelin   Wenzel IV (Vaclav II)
Seneschal   Jean I of Cyprus   Guy of Cyprus   King of Bohemia
of Cyprus   Jean II of Jerusalem   d 1303   1278–1305
                1284–5   King Waclaw I
     ↓   ↓   ↓   ↓

```
                                                              of Poland
                                                              1296–1305
                                                              = Jutta, dau of
                                                              Rudolf of Habsburg

                         Henri of Jerusalem
                         1285–91
                         Henri II of Cyprus
                         1291–1324                      Elizabeth d 1330
Alice —————————————=————— Hugues IV          = John (Jan) of Luxembourg
                         King of Cyprus               King of Bohemia 1310–46
                         1324–59

                    James (Jacques), King of Cyprus    Judith (Bonne) of Bohemia
                    1382–98 (Titular King of Armenia)        1315–49
                            = Esther                   = King John II of France
                                                              1350–64
                         Janus                    King Charles V of France
                         King of Cyprus           1364–80
                         1398–1432                = Joanna, dau of Peter I
                                                  Duc de Bourbon

Charlotte de Bourbon-—=—-John (Jean) II    King Charles VI of France
dau of John I            King of Cyprus     1380–1422
Count de la Marche       1432–58            = Isobel, dau of Stephen II
                                            Duke of Bavaria-Ingolstadt


        ┌─────────────────────────────┐
                                            Catherine de Valois
Charlotte                       Anne        1401–37
Queen of Cyprus                 =Louis      = (2) Owen Tudor of Wales
1458–60                         Duc de Savoy        d 1461
                     ─────────  d 1465

                                            Edmund Tudor (Illegit)
                                Margaret de Savoy   1st Earl of Richmond
                                d 1483             1430–56
        James II                = Peter, Count of  = Margaret, dau of
        King of Cyprus          Luxembourg         John Beaufort, 1st
        1460–73                 d 1482             Duke of Somerset

        James III               Mary               Henry VII Tudor
        King of Cyprus          Countess of St Pol King of England
        1473–4                  d 1546             1485–1509
        = Catherine Cornaro =Francis de Bourbon = Elizabeth of York
        reigned as Queen        Comte de Vendoma  dau of King Edward
        1474–89                 d 1495             IV of England

                                Antoinette de Bourbon  Margaret Tudor
                                1493–1583              1489–1541
                                = Claude, Duc de Guise = James IV Stewart
                                1496–1550              King of Scots
                                                       1488–1513

                                Marie de Guise-Lorraine
                                1515–60                James V. Stewart
                                                       King of Scots
                                                       1513–42
```

1 Guilhelm Makir b. Babylon +Guibourg
  2 Prince Bernard of Septimania +Princess Dhuada (Davida)
    3 Guilhelm d' Aquitaine d.s.p.
    3 Bernard Master of Aquitaine
      4 Louis II Emperor of Italy 855-75
        5 Irmengarde +Count Boso of Vienne
          6 Kunigund +Sigebert of Verdun
            7 Gozelo I Duke of Lower Lorraine 1023-44
              8 Godfrey II Duke of Upper Lorraine d. 1069 +Doda (Davida)
                9 Ida (Saint Ide d'Ardennes) 1040-1113 +Eustache II Aux Grenons Comte de Boulogne
                  10 Eustache III Comte de Boulogne +sister of David I King of Scots 1124-53 Mary
                    11 Matilda=Stephen of Blois
                  10 GODEFROI DE BOUILLON c. 1060-1100
                  10 Baudouin I King of Jerusalem 1100-18
              8 Gozelo II Duke of Lower Lorraine 1044-6 +(mistress)
              8 Geoffroi III d. 1098 illegitimate
                9 Baldwin of Le Bourg Count of Rethul +Ida
                  10 Hugues I de Rethul +Melusine
                    11 Baudouin II King of Jerusalem 1118-31 +Morfia of Armenia
                      12 Melisende Queen of Jerusalem 1131-52 +Fulques V d'Anjou King of Jerusalem 1131-43
                        13 Baudouin III King of Jerusalem 1143-62
                        13 Amaury I (Amalric) King of Jerusalem +Maria of Byzantine Comnenos emperors
                          14 Baudouin IV the Leper King of Jerusalem 1174-85
                          14 Sybille Queen of Jerusalem 1186-90
                            15 Baudouin V King of Jerusalem 1183-6
                          14 Isabella I of Jerusalem d. 1208 +Henri I Count of Champagne
                            15 Alice of Champagne +Hugues I of Cyprus son of Almaric II King of Jerusalem
                              16 Isabella of Cyprus d. 1264 +Henry of Antioch
                                17 Hughes III of Cyprus King of Jerusalem d. 1284
                                  18 Guy of Cyprus d. 1303
                                    19 Hugues IV King of Cyprus 1324-59 +Alice
                                    20 James (Jacques) I King of Cyprus +Esther
                              18 Jean I of Cyprus (II of Jerusalem)
                                  21 Janus King of Cyprus 1398-1432
                                    22 John (Jean) II King of Cyprus +Charlotte de Bourbon
                                      23 Charlotte Queen of Cyprus 1458-60
                                      23 Anne +Louis Duc de Savoy d. 1465
                                        ancestor of Mary of Guise & Mary Queen of Scots

Figure 8. Ancestry of the House of Boulogne and Kings of Jerusalem. Figure by Donald N. Yates.

Chapter 4

Genealogies of the Second Wave of Jewish Families, 1350–1700 C.E.

The families discussed in this chapter are known to have arrived in Scotland after 1350. Most came from the Mediterranean and have been found to have Sephardic-matching DNA.

Caldwell

The Caldwells are believed to have arrived in southwestern Scotland from France around 1550. Their somewhat jumbled origin story is given below. Despite some obvious inaccuracies, what is instructive about it is the report of long-term religious harassment by the Catholic Church in Spain and of the dark, Mediterranean complexions of the Caldwells upon their arrival in Scotland.

Before the name Caldwell came into existence, our ancestors were part of two groups of people living in Italy who called themselves the Albigenses and Waldenses. Both these groups were Protestant in their beliefs and are mentioned often in historical accounts. At this time (i.e., early 1200s),[1] those of Protestant belief were being subjected to heavy persecution by the Roman Catholic Church. Eventually, because of these persecutions, they were forced over the mountainous border that separates Italy from France and settled in a small village called Toulon, near the foot of Mt. Aud (also called Mt. Arid in some accounts). It was here that three brothers, John, Alexander, and Oliver, were born....

The three brothers were originally aligned with the Barbarossa brothers, generally considered pirates of much note at the time. The Barbarossas were of Algerian birth and became the dominant power in Algeria. The name "Barabarossa" is a European one meaning "red beard," which the leader of these pirates (Khaii-ed-din by his Algerian name, who died in 1546) apparently had. Nonetheless, these pirates were themselves defeated by the Governor of Aran when he made a massive effort to end the dominance of the Barbarossas. John, Alexander and Oliver escaped without being captured by the Aranian Governor and returned to Toulon for a short time....

[The Caldwell brothers] put their years of experience on the sea to good use and amassed a naval fleet of their own, one rivaling the defeated Barbarossa's in force. Now, however, Spanish merchants hired John, Alexander and Oliver to do away with the remaining pirates on the Mediterranean. Though hired by the Spanish, King Francis I of France was so pleased with their success that he rewarded the brothers, as well. They decided from that time forward to abandon the high seas and returned to their home in Mt. Aud, France. But on their return there, they found France in a state of turmoil as a result of the persecutions suffered by the Huguenots and Piedmontese, as the Protestants in France were called. They, being Protestant themselves, returned at once to Spain.[2]

> From Spain, they took a merchant ship bound for the coast of Scotland. They landed at a place called Solway Firth. And finding the country (Scotland) in peace under the Protestant reign of King James VI (approx. 1567–1603) who then became King James I, King of England (1603–1625), they determined to settle there. After finding a large landholder, he being a wealthy bishop of the place, they purchased from him a large estate. [They then] sent back to their native land for other relatives and friends and in a few years became numerous and prosperous. But in order to acquire full title to this land, it was necessary that they should gain the consent and signature of the King to their purchase.... The King, upon signing their titles, imposed the following condition; that the three brothers should, when the King required it, each send a son with a troop of twenty men to aid in the wars of the King.
>
> Our forefathers were ... of dark skin, with deep penetrating eyes, [and] high ... foreheads. Although naturally of dark complexion, in mingling with the blue-eyed belles of Scotland through thirteen generations, the younger generations have shown many instances of the fair hair and blue eyes of the mother's family. Thus the blue eyes and the black eyes appear in almost every family.[3]

What is evidenced by this account, despite some obvious historical inaccuracies, is a basically credible story of a French-Iberian family fleeing the Inquisition across Italy and France, becoming pirates during the mid–1500s, and then seeking safe haven with other Iberian refugees in the southwest of Scotland. The story takes pains to portray the family's founders as Protestants, which is possible, yet unlikely. Few Iberian Protestants served as pirates in the Mediterranean during the 1500s, while many Sephardic Jews and Moors did (Benbassa and Rodrique 1995; Fletcher 1992). It also omits mention that at least one branch of the Caldwell line settling in Philadelphia prior to the American Revolution opened a goldsmith and silversmith shop. These skills were usually passed from father to son through apprenticeships and were almost exclusively controlled by Jews and Moors (Fletcher 1992).

Further, paternal DNA tests have matched the Caldwells with known Sephardic families, such as Rodriguez and Cooper. This fact, coupled with the prevalence of Caldwells in Melungeon settlements in the Appalachians, suggests that they were most probably of French-Iberian Jewish, not French-Iberian Protestant, origin.

The entire territory over which the Caldwells purportedly roamed was the same as the land awarded after the fall of Rome to the Visigoths[4] in 419 C.E. It became the Regnum Tolosanum and later the Kingdom of Toulouse (Gibbon II, p. 214). At its center, Toulon is an important naval port on the Côte d'Azur between Marseilles and St. Tropez with the Monts de Maures (Moorish Mountains) looming behind it on the French Riviera. Until the Spanish secured Lombardy and the Duchy of Milan, this area belonged, variously, to Provence, Languedoc, Anjou, and the German Empire. At different times, it also was part of Savoy, Lorraine, Aquitaine, and the Papal State of Avignon.

Significantly, an edict of expulsion against the Jews of Provence was first issued in 1500. Jews in the Kingdom of Naples (which included the duchy of Milan) were partially exiled in 1510. Wealthy Jews in Spanish-ruled Italy were expelled again in 1541. Beginning in 1555, Jews in Italy were ghettoized, a situation that was to last until Napoleon's invasion in 1796. The expulsions of 1515, 1550, and 1575, were to the interior of Italy. In 1572, the Duke of Savoy attempted to give Jews special permission to settle in Nice, but renounced the plan under pressure from Spain and the Pope. Phillip II of Spain ordered the expulsion of Jews from the Duchy of Milan again in 1597, and many took refuge in Protestant Switzerland (Barnavi 1992). From these bare facts it is obvious that Jews living in Toulouse had to keep moving to stay ahead of the changing jurisdictions and policies.

Many anomalies formed in this ambiguous, ever-shifting territory. The Jewish state of Leghorn was established by Portuguese *conversos* in 1593, and the Jewish community of Marseilles managed to maintain a continuous existence until Hitler. The Piedmontese Jews were not relegated to ghettos until the 1730s and 1740s. A splendid Rococo synagogue located between Genoa, Turin and Milan, dating back to 1598, survives as testimony to the past glories of Piedmontese Jewry.[5]

Kennedy/Canaday/Canady

The Kennedys first appear in southwest Scottish history around 1360, shortly after an anti–Jewish pogrom in France (Smout 1969). Their lands were named "Cassilis," which may be derived from the Sephardic name Cassell, and, indeed, Cassell is listed as one of the Kennedy septs.[6] Other Kennedy sept names are Cassilis, Ulrich, Canady/Canaday, and Carrick (because Kennedys married into the Carrick family). DNA analyses have suggested that the Scottish Kennedys and their American descendents are likely of Sephardic ancestry, and that their original name may have been *Candiani* ("from Candy").[7] One of the primary Melungeon researchers in recent years is N. Brent Kennedy (1997). Genealogies of the Kennedy family of Hyannisport, Massachusetts, do not go farther back than to Patrick Kennedy, a prosperous farmer of Dunganstown, County Wexford, Ireland, who was born about 1785 and whose son emigrated to America (*Burke's* 1992). However, there is no reason to rule out a possible French origin for the Massachusetts Kennedys before the family became Irish. Both Cassel and Canady appear on a list of refugee Huguenots to Ireland.[8]

Alexander

The Alexanders arrived in Scotland in the late 1400s or early 1500s, concurrent with the Spanish and Portuguese inquisitions (Roth 1937). Further, both as a given name and surname, Alexander is not indigenous to the British Isles. Rather it is Greek in origin and was one of the most widely used names among Mediterranean Jews in the Middle Ages (Roth 1937).[9] The Alexander family settled in the southwestern portion of Scotland, near Stirling on the English border — a locale with easy access to France and the ports of the Mediterranean. The lineage of the Alexander Earls of Stirling is instructive in showing a pattern of intermarriage with other DNA-confirmed Sephardic-Scottish families (e.g., Forbes, Douglas).[10]

Lineage of the Alexander Earls of Stirling

Thomas ALEXANDER was born before 1505 in Menstrie, Sterling. His son was Alexander ALEXANDER. Alexander ALEXANDER was married to Elizabeth FORBES. Alexander ALEXANDER and Elizabeth FORBES had the following children:

1. William ALEXANDER (Earl of Stirling) was born in 1557 in Menstrie, Sterling, Scotland. He died in 1640 in Scotland. William ALEXANDER (Earl of Sterling) was married to Janet ERSKIN about 1580. William ALEXANDER (Earl of Stirling) and Janet ERSKIN had the following children:

2. John ALEXANDER was born about 1590 in Tarbert, Kentyre, Scotland.
   a. William ALEXANDER was born at Eridy, Donegal Co., Ireland.
   b. Phillip ALEXANDER.
   c. Robert ALEXANDER was born in 1610 in Stirling, Scotland. He died in Drumiquim, Tyrone, Ireland.
   d. John ALEXANDER was born between 1624 and 1653.
   e. Andrew ALEXANDER D.D. REV. was born about 1635 in Co. Coleraine, Ireland.
   f. Archibald ALEXANDER was born about 1614 in Scotland or Co. Armagh, Ireland. He died on 31 Mar. 1689 in Belleghan, Donegal, Ireland.

3. William ALEXANDER was born between 1613 and 1656 in Menstrie, Sterling.

William ALEXANDER was married to Margaret Douglas. William ALEXANDER and Margaret DOUGLAS had the following children:

1. James ALEXANDER was born about 1618 in Menstrie, Sterling. He died 9 Dec. 1691 or 17 Nov. 1704 in Donegal, Donegal Co., Ireland.

James ALEXANDER was married to Mary MAXWELL about 1639/40 in Raphoe, Donegal, Ulster, Ireland. Mary MAXWELL was born about 1634/35 in Raphoe, Donegal, Ulster, Ireland. She died in Cecil C., Md.

James ALEXANDER and Mary MAXWELL had the following children:
   a. Joseph ALEXANDER was born between 1639 and 1660 in Raphoe, Donegal, Ulster, Ireland. He died on 9 Mar. 1729/30 in New Munster, Cecil Co., Md.
   b. William ALEXANDER was born about 1646 in Raphoe, Donegal, Ulster, Ireland. He died in 1715 in Somerset Co., Md.
   c. Andrew ALEXANDER was born about 1648 in Raphoe, Donegal, Ulster, Ireland. He died before 1700 in Cecil Co., Md.
   d. Elizabeth ALEXANDER was born in 1650 in Raphoe, Donegal, Ulster, Ireland. She died between 1714 and 1716 in Manokin Hundred, Somerset Co., Md.
   e. James B. ALEXANDER, weaver and carpenter, was born about 1652 in Raphoe, Donegal, Ulster, Ireland. He died in 1719 in New Munster, Cecil Co., Md.
   f. Frances ALEXANDER was born about 1654 in Raphoe, Donegal, Ulster, Ireland. He died about 1701 in Somerset Co., Md.
   g. Samuel ALEXANDER was born about 1657/58 in Raphoe, Donegal, Ulster, Ireland. He was buried in 1733 in Bethel (Chesapeake City) cemetery. He died on 14 Jun. 1733 in Cecil Co., Md.
   h. Jane ALEXANDER was born about 1659 in Raphoe, Donegal, Ulstger, Ireland. She died on 28 Mar. 1692/93 in Manokin Hundred, Somerset Co., Md.

  i. John ALEXANDER was born about 1662 in Raphoe, Donegal, Ulster, Ireland. He died after 1718 in Cecil Co., Md.
  j. Thomas ALEXANDER was born in 1676 in Donegal, Donegal Co., Ireland. He died in 1749 in Augusta Co., Va.

Note that the Alexander family immigrated to Baltimore, Maryland — the arrival point for many immigrants of Sephardic origin due to Maryland's relatively lax religious constraints. The burial of Samuel Alexander occurred in Bethel Cemetery, likely a Judaic burial ground and not a Presbyterian or Anglican churchyard. Finally, Thomas Alexander, born in Donegal, Ireland, is recorded as having died (1749) in Virginia's Augusta County, believed to be a Melungeon/Crypto-Jewish community (Kennedy 1996).

Additional support for the Alexander's Sephardic and Crypto-Jewish status comes from genealogical information on the family once it had reached the American colonies. Inquiries taken from the Alexander Genealogical Forum on the Internet show a naming pattern for the children which is markedly Hebrew. There was frequent intermarriage with the Houston and Kennedy families, both believed to be of Sephardic descent through DNA testing.

Before leaving Alexander, let us present some additional statistics. According to the U.S. Census for 1990, Alexander is the 96th most common surname in America. If you add the variants Sanders (75th) and Saunders (421st), the frequency climbs to 0.2 percent, rather high in the scheme of things. However, Alexander is even more common as a *specifically Jewish surname*. It is among the top ten researched surnames at the Jewish Genealogical Society of Great Britain, and it figures prominently in Rabbi Malcolm Stern's *Americans of Jewish Descent* (1991), as well as in studies of Jewish tombstones in Barbados and Jamaica by Barnett (1959) and Wright (1976). The Alexander genealogical manuscripts of the American Jewish Historical Society are voluminous. For example, Abraham Alexander, born in London in 1743, came to Charleston, S.C. in 1760 and was *hazan* for that city's Beth Elohim congregation 1764–1784. Several generations of Scottish Alexanders came to the Shenandoah valley from Glasgow, via northern Ireland, to "escape religious persecution" and along with the McKees, Davidsons and Houstons were benefactors of a stone "temple" built near Lexington in Rockbridge County in the mid–eighteenth century.[11] Finally, it was an Alexander who presented Glasgow's Jewish community with an ark (Torah receptacle) for the new synagogue in South Portland Street, the largest in Scotland in 1901 (Collins 1987, p. 104).

The somewhat surprising popularity of the Alexander name among Jews is explained by a legend enshrined in the writings of the Roman Jewish author Josephus (27–95 C.E.; Graves 1975, p. 84):

According to Josephus, when Alexander [the Great] came to Jerusalem at the outset of his Eastern conquests [winter of 332 B.C.E.], he refrained from sacking the Temple but bowed down and adored the Tetragrammaton [the four Hebrew letters for God's name] on the High Priest's golden frontlet. His astonished companion Parmenio asked why in the world he had behaved in this unkingly way. Alexander answered: "I did not adore the High Priest himself, but the God who has honoured him with office. The case is this: that I saw this very person in a dream, dressed exactly as now, while I was at Dios in Macedonia.

"In my dream I was debating with myself how I might conquer Asia, and this man exhorted me not to delay. I was to pass boldly with my army across the narrow sea, for his God would march before me and help me to defeat the Persians. So I am now convinced that

Jehovah is with me and will lead my armies to victory." The High Priest then further encouraged Alexander by showing him the prophecy in the Book of Daniel which promised him the dominion of the East; and he went up to the Temple, sacrificed to Jehovah and made a generous peace-treaty with the Jewish nation. The prophecy referred to Alexander as the "two-horned King" and he subsequently pictured himself on his coins with two horns. He appears in the Koran as Dhul Karnain, "the two-horned."

The surname Alexander was often shortened to Sanders or Saunders and also took the forms Sender, Sand, Andrus, Andros, and Anderson.[12] Numerous surnames beginning with Sand- (e.g., Sandford) are thought to be related (Jacobs 1906–1911).

Cowan/Cowen

Septs: Cowan, Cowen, Cowans, MacCowan, MaCowan, McCowen, McCown
The Clan Cowan Web site states:

Cowan, Cowen, and Cowans are common surnames in Ayrshire, Dumfriesshire, and other Lowland counties. There was a James Cowhen, chaplain in North Berwick, in 1560. There was also an old family in Stirling of Cowane. Cowane's Hospital in Stirling was founded in 1639 by John Cowane, a merchant there. A John M'Coan was in Duchre, parish of Kilbrandon, in 1691. A David M'Kowne was a notary in Glasgow in 1550, and his name was also spelled M'Kownne and M'Kowin.

Some additional commentary on members of Clan Cowan in the American Colonies states:

Alexander McCown, Sr. was shown in VA in 1715. His six sons came to America in 1728. Alexander Sr. was a distinguished Presbyterian minister and his son, George, was a ruling elder of the Presbyterian church. They were Scotch-Irish and suffered religious persecution in Ireland. Alexander McCown's ancestors came to Ireland [from Scotland] in the 1600's....

John McCown, with five brothers, George, James, Malcolm, Alexander, and Moses, emigrated from County Tyrone, Ireland, in 1728. John McCown settled in Calf Pasture, Augusta County, Virginia. James, Moses and Alexander settled in Catawba County, South Carolina, and George in Lancaster County, Pennsylvania [*U.S. Biographical Dictionary — 1876 — Missouri*, p. 723, under McCown, Col. William H., Carthage, Mo.].

Alexander McCown was born in Scotland, and moved to Tyrone, Ireland. His six sons ... came to America in 1728 from Tyrone, Ireland. They were called the Blacks and the Reds, because three of them had black hair and dark eyes and dark complexion. The other three had red hair and light complexion. The sons named were: James, Alexander, Moses, George, Malcolm, and John [Mr. Bobby S. Mullins, of Nashville, Tennessee, in correspondence to Lou Poole dated 29 October 1994].

Despite being Presbyterian by the 1600s, Clan Cowan members were, we argue, Kohanim/Cohens of Sephardic Jewish ancestry. Below is the Colonial American genealogy of a Clan Cowan descendant whose DNA scores were Ashkenazi-Levite:

John Walker III, b. prob. in Wigton (Scotland), married Anne Houston in about 1734, and d. 1778 on the Clinch River, Southwest Territories. They had nine children:
1. Mary, m. Andrew Cowan
2. Susanna, m. Patrick Porter
3. Jane, m. William Cowan
4. Hetty, m. Robert Bell

5. John, m. A. Long
6. Samuel
7. Margaret, m. John Judy (= Yehudi/Jew)
8. Anne, m. Samuel Cowan
9. Martha, m. A. Montgomery

Samuel Cowan, d. 1776, m. Anne Walker. Children:
1. John
2. Robert, m. Susannah Woods
3. William
4. Samuel
5. James, m. Margaret Chrystie Russell
6. Nathaniel, m. Sarah Wilson
7. Anne
8. Elizabeth

James Cowan, b. 1761, d. 1801, m. Margaret Chrystie Russell 1795. Graves at 1st Presbyterian Church in Knoxville, Tenn. Children:
1. Jean Glasgo, b. 10/02/1796, m. David Campbell, d. 13/10/1882
2. Mary, b. 26/10/1799, d. 21/10/1801
3. Margaret, b. 22/10/1799, m. John Greenway, d. 13/10/1882
4. James "Hervey" Cowan, b. 22/12/1801
5. James "Hervey" Cowan, b. 22/12/1801, m. Lucinda Foster Dickinson, d. 25/10/1870. Graves at Old Gray along with others below. Children:
1. Margaret, b. 15/04/1832, m. Charles James McClung, d. 17/11/1883
2. Mary, b. 30/12/1833, d. 9/12/1906
3. James Dickinson, b. 3/6/1839, m. (1) Annie White, m. (2) Jeanette Dodson, d. 13/3/1897
4. Lucinda Foster, b. 9/6/1839, m. (1) Charles Alexander, m. (2) Joseph Finegan, d. 20/8/1910
5. Nancy Estabrooke, b. 19/8/1841, m. John Meem, d. 31/03/1849
6. Perez Dickinson, b. 26/12/1843, m. Margaret Rhea, d. 10/2/1923
7. Susan Penniman, b. 10/02/1846, d. 15/05/1847
8. Joseph, b. 6/4/1848, d. 8/6/1848
9. Isabella White, b. 20/4/1849

Perez Dickinson Cowan, b. 26/12/1843, m. Margaret Rhea 26 Oct 1870, d. 10/2/1923. Children:
1. Margaret McClung, b. 1876, d. 1879
2. Eleanor Rhea, b. 5/11/1885, d. 1972
3. James Dickinson, b. 17/8/1887, m. Elsie Bailey, d. 1930

James Dickinson, b. 1887, m. Elsie Bailey. Children:
1. James Dickinson, b. 24/11/1914, m. Louise Yawger, d. 1995
2. Bailey, b. 23/12/1915, m. Margaret Bergius 7 Mar. 1945, d. 7/7/1994
3. Robert Rhea, b. 25/12/1922, m. Catherine Krieger

Bailey Cowan, b. 1915, m. Margaret Bergius. Children:
1. Dickinson Bergius, b. 30/11/1945, m. Christianne Jane Carlisle
2. Sanda Margaret, b. 1/5/1946, m. Duncan Paul Belcher
3. Jennifer Agnes, b. 14/2/1949, m. Charles Thomas Alexander Helme
4. Sheila Rhea, b. 29/1/1952, m. Roger Gins

Dickinson Bergius Cowan, b. 1945, m. Christianne Jane Carlisle. Children:
1. Christianne Emily, b. 1977, Durban
2. Elizabeth Alice, b. 1979, Durban
3. James Carlisle, b. 1981, Durban
4. Lucinda Bergius, b. 1983, Durban

Notably, the gravestone of the wife of James Cowan, also in the Presbyterian Church graveyard in Knoxville, declares her to be "a mother in Israel."[13] We will discuss in chapter 10 the possibility that Presbyterianism served as a haven for Crypto-Jews from Scotland and Northern Ireland who settled in Appalachia and became known as Melungeons.

Finally, we must consider the coats of arms for the various branches of Clan Cowan. The symbolism in them is quite revelatory. First, all carry the Tau Cabalistic symbol ("X") discussed earlier. Three carry the French fleur-de-lis, derived from the Judaic lily symbol associated with the House of David.[14] Four carry the scallop shell, a symbol that indicates the bearers were Jacobite in their sympathies and supporters of the Royal Stewart (Judaic) monarchy. And one carries the "centered circle" symbol, another Cabalistic sign, standing for the Deity.

With John Cowane of Stirling, founder of the Merchant Guild Hospital in 1639, we have the first readily identifiable figure of a second wave of French and Iberian Jewish families that began to arrive in the sixteenth century, at the time persecutions and expulsions of Jews were stepped up on the Continent. Cowane was a money lender, tax farmer and international trader who owned ships going to Danzig, Hamburg, Sweden and Russia. It is said that his family first arrived in Scotland around 1517. We will have more to say about Stirling and its merchants in a later chapter.

Chapter 5

The Early Jews of France, 700–1200 C.E.

Until the recent appearance of a detailed study of Anglo-Norman Jewry, few people suspected that the Norman capital of Rouen served as a major center of Judaic culture during the High Middle Ages (1000–1300 C.E.). Golb's study in 1998 brought to life the extraordinary story of how Jacob bar Jequthiel, a Jew of Rouen, defied Duke Richard, the grandfather of William the Conqueror, traveled to Rome, secured the protection of the pope for French Jews, and in 1022, at the invitation of Baldwin count of Flanders, migrated with 30 other Rouen Jews to Arras. With ties to Lyon, Paris, Flanders, the Rhineland and places as far away as Cairo, Jerusalem and Babylon, the Jews of Normandy and Flanders had their own schools, cemeteries, properties, privileges, and even a head rabbi, an office transferred to England with the Norman conquest (Golb 1998).

Although several sources state that "Jews came to England with the Norman Invasion" or something akin to this,[1] we have been unable to locate a list of names of these Jewish families, except by inference from the work of Golb and earlier writers such as Adler (1939). Renan (1943, pp. 22–23) writes that most Jews of late antiquity and the early Middle Ages in Italy and Gaul were converts and non–Semitic. It was these Frenchmen who peopled the Jewries of England and Germany.[2] A paper by ha–Levi (1976) lists the names of Jews living in England prior to their expulsion in 1290 by Edward I (see appendix C). However, this list, while useful, shows many Jews identified only by the towns in which they resided in England, e.g., Jacob of London, Isaac of Lincoln, David of York, and because of this it is likely that their original French names were lost. Further, the families we would most like to have listings of are those who came from Europe to England in the Norman entourage of 1100 C.E. It is these families, we believe, who introduced Judaism to Scotland.

Our primary source for this chapter is Esther Benbassa's *The Jews of France* (1999). Benbassa is a Jewish historian, and her book is the most complete and well-documented available on French Jewry. Benbassa describes the Jewish communities known to be present in France prior to 1500 C.E., the time period of most interest to us. This era corresponds most closely to the "first wave" of Jewish arrivals into Scotland. After 1500, we have the "second wave" of Jews coming to Scotland — the Sephardim fleeing the Inquisition — and we will discuss these as well.

As Benbassa notes, Jews from Palestine arrived in Gaul (France) as early as 135 C.E., following the unsuccessful revolt by Bar Kokhba against Roman Emperor Hadrian. At this time, Jews were Roman citizens, and not labeled as "Jews" per se; they could travel freely throughout the Roman Empire, which stretched from Britain to Central Asia.

Benbassa (p. 4) makes several important points on which we will comment:

> (1) The Jews there [in France] did not all come from Palestine; many of them belonged to the diaspora, made up in part by populations converted to Judaism. (2) The Christianization of the Roman Empire under Constantine the Great ... and the restrictions that gradually came to be imposed on the Jews, favored their emigration, particularly to Gaul, which was slower to become Christianized.... (3) The settlement of Jews along an axis following the valley of the Rhône and extending from that of the Saône to its juncture with the Rhine corresponds to the route taken by the Roman legions, which Jews followed as soldiers, tradesmen, or merchants in search of a better life and more favorable economic conditions.

Importantly, Jews were settled where they would have had contact with the Normans, who arrived in Gaul from Scandinavia around 900 C.E. Jews functioned in Gaul and elsewhere as full-fledged Roman citizens, without religious or ethnic hindrance, and were active traders and merchants. Further, they would not necessarily have had Semitic DNA. As we shall argue shortly, many, perhaps most, were converts to Judaism from the French or German regions, so they would have carried primarily R1b DNA. As Benbassa (p. 4) notes, the Jews

> ... dressed like the rest of the population, bore arms, and spoke the local language; even in the synagogue. Hebrew was not the only language used for rituals. Their ancestral names — biblical, Roman, and Gallo-Roman — did not differentiate them from other inhabitants.

During the fifth century, just as Columba was converting the Irish and Scottish Celts to a Christianity that closely followed Jewish practice, Benbassa writes that Jews in France "lacking the Talmud, adhered closely to the text of the Bible and to certain oral traditions. There existed a religious confusion between Judaism and Christianity, both with regard to prescriptions and to worship" (p. 5).

Thus we have a loose compatibility between two monotheistic faiths — Christianity and Judaism — and persons moving back and forth between them up until the early 600s (Benbassa, p. 6). With the establishment of the Carolingian Empire under Charlemagne in 800 C.E., the Jews of France were well treated and socially mobile. Especially in their community in Narbonne, they enjoyed self-governance and moved into the highest political and economic advisory positions.

> Very shortly one finds Jews at the royal court entrusted with diplomatic missions, such as the one carried out by Isaac the Jew on behalf of Charlemagne to the Abbassid Caliph Harun-al-Rashid in Baghdad. Polyglot, and having extensive connections throughout the Jewish communities of the Diaspora, they were in a position to provide indispensable contacts within the young empire. Charlemagne also needed them for economic reasons [p. 6].

Together with the Byzantines and Syrians, Jews in France and elsewhere established international overland and maritime trading routes, controlling the bulk of Mediterranean commerce.

They exported slaves, furs, and silk manufactures to Italy, Spain, and the Levant, and imported to Gaul spices, balsam, garum, dates, brocades, and precious metals. The crossroads of this luxury trade were located in the Meuse and at Narbonne.[3] These traders could be found even in Paris, on the Île de la Cité, near the forecourt of Notre Dame today [p. 6].

By the 800s in France, contemporaneous with the first incursions of the Normans, the Jews constituted an indispensable part of the economy and culture. Benbassa (p. 11) writes:

They did possess buildings, fields, orchards and vineyards, garden farms, and mills. They devoted themselves to agriculture and, in particular, winegrowing in the valleys of the Rhône, the Saône, and in the Paris region. Jewish wine production seems to have been still larger in the ninth century, to the point that it supplied foreign markets....

In addition to being accomplished vintners and wine merchants, the Jews of Gaul also excelled in finance, estate management, medicine, and manufacturing.

A certain number of Jews managed the assets of bishops and abbots. Others were in the service of kings. They played an important role in East-West trade. They also practiced medicine. They were found, too, in trades such as the dyeing of fabric, and the tanning and currying of leather [p. 12].

By 1066, when the Normans conquered England taking several of these French Jewish families with them to establish the new civil administration, the Western world had embarked upon a capitalist economy.

Among the transformations undergone by the West since 1000 [C.E.] was the development of a monetary economy.... Economic development ... made the nobles dependent on cash income. Jews were in a position to meet their demands for liquidity, either through profits made from trade by those among them who practiced it or through recourse to credit [Benbassa, p. 14].

In 1306, for a variety of political, religious and economic reasons, the Jews were expelled from France. (And not coincidentally, we see families such as the "Black" Douglases arriving in Scotland.) This expulsion followed close on the heels of Edward I's banishment of Jews from England and Gascony in 1290, and there were smaller banishings of Jews from cities in Germany and Italy. However, as Benbassa writes (p. 15):

The expulsion in France affected a greater number of Jews (almost 50,000 persons).... Exiles found refuge in Lorraine, Alsace, the Rhine valley, even Poland and Hungary, in the duchy of Burgundy, the Dauphiné, Savoy, Provence, the Comtat Venaissin, and Spain.

We propose that several of these Jewish families made their way, as well, to Scotland, a possibility we will discuss in detail in chapters 7 and 9.

The Jewish Community at Narbonne

Below we present various texts regarding the Babylonian scholar Makhir/Machar and the principality of Narbonne in France during the period 700–900 C.E. It was this Davidic descendant of the Hebrew tribes, carried into captivity by the Babylonians in Biblical times, we suggest, who traveled to Scotland, where he became known as "St." Machar, and likely pioneered the way for some of the earliest Jews to make their way to the north-eastern part of Scotland. From Benbassa's account (p. 7) we learn that

> [t]he Muslim advance into France was checked in 732 at Poitiers by Charles Martel.... His son, Pepin the Short, founded the Carolingian dynasty in 751.... From this moment, the policy of the Carolingian sovereigns was marked by alliance with Rome and indulgence with regard to the Jews.

Pepin's son, Charlemagne, is said to have been assisted by Jews in his conquest of Narbonne, the former Visigothic kingdom, which housed a large Jewish community. Because of their assistance, Pepin made their leader, Makhir (Machar), lord of the new buffer state, and Charlemagne granted additional privileges to the French Jews, especially those of Narbonne. The French Jews, including those of Narbonne, were largely secularized; that is, they had little knowledge of Hebrew or Jewish religious texts. Though the Babylonian Talmud arrived, belatedly, in France,

> even then the Jews did not scrupulously observe its teachings.... Contacts between the Orient [Babylonia] and the Carolingian Empire led a doctor of law named Mahir to leave Babylonia and settle in Narbonne, where he founded a Talmudic school that helped establish Jewish studies in France.... Influences reached France also from Italy and Muslim Spain, where important Jewish cultural centers developed [Benbassa, p. 11].

An Internet site provides another account of Mahir and Narbonne, though this one is substantially more embellished.

The Jewish Rulers of Narbonne

There was once a semi-autonomous principality in Narbonne (southern France) described by Arthur J. Zuckerman (*A Jewish Princedom in Feudal France, 768–900*, New York, 1972). It was ruled by a Jewish prince of the House of David whose offspring intermarried with the aristocracy and royal line of France and [subsequently] with that of Normandy, Scotland, and England.... The first Jewish ruler of the House of David in Narbonne was called Machir. Machir and his sons were probably practising Jews, but most (though not all) of his family quickly assimilated and became Christians.... Machir gave his sister to Pepin and took the sister of Pepin as one of his wives.... William (the son of Machir) ruled over the area of Septimania [an area in southern France where Narbonne is located]. He was made Duke of Aquitaine and is referred to as "King of the Goths," since the area of southern France was a place of Gothic settlement. At one stage many Goths converted to Judaism and the terms "Goth" and "Jew" in southern France were used synonymously.... The wife of William the Conqueror was Matilda of Flanders [and] was descended from Machir. The Dukes of Aquitaine (in western France) were also possibly descended from William, son of Machir [www.kuhnslagoon.net/whitepages/tea_telphi/machir.html].

Here is yet another version of the same narrative:

The House of David in Babylon

The institution of the Babylonian Exilarchate began when King Nebuchadnezzar took Jehoiachin, King of Judah, captive to Babylon in c. 597 B.C.... From Jehoiachin arose a royal

Davidic dynasty in Babylon reigning from their own palace and court over the Jewish communities of the East. They reigned in regal splendor until the beginning of the fifteenth century, when Tamerlane deposed them in 1401, and a branch of the family transferred to Baghdad to lead the Jewish community until 1700.

Gershom and Machir went to Narbonne and founded the Western Dynasty of Exilarchs there. Pepin (king of France) installed Machir, son of the Babylonian Exilarch, as the Jewish King of Narbonne. Machir married a sister of Pepin called Alda. His son Guillame [William] ... was nicknamed "Hook Nosed." He was fluent in Arabic and Hebrew. The heraldic device on his shield was the same as that of the Eastern Exilarchs— the Lion of Judah. Guillame observed the Sabbath and Sukkot during his campaigns. Machir's sister married Pepin and became the mother of Charlemagne [www.kuhnslagoon.net/whitepages/tea_telphi/machir.html].

From these two garbled accounts we glimpse an origin story that, if true, could help account for three unusual circumstances we encountered during our research. First, it would help better explain why HRH Prince Michael Stewart of Scotland so strongly believes he is descended from Davidic Jews, when all the Stewart/Stuart DNA tested thus far has not been Semitic, but rather Sephardic R1b. We believe it is possible that the Babylonian scholar Machir, arriving to instruct the Jews of southern France in the teachings of the Talmud, converted several persons in the surrounding population (as Benbassa noted), which would have been primarily of Gothic R1b DNA.

If Machir also informed these new R1b converts that they were now of Davidic lineage (as he, in fact, was), this would explain Michael Stewart's ancestral French Jewish forebears having this belief. It would also be the likely cause for the enormous (and otherwise inexplicable) number of persons settling in Scotland from 1400 onward surnamed Davidson, Davis, Dawes, Davies, Davison, Davie, Dow, Dowd and the like (for King David), as well for those surnamed Lewis, Low, Law, Lawrey, Lovett and similar forms, based on the Levite tribe from which King David sprang. And, it would help explain the presence of *two* King Davids in Scotland between 1160 and 1290, making it the only country in history, besides ancient Israel, to have a monarch named David.

Further, it could provide an important clue to the identity of the mysterious "St." Machar in Aberdeen, Scotland (exact date and exact religion unknown) and substantiate why the graveyard at St. Machar's church in Aberdeen is typically Crypto-Jewish in style. Is it possible the Davidic Jewish scholar Machir of Narbonne could have visited a Jewish congregation already situated in that city, or perhaps sent an envoy to instruct them?[4] And finally, such a connection could account for why the granddaughter of William the Conqueror through the female line was, in fact, named *Judith* (Yehudi, "female Jew"), a name used exclusively at that time by persons of the Jewish faith. However, these foregoing accounts were not deemed sufficiently cogent for us to draw support from, except in an anecdotal and circumstantial sense.

Most fortuitously, the authors then stumbled across the following entry in the *Jewish Encyclopedia* regarding France (2003, online version). According to this account, during the period 300 to 650 C.E., the Jews residing in France were periodically subjected to fines, restrictions and efforts to convert them to Christianity, with some very interesting consequences (p. 10):

In order to insure the public triumph of the Church, the clergy endeavored to bring the Jews to the acceptance of baptism.... Avitus, bishop of Clermont, strove long but vainly to make converts. At length in 576 a Jew sought to be baptized. [In anger,] one of [the Jew's] former coreligionists poured fetid oil over his head. The following Sunday the [Christian] mob that accompanied the bishop razed the synagogue to the ground. Afterward the bishop told the Jews that unless they were willing to embrace Christianity they must withdraw, since he as bishop could have but one flock. It is said that five hundred Jews then accepted baptism, and the rest withdrew to Marseilles.

By 689 C.E., however, the situation was altered dramatically for Jews in France (p. 11):

But at the south of France, which was then known as "Septimania" and was a dependency of the Visigothic kings of Spain, the Jews continued to dwell and to prosper. From this epoch (689) dates the earliest known Jewish inscription relating to France, that of Narbonne. The Jews of Narbonne, chiefly merchants, were popular among the people, who often rebelled against the Visigothic kings. It is noteworthy that Julian of Toledo accuses Gaul of being Judaized. Wamba decreed that all the Jews of his realm should either embrace Christianity or quit his dominions. This edict, which "threatened the interests of the country," provoked a general uprising.The Count of Nîmes,[5] Hilderic, the abbot Ramire, and Guimaldus, Bishop of Maguelon, took the Jews under their protection and even compelled their neighbors to follow their example. But the insurrection was crushed, and the edict of expulsion was put into force in 673. Still, the exile of the Jews was not of long duration....

From a letter of Pope Stephen III (768–772) to bishop Aribert of Narbonne, it is seen that in his time the Jews still dwelt in Provence, and even in the territory of Narbonne.... This concession is probably connected with a curious episode in the struggle with the Arabs. The "Roman de Philomène" recounts how Charlemagne, after a fabulous siege of Narbonne, rewarded the Jews for the part they had taken in the surrender of the city; he yielded to them, for their own use, a part of the city, and granted them the right to live under a "Jewish king," as the Saracens lived under a Saracen king. Meïr, son of Simon of Narbonne (1240), in his "Milemet Miwah" refers to the same story.... A tradition that Charles granted to them a third part of the town and of its suburbs is partly confirmed by a document which once existed in the abbey of Grasse, and which showed that under the emperor Charlemagne, a "king of the Jews" owned a section of the city of Narbonne, a possession which Charlemagne confirmed in 791.

In the Royal letters of 1364 it is also stated that there were two kings at Narbonne, a Jew and a Saracen, and that one-third of the city was given to the Jews. A tradition preserved by Abraham ibn Daud[6] and agreeing in part with the statement of Benjamin of Tudela, his contemporary, attributes these favors to R. Makir, whom Charlemagne summoned from Babylon, and who called himself a descendant of David. The Jewish quarter of Narbonne was called "New City," and the "Great Jewry." The Makir family bore, in fact, the name "Nasi" (prince), and lived in a building known as the "Cortada Regis Judæorum."

The granting of such privileges would certainly seem to be connected with some particular event, but more probably under Charles Martel or Pepin the Short than under Charlemagne.... It is certain that the Jews were again numerous in France under Charlemagne, their position being regulated by law... They engaged in export trade, an instance of this being found in the Jew whom Charlemagne employed to go to Palestine and bring back precious merchandise.... Isaac the Jew, who was sent by Charlemagne in 797 with two ambassadors to Harun al-Rashid, was probably one of these merchants.... It was said that the Jews, far from being objects of hatred to the emperor, were better loved and considered than the Christians.

A Bishop Agobard also claimed:

The Christians celebrate the Sabbath with the Jews, desecrate Sunday, and transgress the regular fasts. Because the Jews boast of being the race of the Patriarchs, the Nation of the Righteous, the Children of the Prophets, the ignorant think that they are the only people of God and that the Jewish religion is better than their own.

What we learn from this historically documented account is that there *was* a close relationship between the Jews of France and the French monarchy; that the French Jews had a very widespread trading network stretching to Central Asia, and beyond; and perhaps most profoundly, that the French citizenry generally liked and respected Jews. Elsewhere in the article it is noted that there were several instances of conversion to Judaism, even among high-ranking church members.

We believe that it is certainly within the realm of possibility that segments of the French population, especially in the southern and eastern sections of the country, converted to Judaism and adopted surnames consistent with the belief that they were now of the House of David, and of the Tribes of Judah and Levi. These newly-minted, R1b-pedigree Davidsons and Levys would carry their new identities onward to England and Scotland when joining the Norman entourage.

But They Weren't Really Semitic ...

Before leaving France to accompany our new French converts to England with William the Conqueror, we wish to reiterate one point. *Most* of these persons, though practicing Judaism, were *not* Semitic. Rather, they were for the most part R1b Mediterranean, not Middle Eastern in their dominant ancestry. We believe this is why the Scottish clan DNA (e.g., Gordon, Campbell, Forbes) collected and tested in our study is strongly concentrated in the Iberian peninsula and southern France, and why it is not classically Semitic and centered in Palestine or Judea.

If we reexamine the genealogy used by Prince Michael Stewart to establish his descent from the tribe of Judah and compare it to the overview given in the *Jewish Encyclopedia*, we see where a critical error has been made. In the Stewart genealogical chart, a line of descent is drawn from Theodoric IV (720–732) to Guilhelm de Toulouse de Bellone, who is the Davidic sovereign of Septimania (Narbonne). However, there are two mistakes here. First, it was Guilhelm (William) who was given the honorary title Makir (teacher), and not Theodoric. Second, Guilhelm was *not* a son of Theodoric, but rather a foreigner who had been dispatched from the Jewish center at Babylon to Narbonne to establish a *shul* (academy). Thus, the lineage of Pepin, Charlemagne, Louis I, Charles I and their successors was *not* impacted by Judaic/Semitic/Davidic kinship through this source.

A Davidic bloodline does enter later on through Guilhelm, however, when his son Prince Bernard of Septimania, the Imperial Chamberlain of the Carolingian court, marries Charlemagne's daughter, Princess Dhuada. The continuing line through their son Bernard would have carried Davidic and Semitic blood (see fig. 9, Davidic Descent to Kings of Jerusalem).

However, we must also recognize two cultural signs of Judaism already present in the Carolingian dynasty. First, the given name Dhuada means Davida. It is the feminine form of David. To have named a daughter Dhuada and married her to a known Jew strongly suggests that Charlemagne *believed himself* to be of Davidic, or at least Jewish, ancestry. Second, Charlemagne's son, Louis I (814–840), who became king and emperor, married as his second wife a woman named *Judith* of Bavaria, and from that union came Charles II (emperor 867–877). This line continued onward to some of the kings of Jerusalem during the Crusades.[7]

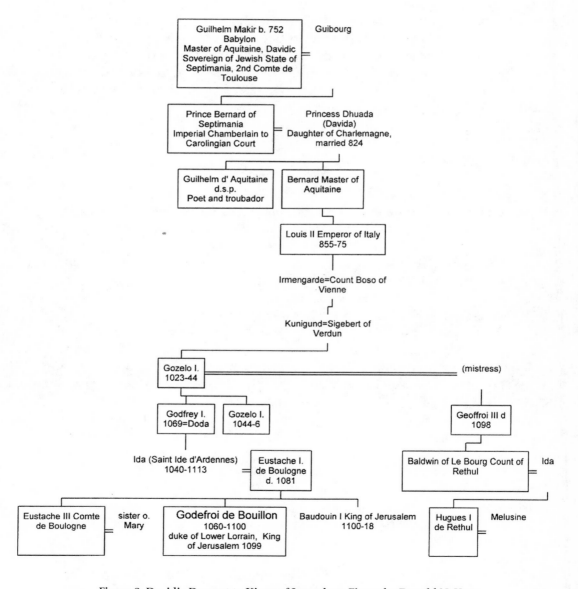

Figure 9. Davidic Descent to Kings of Jerusalem. Figure by Donald N. Yates.

It was also within this Carolingian lineage that the Lion of Judah heraldic device came to be adopted by French, Flemish and Norman nobles. They carried the device to Scotland (for instance, William the Lyon, the Bruces, the Stewarts) and reintroduced it to England with the Plantagenets. We do *not* infer any genuine genealogical support for the presumption among the Bruces, Stewarts and Plantagenets that they were biological descendants of David, nor has DNA testing conducted to date shown any evidence of this. A more feasible conclusion is that among their ancestors during the years between 750 and 900 C.E. were converts to Judaism who instilled in family members a commitment to the *mitzvot* of the faith along with the (erroneous) belief that they were of Davidic descent.

Lest this "We are Davidic" scenario seem farfetched to the reader, we have included in appendix D excerpts from the genealogies of families that also originated in France and believed themselves to be Davidic, but also are not carrying Semitic genes.[8]

Chapter 6

When Did Jews Arrive in Scotland?

Several sources posit that persons from the Levant, North Africa, and even Italy had visited southwestern England near Cornwall before the Common Era (Cunliffe 2001, pp. 302ff.; Finn 1937, pp. 10–11). There were rich tin mines in this region that were exploited by the early Phoenicians (800 B.C.E.), who traded with ports from France and Northern Africa to Italy and Greece (Cunliffe 2001, pp. 302ff.; Thompson 1994, pp. 137–87; Gordon 1971; Casson 1971). Because the Judeans (Jews) often worked with the Phoenicians as trading partners, some could have reached Britain as early as this time. The demography of Cornwall still attests to a significant incidence of J and E3 genes in the region.[1]

According to Brooks (2001), there are numerous well-established geographical links between the Hebrews of the Mediterranean and peoples of the British Isles. The early name of what is now Cornwall and Devon in southwestern England was Dumnoni, Dunmonii, or Danmoni, which antiquarians have glossed as meaning "Dan's Tin Mines" (pp. 89–90). Among others, the distinguished Semitic studies professor Cyrus Gordon suggested that this name, seen also in the Irish myth of the Tuatha (tribe) de Danaan, was identical with that of the Biblical tribe of Dan (Gordon 1971). Finally, the Celtic scholar John Rhys assembled strong evidence of Hebrew colonization of Britain in ancient times. Ireland was known as Iberion, and the ancient name of the Israelites was Ibri or Iberi, derived from the proper name Eber or Heber, the eponymous ancestor of that people (Brooks 2001, p. 90).

Notwithstanding the evidence, many Scottish historians and writers of Judaica seem united in their desire to dismiss any early presence of Jews in Scotland. One goes so far as to maintain:

> There is no record of Jews settled in Scotland before the expulsion of English Jewry in 1290 and, in fact, there is little Jewish history in all of Scotland before the end of the eighteenth century.... [Despite a law promulgated by the bishop of Glasgow in 1181–1187 forbidding churchmen from using their benefices as collaterals on loans from Jews,] it is extremely unlikely that any Jews were resident in the area.... Apart from some Jewish traders and a number of Jewish medical students in Edinburgh [e.g. Mordecai Marx and Levi Myers, both from South Carolina], there were few Jews in Scotland before the formal establishment of Jewish communities in Glasgow and Edinburgh in the early years of the nineteenth century.

There were few Jews in England.... Provincial Jewry remained small and although Jewish communities were formed in Birmingham, Liverpool, Manchester and some smaller English provincial towns during the eighteenth century, no such development took place in Glasgow or anywhere else in Scotland [Collins 1990, pp. 15, 17].

In Edinburgh, the story goes, "Scotland never bore the problems or tested the advantages of a Jewish community within its borders until the year 1816 when twenty Jewish families then living in Edinburgh founded a 'Kehillah' or Congregation of Jews, the first ever to be seen in Scotland" (Phillips 1979, p. 1). Mentions of a "Mr. Wolf or Benjamin of Edinburgh under date 1750," of Masonic Jews in the Lodge of St. David, and of Jewish burials in Edinburgh have been ignored (Phillips 1979, pp. 1–2).

Let us, however, pick up the trail with a group of Jewish émigrés who accompanied William, Duke of Normandy, to Britain in the latter half of the eleventh century. One English historian (Ludovici 1938, p. 2) states:

> The first mention of Jews [in England] is to be found in the "Liber Poenitentialis" of Theodore, Archbishop of Canterbury, A.D. 669. There are also references to Jews in the days of Whitgaf or Wiglaf, King of Mercia, and Edward the Confessor. There can be little doubt, therefore, that long before the [Norman] Conquest, Jews were established over here, though probably not in large numbers. There is, however, no doubt whatsoever that William I was responsible for the influx of a large crowd of Jews into England. They came from Rouen, and the fact that he no doubt granted them extraordinary privileges, which were more or less extended to them by every monarch of the Norman and Plantagenet lines up to the time of Edward, is most significant. It indicates the explanation of a phenomenon otherwise inexplicable — namely, that the crowned head of the land could have held under his protecting wing for over two centuries a community of foreigners.

To this we would add that an even stronger explanation for William's congeniality (and that of subsequent Norman and Plantagenet English monarchs) towards the Jews was the belief that the royal lineage itself carried Davidic Jewish ancestry.[2]

Intriguingly, Ludovici raises, and then abruptly dismisses, the possibility that the majority of these French Jews were converts to Judaism — i.e., that they were not ethnically Semites, but rather European (p. 3):

> Renan, pursuing his customary tactics, tries to imply that since the Jews of the early Middle Ages in England and Germany came from France, and a high percentage of Gallic Jews were converts, a large proportion of the alleged Jews of England and Germany may not have been true Semites at all. The facts, however, are not in harmony with this hypothesis. Neither do Hyamson, Goldschmidt, nor Abrahams — all of them Jewish historians and authors of books on the Jews in England — ever hint at anything of the kind.

We, of course, do propose (and hopefully have shown the reader) that most of the French Jews accompanying William were, in fact, likely carrying R1b DNA, and only a few were genetically Semitic. Ludovici (1938) continues his discussion by noting that these now–English Jews primarily were employed in international trade, banking and medicine,[3] which corresponds with the accounts of other chroniclers (Barnavi 1992). Despite their affluence, the Jews of England lived a precarious existence, primarily serving at the caprice and pleasure of the reigning monarch. Two centuries after they first journeyed to England, the first attacks upon them began. This likely caused an initial movement by some Jewish families across the border into Scotland. As Ludovici (1938, p. 10) says:

At Richard I's coronation in 1189 the first trouble on a large scale ultimately broke out....
There was a riot outside Westminster Abbey, in which the Christian population fell on the
Jews in the crowd, beat them, killed many of them, and pursued the rest to their houses,
which were sacked and burnt, in many cases with their inmates inside them. The king, who
heard of the tumult at his coronation banquet, did his utmost to stop the rioting and protect
the Jews, but in vain. The rioting lasted twenty-four hours, and during the massacre a
minority of Jews secured their safety only by receiving baptism. After the massacre, Richard
I issued an edict menacing punishment to all those who injured the Jews, but before this
edict was published, the Jews of Dunstable, wishing to forestall the possible repetition of the
London incidents in their town, are said to have gone over in a body to Christianity, and the
Jews in other cities are alleged to have done likewise.

It is very likely, we believe, that this 1189 pogrom was the origin of a Crypto-Jewish
presence in England.[4] Ludovici (1938, p. 13) continues:

From this time onwards, throughout the thirteenth century, the condition of the Jews in
England grew steadily worse. John's reign was one of repeated extortions, and under Henry
III the royal demands became so intolerable, and the measures of compulsion so cruel, that
the whole of the Jewish community twice requested in vain to be allowed to leave the kingdom.
    Meanwhile, various measures had been passed which were calculated to destroy the peace
of the Jews in England. In 1218, for instance, they were ordered to wear a distinguishing
badge.... In 1222, Stephen Langton, Archbishop of Canterbury, forbade the Jews to possess
Christian slaves and prohibited all intercourse of Christians with them. Moreover, by certain
laws of Henry III, all sexual intercourse between Jew and Christian was strictly forbidden,
and Jews were not allowed to practise as physicians. All through Henry III's reign, community after community of Jews was ransacked and massacred.... Late in the reign of Henry III,
moreover, disaffection was caused among large sections of the community, owing to the fact
that the Jews had become possessed of land ... one of the last acts of Henry III's reign was to
disqualify all Jews from holding lands or even tenements, except the houses which they actually possessed, particularly in the City of London.

Edward I came to the British throne in 1271 C.E.; he issued in 1290 writs for the
expulsion of all Jews who would not convert to Christianity (Tovey 1967). Likely at this
time yet another set of English Crypto-Jews was created. Ludovici (1938, p. 16) writes:

Sixteen thousand Jews are supposed to have left England—i.e., all those who preferred exile
to apostasy.... Edward I not only allowed them to take their movable property with them and
"all pledges that had not been redeemed," but he also ordered all sheriffs to see that no harm
should overtake them.

It is no surprise we should find additional families with French Jewish DNA making their way to Scotland at this time. And it is also not surprising that they would wisely
choose to practice their religion in secret—pretending outwardly to be Christian, while
adhering to Judaism among their families and close friends. Indeed, Ludovici (1938, p.
30) comments that both Crypto-Jews and the openly Jewish were present in England
from 1290 until their "official" re-entry under Oliver Cromwell in 1654; an assessment
with which others are in agreement (see, e.g., D. Katz 1996).

Not only were there Crypto-Jews (Jews who merely posed as Christians) in England in the
three hundred and fifty years following the expulsion, but also ... there were Jews openly living as such.... Jews as physicians, as philosophers, and men learned in various departments
of knowledge were admitted almost in every reign from the 14th century onwards. Jews are

mentioned in public life under Henry VI; Spanish Jews as having taken refuge in England under Henry VII; eastern Jews as being favoured by Henry VIII; under Elizabeth, Hounsditch was already inhabited by Jews, and two or three Jewish doctors came into prominence, one being physician to the Queen. Jews inhabited England under James I and Charles I, and there was a large influx of them in the latter years of Charles I's reign.

From Ludovici's account, written in 1938,[5] we now turn to *The Jews in the History of England 1485–1850* (1996) by David S. Katz. Katz's research focuses on the period subsequent to the Sephardic Expulsion from Spain and Portugal, which provided the primary impetus for the second wave of Jewish émigrés to Scotland. It was during this period, for example, that the Caldwells are believed to have journeyed from France and Spain to Scotland to find refuge.

Examining Katz's work will also help provide us with some very important clues to the psychological and sociological aspects of Crypto-Judaism. For instance, what religions did Crypto-Jews pretend to practice? What occupations did they follow? Whom did they marry? And perhaps, most compelling, why did the descendants of Crypto-Jews not rush forward and identify themselves as Jews once restrictions regarding Judaizing were removed? We will argue that the patterns observable in England are analogous to those found in Scotland and in most other Crypto-Jewish communities around the globe, namely, the Melungeons in Appalachia and the *conversos* in New Mexico, Cuba, Puerto Rico, and South America.

Presumably the Crypto-Jews who remained in England after the Expulsion in 1290 presented themselves as practicing Christians, which at that time would have meant Roman Catholicism, the prevailing religion in England. They would have "switched" to Anglicanism under the reign of Henry VIII (1509–1547), in order, once again, to conform to external norms.

When Crypto-Jews entered England from Iberia at the time of the Inquisition (1492), they were readily recognizable as Spaniards or Portuguese; hence pretending to be Anglican would not have been a credible cover. Thus, as Katz (1996) reports, these Crypto-Jewish arrivals pretended to be Roman Catholic, the state religion of Spain and Portugal. "The Spanish Jews who had come to London undoubtedly continued as they had done at home, worshipping according to the Roman Catholic rite and behaving outwardly in every respect like any Iberian merchant" (p. 2). By the 1530s, Katz writes, "In the Jewish world, at least, it was possible to speak of a secret Jewish community in London" (p. 4).

What we do *not* know is whether the original English Crypto-Jews—those dating from 1290—were in contact with their Iberian brethren. It is our belief that some Scots were in touch with foreign branches of their family or with trade correspondents and perhaps even attempted to assist these new arrivals using their solid standing in British society. They may have chosen husbands or wives from among the immigrants. A very fruitful path for future research would be to trace public communications[6] on behalf of the new Crypto-Jews by established Englishmen and also document any patterns of intermarriage by these new émigrés into English families.

A glimmer of Anglo-Jewish identity surfaces in the remarkable career of Sir Anthony Ashley-Cooper, who was simultaneously Baron Cooper of Pawlett, Baron Ashley of Wimborne St. Giles, 1st Lord Shaftesbury, Lord Chancellor of the Exchequer, Lord Proprietor of the Carolinas, a member of Charles II's original "Cabal," and author of the Habeas Corpus right in English civil law (1621–1683). What we know of his background, which is rather mysterious, or his life, which was full of intrigues, makes Shaftesbury a very suspect player in our drama.

Simon Cooper was the first of the name to become noted in official affairs in England, being appointed sheriff of London in 1310, shortly after the expulsion of the Jews. This was in the fourth year of the reign of King Edward II. His son, Robert Cooper, became groom of the bedchamber to King Henry V. Descending through several generations, various members of the family held high positions in official life. Sir John Cooper was member of Parliament from the Borough of Whitechurch, Hampshire, in 1586. One of his daughters married Robert Baker, envoy of King James to the Spanish throne. His son, John, was created a baronet on July 4, 1622. John married Anne, daughter of Sir Anthony Ashley, and through her acquired practically all of the vast estates of the Ashley family. The Ashleys were likely also Jewish in origin (Heb. *Asher*, "Assyrian"). American descendants of Sir John Cooper (1598–1630/31) include Daniel Boone's guide, William Cooper, and the name is a familiar one among Melungeon surnames.[7]

A Freemason in the days before this order was openly recognized, Shaftesbury had important connections in Spain, Holland, France, the Caribbean and Scotland. His secretary, John Locke, wrote the first colonial constitution that specifically gave rights of citizenship to Jews (Charter for Carolinas, 1670). Like the Stuart monarch Charles II, Shaftesbury had difficulty producing an heir of his body and rather greater facility in forming scandalous relationships. And like "Old Rowley" and the other Cavaliers, Shaftesbury remained true to his main mistress, after a fashion, and acknowledged the more attractive and ambitious of his bastards. His Nell Gwyn was Lucretia Massey. The illegitimate offspring of this teen-age liaison, evidently his first love, all made brilliant marriages and founded long lines that blended with the First Families of Virginia, specifically Bollings (Boleyn), Howards, Johnstons, Walkers and "Pocahontas' people."[8] Of his first wife, who miscarried four potential heirs, Shaftesbury wrote in his journal, "She was a lovely beautiful fair woman, a religious devout Christian ... *yet* [emphasis added] the most sweet, affectionate, and observant wife in the world."

In a pronouncement later admired by Benjamin Franklin, and enshrined by Benjamin Disraeli in one of his novels, Shaftesbury once answered his critics with a defense that might have been more than just a bon mot. After one of his characteristic alterations of conscience during the Religious Wars, a lady of rank asked him what he actually believed. "Madame," he said, urbanely, "people differ in their discourse and profession about these matters, but men of sense are really but of one religion." So the lady asked, "Pray, my Lord, what religion is that in which men of sense agree?" Shaftesbury replied, "Madame, men of sense never tell it."[9] To us, this seems the classic response of a Crypto-Jew.

At the end of Henry VIII's reign, the Spanish Jews, both Crypto- and openly Jewish, were well established in England. Three of these included Dr. Hector Nuñez, Dunstan Añes, and Simon Ruiz who lived in London and carried on successful professional careers. Nuñez was even made a fellow of the College of Physicians in 1554 and Añes became a freeman of the Grocer's Company in 1557. Nuñez, who presented himself publicly as a Calvinist minister, was in fact the rabbi of the Bristol, England, Jewish community (Katz 1996).

These three men may serve to some extent for us as prototypes of Jewish experience in the mid–1500s in England. One, Hector Nuñez, was so skilled as a doctor as to be allowed to enter the College of Physicians—a pattern we shall see followed in Scotland. Dunstan Añes (Ames) was a merchant in foodstuffs, another typical Jewish profession, and Dr. Henrique Nuñes, the Crypto-rabbi of Bristol, England, pretended to be a Calvinist (Protestant) minister, before fleeing to France. What we will find in Scotland is very similar: Crypto-Jews in the merchant professions, as leading doctors and apothecaries, and as Protestant ministers. What is missing from this list are the several craft skills which the Crypto-Jews possessed — silver smithing, leather tanning, tailoring, weaving, iron mining and smelting, and an orientation toward intellectual pursuits, such as mathematics, chemistry and astronomy.

Meanwhile, the *conversos*[10] outside of England had established an international trading network that linked Eastern Europe, Turkey, Palestine, Holland, Iberia, France and England. The prime movers of this network were Joseph Nasi and his mother, Eva Garcia Mendes Nasi. Joseph also held the titles of Duke of Naxos and Count of Andros and was endeavoring to establish not only a commercial center but also a Jewish homeland at Tiberias in Israel (Katz 1996).

The Crypto-Jewish community in England, which included several prominent physicians and businessmen, affiliated itself with Protestantism. For example, Katz (1996, p. 65) writes that Santa Cruz testified in Madrid, "He knows, as it is public and notorious in London that by race they are all Jews, and it is notorious that in their own homes they live as such observing their Jewish rites; but publicly they attend Lutheran Churches, and listen to the sermons, and take the bread and wine."

In 1649 C.E., under Oliver Cromwell (whom, incidentally, Dutch Jews believed to have Jewish ancestry from the tribe of Judah), the Jews gained quasi-official entry to England, though they were still not enabled to hold office, own land or become citizens. It is very likely the continuation of these restrictions on Jewish social and economic mobility that encouraged the resident Crypto-Jews dating from 1290 forward to remain hidden. For why should they suddenly spring forth at that time and lose their lands, titles, and political and clerical offices? Perhaps they also felt that they could better assist their newly-arrived co-religionists by remaining as they were and had been for centuries— secret Jews, public Christians.

They must also have felt an enormous psychological chasm between themselves and the "real" Jews now immigrating to England. These latter Jews read and spoke Hebrew and Ladino; they knew the appropriate prayers; they attended synagogue, had a rabbi and circumcised their sons. The long-hidden secret Jews of England must have felt both pride and shame regarding their new, public brethren — pride at these newcomers' presence and economic success, yet shame about their own seeming cowardice in hiding and choosing to remain in hiding. Secrets so long kept are excruciatingly difficult to divulge. To our knowledge, none of the hidden Jews of England chose to expose their ancestry at this time. Indeed, if their bloodlines were, as is evident from modern genealogical research, deeply embedded in England's aristocratic peerage and country gentry, they had only to consider the hysteria sweeping Spain and Portugal over "purity of blood" during the 1500s to resolve to remain as they were.

And yet their existence, and that of their fellow Crypto-Jews in Scotland, Switzer-land and France (particularly in the last English foothold around Calais, forfeited only in 1556), was having a transformational impact on the religious world. We will argue in chapter 10 that some of the principle architects of the Protestant Reformation, in partic-ular John Calvin of France and John Knox of Scotland, were descendants of Sephardic Jews. However, we will focus now only on the impact that the Protestant Reformation had on the Western European perception of Jews, particularly in England.

One of the primary tenets of Protestantism is the possibility of a direct relationship between the individual and God. The priests, bishops, cardinals and Pope of the Roman Church are no longer needed as intermediaries. Yet with this possibility of direct con-tact comes the responsibility of individuals to *educate* themselves according to God's laws, as these are revealed in the Bible. This has been viewed by historians (including Katz) as the primary motivation for the Protestant clergy to learn Hebrew, namely, as an entree to the holy scriptures. To us, however, it is pretty flimsy reasoning. We propose that the reason so many leading Protestant clergy "suddenly" began advocating reading in Hebrew and poring over the Old Testament during the 1500s is because they were, in fact, either Crypto-Jews themselves or the sons of Crypto-Jews, and believed that the Old Testament (Torah) in Hebrew was, indeed, the Word of God.

> Katz, however, does not share our suspicions and states the traditional view (pp. 110–111):
> "As was the case everywhere that Hebrew studies flourished, Christian interest in the Old Testament inevitably created a climate of theological opinion that attracted Jews, converted or otherwise.... Sixteenth- and seventeenth-century English religious life was characterized ... by the intense emphasis placed on reading and understanding the Word of God as expressed in Scripture.... [The] "language of Canaan" spoken by God to the Israelites became a tool of biblical scholarship much in demand."

In our view, the reemergence of the Old Testament was actually a "return to the Torah," with recently "Christianized" Jews simply using Protestantism as a guise to practice their traditional faith. (Indeed, in the Melungeon Appalachian Presbyterian church in which one of the authors was raised, Sunday school teachers spent eleven months of the year on the Old Testament [Torah] and only one month on the New Testament [Christian gospels].) Further, by 1535, Thomas Cromwell had required both Oxford and Cambridge to provide public lectures in either Hebrew or Greek. This was ratified by an act of Par-liament in 1530 (Katz 1996).

Notably, Greek was the most common religious language used by Jewish commu-nities in the Diaspora. The Septuagint, a translation of the Hebrew Bible into Greek from the ancient world that remains in use in Greek Orthodox Christianity, still reigned supreme among Jews. Much of the rabbinical literature of Judea during Greco-Roman times had been composed in Greek. The Greek-speaking Romaniot Jews of the Turkish East were still strong, fusing their culture with that of Ladino Jews of Spain and Portu-gal who brought their Judeo-Spanish language to major cultural centers in the Ottoman Empire such as Thessaloniki, Istanbul (Constantinople), Izmir (Smyrna), Rhodes and Crete (Biale 2001, pp. 80–81, 160–61, 328, 864–66).[11]

To understand Crypto-Jews in England and Scotland, we must look at the so-called Marranos of Spain and Portugal. The origin and meaning of the term is disputed, and its use is only sporadic before about 1380, but it appears to have gained great currency in the mid–fourteenth century anti–Jewish riots in Toledo and Cordova that immediately preceded the Spanish Inquisition.[12] Its heyday was the sixteenth century, when Marranos became "Judaizers" outside Spain and Portugal, hounded by the Inquisition through all Europe and the Americas. "The wealthy Maranos, who engaged extensively in commerce, industries, and agriculture, intermarried with families of the old nobility; impoverished counts and marquises unhesitatingly wedded wealthy Jewesses; and it also happened that counts or nobles of the blood royal became infatuated with handsome Jewish girls. Beginning with the second generation, the Neo-Christians usually intermarried with women of their own sect. They became very influential through their wealth and intelligence, and were called to important positions at the palace, in government circles, and in the Cortes; they practised medicine and law and taught at the universities; while their children frequently achieved high ecclesiastical honors" (Jacobs and Meyerling in *Jewish Encyclopaedia* 1906–1911 s.v. *Mutatis mutandis*). The same description holds for the secret Jewish privileged class in Britain.

By 1688, a new day was dawning in Britain. Prince William of Orange, the Protestant ruler of the Netherlands, not only a friend of the Jews in that country but probably of Jewish descent himself,[13] was poised to claim the throne of England from Charles II. The Sephardic community in England, Ireland and the Netherlands coordinated financial and political efforts on William's behalf. As Katz (1996, p. 156) notes, from at least 1674 the chief contractors for provisioning the Republic's land forces were the Jewish firm of Machado and Pereira. "Vous avez sauvé l'état," (You have saved the state), William III wrote to Antonio-Moses Alvarez Machado, and there was probably a good deal of truth in his praise...."

Once Prince William entered England, the Sephardim continued to be instrumental in assisting his military campaign, including even the Battle of the Boyne in Ireland in 1690. As Katz (1996, p. 158) reports, "Isaac Pereira was assisted by Alfonso Rodriguez alias Isaac Israel de Sequeira, son of a man long associated with London Jewry. He in turn was joined by his relative, David Machado de Sequeira, and Jacob do Porto, his grandson. The contribution made by these four men to the success of the Glorious Revolution was outstanding...."

By the 1700s English Sephardim were involved in the transport of diamonds, coral, and silver along a trade route spanning from India to Italy, Amsterdam, London, and Brazil (Yogev 1978). The Sephardim were becoming recognized as valuable members of English society. Defenders of their rights now began to come forward in greater numbers. Sir Josiah Child (perhaps a Crypto-Jew himself) advocated their full assimilation into British society (Katz, p. 176). Another to which we should attend closely is John Toland[14] (Katz, p. 234), who published

"A Defence of the *Jews* against All vulgar Prejudices in all Countries" (1714), Toland's treatise addressed Britain's bishops and archbishops. He stated, "as by your Learning you further know a considerable part of the *British* inhabitants are the undoubted offspring of the *Jews* ... and as you are the advocates of the *Jews* at the Throne of Heaven, so you will be their friends and protectors in the *British* Parliament."

Toland also put forth Jews in England, noting their misfortunes under the Norman kings, and reminding his readers that, after they had been readmitted during Cromwell's reign, under King Charles II "they were conniv'd at and tolerated, being not authoriz'd by Charter or Act of Parliament: nor are they on any terms than permission to this day, tho they have deserv'd much better...."

Most notably for our purposes, Toland expressed the belief that at the time of their expulsion from England (1290) a "great number of 'em fled to *Scotland*, which is the reason so many in that part of the Island have such a remarkable aversion to pork and black-puddings to this day, not to insist on some other resemblances easily observable."

We, of course, agree fully with Toland's arguments and observations. Yes, there *were* many offspring of Jews dwelling in England; yes, many Jews had escaped to Scotland after the 1290 expulsion from England. And yes, many Scots do and did have "easily observable" physical resemblances to Jews. A quick visual inspection of the portraits of prominent Scots presented in chapter 1 will confirm this.

And so, let us now proceed to Scotland.

Chapter 7

To Scotland's Stirling, Ayr, and Glasgow

We focus in this chapter on the western portion of Scotland. Our first task will be to take a look at who was living in this area between 1500 and 1750. It would be very useful to have earlier records, but to our knowledge these do not exist.[1] Therefore, we are going to rely upon lists of burgesses, cemetery inscriptions, lists of guild members, and censuses, the earliest of which date to the late 1500s.

Cemetery Records

Lists 1 through 8 the persons we believe may be of Sephardic ancestry who are buried in local cemeteries in western Scotland. (A complete listing of *all* persons buried in these cemeteries is available in the original works.) Starting with the Cluny Cemetery (list 1), we find several surnames that are either linked with clans already discussed as having Sephardic origins—e.g., Kennedy (fr. Candiani "from Crete, Candy" or Turkish Khandey "king's administrator,"), Forbes (Phoebus/Pharabee, a name from Jewish antiquity) and Gordon (a version of Cohen, Hebrew "priest") or are derived from a Hebrew tribal or given name (e.g., Davidson, Daniel, Robbie, Abel, Adam, Lawrey, Lyon). Others appear to have Arabic or Aramaic names—Carnegie, Ferries, Sherif, Cassie, Malcolm, Norrie ("light, lamp, candle").

Another category of interest is the color names that were usually assigned to dark-complexioned persons (Black, Greig (= gray), Brown). There were also French-derived names: Ramage, Norvel, Rae ("king"), Gall, Gauld, Moir (= Moor), Harvey, Bissett, Barron, Riddell, Noble), and others often carried by persons of Jewish descent: Bannerman (= herald), Copland, Wyness, Slesser ("from Silesia"), Money, Cattanach, Proctor (= administrator, prior), Horne (Hebrew *shofar*), Cromar, Kellock. Except for the clan names, one would hardly expect to find these names lurking around a Scottish graveyard.

Nearby is the Symington Cemetery (list 2), which was founded in 1160 by Simon Loccard, a French émigré, whose name ("family of Lock") became Anglicized to Lockhart.[2] This graveyard contains some names that are strikingly Jewish or Sephardic: for example, Arbell, Pirie (Hebrew "pear tree"; cf. Perry, Perez), Yuille (Hebrew Jehuqiel), Samson, Cown (Cohen), Gemmell (Gamiel, or Gammel, the Hebrew letter), Corseina, Rose, Wharrie, Orr (= gold), Pollock ("from Poland"), Speirs (= a town in Germany from which the Jews were driven in 1180), Currie (Arabic), Hornal, Sangster (Cantor), Akers (fr. Acre, the Crusader capital in the Levant). And again we also see persons from clans discussed earlier as likely to be Jewish: Campbell, Douglas, Kennedy, Fraser, McDougal, and Stewart/Stuart, as well as surnames known to have originated in Flanders or France: Ritchie ("enriched"), Ramage ("branch of vine"), Galt ("money"), Fleming ("from Flanders"), Moffatt (Hebrew for "excellent" and Arabic for "counselor"), Wallace (de Walys, i.e. from Gaul, Wales or Brittany, or possibly Arabic, too, as noted above), Nisket, Colville, Heneage, Bannatine and Kilgour.

The Girvan Cemetery (list 3) is southwards and has some names found in the other two, but some additional ones as well. We find Brown, Davidson, Campbell, Law, Murray, Stewart, Orr and Bissett, and also some new French and Sephardic surnames. Among these are Paton, Alexander (see chapter 4), Muir, Lees, Donell, Lamb (as in Passover), Diamond (a Jewish trade monopoly from antiquity to the present day), McKissock (Isaacson), Caruths, Niven, Bone (French "Good"), Laurie, Tarbett, Hasack, Wasson, Hart (cf. Hirsch in German), Sinclair,[3] Hannah (Hebrew for Ann), Waddell, Ryrie, Jardine, Robinson ("son of Rueben"), Austin, Marshall/Marischal, Cotes (French for Costa, an ancient Jewish family), and Gardiner.

Monkton Cemetery (list 4) is named for the Monck/Mank/Monk/Mock family which is Jewish and has offshoots in Eastern Europe; there were numerous matches of this surname with Caldwell and Kennedy; the name may be a French rendering of Mag, the common designation for "Hungarian." Familiar associated clan names here include Kennedy, Gordon, Stewart, Campbell and Sinclair. The French/Sephardic names show a mixture of new and old: Brown, Muir, Moore, Gray, Law, Blackly, Cowan, Dalmahoy ("from Almohad," the name for a Berber dynasty in Spain), Bone ("good," a common Sephardic Spanish surname as Buen), Purdie, Goldie, Porteous, Hannah, Legge, Gemmell, Tinnion, Alexander, Marr, Lees, Weylie, Howie, Highet (= Hyatt, "life" in Arabic), Nisbet, Bissett, Harvey, Wallace, Dalziel, Frew ("early" in Flemish), Darroch, Currie (Arabic Khoury), Currans, Seaton, Rae, McHarrie, Smellie (I'smaeli), Smee and Howat.

If we move northward to the cemeteries of Geddes (Cadiz) (list 5), Lochaber, and Skye (list 6) we find many of the same surnames: Fraser, Cameron, Sinclair, Garden, Campbell, Davidson, Morice (Maurice, the French form of Moses), but with some novel French/Sephardic entries: Falconer, Rose (an adaptation of Hebrew Rosh "head"), McGlashan, de Moynes, de Glastalich, de Morenge, de Boath, Dollas (D'Allas), de Badzet and Ellis (= Elias). This cemetery was established by one Hugh Rose in 1473 and though located in northern Scotland, it has flat stones and table stones indicative of Jewish burial practices.

The farthest north of our cemeteries, Skye and Lochaber, has not only our Jewish clans Fraser, Cameron, Kennedy, Stewart, Gordon, but also the following remarkable set of Sephardic surnames: McTurk, McMartine, Dow (= Dau, David), Rankin, Rose, Parr (pear), Barnet ("son of Nat"), Fleming, Hannah, Scobie, Matheson, Dallas (= d'Allas, likely Muslim), Davidson, Sansoury, Imry and Tolmie (Egyptian). And, as if to drive home the point, there is a 1699 pyramid tombstone dedicated to Simon, Lord Fraser of Lovat.[4]

Returning to Ayr in the southwest (lists 7 and 8), we find three of the same Sephardic clan names, Kennedy, Caldwell[5] and Stewart. However, what impresses one here is the sheer number and diversity of French/Sephardic Jewish names. Consider these: Black, Ross, Semple, Currie, Vass,[6] Steele (Castille), Givans, Armour, Brown, Hannay, Gouldie, Norvall, Orr, Stobo, Alexander, Jamieson, Wharrie, Cowan, Wise (cf. German Weis "sage"), Savage, Love (Löwe, "lion"), Izat (Arabic), Meikle, Bone, Frew, Hazle, Adams, Doustie, Goudie, Cossar, Affleck (French "with spots/freckles"), Mair, Templeton, Norris (= Noor, "light" in Arabic), Hague (Dutch town), Eccles, Ritchie, Kilgour, Pringle, Samson, Spiers, Peddie, Beaton, Fogo, Purdie, Nimmo ("from Nîmes," in southern France), Lamb, Porteous, Eaton (= Eitan, Hebrew), Wyllie, Dawson, Lash, Bantine, Telfer ("blacksmith"), Gemmell, Highet, Simson, Span ("Spain"), Fleck, Boag, Belfon, Greage (= gray), Pollock ("from Poland"), Adam, Bone, Paton, Gross (German "tall, large"), Arbuckle (Hebrew), Noble, Herkes, Vine, Wharrie, Laurie (= Lurie, Luria, a famous Rabbinic line),[7] Lammie, Imrie, Napier, Goldie, Bowie, Kelso, Guild, Law, Tannock (Hebrew), Lowrie, Beveridge, Muirhead (Moorhead), Parrot (Perrot), Corsane, Ratter ("advisor"), Tarbet, Smellie (Ismailie) and Ferriel ("iron worker").

The frequent occurrence of names ending in–el cannot help but strike us and deserves to be addressed. Jacobs (1906–1911) remarks that the earliest Hebrew names usually incorporate the name of God, as in Samuel, Nathaniel, Daniel, and the like. Most of our Scottish–el names seem to belong to Norman retainers who came over with the Conqueror. Before becoming concentrated in Flanders and Normandy, these families probably lived in the southern part of France, either in the regions of Narbonne, Toulouse or Aquitaine, at a time when the whole southern frontier had just with difficulty been won back from the Arabs. We believe the–el suffix is a sign of southern French Judeo-Arabic roots. In Islam, the word *alah* or Al- is added to names, indifferently designating "man" and "God."

Thus, as far as burials are concerned and on the basis of male family names, we would seem to have significant coverage by persons of Jewish (and likely also Moorish) ancestry from north to south in western Scotland.

Burgesses and Taxpayers

But a sampling of cemetery inscriptions can take us only so far. Many persons living in western Scotland may not have been buried in one of these graveyards and not all inscriptions are decipherable. Thus, lists 9, 10, and 11 show names taken from burgess listings in Stirling and Tron. A burgess was originally an inhabitant of a burgh who held a piece of land there from the Crown (or other superior). Later, a burgess was a merchant or craftsman influential in burgh affairs. Here we find even more surnames from the 1600–1799 time period that appear to indicate Jewish descent. For example, in Stirling between 1600 and 1699, we find persons named Arral, Ana, Bachop, Cassilis,

Gaston, Jak (Jacques, Jacob), Lyoum, Lyon, Mushet (Moses), Orrock, Reoch ("wind" in Arabic), Savin, Shirray (Arabic; cf. shi'ir, Shiraz, a town in Persia), Touch (a Hebrew letter), and Yaire (Hebrew), along with many others previously encountered, are serving as burgesses of this small city. By the period 1700–1799, the list includes Corbet, Corsar, Clugstone, Cassels (Kassel, a town in Germany), Hosie (Hosiah), Hassock, Jaffray (Geoffrey), Oliphant (from "elephant"), Peacock, Runciman, Rattray, Salmond (Soloman) and Yoole (Hebrew Yehuiel).

In nearby Tron Parish in the year 1694 (the first year a census was taken), taxpayers included a Basilly (Greek "king"), Veatch, Berrie, Pouries, Chartres (city in central France), Pyot, Smellum, Mannas (Hebrew Manasse), Hackets, Dejet (*de Jette*, Yates),[8] Rouart ("from Rouen"), Tarras, Arnot (Hebrew Aaron), Lune (Luna, the family of Doña Gracia of the House of Nasi, 1510–1569),[9] Cave, Scougall, Baptie, Antous, Cubie, Bemeny, Lendo, Elphinstone (from Elephantine, a Jewish colony in Egypt), Moncrief, Jolly (French "happy, pleasant"), Montray (Royal Mountain: Spanish), Cant, Buris (Hebrew: Baruch), Riddell (from Arabic *ridda* "warrior"),[10] Scrimjours (Clan Scrymgeour),[11] Eizat (Arabic related to Izod, Izot), Blau ("blue"), Tailfer (Spanish Talliaferro, "blacksmith"), and Picaris (from Picardy) — not names one usually associates with Scotland!

Craftsmen and Seamen

Jews coming to Scotland from Iberia during the 1400s and 1500s (and later) carried with them an ample store of what sociologists term "cultural capital" (Bourdieu 1993). They had valuable knowledge and skills that were incalculable assets to the countries where they settled, notably medical, metallurgical, mining, sailing, leatherworking, glassmaking and mercantile expertise. Unlike their Christian cohorts, European and Middle Eastern Jews of even modest means in the early modern period also possessed literacy and "numeracy," the two requirements for running a business. Some of the craft guilds in western Scotland kept records of these specialties beginning in the 1600s, and it is to an examination of these that we now turn.

Goldsmiths

Virtually all goldsmiths from the Middle Ages onward were either Jews or Moors. Indeed, the surname Goldsmith or Goldschmidt almost always belonged to a person of Jewish ancestry. In Victorian England, Isaac Lyon Goldsmid was the first Jew to receive a hereditary title in 1841; he was made a baronet. When we examine the list of Scottish goldsmiths (list 12) we are struck by the number that are *prima facie* of Jewish origin: Aitken ("from Aix"), Aldcorne, Annand, Argo, Arnot, Bannerman, Bogie (Ottoman Turkish), Burrell, Davidson, Dalzell, Falconer, Gillett, Green, Hector, Houre, Izat, Low, Mossman, Orrock, Pollock, Symonds, Vogil ("bird" in Yiddish), and Zieglar ("sailor" in Yiddish), among many others.[12] We also see surnames from several of the clans previously identified as Jewish in ancestry: Campbell, Christie, Douglas, Gardyne, Gordon,

Leslie, and Stewart. We believe that members of these clans either possessed goldsmithing skills when they first migrated from France and Flanders, or they "adopted-in" persons having these skills, who then took the clan surname.

Clock- and Watchmakers 1576–1800; Glassmakers and Printers

Clock- and watchmaking were, like goldsmithing, virtually a monopoly exercised by Jews and Moors, who closely guarded their valuable trade secrets. Surnames in this industry in Scotland (list 13) prove also to suggest a Sephardic or French Jewish background: Adams, Alexander, Corrie, Currie, Davidson, Gardiner, Given, Jamieson, Low, Muir, Orr, Savell, Seiffert, Sim and Yuill. Early glassmakers (list 14) show the same pattern: Davidson, Dow, Barrat, Wothersponn, Rowan, Gardner and Waddell.

Although printing was developed in Europe only in the latter half of the 1400s and did not spread to many regions until the 1500s, by 1507 King James of Scotland had set up Andro Myllar and Walter Chepman as printers in Edinburgh. In 1520 Thomas Davidson (from Aberdeen) set up a second printing press in Edinburgh. We believe that all three men were of Jewish descent.

Trade Incorporation Records: St. Andrews, Kircaldy, Dunfermline, Fife

List 15 shows the names and dates of persons granted trade incorporation permits in central Scotland. There are several Jewish (and Moorish) names: Alison, Boyack, Ferrier, Leuchars, Syme, Annal, Balmanno, Corsar, Cowan, Norrie, Patie, Sabez, Beaucher, Deas, Davidson, Bruce, Coventrie, Nobel, Balcase, Forbes, Muir and Rennie.

Apprenticeships and Trade Incorporation Records: Fife

Fife is in east central Scotland, so we are moving toward Aberdeen a bit here, yet we still find much the same pattern. Lists 16 and 17 document the surnames of some of the figures to whom trade incorporation and apprenticeship permits were issued. These include Arnot, Lessels, Davidson, Eizatt, Flukour, Simers, Martyne, Angell, Porteous, Douglas, Annan, Bone, Hannah, Riddell, Macara, Balmanno, Pigot, Low, Yule, Salmond and Scobie. Thus, we see that a relatively common set of French and Sephardic surnames was found across central Scotland.

Western Scotland Seamen

Another valuable skill that the French and Spanish Jews brought to Scotland was their navigational and sailing acumen. From the Clyde River near Glasgow, Scottish vessels traded with Mediterranean ports, the Caribbean, and the American colonies. A partial listing of Scottish sailors from 1600 to 1800 (list 18) shows many names recognizable as stemming from French, Spanish, Jewish, Moorish, Hebrew or Arabic: Alexander, Allason, Bisset, Davidson, Dougall, Gemmell, Hammill, Landells, Moor, Pollock, Paltoun, Yoole, Sleiman, Spainzea, Caldwell, Cowan, Glaister (glazier), Gordon, Jargon, Lyon, Nimmo, Sheron (Hebrew: Sharon), Sabaston (Sebastian) and Ure (gold).

Glasgow

Glasgow was founded as early as the sixth century and became a royal burgh in the twelfth century under King David I. The University of Glasgow was chartered in 1451 as the fourth oldest university in the British Isles and counts among its intellectual luminaries the economist Adam Smith, novelist-physician Tobias Smollett, and chemist Joseph Black. Our focus in Glasgow is upon the small set of merchant families who, beginning in the mid–1600s, made vast fortunes in international trade and banking. In particular, they traded with the southeastern American colonies, purchasing tobacco, brokering it to France and Holland, and setting up a series of Tidewater and frontier stores that reached from Maryland to Florida.

Around Glasgow, the merchant shipping trade was an oligopoly highly concentrated (50 percent–80 percent) in the hands of a few families. Among these were the Cunninghames, Glassfords, Dunlops, Oswalds, Donalds, Murdochs, Ritchies, Bogles (Turkish), Speirs, Nisbets and Riddells. As Devine (1975) notes in his detailed work *The Tobacco Lords*, these men were all the sons of Glasgow merchants, not its landed gentry. Most had been sent by their families to live and work for some period of time in the Colonies in order to establish business ties there. In due course, they incorporated themselves into partnerships that in turn formed networks, trading in wine from Lisbon and Madeira, rice and flaxseed from South Carolina, wheat, fish, and tobacco from Maryland, Virginia and North Carolina, and later sugar and cotton from the Caribbean.

To establish such a trading empire required not only large sources of capital, but also contacts who would honor letters of credit, insurance notes, and customs declarations in Portugal, Spain, the Caribbean and Dutch, Danish, French and British colonies, as well as Scotland. Not all of this activity was above board or even legal. The Board of Trade and officially enfranchised merchants in London and Liverpool alternately turned a blind eye on and descried such hugely profitable operations, especially the repeated undercutting of prices to captive planters and the winning by the Bogle Company of the large annual French state contract for tobacco at Le Havre. The canny Scots traders obviously drew on the Auld Alliance with France, but we feel confident that another likely reason for the success of such a network were the blood ties, and shared Jewish ethnicity, of the principles in these Glasgow firms.

This same set of merchant partners formed the Glasgow Arms and Ship Bank in the early 1750s, and around a decade later the Scottish Thistle Bank. In this way, their ventures could be more firmly capitalized and protected from competition. The banks permitted the tobacco lords of the Clyde to loan out money, as well. One bank owner, George

Boyle, extended loans to John Shaw, Lord Cathcart, John Napier and Lady Pollock, among others (Devine 1975).

As was typical of both French and Spanish Jewish families, marriages were almost exclusively endogamous; they occurred only between group members. In-marriage helped to consolidate capital, preserve political power, and maintain cultural ties and identity. By the mid–1700s, most of these merchant families had acquired enough money to buy large tracts of land in the surrounding countryside. Once they became landowners, they were able to select their own church ministers and schoolteachers. This likely proved very useful in perpetuating their Crypto-Judaic heritage, as ministers and teachers could be chosen who were of Jewish descent or sympathy.

Once the American Revolution began, the tobacco trade was disrupted. The Glaswegian merchants hence began to turn to manufacturing. One group, consisting of Andrew Buchanan, William French, John Campbell and George Coats, organized and operated several successful mining ventures, including coal, iron ore and pottery clay — all three of which had been originally perfected by Sephardic Jews and Moors in Muslim Spain. This same group, now including James Milliken, later ventured successfully into leather tanning and sugar refining. Apparently, no great efforts were made to hide their religious identity: a town in the countryside near some of the manufactories was named Succoth — a major Jewish holiday. This town is the ancestral home of the Campbells of Argyll. A portrait of Archibald Campbell, Duke of Argyll, is shown in chapter 1. Also known as the Feast of the Tabernacles, Succoth celebrates the Jews' wandering in the desert; it was the perfect emblem for a migratory waystation a great distance from Israel.

An excerpt from Devine (p. 37) below describes the complexity of these financial partnerships:

> Of the three malleable ironworks in eighteenth century Scotland, the two situated in the Glasgow area ... were financed by tobacco merchants. The first of these was founded in 1734 when a number of traders erected a slitting mill on the banks of the River Kelvin to manufacture nails; this early venture subsequently developed into a major concern producing "nails, adzes, axes, hoes, spades, shovels, chisels, hammers, bellows and anvils" for the colonial market. Thirty-five years after the Smithfield Company was established, Islay Campbell of Succoth, Advocate and M.P. for Glasgow Burghs, feued parts of the lands of Dalnottar to three wealthy merchants, the brothers Peter and George Murdoch and William Cunninghame, all of whom were already fellow partners in a Virginia firm.... Throughout its forty-four years of existence until 1813 it was sold to William Dunn, a leading cottonmaster, the Dalnottar Co. was financed by a series of tobacco merchants....
>
> In 1781, the Muirkirk[13] Iron Co. was set up by the merchants who controlled Smithfield and Dalnottar, together with the partners of Cramond Iron Co. in order to maintain a safe supply of cheap bar-iron at a time when Swedish and Russian prices were rising. It was by a similar process of integration that in the last thirty years of the eighteenth century a tight-knit group of tobacco importers obtained control of almost the entire West of Scotland glass industry and a sizeable proportion of its coal extraction developments.

All of this oligopolistic activity was supported in part by a triangle trade network through the heavily Sephardic Caribbean:

> The West Indies trade was a necessary corollary to the tobacco trade. Most Glasgow houses had correspondents there who supplied sugar, rum and molasses for their North American outlets. Sometimes vessels outward bound from the Clyde were directed firstly to the

Caribbean before proceeding to the tobacco colonies; alternatively merchantmen awaiting a cargo of tobacco were occasionally dispatched to the West Indies to load store provisions.... As planters often paid for their imported articles in wheat and corn, the storekeepers found the West Indies market a profitable outlet for grain. For instance, Neil Jamieson, the chief colonial representative of John Glassford and co., carried on an extensive trade with the Caribbean, particularly Antigua, and with the Azores and the Mediterranean, dealing in provisions, lumber and wine. He also financed shipbuilding and owned coastal shipping and was involved in the salt trade from Bordeaux to Lewiston and in the slave trade to the Carolinas [p. 62].

Just as remarkable was the fact that the primary market for all the Sephardic Scottish tobacco was none other than their original homeland, France. This lucrative market and their own financial contacts provided the Scottish Jewish tobacco lords not only with wealth, but also stability over an extended period of time.

Undoubtedly a major element in providing this was the bulk sales to the French Farmers General, the most important single purchasers in the trade.... Significantly, in the credit crisis of 1772, Sir Robert Herries, the French buyer "was received with open arms" by the great Clyde traders ... [and] in 1762, when it was difficult to procure credit and sales were sluggish, William Alexander and Sons, acting for the French, advanced cash for customs duties to Lawson, Semple and Co....

   Perhaps the most valuable asset possessed by the eighteenth century businessman was not his capital, but rather his reputation and his connexions. The prestige and influence of the well-known families in the Glasgow tobacco trade meant that they ... had little difficulty in securing credit from contacts in other parts of the United Kingdom or Europe. One of the Bogles borrowed freely in London in the 1720's because his father's credit "was as good as ever" and consequently his son "can never want money when you think to borrow it and that without paying Interest on it." James Lawson secured sums of varying amounts from fellow merchants in Bristol, Liverpool and London by drawing bills for between six and twelve months [p. 96].

List 19 (see end of chapter) and the three tables show business dealings and genealogies for the Glasgow merchants.

A Glasgow House of Worship: Ramshorn Kirk

Among Jews, the ram's horn or *shofar* has a special significance. It is used to rally the people, call them to worship, and remind them of who they are and who their God is. It is in perfect keeping with these traditions that a Jewish house of worship would be named for the ram's horn. Ramshorn Kirk (church) on Ingram Street in the old merchant city of Glasgow represents just such a Crypto-Jewish meeting house. First established in 1720, it was the place of worship for the merchants of the city. Its pastors were drawn from among their own kind, and members of the congregation lie buried around its exterior yard.

We took photos of the Ramshorn Kirk during the summer of 2002. The original building was replaced by a new structure in 1828, most unfortunately, and was heavily rebuilt after the dying out of its congregants and eventual acquisition by the university, but even the new stained glass windows are primarily of Old Testament scenes: Abraham and Isaac, Jeremiah, David and Solomon.

However, it is the cemetery that is most remarkable: as the photographs show, it is unlike most cemeteries the reader has probably encountered: there are no upright head-stones (a Christian custom), no crosses of any kind, no citations from the New Testament, and no invocations of Jesus. Instead we see rows and walls of flat tablets stating austerely the names and occupations of the deceased. Significantly, the only images used

Ramshorn Kirk was rebuilt in the 1800s, but stained glass windows still show primarily Old Testament scenes. Photograph by Elizabeth Caldwell Hirschman.

The Ramshorn Kirk cemetery is remarkable; it contains only flat Judaic-style grave markers. There are no Christian symbols. Photograph by Elizabeth Caldwell Hirschman.

on any of the markers are the Book of Life and the Tree of Life, both Hebrew insignia. The names of those interred in the Ramshorn Kirk grounds overlap with those mentioned above, with the addition of explicitly Jewish surnames like Pirie and Davidson.

And Now to Stirling

The town of Stirling was ruled by the Alexander family, which we have argued to be of Jewish ancestry. On a trip in the summer of 2002 we visited Stirling town and Stirling Castle and made two notable discoveries. The first was Cowane's Hospital, founded in 1637 with money left by the Stirling merchant and guild dean John Cowane. As discussed in chapter 2, the name Cowane is analogous to Kohane, the surname carried by members of the Jewish priestly caste traced to Aaron, brother of Moses. Very probably Mr. Cowane was a Kohane. Second, the hospital was actually used as a charity home for indigent guild members, providing them with free room and board. Such an endowment was not common in England at the time, but was *de rigueur* for Jewish communities, which always sought to provide for widows, orphans, unmarried women, pensioners, and other needy members. Examples abound from Bayonne, Bayeux, Amsterdam, Bremen, Copenhagen, Curacao, Hamburg, Barbados, and elsewhere during the Sephardic Diaspora. The custom is grounded on several *mitzvoth* (commandments) concerning almsgiving and halakic conduct (*zedeka*) and later became a cornerstone of the Scottish Presbyterian Church,[14] as noted by Herman (2001, p. 17):

The congregation was the center of everything. It elected its own board of elders or presbyters; it even chose its minister. The congregation's board of elders, the consistory, cared for the poor and the sick; it fed and clothed the community's orphans. Girls who were too poor to have a dowry to tempt a prospective husband got one from the consistory.

This Ramshorn Kirk grave marker shows an open "Book of Life" motif — a Judaic practice. Photograph by Elizabeth Caldwell Hirschman.

This gravemarker for Jane Freeland states that she is the wife of William Gemmell. Gemmell is a Hebrew letter. Photograph by Elizabeth Caldwell Hirschman.

Cowane's Hospital in Stirling, Scotland, was built in 1637 suing a bequest from the Dean of the Guild, John Coawane. He is depicted by the statue above the entry door. Photograph by Elizabeth Caldwell Hirschman.

Of London Jewry, Jacobs (1911) writes:

The Sephardic Orphan Asylum had been established as early as 1703, and a composite society, whose title commenced with "Honen Dalim," was founded in 1704 to aid lying-in women, support the poor, and to give marriage portions to fatherless girls. In 1736 a Marriage Portion Society was founded, and eleven years later the Beth Holim, or hospital, came

This chair within the hospital's main hall carries Cabalah mathematical images and a Ten Commandments motif on the chair back. Note the several forms of triangles and the Tao/Tough symbol. The number 4 was sacred to the Jews. Photograph by Elizabeth Caldwell Hirschman.

into existence, this in turn being followed in 1749 by the institution known as "Mahesim Tobim." Thanks to these and other minor institutions, the life of a Sephardic Jew in London was assisted at every stage from birth, through circumcision, to marriage, and onward to death, while even the girls of the community were assisted with dowries.

The third feature that struck us upon entering the building was that it appeared to have been designed much more as a worship center and Masonic hall than as a hospital

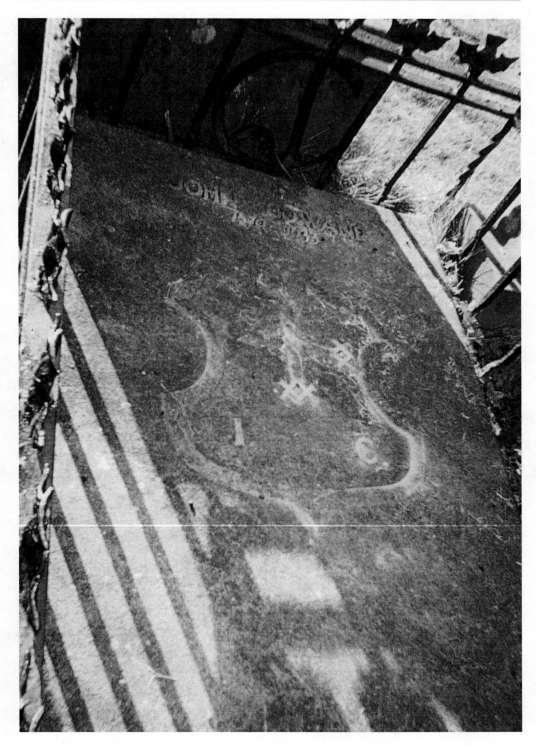

Cowane's grave marker near the hospital (1570–1633) displays the same Cabalistic imagery seen in the building. Photograph by Elizabeth Caldwell Hirschman.

or charity ward. The ceiling was arched and there were few windows to the interior; thus services could have been held without being visible from outside. Fourth, the interior of the building and its original chairs were marked with Masonic emblems. Cowane's grave itself was inscribed with the same Masonic emblems, forming a Star of David symbol.

A Stirling guidebook (*Stirling's Talking Stones*, 2002) provides the following information on John Cowane (1570–1633):

> Stirling's greatest benefactor was born in 1570, a contemporary of William Shakespeare.... His father was a merchant, burgess and indweller in Stirling and a prominent man. He and his wife supplied the Royal Palace in Stirling with goods and their premises would have been the Harrods of the day. John was in business with his father until the latter's death in 1617, when John took over all of his father's business, including running his booth or shop in what is now Broad Street.
>
> Records also show that John Cowane was involved in more than simply selling goods in his booth. He was a substantial landlord in the town and was not averse to evicting non-paying tenants, if the rent was not paid. He was a member of the Town Council and on more than one occasion Dean of Guild, the real source of power in the burgh at that time.... He was also the main banker/money lender in the town....
>
> In addition to his political activities (he was a member of the old Scots Parliament), John Cowane was heavily involved in shipping. [It] was always necessary for a merchant to reach the main Scots export markets of the Low Countries. He could not always rely on trading to make him rich and with empty ships he also acted as a privateer — essentially a pirate with a license.... Kirk records show he did have at least one child by a maid servant.

Even more interesting, however, than John Cowane's seeming litany of Jewish-related business and charitable activities was the kirk altar at which he and the Stirling guild brothers worshiped (Morris 1919, p. 132):

> It was usual for each Incorporation to have a special altar in the Parish church, at which masses were said for behoof of the members, and the maintenance of which was their special duty.... We venture to suggest that the members of the Stirling Merchant Gild [*sic*] constituted the Fraternity of the Holy Blood and were responsible for the upkeep of that altar in the Parish Church. In the published Extracts from the Stirling Town Council Records, there are a good many references to the altar of the Holy Blood. That there was a Fraternity of the Holy Blood is shown by the ... entries [from] 14th February, 1521–2 (Extracts Vol. I., pp. 13–19), 2nd October, 1524 (Trans. Stirling Nat. Hist. and Arch. Socy. 1905–1906, p. 54), 3rd July, 1530, 24th January, 1549–50 (Extracts Vol. I pp. 266, 58, 70).
>
> There is no proof that the Stirling Fraternity of the Holy Blood were the Merchant Gild, but the following facts warrant the suggestion: (1) There was an Altar of the Holy Blood in Stirling Parish Church, and such altars were in Stirling, as elsewhere, supported by Gild Fraternities. (2) There was a Fraternity of the Holy Blood in Stirling. (3) From the analogy of other towns, it is to be presumed that the Stirling Merchant Guild maintained an altar in the Parish Church. (4) On 12th October, 1556, the Town Council of Stirling directed the revenues of the altar of the Holy Blood to be gathered by the Dean of Gild. (Extracts. Vol. I., p. 70). (5) In Dundee the Merchant Gild constituted the Fraternity of the Holy Blood and maintained the altar of that name in the Parish Kirk, their written obligation to do so being still preserved. (*Old Dundee*, Alexander Maxwell, pp. 25, 127). (6) In Edinburgh, also, the Merchants were the Fraternity of the Holy Blood, and were patrons of, and upheld the Holy Blood altar in St. Giles. (Extracts from Edinburgh Records. 10th Dec., 1518, 25th April, 1561.) (7) There were altars of the Holy Blood in the Parish Kirks, with corresponding Fraternities in the following towns, where there were also Merchant Gilds, although the connection in each case is only inferred: Dunfermline (Chalmers, p. 126), Linlithgow (*Ecclesia Antiqua*, Ferguson, pp. 156, 320), Haddington (*Lamp of Lothian*, Miller, p. 177), Lanark (Extracts,

Lanark Records, pp. 15, 16, 326), Peebles (Chaters, Peebles, pp. 73, 300, 348), Aberdeen (Chartulary of St. Nicholas, numerous entries). (8) In Letters of Reversion by Androw Cowane, merchant, father of John Cowane, Stirling's benefactor, granted in 1580 (Fraser Papers, H.M. Gen. Register House), the grant was declared to be redeemable in the "Holy Bluid Ile," situated in the Parish Kirk of Striveling [Stirling]. The fact that Androw Cowane was a merchant and chose Holy Blood aisle as the place for redeeming the debt suggests an association between the merchants and the Holy Blood alter.

Of course, what is remarkable about this testimony is that, when added to the historical record that Cowane supplied the Royal Stewart family with goods, it reveals a close connection between the Cowane family and Stewart monarchy, which claimed to be descended from "the holy blood" (*Sange Real*) of King David. Thus, rather than Christian, we suggest that the Holy Blood altar and fraternity of merchants and guildsmen were, in fact, Crypto-Jewish. The guild hall at Cowane's Hospital has three large scallop shell carvings on the inside above its entryways that strongly hint we are entering a place that was Jacobite, one frequented by supporters of the Stewarts and of the Davidic bloodline the Stewarts embodied. As shall become clear in the next chapter, the cult of the Holy Blood (*Sange Real*) was originally a Templar and later a Masonic practice, with roots in the Cabala. In passing, let us also observe that the Cowanes of Stirling frequently married Alexanders, and that two of the daughters of such unions were named Maisie, the feminine form of Moses.

Venturing up the hill from Cowane's Hospital to Stirling Castle, a Royal Stewart holding, also proved enlightening. In the main building, a similar large sanctuary dat-

The mural on the sanctuary wall inside Stirling Castle, a Royal Stewart residence, is replete with Cabalistic images. The window is designed in a Ten Commandments motif. Photograph by Elizabeth Caldwell Hirschman.

ing from 1628 was found. Around the ceiling border were murals with Old Testament and Mediterranean scenes painted by Valentine Jenkins. While looking at these, it occurred to us that the construction of the "matching" or twin windows at either end of the gallery, unlike windows in churches which typically have three divisions with a central high arch (to symbolize the Holy Trinity) instead consisted of two wide, arched diptyches. The windows on the left had geometrical stained glass panels cross-cut by horizontal lines. As the photograph illustrates, both sets of windows, particularly the ones with the colored glass (perhaps replaced, originally rendering a Hebrew text), seem to represent the Ten Commandments that Moses received from hand of God at Mount Sinai. To all intents and purposes, this could have been a synagogue.

List 1
Cluny Cemetery

McBride	Low	Riddell	Moir
Slesser	Kellock	Sherriffs	Law
Ramage	Kennedy	Emslie	Norvel
Wattie	Davidson	Stephen	Reid
Diach	Adam	Jaffray	Black
Malcolm	Daniel	Copland	Abel
Rae	Christie	Forbes	Cleriheu
Gall	Tough	Lockhart	Henry
Alexander	Money	Ferries	Murison
Bannerman	Barron	Tocher	Noble
Wyness	Cameron	Downie	Horne
Gauld	Eddie	Marr	Norrie
Gordon	Elder	James	
Webster	Cooper	Cassie	
Moir	Lawie	Proctor[15]	
Copland (fr. Jacob)	Glashan	Cromar	
Bissett	Nicol	Law	
Alcock	Robbie	Carnegie	
Forbes	Stuart	Harvey	
Dickie	Cattanach	Greig	
Cundy	Browny	Mackie[16]	

List 2
Symington Cemetery
Founded by a Norman, Simon Loccard (Lockhart), 1160

James Innes	James Watt	Wakelin[17]	John Jamieson
Wilhemina Todd	Robert Loudon	Sarah Muir	Mabel Jessie Blaine
James Ritchie	James Malcolm	Annie Colville	Gray
Robert Paton Pollock	Templeton	Elizabeth Borland	Houston

Joseph Aitken
Euphemia Sillar
William Ramage
Ann Jamison
Elizabeth Douglas
John Galt
Hannah Strathern
Agnes Lyle
Robert King
Janet Layburn
Hector Walker
Sarah Dunn
William Fleming
John Moffatt
Henry Candlish
Adam Campbell
Ellen Mair
James Arbell[20]
Ann Pirie
David Yuille
Arch. Brekinridge

Kennedy
Gordon
David Samson
Daniel Murray
Muir
Cowan
Morrison
McDougal
Corseina
Lamont
Lees
Wallace
Patterson
Alex. Rose
Isabella Bryden
Davidson
Dunlop
Drennan
Wharrie
Nisbet
Parker

Isabella Ogilvy
Stewart
Jessie Dickie
Samuel Cowan
William Noble
Bernard Crosbie
John Jackson
Elizabeth Barton
James Fairlie
Esther Campbell
Elsie Neish
Sandilands
Jane Heneage
Gairdner
Dubbs
Guthrie
George Lister
Margaret Orr
George Akers
Margaret Gemmell
Will Speirs

Bathia[18] Smith
James Steel
Hay
Downie
James Barr
James Currie
Bannatine
Hyslop[19]
Adam Dale
James Landsburgh
Templeton
Stuart
Sangster
Dinning
Fraser
Love
Reid
Lavinia Dennon
Kilgour
John Kelso

List 3
Girvan Cemetery

John Houston
David Henderson
Graham
Robert Jack
Marion Donell
Annie Lees
William Brown
David Philips
Patrick Lamb
Margaret Bowman
Robert Diamond
Thomas Lyle
Sarah Credie
Thomas McKisock
Ann Good
Alexander Roxburgh
Margaret Muir
Alex. Caruths
Robert Niven
Samuel Tait

Abraham Campbell
Elizabeth Laurie
[Assel Cottage]
Andrew Law
Alexander
James Bisset
Andrew Robison
James Austin
Marshall
Jemima McEwen
Annie Russell Cotes
Robert Gardiner
Cath. Tarbett
McGarva
Ballantyne
Mary Hosack[21]
John Bell
John Murray
Stewart
Jessie Davidson

James Lymburner
Rath. Wasson
Robert Leadbetter
Sinclair
Adam Hart
Margaret Caldwell
Andrew Nichol
Robert Hannah
Mary Orr
James Waddell
Moar
Paton
William Kyrie
Agnes Jardine
Bone

List 4
Monkton Cemetery

Jessie Brown	Jessie Muir	Alex Manson	Margaret Smellie
Henry Gordon	William Weylie	Jean Dalziel	James Chalmers
J.M. Cowan	Bessie Barr	John Frew	John Cuthell
Harriet DalMaboy	William Howie	Andrew Guthrie	Archibald Ramsay
Robert Bone	David Dunlop	Elizabeth O'Hare	Bessie Morland
Jane Purdie	Mary Joan Highet	Isa Darroch	Ellen Gray
Moses McFall	Robert Pettigrew	John Currans	Mary Ralston
Mary Hyslop Goldie	David Campbell	Andrew Tait	David Campbell
James Porteous	Isabella Hutchison	John Currie	Abigail Langlands
Agnes Hannah	Mary Blyth	Hector Manson	Robert Law
Elizabeth Black	William Queen	Margaret Goudie	Kate Smee
Henry Legge	James Nisbet	William Heirs	Susan Adamson
James Dow	John Jamieson	Johann Given	Jane Mair
Agnes Muir	William Meikle	David Hendry	Annas Howat
Mary Bryant	Rachel Bissett	George Buyers	James Knox
Janet Gemmell	Mary Wardrobe	Sarah Morrison	Thomas Murray
James Tinnion	William Wallace	George Blackly	John Bicket
Hugh Sillars	Isaac Harvey	John Seaton	William Weir
Jessica Alexander	Charles Gray	Elizabeth Rae	James Hay
James Breckinridge	Jeannie Templeton	Milligan McHarrie	James Edie
Jane Marr	Alex Gardiner	Peter Dallas	Joanna Snodgrass
George Collie	James Kennedy	Samuel Pitt	James Sinclair
Sophia Lees	Sarah Moore	Lilias Drinnon	John Bell

List 5
Geddes[22] (Cadiz) Cemetery (Nairn)*

Hugh Rose 1473	Isobel Garden
David Rose	William Campbell
Fraser	Donald McBean
Scott	Lilias Grant
Anna Maria Twemlow	Joh. Grant de Moynes
Elizabeth Mann	McCulloch de Glastalich
Annie Cameron	Tho. Ross de Morenge
Maggie Chisolm	Alex. Dunbar de Boath
Thomas King	Jaco. McKenzie
Isabella Falconer	Joh. Dollas de Budzet
Ramsay	Rosen
Shaw	Sophia Urquhart
Sinclair	Sophia Ellis
David McGlashan	Anna Morice
John Nicol	Alex. Davidson

Several flat stones and table stones

List 6
Lochaber and Skye Cemetery
Inscriptions (Pre–1855)

Alexander McTurk
Jemima Cameron
Duncan Fraser
Duncan Kennedy
McMartine
Samuel Dow
Anne Rankin
Henry Rose
Isabella Kennedy
William Stewart
James Parr
John Jaffray Block
George Given
James McBarnet
Barbara Matheson

Helen Fleming
Jonathan and Hannah Miller
Janet Scobie
Charles Scobie King
Alexander Marten
James Rhodes
Alexander Lauder
Ann Dallas
John Gordon
Frances Hay
Cameron (many)
George Snodgrass
Alexander Black
Alexander Sandison
Henzel Ferguson

Margaret Pringle
Donald McBean
Donald McGillivray
Thomas Davidson
Colin McIver
Archibald Shennan
Richard Sansoury
James Ballantine
Margaret Imry
Lydia Fowler
John Jamieson
James Inglis
John Tolmie
Pyramid with eulogy to Simon,
   Lord Fraser of Lovat, 1699

List 7
Ayr Old Kirk

Martin, David,
   Isabella Stewart
Margaret Samson
David Limond
Jemima Vint
Grace Aiken
Charles Eaton
Lilias Hamilton
Hugh Wyllie
Jane Eccles
Dugald Campbell
Grisell McAdam
Adam Gladstone
Catherine Lavinia
   Dawson
Robert Davidson
Mary Grace Lash
Andrew Cowan
James Heron
James Burtine
John Bell Telfer

John Ferrie
Agnes Simson
Alexander Dykes
Edith Span
Janet Black Fleck
Samuel Ritchie
Elias Cathcart
Margaret Boag
Helena Belfon
William Turnbull
Jonet Greage
Alex Pollock
Agnes Adam
David Kerr
James Bone
Hannah Kennedy
Walter Jamieson
Robert Paton
Henry Cowan
S.J.B. Gross
David Linton

William Noble
Mary Herkes
John Lauder
Jane Heriot
David Ballingal
William Vine
Agnes Caldwell
Andrew Watt
John Robb
Cosmo Hepburn[23]
J.D. Rowlatt
Alex Gairdner
James Gemmell
Janet Wharrie
Jessie Hendrie
William Laurie
Jeannie Lammie
James Milliken
Thomas Imrie
Rosanna Rillie
Elizabeth Napier

Adamina Smith
Arabella Guild
William Cowan
Bernard Haldan
Margaret Law
Bethea Halden Sloan
Isabella Tannock
David Murray
Elizabeth Lowrie
Marion Hart
Agnes Beveridge
Jean Muirhead
Hugh Parrot
Hamila McVicar
James Shearer
Margaret Corsane
Esther Alexander
George Mirrylee
Euphans Ratter
Isabella Jardine
Janet Tarbet

Margaret Cowan	Robert Highet	Mary Semple[25]	Adam Carnie
Jessie Gemmell	William Arbuckle	Mary Tinnock	John Lambie
Sarah Morrison	Adam McRorie	William Goldie	James Smellie
David Caldwell	Robert Bowie Nichol	David Bowie	
Jessie Tennant	Zearubbable[24] Baillie	Margaret Kelso	

List 8
Secessionist Graveyard at Ayr*

Elizabeth Black	John Jamieson	John Mair	James Dounie
Mary McFadzean	David Wharrie	John Templeton	Lily Peddie
Hardina Ross	Robert Cowan	Jane Norris	Walter Beaton
Elizabeth Semple	Ann Wise	Isabella Kennedy	Jane Fogo
Morris Murray	F. Savage	Janet Hague	William Purdie
David Drynan	Jane Love	James McKissock	Sarah Morley
Jane Currie	Sophia Izat	Ann Dempster	Wm. Bembaridge
William Vass	David Meikle	Thomas Houstan	Andrew Kay
Margaret Steele	David Bone	JaneEccles	Margaret Nimmo
John Givans	Robert Frew	Joseph Ritchie	James Dunlop
Robert Armour	James Hazle	Marion Aitken	William Houat
James Hannay	Dorcas Adams	William Kilgour	Isabella Spark
Isabella Brown	David Poustie	Jessie Brown	Andrew Lamb
Christina Gouldie	John Goudie	Lillias Kennedy	Jane Porteous
Agnes Hannah	Daniel Edie	Thomas Wylie	
Arabella Wilson	Mary Cossar	Mary Rowan	
Agnes Norvall	Anne Tannahill	Jane Pringle	
Agnes Orr	Jacobina Tannahill	Agnes Samson	
John Stobo	William Affleck	Stewart Spiers	
Jacobina McEwen	David Caldwell	John Muir	
Flora Alexander	Gilbert Mein	David Murray	

In "Padanaran," the name of a nearby building, graves are also found.

List 9
Stirling Burgess List, 1600–1699

Malcolm Adam	James Bachop	William Caldwell	John David
Alexander Aiken	James Balfour	John Callander	Peter Davidson
John Aisson	John Balmano	Thomas Cassillo	John Davie
Robert Alshunder	Alexander Barclay	Thomas Christie	Daniel Din
John Ambross	John Benny	William Cossar[26]	David Dog
John Anas	David Birrall	John Cousland	James Dollar
John Arral	Robert Bissett	Adam Cowan	Thomas Dougal
William Aynslie	John Bowie	Walter Cowane	Harry Dow
Alex. Aysounne	David Burrel	James Crocket	Robert Espline

Walter Fairfoul
Alexander Fairie
William Ferrier
George Fogo
Arthur Forbes
Robert Freir
John Frizzall
Gabriel Galbraith
Malcolm Gaston
Robert Gastoun
James Geichan
William Gillies
John Glog
George Gogar
David Gourlay
Gilbert Greinock
Adam Halye
James Hart
Walter Harvie
Andrew Hegie
Robert Hervie
Robert Honeyman
Patrick Houston
James Huitoun
Thomas Jak

Thomas Jalphray
Alexander Jameson
John Junkine
John Kemp
William Kennedy
George Lapslie
John Lawrie
Thomas Leckie
John Leggett
John Leishman
James Liddell
Abraham Lockhart
Joseph Lowrie
James Luttfutt
William Lyon
John Lyoum
Chris Maisson.
David Mane
James Martine
John Matheson
John Max[27]
James Meffit
John Mebine
John Moddrell
Walter Moir

Andrew Muat
John Muirheid
Duncan Murison
Oliver Murray
Adam Mushet
John Napier
Hew Nicoll
John Norvall
Thomas Norye
John Orrock
Robert Pirnie
John Pollock
William Pook
Patrick Provand
Alexander Rack
Henrye Rainy[28]
James Rasay
Alexander Rash
Murdoch Reoch
William Robeine
Alexander Robene
Alexander Robieson
Robert Ross
John Rowchack
James Rynd[29]

John Sands
Robert Sart
William Sator
William Savin
Robert Schirra
John Scobie
Umphra Shaw
Robert Sheran
Andrew Shirray
John Smetoun
James Starrat[30]
John Steel
David Sym
Alexander Touch
Alastair Traquair
Thomas Ure
John Waans
John Waddell
John Wingzett
David Winzet
Alexander Wylie
Duncan Wyse
David Zaire /Yaire
Robert Zoing

List 10
Stirling Burgess List, 1700–1799
David I, 1124–1153, introduced the idea of Royal Burghs to Scotland.
Stirling received its charter in 1226.

John Adam
William Aiken
John Aikman
Charles Alexander
Adam Baad
Tobias Bachop
John Balfour
John Barronet
Andrew Bean
Peter Belch
Michael Belfrage
Charles Bennett
John Benny
William Black

Thomas Bowie
John Brown
James Burges
John Callander
David Cassels
Andrew Chrystie
William Clugstone[31]
Hugh Corbit /Corbet
Alexander Corsan
James Cowan
George Danskine
John Dason
James Davidson
Duncan Davie

John Dawson
Alexander Dollar
James Dow
John Dowies
Thomas Downie
James Eadie
Michael Eason
James Elise
John Ellis
George Esplin
John Fairfoul
James Ferrier
John Fleming
William Fogo

Hugh Forbes
John Forfar
Alex French
Robert Gardner
Robt Garrow. /Guero
Thomas Gaston
John Gentles
Neil Glass
Andrew Glog
John Gourlie
John Govan
Gideon Gray
Robert Haigie
Andrew Hardie

James Harley
John Harrower
Robert Haugh
Walter Hawie
John Hay
John Henieman[32]
James Hogg
James Horn
William Hosie
Kennet Hossock
Francis Houston
Robert Howat
William Hynes
Henry Jaffray
Thomas Jack
Thomas Jamieson
Edward Jarvie
James Junkin
Thomas Kennedy
James Kerr
James Kesson
Daniel King
Robert Knox
Walter Law

John Liddle
James Lockhart
Patrick Lourie
Thomas Lucas
James Luke
Patrick Lyon
William Maiben
James Malice
James Malloch
James Martine
John Mathie
John Mathieson
William Mayne
Malcolm McGilvra
James Meffan
William Mershal
Alex Moffat
John Moffat
George Moir
John Morison
James Muir
John Muirhead
Thomas Murray
David Muschet[33]

Alexander Mushet
George Nairn
Francis Napier
John Nicol
Alexander Norrie
Alexander Oat
William Oliphant
John Paton
Andrew Peacock
Charles Petrie
William Pollock
Patrick Provand
Alexander Ralston
Alexander Rattray
William Reddoch
James Reess
Renny George
William Rind
Thomas Rioch
Robert Risk
John Rob
George Robine
John Runciman
John Russal

George Salmond
Robert Scobbie
Robert Sharp
James Shearer
Andrew Sheddin
James Shirran
Thomas Shirray
John Stiel
James Syme
James Symson
James Telford
John Tower
David Trail
John Turnbull
John Ure
James Ward
William Watt
Robert Weir
Sam Witherspoon.
Andrew Yoole
James Yule

List 11
Tron Parish Poll Tax, 1694

George Sinclair
Anna Alexander
Isobel Douglas
Agnes Basilly
Marjoribanks
Murray
Aikenhead
Hellen Lyon
Hamiltone
Veatch
Hepburn
Murilies
Rutherfoord
Telfer
Moutrey
Maxwell
Rollo
Bennerman
Agnes Berrie

John Kello
Chisley
Nisbet
Kinnear
Elphinstone
Burrie
Wishart
Hays
Lamb
Bruce
Hoiron
Goudie
Speirs
Steuart
Gray
Colt
Sym
Menzies
Keir

Quishinnie
Cameron
Barclay
Fountain
Malcolme
Dinn
Stobo
Davidsone
Caldwell
Ricertone
Gardiner
Drysdale
Hog[34]
Vertue
Pinkertoune
Gledstones
Lammie
Currie
Adamsone

Espline
Brown
Imbray
Marishall
Alisone
Adam
Burtone
Arnot
Bell
Aimersone
Blair
Pendrigh
Legat
Alcorn
Begbie
Aitken
Givan
Mathie
Bower

Lausone	Melvill	Jamisone	Telfer
Robina Lausone	Pitcairn	Rouart	Herriot
Innes	Eistonne	Marr	Watt
Fraser	Murray	Campbell	Cowan
Ramsay	Agnew	Pollock	Forbes
Pouries	Philp	Begry	Bruce
Chartres	Bowis	Padgins	Lune
Grahame	Robsone	Gemmill	Cave
Brown	Hackets	Lawes	Nimmo
Gild	Seatone	Cassils	Abercrombie
Orr	Dyet[35]	Pringle	Douglas
Nicolsone	Fleming	Barclay	Olam
Ross	Bouinack	Purves	Ogilvey
Baikie	Snow	Gray	Houstone
Rankine	Espie	Fleming	Cochrane
Pyot	Douglas	Kello	Naiper
Denham	Inglis	Tarras	Cock
Abercrombie	Dounie	Hay	Barrin
Oliphant	Moris	Baillie	Baxter[36]
Chaplane	Finnie	Holstin	Jacksone
Wintar	Gourley	Chepland	Robinsone
Martine	Penman	Simsone	Black
Kemp	Kerr	Falconer	Scougall
Smellum	Muirhead	Hardy	Vertue
Patersone	Hempseed	Hastie	Ruddoch
Mannas	Alisone	Moncurr	Lamb
Sandry	Balfour	Glass	Hamilton
Lydia Forbes	Jack	Norrie	Baptie
Semple	Bemeny	Swanstoune	Bartram
Grahame	Stabler	Garnes	Simeon Gray
Stevensone	Lendo	Nish	Balfour
Fulton	Lauristone	Afleck	Forbes
Stephensone	Oliphant	Montray	Sibald
Campbell	Atchesone	Coos	Wylly
Currie	Ballenter	Blackie	Bethea Murray
Samuell	Elphinstone	Rob	Penneycook
Gibsone	Ester Campbell	Whillas	Ritchie
Quintance	Jossie	Sword	Smelie
Cathell	Morisone	Chancellar	Dollos
Chartres	Home	Waddell	Paton
Bell	Langlands	Bonner	Winter
Leslie	Samuell	Poltstone	Walkinshau
Marjoribanks	Harve	Skeen	Cant
Bruie	Herron	Trotter	Swane

Callandar	Riddell	Rew	Lownie
Garner	Menzies	Paton	Gib
Walker	Dalrymple	Cant	Isabela Horen
Dounie	Moir	Sands	Eizat
Antous	Moncrief	Fermer	Currie
Yuill	Sethrum	Auchirleck	Gairner
Clow	Elder	Winram	Butler
Govan	Pollock	Binnie	Banantine
Innes	Guthrie	Buris	Masow
Dorrock	Denham	Nisbet	Chaplen
Gellie	Medisone	Bouie	Crisetat
Cubie	Orr	Antonia Brown	Brockie
Magens	Innes	Putherer	Scugall
Murray	Ainslie	Waroick	Stewart
Cowan	Welsteed	Fleming	Darling
Bethea May	Porringer	Riddell	Bowie
Martine	Mein	Seatoune	Benet
Baptie	Kennedy	Wedderburn	Low
Mackie	Blackie	Schaw	Martine
Don	Nimmo	Ripeth	Forbes
Ruthven	Chalmers	Harraway	Russell
Porteous	Marischall	Carnagy	Blau
Spotswood	Jolly	Alisone	Knoris
Stewart	Mow	Davidsone	Purves
Watt	Douglas	Mcarra	Sandilands
Waddell	Urie	Dallas	Muirhead
Tulloch	Anntoun	Kennedy	Cowper
Turnbull	Geills	Leslie	Symenton
Nory	Muir	Gordone	Hepburan
Newall	White	Scrimjours	Picaris
		Adam	Tailfer

List 12
Scottish Goldsmiths, 1600–1800*

Aikman, John 1681	Arnot, James 1589	Bildzing, John 1735
Ainslie, Dalston 1677	Arrot, David 1758	Blackadder, Adam 1763
Aitchison, Alex. 1747	Auchterlony, David 1680s	Blacklaw, James 1752
Aitken, James 1673	Auld, George 1754	Blair, Charles 1745
Aitkenhead, George 1781	Ayton, Andrew 1708	Bogie, William 1752
Aldcorne, Henry 1677	Balfour, David 1721	Boig, David 1660
Annand, James 1592	Bannerman, John 1736	Brock, Robert 1673
Argo,[37] John 1778	Bethune, Henry 1694	Brown, John 1603

*Only one example is given for each surname

Bruce, Alexander 1747
Burrel, Alan 1775
Burrell, Alexander 1641
Callendar, Edward 1735
Campbell, John 1705
Carnegie, Robert 1748
Carruthers, Andrew 1706
Chalmers, Lewis 1738
Cheape, Robert 1713
Christie, William 1653
Cleghorne, Thomas 1606
Clipham, Charles 1774
Coatts, David 1750
Cockie, Archibald 1605
Contenart, John 1694
Cornflute, James 1770
Cruikshank, Robert 1697
Cunningham, James 1638
Dalzell, William 1749
Davidson, William 1733
Davie, Adam 1773
Dennistoun, David 1641
Dertigues, Peter 1694
Dewar, Henry 1717
Douglas, James 1786
Downie, David 1753
Dunlop, David 1710
Durham, Hercules 1711
Eelbick, William 1784
Elphinstone, Robert 1700
Englehart, Casper 1763
Falconer, John 1670
Feddes, John 1761
Forbes, William 1621
Foulis, George 1605
Fraser, John 1625
Gardyne, Patrick 1624
Ged, Dougal 1718
Geddy, Alan 1584
Gilbert, David 1590
Gillett, Nathaniel 17??
Gilmour, Andrew 1703
Gonsale, John 1694
Gordon, Adam 1696
Gottlief-Bildzines, Johan 1716
Graham, Adam 1783
Grant, Murdo 1722
Green, Nathaniel 1696
Grieg, David 1747
Hamilton, James 1730

Hannay, William 1794
Hart, James 1613
Hay, Walter 1605
Hector, Joseph 1805
Hepburn, George 1696
Heriot, David 1593
Horn, John 1801
Houre, Thomas 1651
Inglis, Robert 1686
Innes, Alexander 1715
Izat, David 1786
Jaffray, William 1751
Jamieson, Charles 1797
Jorgenson, Nicolas 1638
Justie, Louis 1696
Keay 1791?
Kerr, Alexander 1708
Kettle, David 1762
Key, Thomas 1753
Lamb, Adam 1619
Lascelles, Edmond 1700
Law, Archibald 1613
Leslie, Andrew 1668
Lindsay, Thomas 1662
Livingstone, Edw. 1792
Louke, George 1680
Low, William 1664
Lowrie, John 1701
Luke, James 1692
Lumsden, Benjamin 1757
Lyon, David 1724
Mair, John 1776
Manuel, Thomas 1765
Marlenes, Hezachris 1690
Marshall, David 1757
Mathie, Peter 1776
McKenzie, Simon 1708
McSymmond, Jas. 1762
Meikle, Samuel 1663
Mellinus, Zachariah 1672
Menzies, William 1755
Michie, Alexander 1797
Mitchell, Alexander 1698
Moir, Gilbert 1734
Moncur, Thomas 1665
More, Archibald 1715
Morison, David 1727
Mossman, John 1592
Muir, George 1696
Murray, Anthony 1745

Napier, James 1720
Nicolls, John 1656
Ochterlony, David 1700
Ogill, Archibald 1662
Old, George 1740
Oliphant, Ebenezer 1727
Orrock, William 1703
Otterbert, Ingleberg 1643
Ottingar, Conrad 1648
Palmer, David 1622
Penman, Edward 1733
Philp, John 1703
Pine, Thomas 1777
Pollock, John 1723
Pringle, Andrew 1708
Rae, William 1673
Reid, Alexander 1622
Ritchie, William 1796
Robertson, George 1643
Rolland, George 1675
Rollo, John 1731
Rose, Arthur 1759
Ross, George 1717
Row, John 1771
Ruddeman, John 1766
Scott, John 1621
Seton, John 1688
Sheriff, Alexander 1750
Skene, Edward 1710
Stalker, William 1607
Stewart, Peter 1741
Storie, John 1796
Strachan, David 1621
Symington, James 1643
Symonds, Paul 1677
Tait, Adam 1745
Telfer, Samuel 1747
Thriepland, John 1747
Tostie, Lues 1696
Trotter, Nicoll 1635
Ure, Archibald 1709
Vogel, John 1748
Waddell, Hercules 1605
Warnock, David 1756
Weir, George 1717
Wemyss, James 1727
Wyllie, James 1791
Yetts, William 1792
Zieglar, Michael 1700

List 13
Clock- and Watchmakers of S-W Scotland, 1576–1900
(Donald Whyte)

James Adair
David Adams
Alexander Aitken
David Alexander
James Beeslizt 1865
David Carruthers
Adam Chisolm
J. Copland 1830
Philip Corrie 1768
Philip Currie 1837
James Davidson
Samuel Dickson 1860
Feren and Comp. 1838
William Fritschler 1825
Samuel Gardiner

James Given 1866
Alexander Gourlay 1860
Alexander Harvey 1811
James Jamieson 1835
Alexander Kerr 1796
James Law 1821
Solomon Law 1748
David Leckie 1795
Ebenezer McGora 1795
Robert McAdam 1812
W. Manerie 1893
James Muir 1760
Archibald Orr 1856
John Reay 1893
Andrew Reed 1798

David Ross 1826
John Sanderson 1715
Thomas Savell (Seville) 1785
Theodore Schweitzer 1851
Charles Seiffert 1876
Frances Sharpe 1831
Robert Sim 1852
William Tait 1830
Samuel Templeton 1837
Robert Watt 1813
Alexander Wylie 1752
Thomas Yuill 1836
James Yuill 1830

List 14
Scottish Glassmakers[38]

James Arbuckle 1801
Nathan Buntine 1803
Andrew Davidson 1785
John Dow 1778
John Arrol 1778
John Barrat 1729
John Bogle 1771
Gavin Wothersponn 1774
William Geddes 1788
Jacob Smith 1788
Thomas Rowan 1779
John Gardner 1765
Peter Verden 1779
James Waddel 1773

List 15
Trade Incorporation Records
St. Andrews, Kirkcaldy, Dunfermline

David Adamson 1664
David Alison 1653
Simon Alison 1761
Andrew Annal 1782
David Annal 1746
David Arnott 1761
John Arrok 1673
Robert Balcase 1816
John Balmanno 1684
David Barnet 1867
Alexander Beaucher 1785
David Bell 1789
Alexander Birrell 1805
John Black 1843
James Bogie 1754
Alexander Boyack 1751
James Boyack 1837
James Braid 1703
Alexander Brown 1792
David Brown 1745
James Bruce /Brus 1743
Robert Buddo 1782
David Buthell 1676
Robert Buttercase 1748
Alexander Chrystie 1677
John Corsar 1668
David Coventrie 1718
Thomas Cowan 1817
David Dalgleish 1633
Alexander Davidson 1790
Andrew Deas 1788

William Diones 1664
James Durkie 1753
Philip Dyshart 1780
David Fairfull 1769
David Ferrier 1610
Andrew Fleming 1793
David Forbes 1775
James Fortune 1778
Thomas Gantone 1682
David Gib 1717
James Gourlay 1691
Alex Govan. /Given 1781
John Gow 1800
John Gray 1610
William Green 1786
James Hardie 1678
Thomas Hartt 1704
David Hay 1775
James Heggie 1798
David Horn 1681
Arch Horsburgh. 1787
William Imrie 1792
Bethune Ireland 1786
George Keddie 1795
Alexander Key 1803
John Lemmon 1676
William Leslie 1790
James Leuchars 1768
James Low 1760
John Mackie 1796
David Mark 1668

George Martine 1705
Andrew Mason 1747
David Mason 1773
David Mason 1788
Charles Morrice 1768
James Morries 1755
John Moys 1793
William Muir 1886
James Murray 1660
Thomas Nobel 1757
David Norrie 1703
John Oliphant 1665
David Patie 18 14
Thomas Peattie 1824
Alex Rankeillour. 1740
George Rennie 1807
Robert Ross 1795
John Sabez 1707
James Seath 1778
William Sime 1829
David Simpson 1810
James Steill 1659
David Swan 1769
David Syme 1746
Thomas Syme 1673
David Tod 1659
David Turnbull 1697
Alexander Turple 1805
David Venison 1610
Laurence Wallace 1799
James Wann 1749

List 16
Fife Trade Incorporation Records

Adams
Adie
Aitken
Alison
Anderson (20)
Angell (1652)
Annan
Aresdel Stouerd

Arnot
Arnot
Bald
Ballmain
Barr
Beanstone
Becket
Begbie

Bell
Benet
Bevrach/Beveridge
Birrell
Bissett
Black
Blair
Blau (1674)

Bone
Bonner
Borland
Braiser
Brous
Browne/Brown
Buist
Bull (1587) (6)

Burrell	Gardner	Marshal	Sands (8)
Burril	Gardner	Martyne	Saybank
Catert	Gay	Maxwell	Scrimgeour
Christie	Glass	Melvill	Sharp
Condie	Gordon	Mercer	Sibbald
Corstopheir	Gourlay	Merchant	Simers
Couss	Grieve	Morris/Moress	Sincler
Coventree	Halliday	Moultrey	Smealls (1820)
Cowie	Hannah/Hana	Muir	Snds
Curer	Heggie	Muirie	Stephen
Currie	Henderson	Murray	Steuart
Dalgleish	Hogg	Nasmyth	Stevenson
Davidson	Honeyman	Ogg	Strang
Davidson	Horsburgh	Oram (1745)	Suttie
Davie	Imbrie	Paton	Symson
Dawson	Kerr (6)	Peddie	Taas
Daykckis	Kilgour	Penman	Taliour
Deas	Kingo (1603)	Perne	Tarner
Dewar	Krey	Pirie	Tayns
Dickie	Kules	Plamer	Tolous39
Don	Lamb	Porteous	Trumble
Dott (5)	Lasone	Pratt	Tullas
Douglas	Lasson	Primrose (1674)	Turnbull
Dow	Law	Prymrois	Veitch
Dowie	Lessels	Rainie	Walloud
Drysdale (9)	Lessels	Reid	Walls
Eingalls	Lille	Rennie/Rainie	Wardlaw
Eizat (1699)	Locke	Rentoull	Wardlaw
Eizatt (1650)	Low	Riddell	Watt
Ellis	Lyell	Robertson	Wylie
Faer	Macara	Rolland	Wyllie
Faulds	Machan	Ronan (1671)	Yeats (1680)
Flukour	Malcolm	Ross	
Fogo/Fege	Mar	Roy	

List 17
Fife Apprenticeships

Adam	Bogie	Davidson (6)	Gordon
Adamson	Bonnar	Dawson	Gorrie
Aitken	Brown (10)	Deas	Gow
Armit	Buddo	Dempster	Gray
Arnot	Chalmers	Doig	Grubb
Balfour	Christie	Dow	Hair
Balmanno	Coventrie	Durie	Hardie
Bar	Currer	Ferrie	Harlow
Barlas/Borlas	Cusine	Fleming	Henderson
Bell	Dalgleish	Forgan	Herd
Black (8)	Dall	Foulis	Horn

Imrie	Maxwell	Rattray	Syme
Ingles	Mories	Reid	Tarvit
Izatt	Morrice	Reiny	Templeman
Jack	Moultray	Rennie	Thallon
Jackson	Muir	Renton	Tod
Jamieson	Murray	Ritchie	Torrence
Jarvis	Napier	Rollo	Tullis
Josana Cumming	Nicoll	Ross	Wallet
Kay	Nimmo	Russel	Watt
Kilgour	Niven	Salmond	Wauchop
Law	Oliphant	Schoolbread	Weir
Lessles	Paton	Scobie	Wishart
Low	Paxton	Seath	Wyllie
Mack	Peadie	Sime	Young (9)
Mackie	Philp	Small (6)	Yule
Marshall (5)	Pigot	Spittal	
Mason	Pratt	Stewart	
Maule	Rae	Swan	

List 18
Mariners of the Cylde and Western Scotland

1600–1700

William Adair
John Aitken
John Alexander
Robert Alison
Jamse Allason
Ronald Ballantine
Thomas Barclay
Alexander Bell
James Bisset
Robert Black
James Blair
James Brown
Isaac Burnes
William Caddie
Samuel Campbell
John Chirrie
Robert Cowan
Arthur Darleith
George Darling
Robert David
Joseph Davidson
Alexander Davie
James Denny
John Dougall
David Ferrie

Robert Ferrier
Andrew Garvin
Robert Gass
James Gay
John Gemmell
Adam Gillies
John Gordon
John Guiland
John Hammil
John Hanna
Alexander Hardy
John Harris
Harry Hart
John Hastie
David Hepburn
John Herries
William Holland
John Horn
Patrick Houstoun
John Jamieson
John Kerr
Andrew Knox
John Lamond
Steven Landells
George Lockhart
Adam Lorimer
Hew Loudoun

William Low
Hector Lyal
Colin Lyon
John Mackie
David Man
Henry Martin
Arch. Mason
John McCoon
Thomas Megonin
Andrew Moor
Chris Morrison.
Andrew Morson
John Muir
Gavin Nickorn
Walter Noble
James Paltoun
George Pollock
James Power
Patrick Prowtie
James Rae
James Rankine
Thomas Riis
John Ritchie
James Robb
John Robison
Duncan Sempill
John Sheills

James Sinclair
Gabriel Sleiman
Andrew Spainzea
Alexander Spittle
John Sta ffan
Walter Sym
Alex. Watson
James Weir
William Yoole
Arch. Yuill

1700–1800

Robert Adam
George Aedie
John Aiken
John Aitken
David Alexander
David Armour
Alexander Auld
David Ballantine
James Barber
David Barclay
Robert Barrie
William Caldwell
Alex. Campbell
Edward Cant
John Caruth

Thomas Chieslie
John Christal
David Conchie
____Coppel
Arch. Corbet
George Corrie
John Cousins
Adam Cowan
Moses Crawford
John Cunison
John Currie
Adam Dalrymple
James Davidson
William Davies
John Dey?es
John Doak
Johnston Dobbie
William Dougatt
James Douglas
William Dow
Jeremiah Downes
John Dunnet
Robert Duthie
Hugh Dyet
Robert Eason
William Eccles
Hugh Fairrie
Robert Fairy
Will. Falconer
Alex. Ferrie
John Fish
Malcolm Fisher

James Fleming
Moses Fletcher
Daniel Galbreath
John Gay
David Gemmill
James Gibson
John Gilmour
Robert Glaister
Joseph Goldie
Samuel Gordon
James Hamilton
Abraham Hastie
Francis Hay
Daniel Henchy
James Heriston
William Heron
James Herrings
Samuel Holliday
Abraham Holme
James Houston
John Howie
Samuel Huie
William Hyndman
Daniel Innes
Arch. Iver
Robert Ja ffray
Jack Jamphray
John Jargon
Robert Kelso
Andrew Kennedy
James King
James Latta

Daniel Leitch
William Leslie
James Lockhart
James Longmuir
Ninian Lorimer
John Love
Stephen Lyall
Andrew Lyon
Robert MacCurry
David MacIver
Hector Mackenzie
William Minnoch
James Monies
Benjamin Moore
Alexander More
Samuel Morkland
James Morris
James Muir
Alex. Nicol
Walter Nimmo
John Niven
James Noble
Arch. Omey
John Orr
____Orrock
James Peacock
John Pollock
John Reid
Arch. Ritchie
John Rollands
David Ross
John Rouet Smollet

John Ryburn
John Ryside
Robert Sabaston
Robert Salmond
William Semple
George Service
John Shaddon
Robert Sharp
William Shearer
Charles Sheddon
William Sheron
William Sim
James Simson
James Sinclair
Alexander Smellie
Robert Speir
Duncan Stewart
James Sturgeon
Andrew Syme
Daniel Symon
Andrew Tarbert
Robert Tod
Andrew Troop
Alex. Ure
John Urie
Hugh Vass
Adam Walker
Umphra Warden
John Weir
Arch. Wyllie

List 19
Glasgow Colonial Merchants and the West of Scotland Sugar Industry

Sugar Houses

South Sugar House (1740s–1796)

King St. Sugar House (1780s–90s)

Easter Sugar House
Wester Sugar House (1773)
Greenock Sugarhouse (1765)

Merchant Partners

Alexander Houston
William McDowall
George, Alesander and James Oswald
James Buchanan
Andrew Buchanan
Thomas Wallace
George Bogle
Alexander Speirs
James Hopkirk
Arthur Connell

Greenock Sugarhouse (1788)	John Campbell sen.
	James Gordon
	Henry Riddell
Port Glasgow Sugar House	George Crawford
	William Crawford
	Andrew Buchanan
	William Cunninghame
	Robert Dunmore
Sugar House Co. of Port Glasgow (1770s)	John Leitch
	Richard Dennistoun
	John Gordon
	David Russell
Newark Sugar Refinery (1809–1817)	Robert Dennistoun
	Alexander Campbell
	James Campbell

Source: Devine 1975

Glasgow Tobacco Merchants and the Leather Industry

Tannery	Merchant Partners
Bell's Tannery	John Coats Campbell, John Bowman, Laurence Dinwiddie, James Dunlop, Alexander Speirs
Glasgow Tanwork	John Bowman, Alex. Speirs, Robert Bogle, Walter Monteath
Francis Hamilton and Co.	Hugh Whylie, Francis Hamilton

The Investments of Some Glasgow Tobacco Merchants

Merchant	Date	Summary of Financial Interests
Alexander Morson	1768	Share in a Boston concern; 1/8 share in the brigantine *Bell*; £503.13 in P. and W. Bogle, tobacco importers; £400 in Jamaica concern with Ebenezer Munro; share in a coal and copper mine; £22.18.15 owed him by Neil Jamieson, merchant in Norfolk, Virginia; £100 in insurance venture; share in a plaiding concern with Ebenezer Munro.
Robert Dunmore	1793	Income in that year; rent of country lands: £7,531.18.4; produce of Jamaica properties £4,500; stock in different concerns, interest and profit accrual:

		£2,626; Virginia debts not yet recovered: £15–20,000.
Alexander Speirs	1770	Stocks in concerns: "Virginia concern": £55,057.4.0; "Maryland concern": £7,410.19.9; Value of landed property: £49,050; Domestic industry and banks: £18,141.3.7½; "Occasional transactions" including canal shares: £1,778.9.4½.
William Cunninghame	1790	Income in that year: John Ferguson and Co. (formerly R. Dunmore and Co.), West India and American merchants: £3,255.6.0; land rentals: £3,696.6.0; East India stock: £436.5.6; government securities: £104.4.5; bills receivable: £13.0.0.
James Somervell	1791	Shares in various concerns: Somervell, Gordon and Co., tobacco and West India merchants: £8,503; David Russell and Co. (West India merchants): £4,936; Money lent on bond to: Findlay, Hopkirks and Co. (tobacco merchants): £1,000; Corbett, Russell and Co. (tobacco merchants): £2,000; Henry Hardi and Co. (linen merchants and printers): £1,000; Muirkirk Iron Co.: £1,000; Port Glasgow Ropework Co.: £3,000; Tanwork Co.: £3,000.

Sample of Sums Borrowed on Bond by Buchanan, Hastie and Co., 1768–1772

Creditor	Amount (£)	Date
William Clavil, landowner	2,000	1768
John Alexander, purser H.M.S. *Panther*	500	1769
James Smollett of Bonhill	100	1771
John Murray of Blackbarony	300	1771
Daniel Baxter, bookseller in Glasgow	400	1773
Factor for children of James Glen, Goldsmith in Glasgow	400	1773
Dr. William Macfarlane, physician in Edinburgh	250	——
Sir Kenneth Pringle of Stithill, Bart	500	——
John Yuill, Shoemaker in Glasgow	600	1772
John Wilson, Town Clerk of Glasgow	600	1772
Marquis of Annandale	1,500	——

Chapter 8

The Knights Templar, Freemasons and Cabala in Scotland

Before we venture to the northeastern section of Scotland, we want to attend to several European and Middle Eastern events that will help place the Jewish migration to Scotland in perspective. Shortly after the Normans invaded England in 1066 C.E., bringing scores of French Jewish families to that country to assist with the civil administration, a holy war was declared throughout western Christendom to regain Palestine from the Muslims. Over the next 300 years, from Pope Urban's bull of 1095 until the close of the 14th century, there was a series of Crusades to the Holy Land.

Prominent French, Scottish and English knights, as well as several of their princes and kings, fought in the Crusades and established fiefdoms throughout the lands we think of as the Levant, or Middle East, stretching from Sicily, Tripoli and Malta to Cypress, Rhodes, Antioch, Tyre and Macedonia. Called Outremer ("Beyond the Sea"), the Norman-French-Scottish domain was ruled by free-standing noblemen and controlled militarily by distinctive "Christian" fighting forces that included the Knights of the Temple of Solomon, or Templars, and the Knights of the Hospital of St. John, or Hospitalers. Although both these military orders began as Christian-soldiered militias, they soon evolved into enormous, profit-making enterprises that owned vast tracts of land, castles, priories, burgs, mills and manufactories, banks, and shipping lanes throughout Europe and the Middle East (Selwood 1999). The persons who managed the vast wealth from this trading empire were not themselves knights, but rather seneschals (retainers), and though the individual knights themselves may have taken Christian vows of chastity or poverty, no such requirements were placed upon the majority of those associated with the order — its estate managers, clerical employees and administrators:

[I]t should not be imagined that armored warriors, largely illiterate, spent their odd hours decoding messages or in the countinghouse maintaining ledgers and checking inventory or out in the barn supervising the annual sheepshearings…. In the Order of the Temple, they were the officer class, and they had as their principal training and occupation direct participation on the battlefield; the army of administrators, native troops, and employees behind them *outnumbered them by as much as fifty to one* [emphasis added]…. The Templar clerics

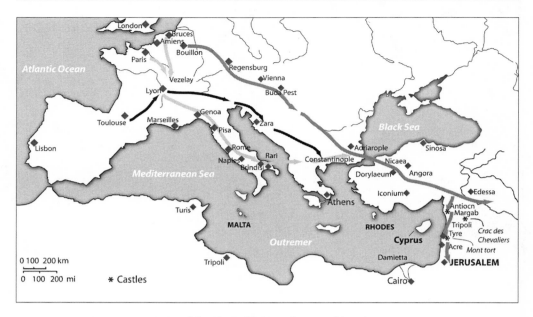

Routes of the Crusades. Map by Donald N. Yates.

were the literate faction, and far more likely to be assigned duties of a managerial or accounting nature, including the drafting of letters in code. Other administrators, supervisors, and scribes were simply employees, and in later years a number were Arabic-speaking [Robinson 1989, pp. 77–78].[1]

Men from several Scottish (and English and French) Jewish families enlisted in the ranks of the Knights Templar, including Bruces, Douglases and Sinclairs. Countless others were involved in the administration of the Templar wealth. Thus, to understand this period of time in Scotland, we must examine the Knights Templar, the Crusades and Outremer.

The Knights Templar

In 1842, a member of the Knights Templar, Charles G. Addison of London, wrote a book titled *History of the Knights Templar* that put forth their origin and history as he understood it. Addison (1892) writes that the Knights Templar were formed around the year 1100 by "nine noble knights" who had committed themselves to protecting pilgrims on the way to Jerusalem. At the time, "Mussulmen" (Muslims) controlled the Holy Land and would frequently attack and rob Christian pilgrims. By 1118, King Baldwin II, a French aristocrat who ruled Jerusalem,[2] granted the knights a headquarters on the Temple Mount. The site was believed to be the location where the Temple of Solomon had stood in remote antiquity; hence the knights came to be known as the Knighthood of the Temple of Solomon. Each knight took a vow of chastity and poverty, yet the order, itself, was permitted to accumulate communal property of unlimited magnitude. On this very site was the ancient Moslem mosque, the Dome of the Rock, dedicated to King

David/Daoud and Allah. Over the centuries, Jews, Muslims and Christians had alternated in tearing down each other's sanctuaries on this holy place and erecting their own.

By 1130 C.E., the Knights Templar order had begun to amass huge amounts of money as well as large estates (Selwood 1999). They were granted holdings by the rulers of Barcelona, Provence, Navarre and Aragon. St. Bernard of Clairvaux, one of the most powerful Christian clerics of the time, promoted their interests with his preaching and writing and swelled the number of knights serving in the order (Selwood 1999). In 1129, Hugh de Payens,[3] the leader of the order, returned to Palestine with a large troop of Templars to battle the Muslim army under its general, Nour-ed-deen (Light of Religion).[4] The Balliol and Barres families of France and Scotland contributed land and money to the Templar cause, as did William de Warrenne, Roger de Mowbray, Ralph de Hastings, Robert Marsel and Gilbert de Lacy.

By 1170, however, the Muslims under Salah-ed-deen (Integrity of Religion, Saladin) with 40,000 soldiers had retaken the Holy Land. Pope Alexander in 1171 issued a bull granting the Templars exemption from prosecution in any religious or civil court of law in return for their support in winning back Jerusalem. The order was now not only fantastically wealthy, but free of any external control over its activities. The only law members were bound by was that of the Master Templar. By this time also, a large part of the Templar force was composed of horsemen called Turcopoles, of Turkish, Syrian and Palestinian descent. These were mercenaries who followed a Middle Eastern lifestyle; they were not Christian, but Moslem or Jewish. Further, the Templars themselves had started to become morally corrupt. When one of their members, Walter du Mesnil, murdered a Muslim aristocrat who had converted to Christianity, he fled for refuge to a Templar priory and the order refused to give him over to the civil authorities.

By this time the resources of the order had become phenomenal. Addington compiles the following (selective and incomplete) list in his *History* (pp. 85–102), which we have tabularized:

Addington's Templar List

Place-Name	Province	Type	Note
Gaza	Palestine	City	"the key to the Kingdom of Jerusalem"
Safed	Palestine	Castle	"in the territory of the ancient tribe of Naphtali"
Castle of the Pilgrims	Palestine	Castle	Near Mount Carmel
Assur	Palestine	Castle	Near Jaffa
House of the Temple	Palestine	City	Jaffa
Faba, La Feue, anc. Aphek	Palestine	Castle	Near Tyre, "the ancient tribe of Asher"
Dok	Palestine	Hill fort	Between Bethel and Jericho
La Cave	Palestine	Castle	Near Acca (St. John d'Acre)
Marle	Palestine	Castle	Near Acca (St. John d'Acre)
Cistern Rouge	Palestine	Castle	Near Acca (St. John d'Acre)
Castel Blanc	Palestine	Castle	Near Acca (St. John d'Acre)
Trapesach	Palestine	Castle	Near Acca (St. John d'Acre)
Sommelleria of the Temple	Palestine	Castle	Near Acca (St. John d'Acre)
Castrum Planorum	Palestine	Castle	Near Acca (St. John d'Acre)
Gerinum Parvum	Palestine	Castle	Near Acca (St. John d'Acre)
Beaufort	Palestine	Castle	Sidon (city purchased by Templars)

St. Jean d'Acre	Palestine	City	"where they erected their temple"
Antioch	Palestine	Temple	Antioch ranked as a principality (princedom)
Aleppo	Palestine	Temple	
Haram	Palestine	Temple	
Tripoli	Tripoli	Principality	One of the eastern provinces
Tortosa, anc. Antaradus	Tripoli	House	Italy, under the Preceptor of Tripoli
Castel-blanc	Tripoli	House	Italy, under the Preceptor of Tripoli
Laodicea	Tripoli	House	Greece, under the Preceptor of Tripoli
Beirut	Tripoli	House	Lebanon, under the Preceptor of Tripoli
Palermo	Sicily	House	
Syracuse	Sicily	House	
Lentini	Sicily	House	
Butera	Sicily	House	
Trapani	Sicily	House	
Piazza, Calatagirone	Sicily	Land	
Messina	Sicily	Priory	Residence of the Grand Prior
Lucca	Italy	House	
Milan	Italy	House	
Perugia	Italy	House	
Placentia	Italy	Convent	Santa Maria del Tempio
Bologna	Italy	House	
Rome	Italy	Priory	Residence of the Grand Preceptor
Monsento	Portugal	Castle	
Idanha	Portugal	Castle	
Tomar	Portugal	Castle	
Lagrovia	Portugal	Citadel	In the province of Beira
Miravel	Portugal	Castle	In Estremadura, taken from Moors
Castromarin	Portugal	Estates	In the Algarve in southern Portugal
Almural	Portugal	Estates	In the Algarve in southern Portugal
Tavira	Portugal	Estates	In the Algarve in southern Portugal
Tomar	Portugal	Priory	Residence of the Grand Preceptor
Cuenca	Spain	House	In kingdom of Castile and Leon
Guadalfagiara	Spain	House	In Oviedo
Tine	Spain	House	In Oviedo
Aviles	Spain	House	In Oviedo
Castile	Spain	Estates	24 bailiwicks
Dumbel	Spain	Castle	In Aragon
Cabanos	Spain	Castle	In Aragon
Azuda	Spain	Castle	In Aragon
Granuena	Spain	Castle	In Aragon
Chalonere	Spain	Castle	In Aragon
Remelins	Spain	Castle	In Aragon
Corgins	Spain	Castle	In Aragon
Lo Mas de Barbaran	Spain	Castle	In Aragon
Moncon	Spain	Castle	In Aragon
Montgausi	Spain	Castle	In Aragon
Borgia	Spain	City	
Tortosa	Spain	City	
Huesca	Spain	City	
Saragossa	Spain	City	
Majorca (Balearic Isles)	Spain	Priory	Subject to Grand Preceptor of Aragon
Hamburg	Germany	House	
Mainz	Germany	House	
Assenheim	Germany	House	
Rotgen	Germany	House	

Mongberg	Germany	House	
Nuitz	Germany	House	
Tissia Altmunmunster	Germany	House	Near Regensberg
Bamberg	Germany	House	
Middlebourg	Germany	House	
Hall	Germany	House	
Brunswick (Braunschweig)		Germany	House
Rorich	Germany	Fiefdom	In Pomerania
Pausin	Germany	Fiefdom	In Pomerania
Wildenheuh	Germany	Fiefdom	In Pomerania
Bach	Hungary	House	
Bohemia, Moravia	Germany	Lands	
Morea	Greece	Lands	Subject to the chief house at Constantinople
Besançon	France	House	
Dol	France	House	
Salins	France	House	
La Romagne	France	House	
La Ville Dieu	France	House	
Arbois	France	House	
Bomgarten	France	House	
Temple Savigne	France	House	Near Corbeil
Dorlesheim Demains	France	House	Near Molsheim, chapel called Templehoff
Ribauvillier	France	House	
Bures	France	House	Near Bercheim
Voulaine les Templiers	France	House	
Ville-sous-Givrey	France	House	
St. Philbert	France	House	
Dijon	France	House	
Fauverney	France	House	
Des Feuilles	France	House	Villett, de Vernay
St. Martin	France	House	
Le Chastel	France	House	
Espesses	France	House	
Tessones	France	House	Near Bourges
La Musse	France	House	Between Bauje and Macon in Burgundy
Paris	France	Headquarters	Residence of Master of the Temple for Fr., Neth.
Treves	France	House	On the Soure River
Dietrich	France	House	On the Soure River
Doberne	France	House	On the Moselle River
Belish	France	House	Near Vianden
Temple Spele	France	House	Near Vianden
Temple Rodt	France	House	Near Vianden
Luxembourg	France	House	
Templehuis	Flanders	House	In Ghent
Alphen	Flanders	House	Near Ostende
Braeckel	Flanders	House	Near Ostende
La Maison de Slipes	Flanders	House	Near Ostende
Temple Caestre	Flanders	House	Near Mount Cassel
Villiers le Temple	Flanders	House	Near Liege, en Condros
Vaillenpont	Flanders	House	Near Arras
Walsberg	Flanders	House	Near Arras
Haut Avenes	Flanders	House	Near Arras
Temploux	Flanders	House	Near Fleury in Namur

Vernoi	Flanders	House	In Hainaut
Temple Dieu	Flanders	House	At Douai
Marles	Flanders	House	Near Valenciennes
St. Symphonier	Flanders	House	Near Mons
Aslakeby	England	House	Lincolnshire
Temple Bruere	England	House	Lincolnshire
Egle	England	House	Lincolnshire
Malteby	England	House	Lincolnshire
Mere	England	House	Lincolnshire
Wilketon	England	House	Lincolnshire
Witham	England	House	Lincolnshire
North Feriby	England	House	Yorkshire
Temple Hurst	England	House	Yorkshire
Temple Newsom	England	House	Yorkshire
Pafflete	England	House	Yorkshire
Flaxflete	England	House	Yorkshire
Ribstane	England	House	Yorkshire
Temple Cumbe	England	House	Somersetshire
Ewell	England	House	Near Dover, in Kent
Strode	England	House	Near Dover, in Kent
Swingfield	England	House	Near Dover, in Kent
Hadescoe	England	House	Norfolk
Balsall	England	House	Warwickshire
Warwick	England	House	Warwickshire
Temple Rothley	England	House	Leicestershire
Wilburgham Magna	England	House	Cambridgeshire
Daney	England	House	Cambridgeshire
Dokesworth	England	House	Cambridgeshire
Halson	England	House	Shropshire
Temple Dynnesley	England	House	Hertfordshire
Temple Cressing	England	House	Essex
Sutton	England	House	Essex
Saddlescomb	England	House	Sussex
Capelay	England	House	Sussex
Schepeley	England	House	Surrey
Temple Cowley	England	House	Oxfordshire
Sandford	England	House	Oxfordshire
Bistelesham	England	House	Oxfordshire
Chalesey	England	House	Oxfordshire
Temple Rockley	England	House	Wiltshire
Upleden	England	House	Herefordshire
Garwy	England	House	Herefordshire
South Badeisley	England	House	Hampshire
Getinges	England	House	Worcestershire
Giselingham	England	House	Suffolk
Dunwich	England	House	Suffolk

In addition to the stunning list given above, there were also several preceptories in Scotland and Ireland, which were dependent on the Temple at London.[5] Addington summarizes:

> The annual income of the order in Europe has been roughly estimated at six millions sterling! According to Matthew Paris, the Templars possessed nine thousand manors or lordships in Christendom, besides a large revenue and immense riches arising from the constant charitable bequests and donations of sums of money from pious persons....

The principal benefactors to the Templars amongst the nobility were William Marshall,[6] Earl of Pembroke, and his sons William and Gilbert; Robert, Lord de Ross;[7] the Earl of Hereford; William, Earl of Devon; the King of Scotland; William, Archbishop of York; Philip Harcourt, dean of Lincoln; the Earl of Cornwall; Philip, Bishop of Bayeux; Simon de Senlis, Earl of Northampton; Leticia and William, Count and Countess of Ferrara; Margaret, Countess of Warwick;[8] Simon de Montfort, Earl of Leicester; Robert de Harecourt, Lord of Rosewarden; William de Vernon, Earl of Devon, etc.

As the reader gathers from this lengthy enumeration of holdings and privileges, the Knights Templar were an enormous, extraordinarily rich and very powerful organization. In essence, they were the first multinational corporation — one over which no court or tribunal had jurisdiction. The seal of the brotherhood featured "a man's head, decorated with a long beard, and surmounted by a small cap, and around it are the letters *Testis V. Magi*" (Addington 1892, p. 106). At this time, Templar masters in England included persons named William de La More and Amadeus de Morestello. Clearly, Muslims, as well as Jews, were in England.

From Addison's (1892) account, we now turn to that of Piers Paul Read, who wrote a critically acclaimed history of the Templars in 1999. Read's work is very well researched, and he delves into the ancient origin of the group, predating the Crusades. He starts by recounting the history of the Jewish people. At the point when King David reconquers Palestine from the Jebusites, we are given great detail concerning David's assembling of materials for a Jewish worship center, the First Temple, built by David's son Solomon around 950 B.C.E.

After Solomon's death, the Jewish state went into decline and was conquered by several eastern nations in succession. In 586 B.C.E., King Nebuchadnezzar, a Chaldean, destroyed the Temple of Solomon and enslaved the Jewish population, taking many of them (including those of Davidic descent) to Babylon. However, by 515 B.C.E., the Persians under their king Cyrus had defeated the Chaldeans and permitted the Jews to return to Judea, where they rebuilt their temple. By the fourth century B.C.E., the Macedonian Greeks under Alexander the Great had swept through the Persian empire and conquered Judea. Upon Alexander's death, his empire was divided, and the Jews were permitted a hereditary high priest, who served both as a secular and spiritual ruler.

In 167 B.C.E, Jews under three Maccabean brothers successfully revolted against the Seleucid government that controlled Judea and founded the Hasmonean dynasty in the land of Israel. The Romans then conquered Jerusalem and the Roman emperor declared Herod Antipas, an Arab who had converted to Judaism, king of Judea, now a semi-independent client state of the Roman Empire. Herod not only rebuilt the holy Temple of Jerusalem into a larger and more magnificent structure, but also extended the state of Israel's influence to cities as distant as Beirut, Damascus, Antioch and Rhodes. Unfortunately, in his later years he became insane (quite likely he was paranoid schizophrenic) and murdered many of his own family members. In 70 c.e, the Jews of Judea again rebelled against Roman rule. The Romans brutally put down the revolt, killing one million persons in Jerusalem and enslaving the rest. To obliterate the memory of a Jewish state, they changed the name of the country, now reduced to the status of being a province, to Palestine.

Concurrent with this turmoil between Jews and Romans over control of the land of

Israel, Jesus, a Jew of Nazareth, was born, preached and was crucified. His band of followers, afterwards known as Christians because they deemed him the Annointed One, started out as heretical Jews, but evolved over the ensuing decades and under Paul of Tarsus into an independent religious sect, by at least 67 C.E. Over time, Rome itself converted to Christianity and began sending missionaries to convert the pagan tribes. Roman dominance began waning rapidly after 200 C.E., resulting in a patchwork of weak city-states across Europe. The European courts of the time period from 200 c.e to the 800s were violent, corrupt and treacherous. There was no law or order that prevailed for any distance or for any length of time.

The papacy in Rome was similarly corrupt and decadent, as reported by Read (1999). Following the last and most devastating invasion of the Langobards in Italy, whole cities were wiped out, and it is thought the population of the Roman capital itself sank to as low as a few hundred people. Powerful Roman families selected popes who would do their bidding; often those chosen were not only mentally incompetent, but also sexually perverted. Some died violent deaths, strangled or stabbed by their bodyguards (Read 1999, p. 58). Priories and bishoprics were usually controlled by powerful local families, who placed their younger sons, or illegitimate sons, into holy offices. The income from these churches and other benefices was diverted to the noble families controlling them, much as we learned to be the case in Scotland.

It was into such a political context that the Normans and their allies entered when they advanced into Italy and the Holy Land in 1060 C.E. A shocking but probably realistic sociological picture of the Crusaders is drawn by Charles Mackay (1841, p. 360):

> The only religion they felt was the religion of fear.... They lived with their hand against every man and with no law but their own passions.... War was the business and the delight of their existence.... Fanaticism and the love of battle alike impelled them to the war, while the kings and princes of Europe had still another motive for encouraging their zeal. Policy opened their eyes to the great advantages which would accrue to themselves by the absence of so many restless, intriguing, and bloodthirsty men, whose insolence it required more than the small power of royalty to restrain within due bounds.

That religious motives were largely a pretext for winning the glory and booty of war became the subject of innumerable satires in France, Italy and England. Moreover, the outcome of the Crusades, especially the ill-fated second one, made them increasingly unpopular and rendered most people back home in Christendom deeply cynical. Over time, the Normans and their Templar Knights developed a congenial living arrangement with the Muslim "foes." As Read (1999, pp. 128–129) describes these events:

> The disillusion in Europe that followed the fiasco of the Second Crusade obliged the Christians in the Holy Land to reach the kind of accommodation with the infidel that would have seemed sacrilegious to the previous generation of crusaders.... The early crusaders had expected to encounter wild savages and depraved pagans in Syria and Palestine; but those who had remained in the Middle East had been obliged to recognize that the culture of Arab Palestine — Muslim, Christian, and Jewish — was more evolved and sophisticated than that at home.
>
> Some had quickly adopted Eastern customs. Baldwin of Le Bourg, having married an Armenian wife, took to wearing an Eastern kaftan and dined squatting on a carpet; while the coins minted by Tancred showed him with the head-dress of an Arab. The Damascene chronicler and diplomat, Usamah Ibn-Munqidh, describes a Frankish knight reassuring a

Muslim guest that he never allowed pork to enter his kitchen and that he employed an Egyptian cook.

Read goes on to report:

There was a large measure of tolerance for the Jews in the crusader states; they were treated much better.... With the [Templars'] capture of the ports on the Mediterranean ... and concessions to the growing maritime powers from Italy — Venice, Genoa and Pisa —considerable trade was stimulated with the Muslims.... The Templars benefited from this prosperity through their fiefs, and they also came to extend a tolerance to the indigenous Muslims which shocked those newly arrived from Europe.

By the latter decades of the twelfth century, joining the Templars had become no longer a sacred calling, but rather a career choice of an entirely lay nature (Read 1999, p. 153). The established nobles in the Holy Land resented the newly arrived knights from Europe who strove to incite warfare with the Muslims in order to carve out their own fiefdoms. For example, Raymond, the Templar master of Tripoli, spoke fluent Arabic and avidly read Muslim texts. To counteract the ambitions of newly-arrived Guy of Lusignaw, Raymond approached Saladin and suggested a collaboration — obviously, the notion of Christian versus Muslim was no longer the operative force in the Holy Land, but rather one power bloc versus another. By the time Richard the Lion-Hearted arrived in the Holy Land in 1191, this fraternization had progressed to the point that the English king offered his sister, Joan, in marriage to the Muslim king, Saladin, suggesting they were both better off jointly ruling Palestine than fighting one another. Saladin rejected the offer (Read 1999, p. 173). However, by 1192 C.E., an accommodation had been reached and Muslims and Christians halted combat, leaving the French, English and other European nobles the opportunity to squabble among themselves.

Although subsequent Crusades were mounted by later popes, they had turned essentially into business enterprises and were no longer holy wars. Suppliers of horses, armaments, food, and apparel made fortunes equipping both sets of warriors; alms were collected across Europe for each effort and diverted to both ecclesiastical and private coffers (Read 1999).

By 1250, the Templars had become a largely secret and closed society. Their initiation rites were hidden from view, as were their operations and internal rules (Read 1999). The majority of persons associated with the order were now estate managers, laborers and international traders and bankers. Even criminals were permitted to join, if they brought some skill or resource of value. In addition, the order had become the primary banking enterprise in the European world. Kings and nobles borrowed money from the Temple treasury; the order also offered financial investments, as well as annuities and pensions (Read 1999, p. 183).

Meanwhile, in Spain, the Templars had reached such a level of accommodation with the Moors that Muslims were allowed to use Temple estates as places of worship (Read 1999, p. 201). Acre became a major trade center, on a par with Constantinople and Alexandria. The 250,000 European-descended inhabitants of the Holy Land purchased exports from both Europe and Asia. In turn, they sold slaves, sugar, dyes and spices to European and Asian markets. By 1250, there were an estimated 7,000 fully initiated Templars, with a corresponding number of associates and dependents that was seven or eight times as large.

Shift in Religion

Remarkably, also by 1250, the Templars had altered their religious creed. Though established initially as Christian soldiers, they now read from the Book of Judges in the Hebrew Bible, or Torah, and had formed a new identity binding themselves to the ancient Israelites (Read, p. 216). At the same time, a new Muslim people swept through the Holy Land. The Mongols under Kublai Khan poured in from the East, while the Mameluks in Egypt attacked from the South. European control of the Holy Land began to collapse. Meanwhile in Europe, the pope, Martin IV, called for a crusade not against the Moslem onslaught in Palestine, but rather against his *Christian* political adversaries in Aragon, and Sicily. By 1290, the Europeans had lost the Holy Land to the Muslims, never to be regained. And at this point, many of the remaining European inhabitants, exhausted by the corruption of Christianity, converted to Islam (Read, p. 248).

In October 1307 C.E., King Philip of France, who had expelled the kingdom's Jews the year before in order to confiscate their possessions, turned his attention to the French Templars. In collaboration with the Pope, he ordered all French Templars arrested, tried for heresy, and executed; he then promptly appropriated their immense wealth and holdings in France. Some of the members of the French Temple became aware of Philip's plan and escaped with a large portion of their treasure (Read 1999). At the same time, a Muslim colony in southern Italy was evicted by Philip's brother King Charles II and appears to have formed something akin to an alliance with the fleeing French Templars and traveled with them to Christendom (Read, p. 272).

A St. Clair tomb at Roslyn Chapel with Ten Commandments motif. Photograph by Elizabeth Caldwell Hirschman.

Tau/Tough symbol window at Roslyn Chapel. Photograph by Elizabeth Caldwell Hirschman.

The French Templar treasure, loaded upon 18 galleys, made its way to Scotland, reportedly to the Isle of Mull. From here, the Templars and their treasure took refuge with the St. Clair family at Rosslyn Castle. Nearby Rosslyn Chapel, built in the 1400s, was, and is, an edifice filled with images and icons drawn from three faiths—Christianity, Judaism and Islam. It contains ample testimony to the "sacred geometry" of the Jewish Cabala, as well as architectural reflections of the St. Clair family's travels and

Ten Commandments motif window at Roslyn Chapel. Photograph by Elizabeth Caldwell Hirschman.

Templar tomb at Roslyn Chapel with Tau/Tough symbol. Photograph by Elizabeth Caldwell Hirschman.

Top: Templar sarcophagus at Roslyn Chapel. *Bottom:* Templar tomb at Roslyn chapel with Lion of Judah motif. Both photographs by Elizabeth Caldwell Hirschman.

Tau/Tough carvings on Roslyn Chapel interior. *Bottom:* Cabalah image of triangle with tetragrammaton inscribed within, in Roslyn Chapel Museum. Both photographs by Elizabeth Caldwell Hirschman.

trade throughout the world, including images of a kangaroo, pineapple, maize, tobacco and other wonders.

> Of course, by the time the Templars arrived, additional Jewish immigrants had already made their way to Scotland. Recall that in 1290 C.E., King Edward I had ordered all Jews to leave England, causing many to flee across the border to Scotland and overseas to France and the Low Countries. Others went underground in England and became Crypto-Jews. It is likely that the subsequent expulsion and proscription of Jews in the French kingdom (1306) caused families with hidden Jewish roots to become even more secretive, if they remained, or else to flee in advance of exposure, as occurred in Nazi Germany. The important Jewish community in Normandy, still an English possession and not yet part of France, must have been in a particularly stressful position. At this point, many English and French Jews doubtless joined relatives already in Scotland. The émigrés could not fail to have included those schooled in the mystical strain of Judaism known as the Cabala, which had been flourishing in Narbonne since the 1100s. As Jews were harried from one country to the next, Scotland emerged as one of the few safe-havens. Thus, by the early 1300s, Templars, Jews and Muslims had likely all sought refuge in Scotland.

Templars, Cabala and Judaism

Before discussing the Cabala, let us turn to additional testimony concerning the historic reality of the Jews in Scotland. The current claimant to the throne of Scotland and holder of the title of Prince of Albany, Michael Stewart, has written extensively about Stuart genealogy and early Scottish history. He discusses the close ties between certain members of the Catholic hierarchy, specifically St. Bernard, the Templars and the Scottish Celtic Church (p. 32):

> St. Bernard [a Cistercian monk] had been appointed Patron and Protector of the Knights Templars at the French "Council of Troyes" in 1128. At that time, he had drawn up the Order's Constitution and had since translated the *Sacred Geometry* of the [Jewish] masons who built King Solomon's Jerusalem Temple.... Also in 1128, Saint Bernard's cousin, Hughes de Payens, founder and Grand Master of the Templars, met with King David I in Scotland, and the Order established a seat on the South Esk.... Both David and his sister mere maritally attached to the Flemish House of Boulogne, so there were direct family ties between David, Hugues de Payens, and the Crusader Kings of Jerusalem....
>
> [The Templars'] Jerusalem excavations had ... led to other important discoveries, including some ancient documentation which enabled them to challenge certain Roman Church doctrines and New Testament interpretation.... Their documentary discoveries were substantial, including numerous books from the East, many of which had been salvaged from the burned library of Alexandria [Egypt]. There were ancient Essene works predating Jesus Christ and volumes from Arabian and Greek philosophers, all of which were destined to be condemned by the Church. There were also countless works concerning numerology, geometry, architecture and music, along with manuscripts pertaining to metals and alloys. In all, the Templars returned to Europe with the combined knowledge of thousands of years of study.

Thus, by the early 1100s a substantial amount of Middle Eastern knowledge, learning and mysticism had been transferred to Scotland. It was little surprise, then, that the Knights Templar, Jews, and Muslims would have chosen to cooperate in seeking refuge in Scotland, once they were exiled from Christian countries. Stewart (p. 33) also writes:

Scotland was the perfect haven for the Knights Templar of Jerusalem. The Stewart kings, the Setons, and the Sinclairs were all hereditary Knights Templar, and Scottish Rite Freemasonry was later created as a sub-structure of the organization. The hereditary right of the Stewarts came by virtue of Robert the Bruce having granted the Knights asylum in Scotland. The Sinclairs gained their privilege because they had afforded half the Templar Fleet safe anchorage at Orkney, and the Setons had given valuable financial assistance during the Order's hour of need.

Stewart also traces the origins of the St. Clair/Sinclair family from France to Scotland, specifically mentioning their role in the Templar Order (p. 102):

One of Scotland's most prominent families of the early Stewart era was the old Norman family of St. Clair, who had arrived in the 11th century, sometime before the Norman Conquest of England. In 1057, they had received the Barony of Roslin, south of Edinburgh, from Malcolm III Canmore.... William Sinclair, [St. Clair] Earl of Caithness and Grand Admiral of Scotland, was appointed Hereditary Patron and Protector of the Scottish Masons by King James in 1441....

The masons of William Sinclair were not the speculative freemasons that we know today, but operative stonemasons privy to the Sacred Geometry held by the Knights Templar. Because of this, William was enabled to build the now famous Rosslyn Chapel; the overall work, with its abundance of intricate carvings, was begun in about 1446. In 1475 a Charter ... was ratified, and Rosslyn became known as "Lodge Number One" in Edinburgh. The magnificent Chapel — still used by Knights Templar of the Scottish Grand Priory, and by the Scottish Episcopal Church — stands above the Esk Valley, near the original Templar center at Ballantradoch (House of the Warrior).

Stewart (p. 117) continues:

In respect of the Masonic patronage granted to Sir William Sinclair in 1475, ... there were trade and craft Guilds in Scotland at that time.... King James III had granted numerous Charters in Edinburgh that year, as did his successors thereafter:

Date	Guild	Chartered by
1475	Weavers, Cordwainers (leatherworkers and shoemakers), Wrights (artificers and metalworkers), Masons (stone-workers and builders), Bowyers (bow-makers), Glaziers, Upholsterers, Painters, Slaters, Sievewrights (sieve- and basket-makers), Coopers (barrel-makers)	James III
1483	Hammermen (blacksmiths, goldsmiths, saddlers, cutlers and armourers), Fleshers (butchers)	James III
1500	Wakers (clothiers and millers)	James IV
1505	Surgeons, Barbers	James IV
1530	Bakers, Bonnet-makers	James V
1581	Goldsmiths (separated from Hammermen)	James VI
1586	Skinners	James VI
1635	Post Office	Charles I
1640	Dyers (incorporated with Bonnet-makers)	Charles I
1672	Hatters (incorporated with Wakers)	Charles II
1681	Merchant Company	Charles II

From the ranks of the newly created, operative Guilds, the Knights Templars selected certain members who were keen to extend their minds to matters of science, geometry, history and philosophy, as detailed in the ancient manuscripts which the original Order had brought out of Jerusalem and the Holy Land.... Scotland became a beacon of enlightenment. The new brotherhood of "Free" Masons supported their less fortunate neighbours, and their respective Guilds set money aside for the poorer members of society, thereby beginning the establishment of charitable organizations in Britain.[9] King James VI became a speculative Freemason at the Lodge of Perth and Scone in 1601, and on becoming James I of England two years later, he introduced the concept south of the Border.

Stewart further reports that the Scottish Guilds were given access to the Templar banking system, which enabled them to construct and maintain their international trade network. Aberdeen, with its very broad-based trade channels, founded Freemason Guilds on the French model in 1361, according to Stewart (p. 117–118):

> [Further,] quite apart from the Guilds, the Knights also received lay-people into their allied confraternities and, for a small annual subscription of a few pence, men and women alike were afforded numerous privileges by way of personal and family support in times of need. This was, in fact, the beginning of the insurance and life assurance industry, and it is the reason why so many of today's leading British underwriting institutions emanated from Scotland.

The Cabala

We will close this chapter with a section designed to segue between what has been presented about the Templars and what will be covered in chapter 9, on Aberdeen and northeast Scotland. This has to do with a branch of Judaism termed the Cabala. The Cabala originated in the Holy Land around 70 C.E. and incorporated Judaic religious ideas together with geometric principles developed much earlier, very likely at the time of the building of the pyramids of Egypt. The same architectural and mathematical principles were applied to the construction of the Temple of Solomon in Israel.

As we shall see, the theorems behind both the pyramids and the First Temple are based on the discovery of pi, phi, a number of Pythagorean theorems, and other geometric principles emanating from Eastern learning. They are not magical or mystical, per se. Yet, to the human minds capable of grasping them, they must have seemed God-given and divinely-inspired. Their perfection, symmetry and consistency would have produced awe and amazement among those gifted enough to comprehend and use them. This same set of mathematical principles also had enormous pragmatic utility in fields as diverse as astronomy, architecture, navigation and land measurement. Because of the precious intellectual capital they represented, these geometric theorems were closely guarded, shared only among a select group of Middle Eastern cognoscenti.

The Templars embraced this body of knowledge eagerly, more particularly since it had been the subject of earlier philosophical, scientific and religious speculation in Greece, Rome and Moorish Spain, and it became one of the spoils of conquest when they seized control of the ancient civilizations of the East. In medieval Palestine, the principles had been combined with a mystical numerical system which assigned each letter in the Hebrew alphabet to a number or digit. By recasting Torah texts as numerical sequences, the Jews created elaborate mathematical metaphors that were used to give additional levels of meaning and correspondences to their sacred scripture. In the Diaspora after 100 C.E., these notions were elaborated and embroidered in Cabalistic centers of learning, first in Provence in southern France, then in Spain, and by the 1500s, cycling back to the Holy Land and other Levantine centers such as Alexandria, Istanbul and Salonica.

As Benbassa (1999, p. 38) notes, the spread of Cabalistic doctrines occurred within the larger context of the cross-translation of important philosophical and scientific treatises in the Mediterranean area:

> The [French-Jewish] Kimhi and Ibn Tibbon families distinguished themselves in the domain of translation. In the one, Joseph Kimhi (1105–70) and his son David (1160?–1235), and in the other, Judah ibn Tibbon (1120–90) and his son Samuel (1150–1230), translated the great classics of Judeo-Arabic thought from Arabic into Hebrew, including the works of Saadya Gaon (882–942), Ibn Gabiron (1020?–1057?), Judah Halevi (before 1075–1141), and Bahya ibn Pakuda (second half of the eleventh century).... They also devoted themselves to the translation of Greek and Arabic scientific works, particularly in medicine. The texts of the Muslim physician, philosopher, and mystic Avicenna (980–1037) and, especially, of the philosopher Averroes (1126–98) were translated from Arabic into Hebrew.[10] Spanish Jews trained in their homeland in Arabic astronomy brought it with them to Provence; some invented astronomical instruments, others translated works from Latin.... Samuel ibn Tibbon produced a translation of Maimonides' *Guide for the Perplexed* (1200) that appeared before the author's death in 1204.... Indeed, Provence was also the homeland of Levi ben Gershom, commonly known as Gersonides (1288–1344).... At once a philosopher and theologian, commentator on Averroes and biblical exegete, talmudist, mathematician and logician, he was also the inventor of an astronomical instrument....
>
> Provence, land of philosophy, was also a land of mysticism. It is there that the *Sefer-ha-Bahir* (Book of Brightness), the first document of theosophic kabbalism, was compiled on the basis of oriental sources between 1150 and 1200.... Abrah ben Isaac, president of the rabbinical court of Narbonne (d. 1180), and especially Isaac the Blind (1160?–1235)—grandson of Abraham ben Isaac ... developed a contemplative mysticism. Born in Provence and along the coast of Languedoc, the kabbalah was rapidly transplanted to Catalonia, which maintained close political and cultural ties with these regions.

The earliest known mention of the Cabala comes from the first century of the Common Era, in Judea. Here, four of the classical texts were written: (1) Heikalot Books, (2) *Sepher Yetzirah* (Book of Formation), (3) the *Zohar* (Book of Splendor), and (4) the *Bahir* (Book of Brilliance) (Bernstein 1984). The Heikalot Books are based on the biblical Book of Ezekial, which uses the Throne of Glory and the Heavenly Chariot (Merkabah) as central symbolic devices. The Book of Ezekial and the Book of Genesis both were popular religious texts within Judea from 538 B.C.E. to 70 C.E., that is, during the Second Temple period. Commonly, the wheels of the heavenly chariot are drawn to incorporate the Pythagorean theorem; metaphorically, this means that mathematical wisdom could raise mankind to a perfected state (Bernstein 1984).

The *Sepher Yetzirah* (Book of Formation) is the oldest non–Biblical treatise of Judaism, having been written down in the second century (Bernstein 1984). This book develops the theme of the ten Sephiroth or primordial numbers and the 22 letters of the Hebrew alphabet. Some of its main images are the ladder of wisdom, with each step leading to a higher level of knowledge, and the tree of life, which combines aspects of the ladder going upward from Earth to Heaven with the additional symbolism of "above ground tree, below ground roots," or, "As Above, So Below."[11] The tree metaphor posits that activities on Earth are reflections of actions in Heaven. An important theme through-

Table of Hebrew Letters

Order	Sound	Hebrew Letter	Numerical Value	Latin Letter	Name	Signification of Name
1.	*a*	א	1, 1000	A	Aleph	Ox
2.	*b, bh, (v)*	ב	2	B	Beth	House
3.	*g. gh*	ג	3	G	Gimel	Camel
4.	*d, dh*	ד	4.	D	Daleth	Door
5.	*h*	ה	5.	H	He	Window
6.	*v, u, o*	ו	6	V	Vau	Peg, nail
7.	*z, dz*	ז	7	Z	Zayin	Weapon, sword
8.	*ch (guttural)*	ח	8	Cʜ	Cheth	Enclosure, fence
9.	*t*	ט	9	T	Teth	Serpent
10.	*i, y*	י	10	I	Yod	Hand
11.	*k, kh*	דכ	20, 500	K	Caph	Palm of the hand
12.	*l*	ל	30	L	Lamed	Ox-goad
13.	*m*	ממ	40, 600	M	Mem	Water
14.	*n*	נן	50, 700	N	Nun	Fish
15.	*s*	ס	60	S	Samekh	Prop, support
16.	*O, aa, ng*	ע	70	O	Ayin	Eye
17.	*p, ph*	ףפ	80, 800	P	Pe	Mouth
18.	*ts, tz, j*	צץ	90, 900	Tz	Tzaddi	Fishhook
19.	*q, qk*	ק	100	Q	Qoph	Back of the head
20.	*r*	ר	200	R	Resh	Head
21.	*sh, s*	ש	300	Sʜ	Shin	Tooth
22.	*th, t*	ת	400	Tʜ	Tau	Sign of the cross

out is the perfectibility of the world through human endeavor, often expressed in Judaic tradition as Tikkun Olam ("perfecting the universe").

The *Zohar* (Book of Splendor) is a collection of many different writings on various religious topics. Possibly authored by Rabbi Simeon ben Yohai (160 C.E.), it is the most influential of the Cabalistic writings. It was first published in its entirety by Rabbi Moses de Leon of Guadalajara, Spain, around 1290 C.E. (Bernstein 1984). Rabbi Simeon was known as "the Sacred Light," and we see this name carried forward to the Saint Clair/Sinclair/Sanctus Clarus family of France and Scotland. Further, we will find in Aberdeen many persons having the surname of Norrie/Noory/Nory/Norris, which is Arabic for "light" or "illumination." The *Zohar* proposes that the Torah is actually a series of numerical codes that reveal a much deeper level of divine meaning than the "surface" letters, words and stories.

The *Bahir* (Book of Brilliance) was also produced in the early Talmudic period (ca. 100 C.E.) and almost lost as a text, only to reappear in Provence, France, during the 1200s. The *Bahir* introduces metaphors of reincarnation and the masculine-feminine nature of God. The Jewish scholar most closely associated with the tradition of the *Bahir* is Rabbi Isaac Luria, known as the Ari, who led the Safed school of Cabala in the Holy Land, 1534–1572. Luria was the descendant of Sephardic Jews who had been expelled from Spain in 1492. Prominent in the symbolism of the *Bahir* is the iconography of Light and Darkness. Within Moorish Spain were two other major figures of Cabalism: Rabbi Abraham Abulafia (flourished 1240 C.E.) and one of his students, Rabbi Joseph Gikatilla of Castile.

Mathematics of the Cabala

We turn now to a discussion of the mathematics of the Cabala. The ancient Hebrews used anagrams, termed Temura, and Gematria, a system whereby each letter of the alphabet was assigned a number or digit, creating secret codes and metaphors. Under Cabalism, these codes and metaphors became very highly refined and were communicated only to those initiated into the traditions. Similarly, within the Templar Order, the same set of codes and metaphors was used and it was relayed only to initiates into the order. To represent God, the Cabalists used, at various times, an Aleph (א), a Yod (י) or a Shin (ש); sometimes God would be represented by a point within a circle or a triangle. Hence the intersecting triangles of the Star of David, standing for God's heavenly and earthly presence (above and below).

The Cabala also developed a series of images and calculations based on what is termed "sacred geometry": the principles of Pi (π), Phi (ϕ), ∂ (the base of natural logarithms), and i (-1). It is very likely that the Jews of ancient Judea originally acquired this knowledge from the Greeks when they were conquered by Alexander the Great in the 4th century B.C.E., though some may have been acquired from the Egyptians. After the Greek conquest and during the rule of the Antiochene successors to Alexander's empire, many Jews became Hellenized, even adopting Greek names, customs, language and literary conventions (Biale 2002, pp. 77–134).

Also incorporated within the Cabala were Fibonacci numbers, the geometric progressions that govern the natural growth of populations, for instance, cell division. The Cabala also featured geometric figures such as the pentagram, pentagon, and "golden" isosceles triangles, which make use of phi mathematics. The decagon, or ten-sided figure, also adhered to the phi principle. Further, the Pythagorean theorem, the Golden Mean and the Golden Right Triangle of Phi were well known by the Cabalists and favored in their designs. From these were developed what are perhaps the most profound Cabalistic symbols: the Pyramid/Tree of Life and the Sephirotic Tree. These symbols were enlarged to incorporate the Star of David equilateral triangles.

If you will refer to chapter 7 on Glasgow and environs and re-examine the images in the photographs of Cowane's Hospital and cemetery in Stirling, you will see that some of this symbolism appears in them. In the next chapter we will find several more examples of Cabalistic emblems and designs, including the ceiling at Fyvie Castle outside Aberdeen.

Chapter 9

The Judaic Colony at Aberdeen

It is now time for us to venture up to Aberdeen in the northeast corner of Scotland. As seen on the accompanying map, Aberdeen is bordered by the North Sea and has direct shipping channels to Norway, Sweden, France, Denmark, Russia, the Baltic Sea, Germany and Poland. From the 1100s onward — and perhaps even before — Aberdeen was trading with all of these countries and had established companies, even factories, in each. By 1200 C.E., it was the third wealthiest city in Scotland, despite its northern location, relative isolation from the rest of Scotland, and having only the eighth rank in population. Why?

We propose that Aberdeen's phenomenal growth as a trading center and financial capital was due to the fact that it was a Crypto-Jewish burgh. It is very likely that *all* the dominant families in the city, from 1100 to the 1800s, were of Jewish descent, originating early on from southern France, then from England after the 1290 expulsion, and finally, 1492 onward, from the Iberian peninsula and shifting safe-havens of the Sephardic Diaspora. The DNA results from prominent Aberdeen families discussed in chapter 2 already support this proposition, but we will now develop a different line of evidence, one based on religious practices, marriage patterns and burial customs. This evidence, we believe, will document conclusively that Aberdeen and its environs were solidly Judaic in culture.

Let us begin with the mysterious "St. Machar," to whom not one, but two, parishes were dedicated in the dawn of Aberdeen history (Morgan 2000). As Morgan cogently observes, there is *no* written or archeological record of a saint named Machar, at least no Roman Catholic St. Machar, ever setting foot in Aberdeen, or Scotland for that matter. What does exist, however, is a church in Old Aberdeen dedicated to a "St. Machar" around which prominent members of the citizenry have been buried since its founding, this despite the fact that "we can never know exactly how, when or by whom St. Machar's Cathedral was established" (p. 13). We can only make educated guesses.

The candidate we would like to examine is the Davidic-descended master teacher of the Jewish community in Provence in southern France whose title was, in fact, *Machar* (Benbassa 1999) and who was active there during the appropriate timeframe.

This spiritual leader, Machar, would have been the central figure to persons practicing Judaism in France in the time just before the migration by Jews to Britain with William the Conqueror in 1060 C.E. To dedicate a religious center to this man would be very much in keeping with contemporaneous Talmudic practice of naming religious sites after their

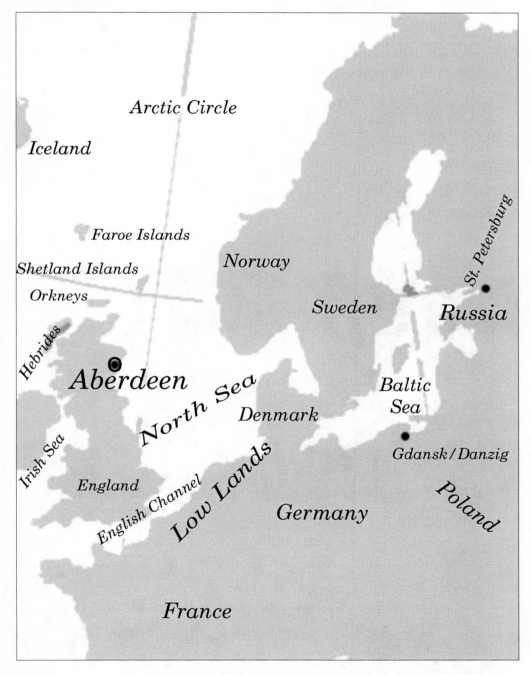

Aberdeen, Scotland, probably had a strong Crypto-Jewish presence. Map by Donald N. Yates.

founders. The sole remaining artifact from the original place of worship (ca. 1100) is a section of stone from the top of a column carved in a "dog-tooth" pattern (Morgan 2000, p. 16). This pattern is consistent with contemporaneous images found in Islamic and Jewish manuscripts and mosaics.

Images of a Jewish Presence

We will next present a series of images found in and around Aberdeen and place them in a context of Judaic/Islamic aesthetics. We believe a compelling case can be made that Aberdeen did serve as a center of Jewish worship and culture during the time period 1100–1750 C.E., in other words, from Norman to Georgian times, when the status and number of Jews in the British Isles was first brought into the open and they began to be integrated into a "desacralized" British state (Endelman 1979).

At the time the "Jew Bill" was debated in England around 1750, many Scottish Crypto-Jews must have preferred to remain underground, especially as they already enjoyed not only full rights as citizens, but an active engagement in politics and nationalism denied to their counterparts in other countries. Others undoubtedly lapsed or converted, without ever becoming labeled "ex–Jews." In Spain and Portugal, on the other hand, Jewish origins had long become enshrined in the caste system. Jews were branded as *conversos* or remembered as coming from "New Christian" families for more than 400 years.

Kings College Chapel

On page 85 of Morgan's 2000 study is an illustration of a carving completed on the north side of Kings College Chapel at Aberdeen University in 1506. The text labels this as a "conservation cross," but it is in fact a Cabalistic image. Also within Kings College Chapel are other carvings on wooden panels in prominent Judaic and Islamic motifs (Morgan 2000, pp. 93, 96). Similarly, the Findour Panel from the Great Hall at Kings College (now in the Chapel) has an Islamic/Judaic motif, together with a Templar geometric symbol on the heraldic shield.

Within St. Machar's Church nearby is a heraldic ceiling with geometric squares, triangles and rectangles which is also Judaic and Islamic in inspiration. A patterned ceiling closely resembling it was constructed by the same craftsman, believed to be from the Netherlands, John Fendour or Ferdour, in St. Nicholas Kirk in Aberdeen around 1510. Keith (1988, p. 53) reports that in 1740 the grave at St. Nicholas Kirk of a Sir Robert Davidson, who died in 1411, was opened during construction "and his remains found, with a small silk skull cap that had been on his head when he was buried. The cap, unfor-

---

Opposite top: "Dog-tooth" column fragment from St. Machar Cathedral, ca. 1100 C.E. Sketch by Elizabeth Caldwell Hirschman. *Bottom:* Contemporaneous "dog tooth" mosaic patterns from the Moorish Real Alcazar, Granada, Spain. Photograph by Elizabeth Caldwell Hirschman.

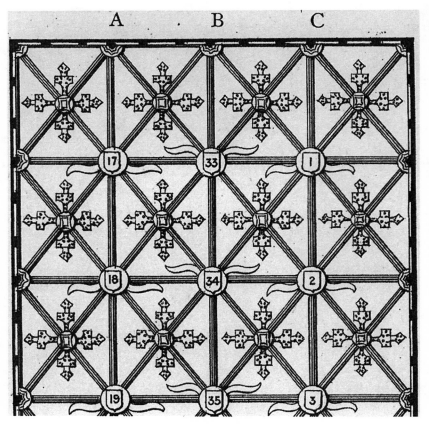

Top: "Conservation Cross"/Moorish-Judaic motif, Aberdeen University, 1506. Sketch by Elizabeth Caldwell Hirschman. *Bottom:* King's College ceiling decor. Courtesy of Aberdeen University.

tunately, was given away." The cap's description corresponds to that of a kipah, the Jewish male's headgear worn in temple visits, during prayer and upon his death. The kirk apparently was being used for Jewish burials.

Fyvie Castle

Fyvie Castle, just outside Aberdeen, was owned by the Gordon and Seaton families dating from the 1300s. We found it to be a virtual trove of Judaic, Cabalistic and Islamic imagery. Several Islamic crescents were carved or painted at prominent places in the castle, including on coats of arms, above stairways, and on wooden divider panels and screens. The ceilings at Fyvie were also remarkable for their geometric and floral Islamic and Judaic designs. But the most intriguing of the ceilings is in the entrance hall. Inside a set of interlocking equilateral triangles are clearly depicted symbols of the Cabalah Sephirotic Tree. Compare these with the Cabalistic adaptation of the same image (chapter 6).

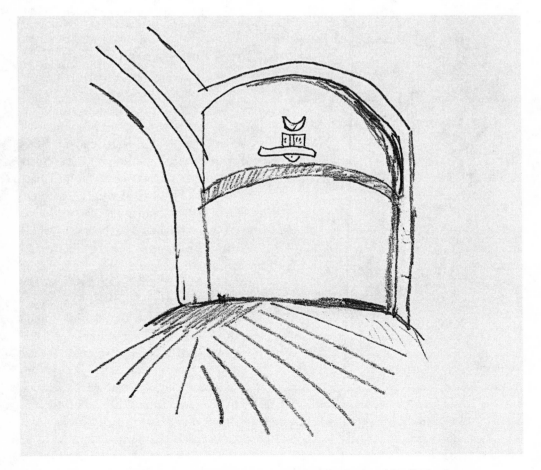

Fyvie Castle stairway: carved crescent. Sketch by Elizabeth Caldwell Hirschman

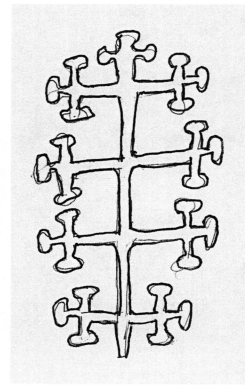

Top: Fyvie Castle wood panels with Islamic crescents and 5 points of Islam flowers motif. *Left:* Sephirotic Tree Cabalah image. Fyvie Castle entrance hall. Both sketches by Elizabeth Caldwell Hirschman.

Royal Images and Coins

Also suggestive of a Judaic or Cabalistic orientation are portraits and coins of early Scottish royalty. For example, William the Lyon (King of Scotland 1165–1214) and David I the Saint (King of Scotland 1124–1153) are depicted on the Charter of Abroath in 1320 with a complete absence of Christian symbolism. Rather, two entwined snakes (a Cabalistic symbol) surround the figures. King William and King David, his grandfather, both have crossed legs in the form of the Templar/Cabalistic X mark, and William holds what appears to be a fruit, possibly a pomegranate from the Song of Songs of Solomon, builder of the First Temple. An oak tomb effigy in Gloucester Cathedral dated about 1250 of Robert Curthose, Duke of Normandy, the crusading eldest son of William the Conqueror, shows him to have the same posture (Douglas 2001, plate between pp. 108 and 109). A coin from the reign of Alexander III (1249–1286) carries equilateral triangles in the form of six-pointed stars.

The Stewart monarchs, said by the latest claimant, Michael Stewart (2000), to be of Davidic descent, use as their principal symbols the "Lion rampant" and "St. Andrew's Cross." We have argued that the latter represents the Judaic or Templar X mark, used to commemorate ties with the Holy Land. The Scottish royal lion, we believe, is a direct representation of the Lion of Judah ("The scepter shall not depart from Judah, Nor the ruler's staff from between his feet," Gen. 49:9), widely adopted to indicate the divine right and supremacy of Davidic royal descent. For purposes of comparison, let us now examine some markedly Sephardic iconography from roughly the same time period. They include five coats of arms for Sephardic Jewish families, prior to their expulsion from Spain. Notably, the symbols used include the crescent, tau symbol, lion rampant, tree of life, Star of David, Cockle Shell (a Jacobite icon) and three towered castle.

Bishop's Emblems and the Fraser Coat of Arms

Another very significant group of symbols can be found on the emblems of the Bishops of Aberdeen and St. Andrews. The seal of Bishop Elphinstone of Aberdeen depicts on one side three steeples that may symbolize the holy trinity of Christian faith; they are set atop what appears to be a structure containing the tablets of the Ten Commandments. The obverse has a holy man wearing a crown, holding a shepherd's crook and flanked on one side by a crescent moon and on the other by a six-pointed star. Our interpretation of this imagery is that all three faiths were permitted to be practiced in the city.[1]

Templar tomb carving showing crossed legs in Tau/Tough image. Sketch by Elizabeth Caldwell Hirschman.

The Fraser family, which we have argued to be carrying Sephardic and Ashkenazic DNA, produced a bishop of St. Andrews, William Fraser, who served from 1279 to 1297. His two seals feature a bishop arranged within an arch with the tell-tale "X" mark in the center and a flower etched on either side. The second shows the same holy man, but this time in an "X" posture, flanked by a crescent moon and a six-pointed star, as we observed earlier. Again, our interpretation is that all three faiths—Christian, Jewish, Muslim—were tolerated and practiced in the diocese of St. Andrews.

Turning to the Fraser coat of arms, itself, and Fraser banner (1300), we detect additional resonances with a Judaic heritage. The banner displays six five-petaled strawberry flowers in a triangular pattern — a rebus or pictorial pun on the French meaning of the Fraser surname, "strawberry grower." Related floral designs are found on an Italian Hebrew Bible, also from 1300, and on a Hebrew prayer book from Germany, ca. 1380. The arms of the chief of Clan Fraser, a centered square with three strawberry flowers in another triangular pattern, bolstered by two angels, also resembles contemporaneous Judaic images.

Edward Raban Psalter, 1623

The most startling image of Judaic culture from Aberdeen emerges in the cover of the psalm book printed by Edward Raban for the Town of Aberdeen in 1623. Raban was from a Jewish-descended family in Germany and had been active briefly as a printer in London, Glasgow and Edinburgh, before coming to Aberdeen at the request of the city burgesses in 1621. He was the first printer to work in Aberdeen. The first book he produced for the burgesses was the Psalms of David, published in 1623. Strikingly, the title page to this work not only invokes the name of "the Princelie Prophet David" but also carries the Hebrew letters standing for the name of God. These letters, appearing in the upper center section of Raban's page layout, were the pri-

Opposite and above: Sephardic Jewish coats of arms. Courtesy of Harry Stein: Sephardim.com.

mary meditative device among Cabalistic Jews. Notably, Raban's printing of the Tetragrammaton (YHWH) is without vowels, but using an extended final letter. This pattern comes directly from the Torah. Further, the decorative border around the page is Moorish Arabesque in pattern, and the arms of Aberdeen City itself incorporate two leopards (an Oriental symbol for splendor) holding a shield with three towers or columns, a Templar allusion. Arabesque motifs from Sephardic and Moorish inscriptions in Andalusia are shown for comparison.

Kings College and Aberdeen University

We now want to take a look at the intellectual and educational activities of Aberdeen and focus on Kings College and its founder, Bishop William Elphinstone. The surname itself was a common Medieval Jewish surname meaning "ivory": most dealers in "elephant stone" in the Middle Ages were either Jews or Arabs. Morgan (2000, pp. 42–42) gives us some excellent insight into Elphinstone's origins and career:

> In April 1488, William Elphinstone, then fifty-seven years of age, was consecrated Bishop of Aberdeen at St Machar's Cathedral, in the presence of King James III. Unlike many of his predecessors and his successor Gavin Dunbar, he was not a member of a mighty or powerful family, but was the leading civil and canon lawyer in the kingdom and one of the monarch's most skilled ambassadors. He was dogged, hard-working and ambitious.... Born in Glasgow in 1431.... His mother is something of a mystery, though she is thought to have been Margaret Douglas, daughter of a Laird of Drumlanrig. Elphinstone was subsequently dispensed from illegitimacy by the pope in 1454 to allow him to take holy orders....
> His career was not typical of an ambitious churchman. He ran the family estate for a

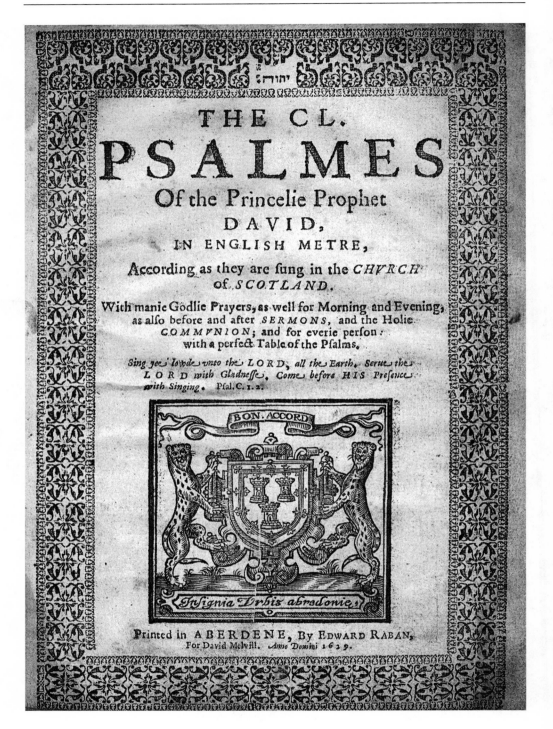

Title page from psalter printed by Edward Raban in 1629 for the City of Aberdeen. The tetragrammaton uses Torah-style lettering forms. Courtesy of University of Aberdeen.

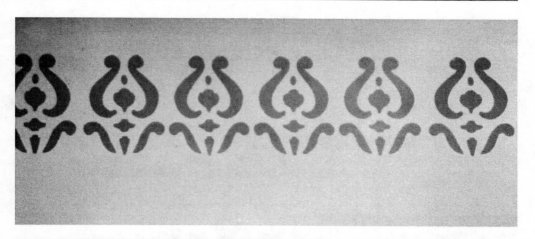

Arabesque motifs from Jewish and Moorish Andalusia. Photographs by Elizabeth Caldwell Hirschman.

time, graduated in arts at Glasgow University in 1462 at the age of thirty-one, then went on to study canon law there and pled in the consistorial court.... Elphinstone pled especially for the poor, the *personae miserabiles*, "not for a fee but for the sake of equity and justice," wrote Hector Boece in his *Lives of the Bishops....*

[W]ith a little persuading from his uncle, Laurence Elphinstone, [he] set off for the University of Paris to resume his studies in canon law. His aptitude for legal argument caught the attention of his masters and after graduating he was made reader (lecturer) in that subject. Next Elphinstone passed to Orleans to study civil law.... He returned home in 1471 after less than a year at Orleans, possibly alerted by his father, still a canon of Glasgow Cathedral, that the post of official of that diocese was about to fall vacant. He was duly appointed, then following in his father's footsteps, was elected Dean of Faculty of Arts at Glasgow University.

Elphinstone next turned his attention to Aberdeen and decided to establish a university there. Aberdeen had been a royal burgh since the 1100s and a commercial trading partner with Danzig, Poland and the Netherlands; by the 1500s, it had a population of 4,000. As Morgan (p. 47) writes, "A university would add to the burgh's prestige and there was no reason to suppose that the burgesses ... would not assist financially in its funding."

At its founding, Keith notes (p. 128) that Kings College employed

besides the Chancellor (Elphinstone) and the Rector, who were unpaid, thirty-six persons [who] were to reside within the college and receive emoluments of some kind from its endowments. The Principal, who had to be a master of theology, was the administrative head, lectured on theology and preached.... The Mediciner was the first professor of Medicine to be appointed in Britain. Cambridge did not have one until 1540, Oxford till 1546. The Sub-Principal, a Master of Arts, deputized for the Principal and lectured on the liberal arts; the Grammarian, also a Master of Arts, instructed in grammar.... The subjects were: First Year: Logic; Second year: Physics and Natural Philosophy; Last year and half: Arithmetic, Geometry, Cosmography and Moral Philosophy.... The Grammarian taught Latin, and at a remarkably early date ... he or one of his colleagues instructed in Greek.

The headmaster, or principal, of Kings College was a man named Hector Boece (i.e. Boethius, a commonly adopted Roman surname equivalent to Ezra among Jews of the Hellenistic and Roman periods). Morgan (p. 67) notes:

Elphinstone had head-hunted Hector Boece, of whom he had good reports from his continental contacts, as a potential principal. A St Andrews graduate in his early thirties, a Christian humanist with a reputation as a skilled writer of Latin prose, Boece was teaching philosophy in Paris at that time. He had a minus point in that he had no degree in theology, the latter a requisite for the principalship, but a plus in that he had begun the study of medicine in Paris, the very subject that Elphinstone and King James sought to promote.

She then asks (p. 67):

With learned doctors of divinity on his doorstep, why did Elphinstone lure this stranger, not yet even a bachelor of theology, from Paris? It was, perhaps, part of his aim to distance his new university from the Chanonry and its "college of canons," which was purely a theological college. Within a few years it seems that Boece had not only gained his first degree in theology, but was running the university.... In spite of a heavy workload, Boece found time to continue his study of medicine and to write two works, both in Latin, which were famous in their day....
  By the mid–1500s, Kings [University] was teaching not only Greek and Latin, but also Hebrew, Syriac and Chaldean.... The inclusion of Hebrew, as well as the Mid-Eastern languages of Syriac and Chaldean, suggests a preoccupation with scientific rather than theological texts, since Syriac and Chaldean (non–Biblical languages) were the threads by which a large part of the corpus of Aristotle's works, as well as unique Platonic and Neo-Platonic treatises, were preserved, entering Western thought and learning through the stream of "Averroeism," a materialistic philosophy created by Jews and Moors in northern Spain.

As many as three centuries later, when the Scotsman Adam Smith published *The Wealth of Nations*, Hebrew still was not part of a common university education in *England*, yet the *Scots* had pioneered its place in the curriculum. We would argue that in addition to permitting the study of Judaic and Islamic *scientific* texts, the teaching of Hebrew, Syriac and Chaldean also opened access to Palestinian and Babylonian *philosophical* and *religious* writings, a desirable skill for persons of Jewish and Muslim heritage.

Tellingly, when Elphinstone first became bishop of Aberdeen in 1488, he halted use of the traditional Roman Catholic breviary in that city. In its place, and with the support of King James IV, he had a new breviary printed in Edinburgh by a "wealthy merchant burgess," Walter Chapman, and Andrew Myllar, a bookseller. Concurrently, James IV banned the use of the Roman Catholic breviary throughout Scotland. Unfortunately, only four partial copies of this work survive. We believe that it too would prove to be a Crypto-Jewish devotional text, akin to Raban's Davidic Psalm book. From this overview, we see that a university education in Aberdeen during the 1500s certainly did not follow a Christian, Catholic or even theological tradition. Rather, it resembled the "open" scholarship of the Babylonian Talmudic academy in Provence and of centers of secular learning in Muslim Spain and the more tolerant northern Christian kingdoms of Aragon and Catalonia.

As is well known, many intellectual Jews in the anti–Semitic climate of Spain and France following the pogrom of 1389 nominally or genuinely converted to Christianity and became clerics, monks and even bishops, so they could retain access to Hebrew books, which were otherwise forbidden. For instance, according to Gitlitz (2002, p. 475), "The *converso* Pedro Alfonso was so well known as a Jewish scholar in Valencia in the 1480s that 'when a Jew who was carrying a Hebrew book was asked who in Valencia could read it, he answered, Pedro Alfonso.' Alfonso was even reputed to speak Hebrew at home with his wife (Haliczer 1990, 212)."

What Are Hebrew Letters Like These Doing in a Place Like This?

As we did for the western region of Scotland in chapter 5, we now examine who was living around Aberdeen from 1200 onward. Several aristocratic families whose ancestral homes are near Aberdeen we have already identified as being of probable Jewish ancestry. Among these are the Gordons, Frasers, Forbeses, and Leslies. They arrived in Scotland during the first Jewish in-migration, 1066–1250 C.E. The 1400s and 1500s brought a new influx of families bearing Sephardic and French Jewish surnames, such as Menzies/Menezes (originally from Hebrew Menachem),[2] Davidson, Arnot (from Aaron), and Perry (from "pear" in Spanish [Jacobs 1911]). Perhaps most blatantly, some of the incoming families had surnames that were actually the names of letters in the Hebrew alphabet: Gemmell (representing a camel), Hay (life) and Taw (*tau,* cross or saltire).

Elgin

The earliest records available for Northeast Scotland are for Elgin[3] ("God's spirit" in Aramaic). A list of provosts (mayors) of the town begins with a Wisman in 1261 and goes forward to a series of Douglases from 1488 to 1530. The Douglas family we already have proposed to be Jewish. A new surname, Gaderer, then enters the list and alternates with Douglas and Innes (Gaelic for "isles") and Annand (Hebrew).[4] By the 1600s the Pringill (Pringle) family appears on the list, together with several occurrences of Hays and Seton. We believe the Hay surname (which is common even today among Jews) to be derived from the name of the Hebrew letter Heh (pronounced "hay"), which corresponds to the numeral 5 and symbolizes life (*hayyim*; *hayat* in Arabic).[5] The Seton family is the one we encountered earlier at Fyvie Castle: the Seton coat of arms displays three orange crescent moons.

Provosts of Elgin

1261, August	Thomas Wisman, prepositus
1272, December	Adam, filius Stephani and Patricius Heroc, prepositi
1330, December	Walter filius Radulphi, major
1343, March	Walterus, filius Radulphi, prepositus
1488, October	Jacobus Douglas de Pittendreich, prepositus
1521–25	David Douglas of Pittendreich, alderman
1529–30	William Douglas
1538–39	William Gaderer, elder
1542–43	John Young, elder
1540–42	William Gaderer, elder
1547–48	St Giles
1548–49	William Hay of Mayne
1549–53	Alexander Innes of that ilk
1553–54	William Innes
1554–57	Mr. Alexander Douglas
1557–58	William Gaderar
1559–61	Mr. Alexander Douglas
1565–68	John Annand
1568–69	Mr. Alexander Douglas
1569–74	John Annand of Morristoun
1574–75	Mr. Alexander Douglas
1575–83	John Annand of Morristoun
1583–84	Thomas Young
1584–85	James Douglas of Shutting Acres
1585–86	John Annand of Morristoun
1594–1600	Alexander Seton, Lord of Urquhart and Fyvie
1600–01	James Douglas of Shutting Acres
1601–07	Alexander Seton, Earl of Dunfermline
1609–10	James Douglas of Barflethills
1610–11	Alexander Pringill
1611–12	James Rutherford
1612–13	Alexander Pringill
1613–15	James Douglas of Bartlethills
1615–23	James Rutherford

1623–31	Mr. Gavin Douglas of Shutting Acres
1631–43	Mr. John Hay
1643–45	Mr. Gavin Douglas of Morristoun
1645–50	Mr. John Hay
1650–53	Mr. John Douglas of Morristoun
1653–55	Mr. John Hay
1655–58	Mr. John Douglas of Morristoun
1658–64	George Cuming of Lochtervandich
1664–65	William Cuming
1665–68	Thomas Calder
1668–87	George Cuming of Lochtervandich
1687–88	Sir Alexander Innes of Coxton
1688–89	David Stewart
1689–90	William Calder of Spynie
1690–1700	William King of Newmill
1700–05	James, Lord Duffus
1705–08	William Sutherland of Mostowie
1708–11	William King of Newmill
1711–14	George Innes of Dunkinty
1714–17	Mr. Archibald Dunbar of Thunderton
1717–20	Robert Innes MD
1720–23	James Innes MD
1723–26	Robert Innes MD
1726–29	James Innes MD
1729–31	James Anderson of Linkwood
1731–34	James Innes MD
1734–37	John Robertson, merchant
1737–40	James Innes MD
1740–43	William Anderson of Linkwood
1743–46	James Stephen, merchant
1746–49	John Duff, senior, merchant
1749–52	Alexander Brodie of Windyhills
1752–55	James Robertson of Bishopmill
1755–58	Alexander Brodie of Windyhills
1758–61	James Robertson of Bishopmill
1761–64	Alexander Brodie of Windyhills
1764–67	James Robertson of Bishopmill
1767–70	Alexander Brodie of Windyhills
1770–71	Thomas Stephen, merchant
1771–74	John Duff, merchant
1774–75	Alexander Brodie[6] of Windyhills

Elgin's Burgess Roll is similarly expressive of a strong Jewish presence and also hints at some Islamic origins. It includes Sephardic surnames such as Arnot, Baron, Braco,

Cadell,[7] Livie (Levy, Levi), Martine, Masson, Morrice (Morris, a form of Moses), Pirie (Perry), Tarris and Troupe.

Elgin Burgess Roll Surnames

Adam	Gray	Murray[8]
Alves	Greenlaw	Naughtie
Appie	Hardy	Nicholl
Arnot	Hay	Panton
Baron	Innes	Petrie
Black	Jack (= Jacob)	Pirie
Blenshell ("white, blonde")	Junken	Proctor[9]
Bonyman[10]	Kay	Rainey
	Knox	Reid
Braco	Kynoch (Gael. *dark*)	Abraham Ridge 1644
Brodie	Laurie[11]	Roche
Bruce	Leslie	Rose
Cadell	Livie	Rosehaugh
Chrystie	Aeneas Mckay	Sellar
Davidson	Malcolm	Sinclair (St. Clair)
Denoon	Martine	Skeen
Ellis	Masson	Smeill (Smeal, Ismael)
Falconer	Mathieson	Steal
Fraser	May	Stewart
Gaderar	Mellice	Symson
Geddes (Cadiz)	Missan	Tarris
Glass	Minty	Troupe
Cosmo Gordon	Mories	Hierom (Hiram) Tulloch 1651
Isaac Grant	Morrice	

Aberdour, Alford, Alvah and Alves

These four towns are also in northeast Scotland, and their cemetery inscriptions provide additional evidence of a large French/Sephardic Jewish (and possibly Islamic) population. Indeed, Alves is the name of a city in Spain from which many Sephardic exiles departed in 1492. Alvah is Hebrew and Arabic for "sublime." In Aberdour, we find a woman named Bassilia Cameron, also Davidsons, Riddells, Addan, Clyne (Klein), Peirie, and Gall (Gaul). In Alford are buried persons named Imlah, Tawse (Hebrew letter Tau = 400), Morrice (= Moses), Benzie (= Ben Zion), and Bandeen (Ben Din = "Son of Religion" in Arabic). There are seven Templar tombs listed for the Farquarson family. Presumably, this surname is derived from the common Arabic occupation name Al-Fakhkhar, "potter." In Alvah are found gravestones for Sherres (Sheretz), Ferrier ("iron worker"), Caies, Dow (David), Davie (David), Massie and an Abram Syme (Simon). And in Alves we find stones for persons surnamed Hosack, Aster ("one from Asturias in Spain"), Gilzean and Mallies.

Aberdour Cemetery

Cruden
Gordon
Black
Shand
Basslia Cameron
Murcar
Dounie
Stewart
Davidson
Watson
Riddel
Shirran
Kidd
Addan
King
Murray
Robertson
Gardiner

Forsyth
Bruce
Reid
Panton
Finlator
Gerard
Gall
Simpson
Jamieson
Callum
Duncan
Chapman
Baird (1593)
Keith (Kieff)
Walker
Gatt
Ramsay

Brown
Park
Bartlett
Milne
Clyne
Sheran
Watt
Wells
Campbell
Whyte
Peirie
Jaffrey
Leslie
Jack
Cowrie
Watt
Pirie

Alford Churchyard

Gordon
Imlah
Lawson
Reid
Sutherland
Tawse
Black
Lobban[12]
Hosie (= Hosea)
Syme (= Simon)

Gauld
Christie
Mortimer
Mitchell
Bruce
Benzie
Berrie
Marnock
Berry (Moses)
Watt

Ferries
**Templar Slab
  Tombs:**
Farquarson (7)
Elmslie
Adam
Bandeen
Gordon
Stewart

Alvah Churchyard

Dougal
Morrison
Cameron
Barclay
Deeson
Ruddiman
Carnegie[13]
Leslie
Chrystal

Jamieson
Inglis
Caies
Aven
Cowie
Rennie
Marr
Christie
Panton

Massie
Joase (Jewish
  grave) 1665
Grant
Sinclair
Ellis
Joass
Minty
Brown

Davidson	Oman	Davidson
Sherres	Allerdice	Steinson
Smollet	Dow	Robb
Duffes	Davie	Findlater
Anton	Hay	Lobban
Murray	Gray	Kennedy
Watt	Barclay	Reid
Henry	Brodie	Abram Syme, 1735
Ferrier	Brebner (fr. Brabant)	Currie
Chapman	Robson	Wallace
Mackie	Chalmus	Bisset
Greenlaw	Carruth	Steel[14]
Adam	Rae (It., Sp. "King")	Shearer
Stewart	Hacket	Hatt (Hyatt)
Cruikshank	Pirie	
Kelman	Fraser	

Alves Cemetery

Arnot	Gillan	Leslie
Paul	Petrie	Fraser
Mallie	Collie	Rhind (German "bull")
Phillip	Sim	Fimestar
Duglas	Innes	Austie
Dormie	Black	Buie
Murray	Watson	Sinclair
Masson	Gordon	Davidson
Gilzean	Cowie	Sleat
Cruickshank	Hay	Anderson
Rose	Royan (Rouen?)	Gordon
Cobban	Nicol	Hosack
Adam	Asher	Fordyce
Falconer	Russell	Ross
Dempster	Robb	Begg (Khazar "king"
Hieronymous Spens 1585	Petrie	Dow

Cowie, Daviot, Dyce, Echt, and Fyvie

At the Cowie cemetery we find some new Sephardic surnames. These include Lees, Neper (Napier), Lyon (= Judah), Dallas, and Perrin (= Perone). The Daviot churchyard takes its name from the French form of David; it has stones for Pape (Avignonese Jews belonged to the Pope and often bore that name, as English and Italian Jews employed by royalty often took the name King or Re, Reyes), Ritie, Valentine, Diack, Chesser (= Hezer) and Kellas, among others. Dyce cemetery has several Sephardic surnames; among them are Reiach ("wind" in Arabic), Low (an Askenazic form for Joseph), Raffan, Abel, Forbas, Annan, Dalgarno and Jolly (French *jolie*, "happy").

Echt cemetery includes surnames such as Russel, Achnach, Lyell, Norrie, Ferries and Shewan (*schön* is German and Yiddish for "beautiful," for which the Arabic popular name was Jafeh). And Fyvie has the surnames Barrack,[15] Rainie, Joss, Florance (Florance, Italy), Castel (from Castille), Gamack, Gabriel and Cassie. We also notice the popularity of Alexander — in Gaelic, Alistair.[16]

Cowie Cemetery

Spark	Christie	Davidson
Fraser	Lees	Masson
Brown	Taylor	Neper
Lyon	Jamieson	Duthie
Strachan	Burnet	Napier
Orchie	Brodie	Cadonhead
Adam	Lees	Dallas
Falconer	Reith (*Ger.* Reuth)	Perrin
Wood	Moir	Brebner[17]
Smart	Mitchell	Henderson
Masson	Innes	Sheret
Robb	Carnegie	

Daviot Churchyard

Shepherd	Diack
Bruce	Cruikshank
Paul	Fraser
Topp	Carr
Keith	Christie
Coutts	Seton
Pape	Phillip
Moir	Kynock
Gray	Pierie
Kennedy	Muray
Rothnie	Kemp
Singer (2, Latin *Cantor*)	Valentine
Mailand	Davidson
Hardie	Benzie
Chesser	Kellas
Stewart	Marr
Law (cp. Low, Lau)	Falconer
Lyon	Gray

Dyce Cemetery

Alexander Kynoch
Will. Leslie
Harriett Adams
Ruth Beveridge
Robert Sandison
William Low
Norman Raffan
Mary Matheson
Elizabeth Shivas Scott
Alexander Norrie Scott
Margaret Chrystal
William Cowie
Isabella Lawson
Christian Hervey
Alexander Abel
Sophia Abel
Mary Leslie
John Moir
Barbra Runcieman
Joseph Dalgarno ("from the Algarve")
Isabella Jolly
Isabella Pirie
Isabella Gill (Heb. "happy")
Isabella Sang (Fr. "blood"?)
James Bisset
William Riddell
Alex. Sharp
Margaret Barclay
Charles Adar (Heb. month)
Bothice Simpson (Boëce = old Heb. name)
Robert Esson
Eliz. Jardine (Fr. "garden")
William Hector (Greek surname)

Alexander Reiach (Ger. *Reich* "rich"?)
Isabella Young (*Jung, Jeune*)
Bella Gordon
John, Isabella and David Napier
James Davidson
John Petrie
Alex Annand
Elizabeth Diack
Isabella Morrison
James Forbes
William Rea
Alex. Chapman
Elizabeth Morrice
Isabella Sangster
Peter Sim
William Forbas
Alexander Watt
Anne Mackie (fr. Kay)
Robert Annan
Jessie Forbes
Jessie Kempt
Elizabeth Godsman
Albert Cushnie
William Greig
Mary Mackie
Catherine Ellis (fr. Heb. Elias)
Gordon Marr
Isobel Barioch
James Gauld (Gold)
Reva Priscilla Raby[18]
Jeannie Tawse
Robert Christie

Echt Churchyard

Kerr
Innes
Greig
Mathieson
Ross
Farquhar
Soutter

Kempt
Law
Sandison
Russel
Coutts
Watt
Wagrel

Shewan
Calder
Guild
Abel
Bruce
Gibbon
Christie

Wyllie
Gordon (2)
Anderson
Gaven
Forbes
Pirie
Niven (Fr. "snowy")
Philip
Tough
Abel
Adam
Kennedy
Hogg (Heb. Haag = "holiday")
Leith
Aitken

Achnach
Alexander
Kyd
Adam
Snowie
Campbell
Carnie (2)
Lyell
Roob (Rueben)
Elphinstone ("ivory")
Kinghorn
Barclay
Ferries
Barrow (Baruch)
Noble

Eddie
Copland
Barron
Skene
Davidson
Collie
Riddel
Norrie
Nicol
Lawrie
Sangster
Cooper[19]
Raeburn (Rueben)
Craib
Hird (Ger. "deer")

Fyvie Churchyard (near Fyvie Castle)

Barrack (Heb.)
Petrie
Gray
Davidson
Beaton
Gordon
Joss
Kennedy
Jamieson
Grieve
Norrie
Sorrie
Aiken
McRobb
Black
Rattray
Bean
Lyon
Gerrie
Campbell
Lindell

Mackie
Pratt
Hatt
Bruce
Horn (Heb. *shofar*)
Florance (city in Italy)
Burr
Florence
Hay
Leask
Shand (Ger. "shame")[20]
Nicol
Cruickshank
Gamack
Gabriel
Beverly
Alexander
Rose
Riddell
Knox
Leslie

Singer ("Cantor")
Rainie
Cowie
Shearer
Duguid
Chene (Ger. *Schön*)
Murray
Richie (Fr. "rich")
Christie
Castle/Castel
Watson
Diack
Sherren
Scorgies
Murray
Jaffray (cp. Joffré)
Beaton
Marr (Lat. *Maurus*, Moor)
Cassie
Massie
Fiddes

Leslie, New Machar, Rathen, Rhynie

These four cemeteries are all named either for families of proposed Jewish paternal descent (e.g., Leslie/Ladislau) or utilize Hebrew/Jewish surnames, i.e., Machar, Rathen, and Rhynie. In Leslie cemetery we find Riddells, Toughs (Tow), Benzie (Benzion), Hay and Norrie. New Machar has tombstones carrying surnames such as Gill, Catto (Italian and Spanish for "cat": the German form, Katz, though actually formed from a Hebrew anagram, is the most common Jewish surname today), Singer, Kiloti, Argo and Sherriff (= Arab. *sherif*). Rathen is smaller, but has several Sephardic surnames including Cheves, Lunan, Shirras, Yool and Esslemont. Rhynie, smaller still, has Symon, Castell, Tocher, Jessieman and Riach.

Leslie Churchyard

Forbes	Dawson	Connon
Norrie	Brown	Weir
Innes	McGilvray	Riddell
Mackee	Leslie	Green
Chrystall[21]	Alexander	Sim
Ferries	Jervise (Fr. Tanner)	Davie
Tough	Mitchell	Morrison
Benzie	Hay	Mair
Petrie	Pirie	

New Machar Churchyard

Gill	Chapman	Lamb
Murray	Sangster	Catto (= Katz)
Philip	Black	Moir
Elrick	Low	Jamieson
Mathison	Rae	Collie
Singer	Stephen	Bennerman
Keith	Seymour	Barrack
Duguid	Sym	Kiloh
Petrie	Aiken	Gawn (cp. Goen)
Norie	Lyall	Proctor
Christie	Skene	Bisset
Harvey	Hardie	Massie
Ritchie	Lyon	Sime
Campbell	Davidson	Mathieson
Cassie	Chesser	Barclay
Barrack	Sherriffs	Topp
Black	Paton	Argo ("merchantman")[22]
Wyness	Cowie	Masson (Fr. "house")
Adam	Greig (Gray)	Duguid
Cheyne (Yiddish *sheyn*)	Forbes	Rae ("king")

Rathen Churchyard

Bruce	Greig	Davidson
Murray	Jamieson	Cheves
Brown	Fraser	Alexander
Pirie	Cadger (Isaac)	Robb
Lunan	Nicol	Bisset
Yule (Heb. *Yehuel*)	Cumine (Lat. *Cuma*)	Perry
Mair (Heb. Meïr)	Shirras	Cowie
Morrice	Lamb	Laurance
Cheyne	Murray	Dawson (David's son)
Willox	Hay	Mowat (Arabic)
Gall	Yool	Knox[23]
Esslemont (town in Flanders)	Marr	

Rhynie Churchyard

Symon	Riddell	Gordone
Castell	Tocher (Heb.)	Rhind (Ger. "beef")
Leslie	Joss	Pirie
Kynoch	Dallas	Bannerman[24]
Glass	Jessieman	Roper (Sp. "old clothes dealer")
Innes	Glases	Riach (Arabic "wind")
Gordon	Bruce	

Skene, Tarves, Turriff, Tyrie

Again, these are cemeteries whose names are strongly redolent of the Mediterranean world. Tyrie is likely named for Tyre, the ancient capital of Phoenicia (now Lebanon), and Tarves invokes Tarshish, referred to in the Bible, located by some in southern Spain, the homeland of the Sephardim.[25] Buried at Skene, just north of Aberdeen, are persons named Low, Massey, Hector, Davnie, Kellas, Menzies, Gammie and Tawse (Thow). An unusual feature of many of these names is their evident Greek origin. One might speculate that so much Greek in one place bears testimony to the vestiges of a colony of Romaniots (Greek Jews), perhaps displaced to faraway Scotland by the fall of Byzantium in 1453.[26]

At Tarves cemetery several graves had flat stones and "open book" designs indicative of Jewish burial practice. Names found here were Tough (= Thow), Godsman, Perry, Norrie, Luias, Argo, Cassie, and Cheyne (= Hebrew letter Shin, with a pun on *schön*, "beautiful"). Turriff cemetery also had several flat stones and names such as Chessar (Hezar), Imlach, Taws, Shirof (Sharif), Grassie (= Grassi, Garcia, Gracia, the ancestral village of a famous noble Sephardic family from the area of Barcelona), Chivas, and Loban (perhaps from Lobbes, a commercial center in the Low Countries). Finally, Tyrie graveyard had several Semitic surnames: Pirie, Lyon, Lee, Lovie,[27] Lowe (indicative of lion/Loewe, for the tribe of Judah), Shirran, Lunan (Sp. de Luna) and Chivas.

Skene Churchyard

Low
Massey
Hector (Gr.)
Leslie
Davnie
Ruddiman
Moir
Brebner
Christie
Menzies
Abel
Jamieson
Daniel
Norie
Lyall
Chalmers
Kynoch
Esson

Law
Davidson
Sim
Bathia Rae
Black
Fraser
Lyon
Milne[28]
Wisely
Kellas[29]
Brechen
Valentine
Sangster
Imray
Gammie
Kiloh (Greek "thousand")
Malcolm
Riddell

Polson
Hardie
Booth
Mensal
Barron
Lobban
Stewart
Pirie
Kilgour
Kennedy
Kemp
Watt
Gellon
Vass
Mellis (Greek "honey")
Wyness
Gill
Tawse

Tarves Cemetery

Knox
Tough
Skinner
Catto
Robb
Norrie
Shepherd
Luias
Argo
Simmers
Toquhoun
Kynoch
Marr
Strath
Scrogie
Davie
Brechen
Campbell
Chyne
Coull
Barrack
Hay
Sim
Argo

Norrie
Florence
Thom
Annand
Pirie
Perry
Sutherland
Davidson (many)
Dickie
Wallace
Fraser
Hardie
Kiloh
Aiken
Burr
Gaven
Bean
Hatt
Leslie
Jack
Leask
Cassie
Campbell
Troup

Mann (fr. Menachem)
Hay
Godsman
Barron
Chapman
Mair
Riddel
Brown
Legg
Loggie
Rannie
Garden
Moir
Allardyce
Gray
Petrie
Duguid
Tomb: Forbes/Gordon 1589
Nory
Moir
Gelon
Black
Lind
Duthie

Tarriff Cemetery
(several flat stones)

Tarras	Jamieson	Murray
Hepburn	Adam	Milne
Rainie	Pratt	Panton
Imlach	Black	Brown
Skene	Cowie	Mouat
Pirie	Davidson	Grieve
Taws, Tawse	Mavor	Shirof
Gaule	Gordon	Taes
Barclay	Jolly	Tough
Lepper	Grassie	Leslie
Forbes	Dalgarno	Towie
Crombie	Barclay	Dallas
Mowat (1558)	Fraser	Gall
Murray	Milne	Caeie
Hay	Cruickshank	Lyon (1541)
Leggat	Lawson	Alexander
Forrest	Joss	Cheyne
Gallen	Mackie	Kemp
Fowlie	Tyloar	Chivas
Cumine	Chapman	Custinie
Gray	Hay	Mair
Allardice	Tarras	Hebren (Hebron)
Morrison	Catto (= Katz)	Barnet (fr. Issachar)[30]
Bathia Sim	Jacobina Cheviz	Stoble
Pirrie	Diack	Loban

Tyrie Churchyard

Murray	Fowlie	Pirie
Lyon	Lee	McRobbie
Trail	Gray	Wallace
Burnet	Cruickshank	Davidson
Davidson	Tocher	Dickie
Rettel	Michie	Lovie
Bisset	Sinclair	Sangster
Campbell	Pratt	Watt
Lowe	Esslemont	Anderson
Simpson	Shirer	McKessar
Fraser	Forbes	Shirran
Bruce	Gallan	Merson
Barron	Greig	Massie
Lovie	Duffus	Birnie (Ger. "pear place")

Mercer (French "merchant")	Giles	Gammack
Mowat	Wallace	Slessor ("one fr. Silesia")
Black	Corbett	Knox
Jaffray	Beaton	Chivas
Lunan	Hepburn	

Aberdeen

We now turn to the population of Aberdeen proper, the earliest useful record for which is the list of merchant and trade burgesses, beginning 1600–1620. To become a burgess required social, political and economic standing in the community. It was a hereditary status, passed from father to son and not granted to outsiders unless they married the daughter of a burgess. The names of several burgesses in Aberdeen from 1600 to 1620, 1631 to 1639 and 1640 to 1659 are listed below. As the reader will see, they include a great many names that are, *prima facie*, Sephardic, French Jewish and even Islamic.

From 1600 to 1620, for example, we find Allies (= Ali, *Arabic* for "man"), Balmanno, Frachar, Gareauche, Horne (cp. Hebrew *shofar*), Menzies, Pantoune and Zutche. From 1621 to 1639, names such as Alshinor, Ezatt, Goldman, Omay, and Zuill appear on the list. The time period of the 1640s and 1650s sees Arrat, Daniell, Dovie, Izods, Pittullo and Yair added. By the time of the first Scottish national census in 1696, additional Jewish and Islamic surnames had made their home in Aberdeen, including Deuran (cp. the rabbinical family of Duran), Orem, Lucas, Scrimgeor, Monyman, Aeson, de Pamaer, and Lorimer. By the late 1700s (1751–1796) a list of apprentices in Aberdeen included Chillas, Gillet, Kemlo, Silver, and Tilleray.

1696 Census: Aberdeen Environs

The 1696 census also sheds light on who was living in the areas around Aberdeen. For example, in Belkelvie and New Machar we find Barok, Brockie, Salmon, Talzor, Cowane, Hervie, Wysehart, Pyet and Essell (Heb. Assael). And in nearby Daviot, Bethelnie and Bourtie, there are the surnames Hebron, Gammie, Lunan, Shivas, Shirres, Argoe, Currie, Yool, Benzie and Japp.

Although we have not listed all the surnames in the northeast section of Scotland, we have given a representative sampling in the lists published here. What is striking is the very low incidence of "traditional" Scottish surnames (once the origin of aristocratic Jewish families like Gordon, Fraser, Leslie and their ilk is factored in). The candidate population for a significant paternal genetic legacy in Aberdeen strongly resembles the Sephardic Jewish contribution to the founders of Colombia, a Spanish colony established in South America at about the same time.

The male and female lines of the Colombian population were genetically mapped in exacting detail by Carvajal-Carmona and his team of geneticists at the University of Antioquia (2000). They found an unusually large (16 percent) frequency of paternal

Semitic ancestry, including the Cohen modal haplotype of Jewish priests (p. 1290). Similarly, the correspondence between Jewish names mentioned in the records of the Spanish Inquisition and reflected in the Aberdeen burgess and merchant lists is much too high to be coincidental. In both records one can trace the path of Jewish refugees fleeing the Iberian Peninsula in order to escape the long arm of the Holy Office. If readers were to tabulate the *complete* listings in the original documents we cite using the surname touchstones we have argued for in these pages, around 50 percent of the surnames would fall into the French-Jewish/Sephardic/Islamic column.[31] Those marked with an asterisk appear in the same form in a contemporaneous record of Jewish surnames compiled by the Spanish Inquisition.[32]

Aberdeen Merchant and Trade Burgesses, 1600–1620

Adam*	Cristia[n]*)	Vida(l)*)
Adie	Crukshank	Herauld (Ila)
Aiken[33]	Curror (cp. Curuyra*)	Hervie
Aillies	Cuschny	his majesty
Aittour	Davidson (cp. David*)	Hoip
Alschenor	Dolas (cp. Dola,* Dols,* Dolz*)	Horne (cp. Trompero*)
Anderson	Dougall	Innes (cp. Islas*)
Annand (cp. Anna*)	Dower	Jaffray
Bairres	Duvie	Jameson (cp. Jacobei,
Balfour	Enzie	Jaimes/z)
Balmanno	Espline (cp. Esspina/o*)	Junkyne
Banerman	Falaquero* "potter")	Kay (cp. Caes*)
Barbor (= "Berber")	Farchar (Abraham, cp.	Kello
Barcar	Farfar	Kempt ("one from Kempes")
Bethun (fr. Béthune)	Ferrie (cp. Ferriz*)	Kynnoir
Bissett	Flesher (cp. Carneiro* etc.)	Lamb (cp. Lamo*)
Black	Forbes (Sp. Febos*)	Lautie
Boduall	Fraser	Leidis
Brabner ("one from Brabant")	Fresser (Lat. Frisius* "one	Leslie
Brown (cp. Pardo)	from Frisia")	Lillie
Bruce	Freynd (= Ger. Freund,	Logie
Burrie	"friend")	Low (cp. Leo*)
Calder (cp.	Gairdyn	Lyell
Caldera, Calderone)	Gallant (cp. Galante*, fr.	Maissoun
Calvelay	Ital.)	Makkie
Cant (cp. Cantos*)	Gareauche	Malice
Carkeall	Gelly	Manteith
Chalmer	Gerard	Marr
Cheine (cp. Bel*)	Gib (cp. Gibre*)	Martine*
Chessure	Gordon (cp. Gordo*)	Mayne
Chives (cp. Chaves, Heb.	Gorine	Menzies (cp. Menezes*)
"friend")	Gray (Sp. Gris*)	Mercur
Chrystie (cp.	Guild	Merschall
Cp. Gutierrez*	Guthrie (Hercules)	Merser*
Cristell (= crystal)	Hay (cp. Haym,* Hayon,*	Moir (cp. Pardo*)

Morrison
Mowat (Heb. "excellent")
Murray (= Moiré)
Narne (Heb. candle)
Nauchtie
Norvell
Olephant
Paitrie ("pear tree," Peirera*)
Pantoune
Perrie (cp. Pere*)
Puiridok
Ranye (= Rainey)
Richie (cp. Rich,* Rico*)

Ross (cp. Rojas* "red")
Sandelands
Sanderis
Schand (Ger. "shame")
Scherar (cp. Serra*)
Schewane (cp. Bello*)
Sengzor (cp. Sanger*)
Settoun
Stewart
Sym (cp. Simo*)
Symsoun
Taysche
Toshe

Touche
Toux
Troup
Ussey
Vilguis
Waldgrew
Watson
Wolffrumber, John (1617),
   apothecary to
Yester
Zutche

Aberdeen Merchant and Trade Burgesses, 1621–1639

Adam
Aickyn
Aillies
Aittoun
Alexander
Allaides
AlShiror
Annand
Astian
Bachup
Balfour
Barclay
Barnet (Assyrian)
Bastardus, Rochus (fr. Zee-
   land)34
Brabner
Brown
Bruce
Burnet
Burrie
Caddell
Callendar
Cassie
Castell, David
Chessur
Cheyne
Christall
Cruikshank
Cushnie
Dalgarno
Daskorie
Dason
Davidson (many)

Divinnes
Douglas (many)
Duncan
Ellis
Elphingstoune
Ezatt
Falconer
Ferrar ("one from Ferrara")
Fiddes
Fleming
Forbes (many)
Fraser (many)
Gairdyn (many)
Galliar
Gardauch
Garioche
Geddes
Gilzean
Goldman
Gordon (many)
Gourlay
Gray
Greyushead
Gudeaill
Guthrie
Hackett
Hamman
Hay (many)
Hervie
Higgein
Horne
Innes
Irving

Jaffray
Jack (= Jacob)
Keith
Kelo
Kempt
Kennedy
Ker
Low
Lunan
Lyon
Macky
Mair
Maleis
Malice
Mar
Marischal
Massie
Maule
Mayen (fr. Mainz)
Meiser
Menzies (many)
Mihie
Moir
Moncreiff
Mowatt
Muirhead
Murray
Musset
Norie
Oliphant
Omay
Ord
Paip

Panton
Pattoun
Paulitius
Peires
Pendillberie
Petindreiche
Pirie
Pouters
Prymrois
Raff
Raithe
Rattrau
Ray
Reid
Rickard

Ridge, Abraham
Rogie
Rollok
Rose
Ross
Sanders
Sandilands
Scherar
Seton
Sibbald
Simon (Master of Lovat)
Sinclair
Skeyne
Spottiswood
Stavines

Stewart
Storie
Strachan
Sym
Tarres
Thoiris
Tillie, Arrell
Touch
Toux
Vallange
Vas
Wear
Whippa
Zuil

Aberdeen Merchant and Trade Burgesses, 1640–1659

Abercrombie
Adam
Aikinhead
Alder
Alexander
Allardes
Ardudill
Arnot
Arrat
Banar
Banerman
Barclay
Barham
Barnet (Assyrian)
Bisset
Black
Brown
Bruce
Bucas (Abraham)
Burrell
Campbell
Chapman
Chaser
Chessor
Chisenis
Christie
Couper, Elias
Couzies
Cushny
Cymer
Dalgarno

Dalgleish
Daniell
Davidson
Davie
Dazell
Desburrow
Divy
Dobie
Dougall
Douglas
Duffus
Duighet
Dune
Durat
Duvant
Eisot
Eresot
Ergo
Falconer
Fermor
Forbes
Gordon
Gray
Guidall
Harvie
Hayter
Heres
Herone
Horne
Hydmoir
Innes

Izods
Jaffray
Jamieson
Keilo (Gr. Kilo)
Kempt
Kennedy
King, Hans Jacob
Law
Leslie
Liewe (Flem. "one fr. Lou-
    vain")
Lillie
Logie
Love
Low
Makie
Marno
Massie
Massonet
Massoun
Melville
Menzies
Merser
Mershaell
Metcalf, Hadrian
Mirrelou
Moir
Moncur
Morrell[35]
Mosley
Moss (Moses)

Mowat (merchant in Paris)	Robson	Stoker
Peirie	Sandelands	Tarves
Petrie	Schivell, David	Titus
Peugue	Scrogie	Tosch
Pittullo	Shirron	Troup
Progeris	Sibbald	Urrie
Purvie	Silvester	Valor
Raven (cp. Corvo, Raban)	Simson	Wachop
Reniken	Sinclair	Watt
Rhind	Skene	Weir, Jasper
Riauch	Skougall (David)	Winzet
Ritchie	Steinson	Wyllie
Ritter, Elias	Stewart	Yair

Aberdeen and Freedom Lands Census, 1696

Abell	Davidsone	Joss
Adam	De Pamaer	Keilo
Adam	Deuchars	Keith
Aeson	Deuran	Kempt
Aisone	Divvie	Kennedie
Alexander	Downie	King[36]
Allardes	Duffus	Kynach
Annand	Falconer	Lamb
Austeen	Forbes	Lawson
Bannerman	Forbes	Leonard
Barnet	Forbesses	Leslie
Binny	Foullar	Leys
Birnie	Fraser	Liddell
Bisset	Gall	Lilly (Arab. Sason)
Blacbree	Gallan	Logie
Black	Garden	Lorimer
Black	Garioch	Low
Blaire	Gibb	Low
Brans	Gillo	Lowrie
Brown	Godsman	Lucas
Bruice	Gordon	Lyall
Carnegie	Gray	Mackie
Cassie	Gray	Malis
Castle	Harrow	Mann (Heb.)
Catto (= Katz)	Harvie	Mark
Cheyn	Hay	Marr
Christall	Hay (several)	Martein
Christie	Hendrie	Martine
Coupland	Honyman	Massie
Cowie	Hosack	Matheson
Cruickshank	Innes	Maver
Cushnie	Jack	Mavor
Dalbarno	Jamesone	Mellon

Melvill
Menzies
Mercer
Milne
Moffet
Moire
Moire
Mollyson
Monecht
Mowat
Mowat
Murray
Neper
Nicholl
Noble
Norie
Oliphant
Orem
Paip
Panton
Peacock
Pedder

Peirie
Phanes
Philp
Pirie
Proat
Rae
Ragg
Reed
Riach
Rickart
Ritchie
Rolland
Ross
Sandilands
Sangster
Sangster
Schand
Scrimgeor
Scrogie
Seaton
Sharp (Ger. Kuhn)
Shewan

Shirres (fr. Shiraz, Persia)
Simer
Smellie
Snawie (cp. Cano, Niveaux, Whitehead)
Soupar
Speed
Speidie
Strachan
Stuart
Taite
Thow
Toash
Touch
Toux
Toux
Troup
Wallace
Watt
Yeats
Yooll

Aberdeen Apprentices, 1751–1796

Abel
Adam
Allardyce
Barclay
Barron
Bean
Bennet (Heb. Baruch)
Black
Burnett
Caie
Cassie
Catto
Chillas
Christie
Clerihue
Collie
Courage
Cowie
Cromar
Cruikshank
Cushny
Dalgarno
Davidson
Diack

Duncan
Dyce
Esson
Falconer
Fettes
Fleming
Forbes
Frazier
Gall
Gillet
Gordon
Greenlaw
Hacket
Harvie
Hogg
Horne
Howie
Imlay
Izat
Jaffrey
Kemlo
Kemp
Kiloh
Law

Legate
Levie
Leys
Low
Lunan
Lyell
Mair
Marnock
Mass
Massie
Mathieson
Menzies
Mercer
Moir
Morice
Morison
Murray
Napier
Nowall
Petrie
Pirie
Rae
Rainee
Rhind

Riach
Riddell
Robb
Ross
Sang
Sheriffs
Silver

Singer
Stark (German form of
  Amos)[37]
Stewart
Stillas
Symers
Tilleray

Tocher
Tough
Troup
Turriff
Watt
Wishar

Belhalvie and New Machar Census

Adie
Aiken
Anand
Annand
Bannerman
Bannerman
Barok (Heb.)
Barrok
Benzie
Bisset
Black (2)
Brockie
Broune
Catow
Catto
Caye
Chyn (Shin, schön)
Cockee
Couie
Courag
Cowane (= Cohen)
Cristall
Crocket (= Crocquetaine)
Crystie
Currie
Dallas
Daniell
Darg
Davedson
Davedson
Davie
Dewar
Essell

Gill
Gordon
Gray
Gray
Harvie
Hergeries
Hervie
Hervie
Innes (2)
Jacksone
Jafray
Jameson
Jamieson
Jesseman
Kemp
Ker
Lamb
Leslie
Logie
Lucas
Lyon
Lyon
Lyon
Mackie
Mairtine
Man
Menzies (2)
Moir
Morres
Murey
Mury
Naper
Pantoun

Peirie
Peirie
Peiris (Sp. Peres)
Petrie
Pirri
Pirrie
Pyet
Reanie
Rhaney
Robb
Roch
Salmon
Salmond (2)
Salmone
Samson
Sangster
Seymour (Heb.)
Shirreff
Shirres
Shirres
Shirris (2)
Sim
Simsone
Symon
Taillior ("fringer")
Talzor
Talzor
Tempell
Tyrie
Viccar
Walentine
Warrock
Wysehart

1696 Census: Daviot, Bethelnie, Bourtie

Adam Syme	Forbes	Morress
Annand	Gammie	Norvell
Annand	Gellas	Panton
Argoe	Gellen	Panton
Austian	Gray	Petrie
Bannerman	Harvie	Pierie
Banon	Hebron	Pierie
Banzie	Hebron	Rae
Barrie	Imblae	Rainie
Benzies	Jack	Rerie
Birnie (Ger. "peary")	Jamesone	Sewan
Black	Japp	Shirres
Black	Joss	Shirres
Brick	Kemp	Shirres
Broune	Kempe	Shivas
Chassier	Law	Shives
Christie	Lesly	Sime
Cristell	Lunan	Stark
Currie	Lunan	Steinsone
Davidsone	Lunane	Sympsone
Davidsone	Lyon	Tappe
Davie	Lyon	Watt
Dounie	Mackie	Wican
Dysart	Mathewsone	Yool
Elphinstone	Merchant (= Heb. Jacob)[38]	

Further, there is also surname evidence that this exotic population extended north to the Orkney Islands. The Orkneys were ruled by the Sinclair family—of Templar fame—and thus it would make sense that they would permit Templar-linked refugees to settle on their lands. In the Yell Cemetery on Orkney, likely named after the Hebrew Jehiel ("God lives")—there is also a Yell County, Arkansas, incidentally—we find, for example, a Hosea Hoseason, a Basil Pole, a Jemima Jeromson and a Janet Tarel—all domiciled there quite recently.

The Orkney Island surname genealogy listings include Annal, Arnot, Esson, Gorrie, Lyon, Davie, Gullion, Holland, Hourie and Omand as "native born." Patterns such as these call into serious question the presumption that even these northernmost portions of Scotland were inhabited by persons primarily of Viking/Scandinavian descent. Indeed, genetic investigations of the population in the remote north of Scotland have found the gene pool there surprisingly low in "Viking genes," though how much of the dominant Atlantic Modal Haplotype (AMH) is Celtic and how much is Iberian has not yet been reliably determined; see, for instance, Wilson et al. 2001, also Helgason et al. 2000.

Mid- and South Yell: Orkney Cemetery

Tamar[39] Nisbet 1947
Robina Stewart
Daniel Moar (= Moor) 1896
Jakob Sualland 1905 (Scandinavian)
Hannah Scollay 1979
Johanna Hoseason 1922
John Green 1945
Jemima Grace (fr. Garcia, Gratia) 1947
Hosea Hoseason 1824
Williamina Omand 1966
Thomasina Mouat 1958
Basil Pole 1874

Jemima Mann 1957
Laurina Jamieson 1972
Marabella Henderson 1906
Jemima Jeromson 1902
Lillias, Tamar Gilbert 1941, 1985
Davina Hoseason 1976
Davina Brown 1997
Jessamine Stewart 1972
Basil Sinclair 1904
Alexander Danielson 1931
Hose Moar 1900
Janet Tarel 1907

Surnames from Orkney Genealogy

Annal
Arcus
Arnet
Arnot
Balfour
Ballantyne
Baikie
Barnet
Berger
Burghar
Berstan
Bichan
Black
Bremner ("from Bremen")
Brock
Brown
Calder
Corrigal
Corsie
Copland
Cowper
Cruickshank
Cumming
Dass
Davidson
Davie
Delday

Esson
Fea
Flett
Foulis
Fraser
Garrioch
Gibson
Goar (Heb.)
Gorn
Gorrie
Gray
Grieve
Gullion
Gunn (Heb.)
Guthrie
Harvie
Hepburn
Hercus
Holland
Horrie, Hourie
Irvine, Irving
Isbister
Kemp
King
Lamb
Lennie
Leslie

Melville
Michal
Michael
Milne
Mitchell
Moar
Morwick
Mowat
Muir
Murray
Nesbit
Nicolson
Nisbet
Omand (Turk.)
Paplay
Pauvy
Peace
Petrie
Reid
Rich, Ritch
Robertson, Robson
Rosie
Ross
Sandison
Shearer
Stuart
Towrie

Dennison	Linay	Vallion
Dick	Lyon	Velzian
Durran	Marwick	Watt
Ballenden	Matheson	Wishart
Bews	Mathewson	Young

Source: http://www.cursiter.com/pages/origins.htm

Aberdeen and the World: 1200–1750

We believe that it was this Judaic community that provided Aberdeen its large role as an international center of trade from the 1200s onward. Keith (1974, p. 46–47) writes:

As commerce went in those days, Aberdeen plied a busy trade in the fifteenth century with both the Netherlands and the Baltic ports, Danzig and Poland particularly. The Danzig business developed sharply after 1500 [when additional Sephardim would have arrived there from Iberia], and during the next 200 years the number of *Scotsmen* trading in Poland was so large as to become proverbial. Several observers put them at 40,000.... After 1500 there were Aberdonians of the name of Skene with cloth mills and sugar refineries in Poland.... The older and steadier commerce was with the Low Countries. Bruges, Middleburg, and Campvere were in turn the Scottish staple there — the clearing-house for all Scottish imports....

There were about half a dozen great Aberdonian shipping families — the Cullens, Blindseles, Rattrays, Fiddeses and Pratts. Greatest of all the town's merchants were Andrew Cullen and Andrew Buk. Cullen was Provost in 1506 and 1535.... Even Bishop Elphinstone engaged in the overseas trade, though as a priest he must have procured a special licence to do so (!). When he was building King's College he sent abroad wool, salmon, trout, and money, receiving in exchange carts, wheelbarrows, and gunpowder — to quarry and transport the freestone from Elgin which he was using in Old Aberdeen.

Royalty also was closely aligned with Aberdeen. David II had opened a mint there for the making of coins and his sister Matilda was married to Thomas Isaac (obviously Jewish), a clerk and burgess of the city. By the early 1400s, a Sephardic family, the Menezes/Menzies, had arrived. Keith (1974, p. 67) comments:

In the first half of the fifteenth century, a new family appears upon the scene. The Chalmerses [from de Camera, Cameron, Chambers, meaning "chamberlain"] were still at the height of their influence when the first member of this house, which was to rule the destinies of Aberdeen for 200 years, made his appearance in the provost's seat. This was Gilbert Menzies, surmised to have been a son of Sir Robert Menzies of Wemyss. Gilbert came from Perthshire[40] to Aberdeen about 1408.... No more brilliant autocratic family than the Menzies ever resided in Aberdeen. They held their heads high before royalty; they lived side by side with the most opulent of the nobility.

Also prominent among Aberdeen's leading families were the Bannermans, one of whom, Alexander Bannerman, was physician to David II. Yet another was Robert Davidson. John Barbour (= Berber) became archdeacon of Aberdeen in 1357. Keith (1974, p. 95) notes he "was a scholar and a man of business, as well as a priest and a poet ... and above all, he was a historian.... He several times audited the King's household accounts and those of the Exchequer.... He twice traveled in France. Both David II and Robert II gave him pensions." Another Aberdeen provost, in 1416, was Thomas Roull (= Raoul), mentioned by Keith (p. 97).

Keith also records (p. 104) that an Andrew Schivas was the "Master of Schools" for Aberdeen. And the same Skene family that was operating linen factories and sugar mills in Poland also produced Gilbert Skene, who held the chair of medicine at Kings College in 1556 and became physician to King James IV. Skene also authored the first book on medicine in Scotland. Even earlier, Bernard Gordon had written an excellent treatise on the subject (1305 C.E.), and this text was still in use at the renowned medical school of Salerno (Italy) in 1480.

Another Gordon, one named Patrick, held the Hebrew chair at Marischal University in Aberdeen in 1642. Keith (p. 176) informs us he "learned Hebrew from a Jew": most likely, he already knew it. And yet another Gordon, Thomas, was making regular trips to the island of Leghorn in Italy during the early 1600s. At this time, Leghorn, or Livorno, had a large and prosperous Jewish population, thanks to licenses and special dispensations by the de Medici rulers of Florence; it was also the center of the coral export trade with India (gems and metals were the import goods). John Burnet, another Aberdonian, was already engaged in the tobacco trade with Maryland and Virginia. In English eyes, the Scottish tobacco trade was illegal. It was carried out behind the backs of the merchants of the Royal Exchange in London, becoming enormously profitable in years when Aberdonian and Glaswegian traders managed to undercut the state contract with France.

A wealthy Scottish merchant and financier in Danzig, Robert Gordon, left £10,000 for the establishment of a school for indigent boys in Aberdeen. Another Gordon from London, William, was the doctor of medicine at Kings College from 1632 to 1640. He had been educated at Padua in Italy and studied dissection, which he introduced into the medical curriculum. He also served as the business manager for the college (Keith, pp. 306, 339).

Not all the scions of Jewish-descended families in the North of Scotland, however, were pillars of polite society. Several were smugglers (Wilkins 1995). In France, an Alexander Gordon of St. Martins and a Robert Gordon of Bordeaux supplied John Stewart of Inverness, Scotland, with contraband salt and liquor. Similarly, Andrew Cruikshank, John Sutherland, and Alexander Brodie smuggled tobacco from Port Hampton, Virginia, to their factory in Gourdon during the American War of Independence, proving perhaps once again that money outbids politics when it comes to power.

Finally we must ask the question: Did these Aberdonian families still maintain social and economic ties with their ancestral families in France and with other Crypto-Jews in that country or elsewhere? We believe the answer is a resounding Yes and will use the overseas suppliers of Stewart et al. shown as a case in point. First, the reader is invited to take at look at the list of cities with which these Scots had trading relationships. They range from Scandinavia (Copenhagen, Stockholm, Bergen) to Holland (Rotterdam), to France (Rouen, Boulogne), to Spain (Barcelona), to Italy (Livorno) — all places of Sephardic Crypto-Jewish settlement after the Inquisition. Further, the trading partners used in these cities included not only persons with relatives or ancestors now in Aberdeen (e.g., Robert Gordon and John McLeod in Bordeaux; Campbell in Stockholm; Farquhar in Bergen, Norway), but — very importantly — Jewish trading houses which would usually only trade with other Jewish companies. For example, Jacob Ferray in Le Havre; Shalet, Vonder and Ferrant in Barcelona; and Rosenmeyer, Flor and Co. in Frederickswaag. This, we posit, is strong evidence of a common Judaic awareness and ethnic identity recognized on an international level.

Overseas Suppliers Used by John Stewart, William Watt Jr. & Co., and Alexander Bain Jr. & Co.

Stockholm: Nelleton & Campbell, Montgomery Mould & Fenick, Campbell, Gerrard & Dobson

Gothenburg: Hugh Ross

Danzig: Marjoribanks & Coutts, Francis Grant

Hamburg: David Barclay, Bartholomew Bludworth

Copenhagen: Alexander Ross

Amsterdam: Jackson & Bradley

Rotterdam: Alexander Andrew, Robert Gerrard, John Gordon, Robert Mackay

Campvere: David Gregory

"In Holland": John MacDonald

Boulogne: Charles Smith

Rouen: Robert Arbuthnott

Havre: Jacob Ferray

St Martins: John Souper, Alexander Gordon

Bordeaux: Robert Gordon, John MacLeod

Bilbao: Ivan van Duffel

Barcelona: Shalet, Vonder & Ferrant, Winder & Ferrand

Leghorn/Livorno: Aickman & Winder, Godfrey & Hudson

Bergen: William Farquhar, Jesper de Fine

Rotterdam: William Murdoch, George Gibson

Frederickswaag, North Faro: Rosenmeyer, Flor & Co

Gothenburg: Low & Smith

Dunkirk: Alexander Hunter

Equally eloquent of Scottish Jews' ties to other countries are the names of Scots who served in the Russian military or operated businesses in Russia during the 1600s and 1700s. Russia at this time was extremely accommodating to Jews from a variety of countries, Poland, Germany, Pomerania and Hungary among them, in an effort to internationalize its economy. Virtually all of Scotland's leading families sent members to Russia. Among the most noteworthy were the Gordons and Davidsons. The latter became Davidoffs/Davidovs, and both of them have Russian (and doubtless also Israeli) descendants recognized as Jewish. Indeed the two Russian Jewish Gordons whose DNA we tested both carried the Kohanim gene.

Scots Serving in the Russian Army or Operating Businesses in Russia, 1600–1800

Sir Robert Adair 1791
James Adamson 1600s
John Adie 1632
James Afflech 1632
Adam Aikman 1600s
James Alexander 1690s
Alexander Annan 1631
John Annand 1660
Andrew Arbuthnot 1606
John Arnot 1600s
James Balfour 1770
James Bannatine 1632
_____ Bannerman 1661
Peter Barclay 1664
Achilles Beaton 1632
John Bell 1691
Robert Bowie 1771
David Broun 1600s
Andrew Bruce 1632
James Daniel Bruce
   1686–1698–1726
William Bruce 1647
Lewis Calderwood 1755
Charles Cameron 1772
John Carr /Kar 1618*
Robert Carr /Kerr 1610*
David Carran 1529
William Carrick 1783
John Christie 1790s
Alexander Clerk 1722
   (= Schreiber)
William Colley 1795
David Cooper 1632*
Thomas Dalyell 1656
Vladimir Davidov 1809
   (Davidson descendant)
Gilbert Davidson 1632
Peter Davidson 1479
William Davidson 1632
Alexander Davie 1761
Francis Douglas 1634
Simon Douglas 1710
Kenneth Duffus 1732

James Duncan 1630
John Elphinston 1769
Gabriel Elphinstone 1500s
Robert Erskine 1704
Henry Farquharson 1698
Robert Fleck 1632 (Ger. for
   Fr. moir "spotted")
George Forbes 1675
James Forbes 1633
William Freer 1768
Andrew Gardyne 1650
Thomas Garvine 1690
Charles Gascoigne 1737
Isaac Geddes 1630s
Hay George 1763
David Gilbert 1625
John Gilbert 1637
Alexander Gordon 1632
Alexander Gordon 1632
Alexander Gordon 1695
Alexander Gordon 1710
Alexander Gordon 1739
George Gordon 1690s
Harie Gordon 1691
Henry Gordon 1784
James Gordon 1632
James Gordon 1689
Patrick Gordon 1661†
Robert Gordon 1632
Theodore Gordon 1681
Thomas Gordon 1717
William Gordon 1632
William Gordon 1692
William Gordon 1764
David Graham 1639
Mungo Graham 1730
Gilbert Gray 1632
Samuel Greig 1735
James Grieve 1733
John Grieve 1778
William Guild 1685
Thomas Guthrie 1632
Alexander Hamilton 1661

Alexander Hamilton 1670
Andrey Hamilton 1647
Ivan Hamilton 1705
Johan Hamilton 1660s
John Hamilton 1629
John Hamilton 1678
Mary Hamilton 1690s
Peter Hamilton 1715
Thomas Hamilton 1542
David Hay 1630
Gelenus Hay 1784
John Hay 1725
Thomas Hay 1650s
William Hay 1661
William Hay 1718
L. Isaac 1784
Gabriel Kar*
George Keith 1650s
George Keith 1661
James Keith 1696
Robert Keith 1774
William Keith 1632
Alexander Leslie 1618*
_____ Lewis 1700s
John Livingstone 1630s
Archibald Lovell 1632
Peter Lyall 1632
Peter Lyon 1632
James Main 1659
Thomas Marr 1632
John Menzies 1670
Thomas Menzies 1660
William Menzies 1670
John Moubray 1600s
John Muir 1661
Andrew Murray 1632
Ethan Murray 1632
James Murray 1632
Peter Murray 1632
William Murray /Morea
   1636
George Napier 1730s
George Ogilvy 1648

*Still many descendants in Russia.
†Served Tsar Peter the Great, Jacobite, left many sons and kinsmen in Russia.

Alexander Orrie 1632
Archibald Primrose 1632
David Primrose 1632
James Ramsay 1646
George Rattray 1632
William Riach /Reach 1632
David Ruthven 1600s
Anthony Saunders 1632
William Scrymgeour 1632

Walter Sharp 1752
Malcolm Sinclair 1709
George Skene 1617
Albert Stewart 1678
Gile Stewart 1632
Neill Stewart 1739
William Stewart 1610**
John Stranack 1770s
  (Freemason)

Alexander Swan 1632
Henry Wallace 1632
James Wardlaw 1632
Robert Watson 1632
James Wauchop 1630
James Wemyss 1629
Job Wood 1632
Peter Yuille 1615

**A number of Stewarts became noblemen in Russia and Sweden.*

Chapter 10

The Religions of Scotland: Did Presbyterianism Have Crypto-Jewish Origins?

This book began with a provocative idea: Scotland is, or was, Jewish. The previous chapters have explored the Jewish ancestry and culture of some of Scotland's leading families and much of her population. We now present an equally unlikely thesis, which we nonetheless believe is correct: that the origins of the Protestant Reformation and especially the particular form it took in Scotland — Presbyterianism — also lie in Judaic influences. Both authors of this investigation were not only told growing up that we were of Scottish origin, but we were also raised in the Protestant faith. Just as we subsequently discovered that our "Scottish" roots were not Celtic, but Sephardic and French Jewish, so also were we led to question the traditional origins of Scottish Protestantism.

As was the case with us, most readers probably "learned" that Scotland began as a pagan country, Druidic, worshiping nature and the sun. And then, around 560 C.E. St. Columba (Columcille, born around 521, died 597)[1] arrived from Ireland, established the first Christian monastery at Iona and began converting the surrounding countryside to Christianity. Ostensibly, the entire land was then won over to Roman Catholicism and remained loyal to that form of Christianity until John Knox and other reformers led Scotland to Protestantism in the 1560s.

As we saw in chapter 1, however, the actual history of religion in Scotland is much more equivocal and unsettled. Modern-day pilgrims who visit "St. Columba's abbey church" on the remote island of Iona to revel in its Celtic past usually do not stop to think that the cruciform structure actually dates from the ninth century, four hundred years after Columba lived, and was built as a monument to mark the triumph of Roman Catholicism over the Celtic religion, which was then consigned to oblivion. There are very few artifacts preserved of the original Celtic church, and almost no texts that have not been overlaid with subsequent (and suspect) traditions of orthodoxy. The oldest authentic symbols that can be tied to the Columban church occur on the Monymusk reliquary, which lacks any depiction of a cross, Chi-Ro, or other Christian iconography, exhibiting only a zoomorphic form of decoration similar to that of the surrounding "pagan" population.

Indeed, Donald Meek, professor of Celtic Studies at the University of Aberdeen, has suggested that the great bulk of what we think we know about the Celtic church is a romantic construction, the creation of poets like the eighteenth-century "Ossian" and, more recently, of "feel-good Celticists" and New Age enthusiasts (2000, chapters 1–6).

Moreover, the term "Celtic" lay dormant from antiquity until it was revived by the humanist George Buchanan, the tutor to Mary Queen of Scots and later to her son, the future James I of England (Atherton 2002, pp. 24–28). The label itself is a misconception, and recent critics have even withdrawn the use of the word "church" from the phrase "Celtic church" on the grounds that it implies a hierarchy and organization that never existed (pp. 51–52).

There are glimmers of Judaism as a precursor and companion to Christianity in the British Isles. Deansley (1963) notes that the earliest Roman-era saints were named Alban, Aaron and Julius, though they do not appear in official martyrologies (p. 6), while we have remarked previously on the unique status of Wales's St. David. We have also seen that the earliest saint of the Irish church, Ninyas, was perhaps so named because he came, via Gaul, from Ninevah in the Middle East. There is some evidence of relations with Mediterranean Greeks, Jews and Syrians in the Roman period, increasingly so in the sixth century and later. Moreover, the greatest point of difference between the old-style "Celtic" monks and those of Anglo-Saxon England revolved around the celebration of Easter: the Scots "reckoning like Jews ... [even though] they knew that Christians always celebrate the Resurrection on the first day of the week" (p. 85). The Scots and "northern Irish" long clung to their custom of celebrating Easter (Latin *Paschua*, "Passover") on the same day as Jews, even after the Synod of Whitby attempted to settle the controversy in 664 C.E. (pp. 85–90). Finally, we should raise the possibility that the second point of divergence often emphasized by scholars, the "Celtic" tonsure in which the front of the head, rather than top, was shaved, may have been inspired by a literal adherence to the injunction of the Torah to signal one's Jewish identity to other nations by ensuring that the Shema (creed) and Commandments "serve as a symbol (frontlet) on your forehead" (Ex. 6:8). This peculiar badge of faith and ethnicity also persisted in Scotland, down to the age of the Templars, and nowhere else in all of Christendom.[2]

As for the underlying paganism that both Judaism and Christianity fought, forms of nature worship such as the Green Man fertility cult can be found in castles and kirks across Scotland. Indeed, paganism died a hard, slow death in Celtic lands, which developed a religious identity of their own and often proved immune to the militant Christianity on the continent, according to Jones and Pennick (1995, pp. 96–110):

> In Wales, Scotland, Ireland and Brittany, the old gods, worshipped sometimes under the guise of Celtic saints (i.e. those not canonized by the Pope), were revered in truly Pagan fashion.... In 1589, John Ansers reported that bullocks were sacrificed "the half to God and to Beino" in the churchyard at Clynog, Lleyn, Wales.... Such cattle were ... sold for slaughter by the churchwarden on Trinity Sunday. The custom fell into disuse in the nineteenth century.... Pagan observances continue in the twentieth century in Celtic countries. A Pagan prayer, collected around 1910 by W.Y. Evans-Wentz from an old Manx woman, invokes the

Celtic god of the sea.... In the Scottish Highlands, libations of milk are poured on a special hollowed stone ... in honour of the Gruagach, a goddess who watches over the cows.... Until modern times in Iona similar libations were poured to a god corresponding to Neptune....

Paganism flourished in Scotland after the break-up of the Catholic Church. In the region of Gaerloch, Wester Ross, the "old rites" of the divinity Mhor-Ri, the Great King, transformed into St Maree, Mourie or Maelrubha, were observed until the nineteenth century. In 1656, the Dingwall Presbytery, "findeing amongst uther abhominable and heathenishe practices, that the people in that place were accustomed to sacrifice bulls at a certaine tyme upon the 25 of August, which day is dedicate, as they conceive, to St Mourie, as they call him ... and withal their adoring of wells and uther superstitious monuments and stones," attempted to suppress the observances of Mhor-Ri, which, according to the Presbytery Records, Dingwall, included "sacrificing at certain times at the Loch of Mourie ... quherein [wherein] ar monuments of Idolatrie," also "pouring of milk upon hills as oblationes." Strangers and "thease that comes from forren countreyes" participated in the "old rites" of Mhor-Ri.

The attempted suppression failed. Twenty years later, in 1678, members of the Mackenzie clan were summoned by the Church at Dingwall for "sacrificing a bull in ane heathenish manner." ... In 1699, a man was arraigned before the Kirk Sessions at Elgin, Morayshire, charged with idolatry.

Such belated eradication of idolatry, much of it rooted in Roman, pre–Roman, and matriarchal Middle Eastern customs such as the worship of the Triple Goddess (Graves 1975), speaks to Scotland's general record of religious tolerance, as well as to the diversity and amalgamation of its religions over the course of centuries.

When Malcom Canmore, the Scottish king, and his Hungarian-born consort, Margaret, were married in 1069, the ceremony was performed by a Culdee,[3] or Celtic, priest, named Fothad. The Celtic church had its own priests and religious practices, which, as we discussed in chapter 1, corresponded more closely to Judaic customs and beliefs than to the Roman rite. Culdean priests continued to officiate in Scotland at most churches well into the 1200s (Howie 1981, pp. 4–8), at which time, we maintain, a large contingent of Crypto-Jewish aristocrats, nobles, merchants and tradespeople dwelt in Scotland and were "alive and well."

There is evidence to show that some of the houses of worship even after 1200 were staffed by Jewish or Crypto-Jewish personnel. The list below shows known priors for Inchmaholme Abbey in south central Scotland. The list is incomplete; notably, it has gaps caused by the destruction of records in the age of iconoclasm under the Tudor kings. But take a look at the names that do survive. The first prior was named Adam (1296), a Hebrew name rather than a saint's name or one coming from the New Testament; the second was named Maurice, a common French Jewish version of Moses. From 1419 to 1469 we find surnames listed in the French, or Norman, style (e.g., *de* Port). A second Maurice/Moses appears in 1445, a Gilbert de Camera (Sephardic) in 1450–1469, and a David Noble (Nobel, also French Jewish), in 1468.

A List of Known Priors of Inchmaholme Abbey

Adam	1296
Maurice	1297–1309
Cristin	1309–1319
Patrick de Port	1419

Patrick de Cardross	1419–1445
Thomas de Arbroath	1419–11420
Maurice de Cardross	1445
Gilbert de Camera (Chalmers)	1450–1468, 1469
David Noble	1468
Thomas Dog	1469–1477
John Cavers	1470–1473
Alexander Ruch	1474–1479
Walter Drummon	1477
John Ruch	1479

The known bishops and archbishops of St. Andrews Cathedral, where several Templar tombs and the famous David sarcophagus were found, appear below. Among them we see a series of Chuldee/Celtic religious leaders: Maeldwin, Tuthald, Fothad, Turgon, a gap, then a Robert, an Arnold, a Richard, a John Scot, and another Roger. But in 1202 something very interesting happens: William Malvoisin (1202–1238) succeeds, and his surname is French. He is followed by David de Bernham (with a Hebrew given name), Abel de Colin (Hebrew again), Gamelin (Hebrew), a Wishart, a Fraser (Crypto-Jewish family), and, in 1328–1332, James Ben (Jewish surname). In 1478–1497, for nearly 20 years, the see was ruled by William Scheves (Jewish surname). He was followed by several Stewarts, Beatons, a Douglas, and an Adamson. With the arrival of the Reformation, we find a George Gledstanes (Gladstone, often Jewish). The Spottswood family, which follows, included more than one physician and had ties to Morocco; a lieutenant governor of Virginia of the same name settled countless of his countrymen and co-religionists in that colony to explore for precious metals and develop trade and industry.[4]

Bishops and Archbishops of St. Andrews

Maeldwin	?c. 1028–1055
Tuthald	?1055
Fothad	c. 1070–1093
Turgot	c. 1107–1115
Robert	1123–1159
Arnold	1160–1162
Richard	1163–1178
John Scot	1178–1188
Roger	1189–1202
William Malvoisin	1202–1238
David de Bernham	1239–1253
Abel de Golin	1254
Gamelin	1255–1271
William Wishart	1271–1279
William Fraser	1279–1297
William Lamberton	1297–1328

James Ben	1328–1332
William Landallis	1342–1385
William Trail	1385–1401
Henry Wardlaw	1403–1440
James Kennedy	1440–1465
Patrick Graham (archbishop 1472)	1465–1478
William Scheves	1478–1497
James Stewart	1497–1504
Andrew Forman	1514–1521
James Beaton	1521–1539
David Beaton	1539–1546
John Hamilton	1546–1571
John Douglas	1571–1574
Patrick Adamson	1575–1592
George Gledstanes	1604–1615
John Spottiswood	1615–1638
James Sharp	1661–1679
Alexander Burnet	1679–1684
Arthur Ross	1684–1689

Equally remarkable are the names of the bishops of Dunblane Cathedral, situated just above Stirling. We find the usual early entries of Culdee/Celtic names (S. Blane, Colum), but then, incongruously, a Daniel appears in 640–659, followed by a Ronan (689–737), a Maelmanach (possibly Aramaic or Arabic, 737–776) and Noe (Portuguese Sephardic, 776–790). A large 300-year-plus hiatus occurs next, when the list resumes with a Lawrence (French) succeeded, remarkably, by a Symon (Hebrew), a W———, a Jonathan (Hebrew), and an Abraham (1212–1225). The latter would certainly seem to be Jewish, and he served for 13 years.

Bishops and Ministers of Dunblane Cathedral

S. Blane	602–?
Colum	640
Daniel	640–659
Iolan	659–689
S. Ronan	689–737
Maelmanach	737–776
Noe	776–798
M ——?	1155–?
Lawrence	1160–1178
Symon	1178–1196
W ——?	1196–1197
Jonathan	1198–1210
Abraham	1212–1225
Ralph	1225–1226

Osbert	1227–1230
St. Clement	1233–1258
Robert de Prebenda	1258–1284
William	1284–1296
Alpin	1296–1300
Nicolas	1301–1307
Nicolas de Balmyle	1307–1319
Maurice	1322–1347
William	1347–1361
Walter de Coventre	1361–1371
Andrew	1312–1380
Dougal	1380–1403
Finlay Dermoch	1403–1419
William Stephan	1419–1429
Michael Ochiltree	1429–1447
Robert Lawder	1447–1466
John Hepburn	1466–1486
James Chisholm	1487–1526
William Chisholm	1526–1564
William Chisholm	1561–1573
Robert Pont (du Pont)	1562
Thomas Drummond	1564
Adam Bellenden	1615–1635
William Fogo[5]	1619–1623

Keep in mind these patterns of office holding *predate* the enormous out-migration of Iberian Jews due to the Inquisition. Indeed, religious scholars have pointed out that it would be foolhardy to assume that the estimated 200,000 Jews expelled from Spain and Portugal after 1492, added to the millions of others who had already converted, genuinely or not, to Catholicism, had no impact upon the religious practice in the countries to which they migrated (see Lavender 2003, p. 1). How could they fail to have a rather large one? They were well educated, in many cases more steeped in learning and better trained in the professions than the Christian majority. They were multilingual, well traveled, and socially active, often holding key positions in government, finance and civil administration. (For instance, John Mossman was royal treasurer to James IV of Scotland, and an architect-master mason named Moise Martyne designed the East Range façade of Falkland Palace for James V.) Their numbers included a high proportion of physicians, professors, artists, philosophers, international traders, astronomers, manufacturers, craftsmen, cartographers, ship builders, architects, bankers, brokers, metallurgists, jewelers, smiths, glaziers and chemists. Some moved in the upper ranks of society, becoming counselors to kings and emperors, popes and princes; indeed, not a few had careers within the Catholic Church (Gitlitz 2002, pp. 563–69).

In all these social roles, their private religious beliefs must have influenced their discourse, actions and counsel. Lavender (2003), who recently uncovered the Sephardic ancestry behind his family's French Huguenot roots in Charleston, S.C., draws attention to the fact that the Huguenot Seal of 1559 has the same four Cabalistic Hebrew letters, YHVH (the Tetragrammaton),[6] engraved upon it — within a burning bush, no less — as we found emblazoned on the title page of the Edward Raban psalter in Aberdeen in 1623. Many of the Huguenots were formerly Jews and Moors (Roth 1932), and in France, the persecution of Jews and Huguenots went hand in hand. The King's dragonnards came after both with equal ferocity, and often the same legislation was used to condemn them

This headstone from the Dunblane Cathedral cemetery has a Judaic Ten Commandments motif. Photograph by Elizabeth Caldwell Hirschman.

This headstone, also from Dunblane Cathedral cemetery, displays the Judaic dove and olive branch symbol. Photograph by Elizabeth Caldwell Hirschman.

in the courts and seize their assets. Could it not be more than merely fortuitous that the Protestant Reformation sprang from those very countries to which Sephardim fled — France, Switzerland, Germany, Holland, England and Scotland?

Remarking on the main difference between the Reformation in Scotland and in England, M'Gavin wrote:

> England ... retained many of the ceremonies, the habits, and almost all the frame-work, of the previous [Catholic] establishment. In Scotland, these were generally swept away; and an order was established, simple and unostentatious, having more of a spiritual kingdom, and much less of the splendour of this world, than our neighbour in the south [Howie 1981, p. xi].

Curiously, few scholars have actively pursued this angle of investigation in exploring the origins of Protestantism. We suspect it is for the same reasons Scottish history is normally told as a monothematic battle for independence from the British "elephant" that one popular writer finds himself "in bed with" (Kennedy 1995) — told with such partisan zeal, in fact, that "Scots" and "Scottish" come to be defined only as a counterfoil to "British," eclipsing all other strains of nationality and culture that went into the making of modern Scotland. We propose that the Reformation, beyond being a movement *against* Catholicism, should also be seen as a movement *toward* Judaism.

John Calvin/Cauvin (1509–1564)

John (Jean) Calvin was born in 1509 in Picardy, France; the family name was perhaps actually Cauvin. John's father, Gerard, was employed as an attorney by the Lord of Noyon. Of John's youth we know only that he served the noble family of deMontmor and studied for the priesthood. In early adulthood, Calvin moved to Paris, where he became friends with the two sons of the French king's physician. Given their surname and their father's occupation, Nicholas and Michael Cop were likely of Crypto-Jewish descent. Calvin's father persuaded him to abandon training for an ecclesiastical career and instead pursue an education in the law. However, in 1529 Calvin decided instead to seek an education in the humanities under scholar Andrea Aciate[8] in Bourges, France. Calvin was joined there by a friend from Orleans, Melchior Wolmar. Wolmar instructed Calvin in Greek and later in Paris, Calvin became proficient in Hebrew, as well.

From 1532 to 1534, Calvin experienced a religious epiphany, turning to Protestantism. Concurrently, his friend Nicolas Cop was elected rector of the University of Paris. Calvin helped prepare Cop's inaugural address which was strongly Protestant in tone. As a result, Cop was ordered to appear before the Parisian Parliament, but fled instead to Basel, Switzerland — a Protestant stronghold.

At the time, a war was in progress between Francis I and Charles V, so Calvin was forced to make his own way to Switzerland through Geneva. In Geneva, William Farel[9] (bearing a Sephardic surname), founder of the Reformed Church in Geneva, convinced Calvin to stay and help preach the new Protestant theology. Calvin obliged and set up several Protestant religious schools in the city.

However, theology within the new Protestant movement was in flux; a diversity of theological positions was present even from the earliest days, perhaps due to the desire to overthrow the strict orthodoxy of the Catholic doctrine. Thus Calvin's views were shared by some but not by all Reform theologians of the time period. Calvin next moved on to Strasbourg where he married a widow, Idelette de Burre, in 1540. He continued to preach, write and teach in Strasbourg, establishing himself as one of the prime movers of the new theology.

From this capsule biography we learn that Calvin's father was an attorney in Picardy, which contained at the time a flourishing Marrano colony.[10] Obviously his father was literate and well-educated; he was also an advisor to nobility—common traits of Crypto-Jews. Gérard Cauvin was clearly ambitious for his son, guiding his career with an eye toward social and economic advancement. He was *not* a force of Catholic religious fervor or conventional piety.

We read also that John chose to learn both Greek and Hebrew, languages which would have permitted him to read the Old Testament (i.e. Torah) in its original ancient form, rather than relying upon Christian translations into Latin. We perceive as well that he favored universal literacy, a Judaic value, that two of his closest friends, Cop and Farel, both had Sephardic surnames, and that he married a woman named Idelette de Bure, evidently of possible Sephardic descent. A surviving sketch of John Calvin shows him with leather head covering, full beard and dark features. While we do not presume to judge the sincerity or Christian orientation of his beliefs, we do hold that he was of Crypto-Jewish descent, that he moved in circles that included Marranos, and that his theology would naturally have been influenced by these ancestral and communal ties.

John Knox (1513/14? to 1572)

Details of John Knox's childhood and even his birth date are unknown. Historians believe he was born around 1513 or 1514 in Haddington, Scotland. It is known that Knox attended a university, but unknown whether it was St Andrews or the University of Glasgow.[12] It appears unlikely that Knox graduated, choosing instead to take up the priesthood as a career around 1540. By the early 1540s he was serving as a theological lecturer and by 1545 had come under the influence of George Wishart, a Lutheran-oriented minister.

In March 1546, Catholic Cardinal Beaton ordered Wishart burned at the stake for heresy and Scotland entered the bloody throes of the Reformation. The Cardinal himself was killed by an angry mob of Protestants, among them John Knox, who stormed his castle at St. Andrews.

The Protestant radicals were soon defeated, however, and Knox was sent in chains to serve as a galley slave in France for 19 months. When pro–Protestant King Edward VI of England obtained his release, Knox made his way back to the Scottish borders, serving as a royal minister in Berwick and New Castle. Sickly Edward soon died, however, bringing the staunchly Catholic Mary Tudor ("Bloody Mary") to the throne of England. Knox fled to Europe, first to Frankfurt, Germany, and then on to Geneva, Switzerland, where he joined forces with John Calvin and also assisted in the translation of the Bible from Latin to English, resulting in the Geneva Bible. It was also in Geneva that Knox wrote the tract "Faithful Admonition" (1554) which advocated the violent overthrow of "godless rulers" by the populace. He became pastor of the English Reformed Church in Geneva (1556–1558) and subsequently published his tract "First Blast of the Trumpet against the Monstrous Regiment of Women," which attacked the policies and right to rule of Catholic monarchs Mary of Guise (Scotland) and Mary Tudor (England).

In 1557, several Protestant Scottish noblemen, including James Stewart, the Earl of Moray (see chapter 1), signed a covenant declaring Protestantism the national religion of Scotland. Knox had been in correspondence with them and returned to Scotland at their request in May 1559. With Knox's leadership, the Scottish Parliament declared itself a Protestant nation and adopted the "Scots Confession"; Catholicism was banned from Scotland.

In 1560, a general assembly was held to assist the reformation of the Scottish church. By 1561, the "Book of Discipline" was adopted by the Scottish Parliament, placing Calvinist Presbyterian structure at the center of church governance. In this treatise, Knox outlined a system of education and welfare covering the entire Scottish population that was to be financed by the sale of former Catholic properties.[13] Knox also re-designed the content of the worship service itself, determining that all rites and practices must be based in scripture.

To go a little more deeply into Knox's theology, let us have a look at the recent biography by Rosalind Marshall (2000). While Marshall never doubts that Knox was a wholehearted Christian, she characterizes him as modeled largely after the Old Testament prophets. In her narrative, Knox emerges as a Biblical purist, much like the Jewish Karaites. He believed that the Bible was the word of God and that only the scriptures should serve as a religious guide. Among his favorite texts were the Book of Daniel, Psalms (especially Psalm 6), Exodus and passages describing David and Moses. He was virulently anti–Catholic and anti–Spanish, viewing both Mary Stuart Queen of Scots and Queen Mary of England as "idolatrous harlots" and "Jezebels." He advocated that "God should send a *jehu* to slay Mary Stuart."[14] He once threw a painting of the Virgin Mary into the river saying (p. 25), "Such an idol is accursed and therefore I will not touch it."

He railed against women as monarchs, especially Mary of England, stating that under her rule the English were "compelled to bow their necks under the yoke of Satan and of his proud mistress, pestilent Papists and proud Spaniards" (Marshall 2000, p. 107).[15] His exhortations to his congregants were likewise rooted in the Old Testament (p. 145). For instance, he applied Psalm 80 ("Turn us again, O Lord God of Hosts, cause thy face to shine and we shall be saved") to current events, equating his present congregation to the ancient Israelites.

Knox also urged the adoption of *Mosaic law* as the governing rule of Scotland. Under it, "certain crimes [including] murder, blasphemy, adultery, perjury and idolatry" (Marshall 2000, p. 67) would be punishable by death. He further proposed that Scotland create *a universal system of education* so that every individual in the population would be literate and able to read the scriptures; he also envisaged a *universal charity system* to care for the indigent, ill and disabled. All three of these concepts are rooted in Judaic tradition, not in Christianity. Knox described the resulting society as one in which *events on Earth would mirror those in Heaven*— a metaphor which Marshall attributes to St. Augustine, but which could just as easily, and more immediately, be derived from the Cabalistic tradition in France. In Knox's view, Scotland was "a new Israel dedicated to upholding God's law" (Smout 1969).

By 1656 the Scottish Parliament had institutionalized Sabbatarianism, "forbidding anyone to frequent taverns, dance, hear profane music, wash, brew ale or bake bread, profanely walk or travel or do any other worldly business" on the Sabbath (Smout, p. 79). Also forbidden on the Sabbath were "carrying in water or casting out ashes," a provision that had been in effect in Aberdeen as early as 1603, according to Smout (p. 79). These restrictions echo in remarkable detail the Jewish mitzvoth regarding the keeping of the Sabbath (Gitlitz 2003, pp. 317–354).

Knox also developed very detailed guidelines for the religious training of ministers. "Trainee ministers would study not only theology, but Hebrew, mathematics, physics, economics, ethics, and moral philosophy" (Marshall 2000, p. 153), a curriculum that appears to be patterned more on the Islamic and Jewish ideals emanating from Spain and southern France than on any prior Christian educational scheme.

Knox advocated that every household have its members instructed in the principles of the Reform religion, so they could sing the psalms at Sabbath services and hold household prayer services morning and evening in their homes (Marshall 2000, p. 153). Both parents were to "instruct their children in God's law" (p. 29); highly reminiscent of the familial worship practices of Orthodox Jews. Virtually the only exceptions to the Judaic nature of his religious ideology were the absence of dietary rules, or kashrut (for instance, a prohibition of pork); and the requirement that males be circumcised.

Examining Knox's family and friends helps shed some additional light on his thinking and sympathies. Among his most ardent supporters was Thomas Lever, formerly master of St. Johns College in Cambridge and later a Protestant minister living in Zurich. Lever is a surname of Semitic origin. Descendants of this same family afterwards immigrated to the American colonies and established the Lever Brothers Corporation; they were practicing Jews. Also among the early Protestants in Frankfurt, Germany, with one of the largest Jewish communities in Europe, were Thomas Parry (a common Sephardic surname) and John Foxe (= Fuchs, an Ashkenazic surname). When Knox returned to Scotland, he lodged in the house of a "well-known Protestant merchant, James Syme" (Marshall 2000, p. 89), and had for his assistant another Scot, James Barron (both, of course, are Sephardic surnames).

In 1652, Knox performed the wedding ceremony uniting Lord James Stewart and Lady Agnes Keith, the former a man who was self-consciously of Jewish descent and the latter a woman from an Aberdonian family that we have suggested was also of Jewish origin. Knox himself had married Marjorie Bowes (the surname Bovée is French Jewish), and the couple named their two children Nathaniel and Eleazer, Old Testament Hebrew names uncommon among Christians at the time. When Marjorie died in 1560, she gave her sons her blessing, "praying that they would always be as true worshippers of God as any that ever sprang out of Abraham's loins" (Marshall 2000, p. 155)—a strange injunction for a Christian mother.

In 1564 Knox remarried at the age of 50 to Margaret Stewart, age 17, a member of the royal Stewart family. Of course, because of its linking of a noblewoman with a commoner (especially one who had presided over Catholic Mary Stewart's downfall), and because of the pairing of a young woman with an elderly man, this marriage makes little sense — unless it is viewed from a Judaic perspective. As Marshall (2000, p. 199) explains, Knox was the "leading minister" in Scotland at that time. If we recognize Knox as the Head Rabbi, then his marriage to a woman of the ruling house, and of Davidic descent, makes imminent sense.[16]

So, can we *prove* that either John Calvin or John Knox were of Marrano descent? No. But we can sum up our case by pointing to the preponderance of the evidence, which suggests that their ancestors *were* Jewish and that they, themselves, were aware of this. If we are correct in this inference, then perhaps the ultimate irony is that the Spanish Inquisition — intended to crush Judaism and send Spain's Sephardim into ignominious exile — actually had the opposite effect. The displaced Jews, like so many tiny floating seeds from a milkweed pod, landed on fertile ground in Holland, France, Scotland, Germany, Switzerland, and England, where they grew into the Protestant Reformation.

Chapter 11

Jews in the National Consciousness of Scotland: Scott's *Ivanhoe*

Significantly, it was a Scottish lawyer and antiquary who fired the first salvo in the public debate over Jews in Britain; this debate intensified with the Reform Movement in national politics and eventually led to their emancipation in the 1830s. And just as significantly, the Jews were Sephardic.[1] He was Sir Walter Scott, Edinburgh publisher, national champion of Scots culture and author of the immensely popular Waverly novels (1771–1832). It may be surprising to learn that the best-paid author in Britain in the first decades of the nineteenth century was a Scotsman.[2] *Scottish Border Minstrelsy,* ballads that Scott collected on journeys through his native Borders country, had catapulted him to fame in 1802, and *The Lay of the Last Minstrel* sealed it. Now he turned to prose, and with *Waverly* in 1814 he created a new literary genre, the historical novel, an invention that would inspire "Jane Austen, Charles Dickens, William Thackeray, George Eliot, Anthony Trollope and other accomplished Continental writers of nineteenth-century literature, such as Balzac, Hugo, Flaubert, and Tolstoy" (Herman 2001, pp. 309–310), not to mention the American writers Irving, Hawthorne, Melville, Cooper, Twain, and Wallace.

The debt author Washington Irving owed to Scott, and vice versa, is especially noteworthy, for Scott's Rebecca of York was apparently inspired by Rebecca Gratz, a member of Philadelphia's elite and widely regarded as the foremost American Jewess of her day (1781–1869).[3] The story is told by Stephen Birmingham in *The Grandees* (1971, pp. 160–62):

A particularly close friend of Rebecca Gratz's was Matilda Hoffman. It was in the office of Matilda's father, Judge Ogden Hoffman, that Washington Irving studied law, and presently Miss Hoffman and Washington Irving became engaged. But before the pair could marry, Miss Hoffman became ill with "wasting disease," a common affliction of the day, and Rebecca went to live at the Hoffmans' to help nurse her friend. Rebecca was there to close Matilda's eyes at the end.

The devotion of one young woman to another impressed Irving. When he went to England to try to forget his sweetheart's death, Rebecca Gratz and her kindness to Matilda became almost an obsession with him.... One of the people he told the story to was Sir Walter Scott.... [W]hen *Ivanhoe* was published ... Scott wrote Irving a letter saying ..."How do you like your Rebecca? Does the Rebecca I have pictured compare well with the pattern given?"

Thus a vivacious and emancipated Sephardic Jewish American served as the model for Ivanhoe's Rebecca, infusing contemporary meaning and life into the ancient tale.

It is counter-intuitive for many of us to realize that Scotland at that time was far more literate and literary than England. In 1696, Scotland's parliament had passed the country's progressive School Act calling for the establishment of a school in every parish nationwide.

> In 1790 nearly every eight-year-old in Cleish, Kinross-shire, could read, and read well. By one estimate male literacy stood at around 55 percent, compared with only 53 percent in England. It would not be until the 1880s that the English would finally catch up with their northern neighbors. Scotland became Europe's first modern literate society [Herman 2001, p. 23].

While intellectuals such as Adam Smith and David Hume held sway in the seats of learning, townspeople flocked to public lectures at the universities and Scotland's working classes read avidly. Patrons of lending libraries included bakers, blacksmiths, coopers, dyer's apprentices, farmers, stonemasons, tailors and servants (Herman, p. 23). "An official national survey in 1795 showed that out of a total population of 1.5 million, nearly twenty thousand Scots depended for their livelihood on writing and publishing — and 10,500 on teaching" (p. 25). With its passion for education and high literacy rate (not neglecting its mathematical counterpart, computational ability), Scotland was uniquely prepared to inform the literary tastes of the masses and set the tone for public discourse. No one was better positioned to lead the popular groundswell that blended nostalgia with progressiveness than Sir Walter Scott, whose family came of the same background as the Stewarts, Leslies, Frasers, and Campbells.

In 1819, Scott published the first of his novels in which he adopted a purely English subject.[4] *Ivanhoe* introduced a set of characters based on a defining moment in English history, the late twelfth century, and its protagonists and antagonists were all English, from Richard Lionheart to Robin Hood.[5] Saxons and Jews represented the "other" in this sweeping book about cultural conflict, while Scots were conspicuously absent. With its pathos-laden figures of Rebecca the Jewess and her father Isaac, Ivanhoe attacked the prevailing stereotypes of English history at a time when the experiment in government called Great Britain was going through "a crisis of acculturation and assimilation ... [when] the fabrication of the (Scottish or Jewish or Irish) Briton through parliamentary legislation led to a variety of reactions: the attempt by these minorities to reinvent themselves, or their rejection of their new identity, or their rejection by so-called true-born Englishmen" (Ragussis 2000, p. 775). Moreover, in Ivanhoe's climactic scene, "Scott rewrites English history as Anglo-Jewish history" (Ragussis 1995, p. 113). Scott also accords a central role to Templars in the national consciousness and sets his tale in York, about as close to Scotland as one can get without being in the Borders. Did he know something?

A recent writer on collective memory and cultural "forgetting" has demonstrated that ancestry, pedigrees, dynasties, genealogies and ethnic origins are social constructs. Like time periods, these notions take shape through a process of collective cognition, the organization of unrelated and discontinuous events into coherent and meaningful narratives (Zerubavel 2003). Many people, for instance, conceive that the Roman Empire ended in 476 C.E., even though its Eastern part, known as Byzantium, continued for another thousand years. Nationalities are constructed around the genealogies of their ruling families (Zerubavel, pp. 32–43). Sometimes the dynastic pedigrees have to be reinvented or refashioned, as was the case with Saxon England's Norman invaders, who had to be recast as British and Celtic in the historiography of Geoffrey of Monmouth and William de Newbury. To take a modern example, the House of Saxe-Coburg[6] that occupied the British throne was converted into the House of Windsor in short order at the beginning of hostilities between Great Britain and the German Empire in 1914. A similar process erased the dynasty's Scottish links under the Hanoverians in the eighteenth century. In this spirit, we can appreciate Scott as one of the inventors of British culture. Notably, it is a culture that includes Jews and is not born in London, the capital, but rather in a northern province.

The city of York was long associated in the minds of Jew and non–Jew with the pogrom that took place there in the year 1190, the precise timeframe of Scott's *Ivanhoe*; in the words of Joseph Jacobs, a pivotal year that brought "the first proof that the Jews of England had of any popular ill-will against them" (1911, s.v. "London"). While King Richard (a philosemite) was away at the Crusades, a number of local Crusaders under Sir Richard Malebis seized the opportunity to erase their debts by murdering Jews. Those who escaped took refuge in the King's castle, where, inspired by one of their celebrated poets, the visiting French rabbi Yom Tob of Joigny, they committed collective suicide (Barnavi 1992, p. 98). Before that disaster, York Jewry enjoyed a high degree of prosperity. Unlike Jewish communities in the rest of England, there was no Jewish quarter in York; rather, Jews lived betwixt and between the Christian inhabitants (Adler 1939, p. 132).

Knights, fair maidens in distress, bloodthirsty Templars who say things like "Back, dog!" and dark heroines whose "long silken eyelashes ... a minstrel would have compared to the evening star darting its rays through a bower of jessamine" (Scott 1988, p. 249) are apparently no longer in the step of literary fashion. Though generations of Southern belles and beaus may have been nursed on *The Lady of the Lake*, our local libraries could not produce *one* copy of the works of the author credited with inventing historical romance and reviving clans and tartans. Assuming our readers would face some of the same difficulties, we will save them the trouble both of tracking down this classic and actually reading it. We provide here a plot summary of *Ivanhoe*. We will then be able to look at some of the scenes and characters which hark back to a time "when Scotland was Jewish."

Wilfred of Ivanhoe, son of Cedric, a noble Saxon, loves his father's ward, the lady Rowena, who also traces her descent to Saxon King Alfred. Cedric is intent on restoring the Saxon line to the throne of England, now occupied by Norman King Richard the Lionheart, and he hopes to accomplish this by marrying his daughter Rowena to Athelstane of Coningsburgh. He has banished his own son, Ivanhoe, who has joined King Richard on the Crusades. In Richard's absence, his brother Prince John rallies the lawless, dissolute Norman vassals to his own cause, intending to depose Richard. Among the knights in John's party are the fierce Templar Sir Brian de Bois-Guilbert and Sir Reginald Front-de-Bœuf.

The story centers around two events. At a great tournament at Ashby de la Zouch, Ivanhoe together with King Richard defeats the Templars, but is wounded. It is at this point, more than halfway through the novel, that Scott introduces Rebecca the Jewess, who will upstage Rowena as the love interest for both Saxons and Normans and become the intrinsic heroine of the tale. The Templars carry off Cedric, Rowena, the wounded Ivanhoe, Rebecca and her father Isaac to the castle of Torquilstone, where, after an exciting assault by King Richard and a band of Saxon outlaws led by Locksley (Robin Hood), the prisoners are rescued — all except for Rebecca, with whom Bois-Guilbert falls in love and carries off to the Templar Preceptory of Templestowe.

We relate the rest of the story in the words of *The Oxford Companion to English Literature* (Drabble 1985, p. 499):

> Here the unexpected arrival of the Grand Master of the order, while relieving Rebecca from the dishonourable advances of Bois-Guilbert, exposes her to the charge of witchcraft, and she escapes sentence of death only by demanding trial by combat. Ivanhoe, whose gratitude she has earned by nursing him when wounded at the tournament of Ashby, appears as her champion, and in the encounter between him and Bois-Guilbert (on whom has been thrust the unwelcome duty of appearing as the accuser), the latter falls dead, untouched by his opponent's lance, the victim of his own contending passions. Ivanhoe and Rowena,[7] by the intervention of Richard, are united; the more interesting Rebecca, suppressing her love for Ivanhoe, leaves England [for Spain] with her father.

When the book first appeared in 1819, many criticized its author's sense of history as wrong-headed. He should not have pitted the indigenous Saxons against the Norman invaders at so late a period, for by the twelfth century both peoples were well assimilated with each other. There was no rear-guard Saxon resistance, and Robin Hood belonged to another era entirely, the fourteenth century and later. Scott anticipated his detractors with a mock dedicatory epistle humbly addressed to the lofty antiquary "the Reverend Dr. Dryasdust" and back-dated to 1817. He also fitted later editions of *Ivanhoe* with a long introduction, defending his theme and fictional mode of operation (p. vii):

> The period of the narrative adopted was the reign of Richard I, not only as abounding with characters whose very names were sure to attract general attention, but as affording a striking contrast betwixt the Saxons, by whom the soil was cultivated, and the Normans, who still reigned in it as conquerors, reluctant to mix with the vanquished, or acknowledge themselves of the same stock.

It is clear then that *Ivanhoe* is about national identity and the ethnic "Other." Lest the point be lost, Scott has his author, in the plodding and subservient persona of Laurence Templeton, apologize for deserting the easy fables of Scotland to venture into the more treacherous ground of English myth-making:

> In England civilization has been so long complete, that our ideas of our ancestors are only to be gleaned from musty records and chronicles, the authors of which seem perversely to have conspired to suppress in their narratives all interesting details, in order to find room for flowers of monkish eloquence, or trite reflections upon morals. To match an English and a Scottish author in the rival task of embodying and reviving the traditions of their respective countries would be ... in the highest degree unequal and unjust [p. xvii].

Scott, therefore, will tell the *real* story of English nationhood, which is not found in any of the history books. His tale includes not only the noble yet "homely" Saxons along with the merry band of Robin and his thieves, but also usurious Jews, good and bad Templars, indifferent kings, and learned Jewesses.

Virginia Woolf remarked that there was more originality to Scott's novels than met the eye. "Part of their astonishing freshness, their perennial vitality, is that you may read them over and over again, and never know for certain what Scott himself was or what Scott himself thought" (Herman 2001, p. 310). The man himself was a bundle of paradoxes, a Tory among the Whig heirs to the Scottish Enlightenment then getting their second wind, a painstaking antiquarian and confirmed reactionary with a flare for modernity, "the last minstrel" and first promoter of the Edinburgh municipal gas company. He called himself "half-lawyer, half-sportsman ... half crazy ... half-everything" (p. 291).

Of all Scott's ethnic types, it is Rebecca, a woman and a Jew, who is at once "most Other," yet at the same time, the quintessential ingredient. When she sails away to Spain at the end of the novel, suppressing her love at the moment of its requital by the hero Ivanhoe, we sense the departure of Jews from English shores and experience a void that can only be filled with nostalgia, wonder and guilt. Scott's readers did not like this ending:

> The character of the fair Jewess found so much favour in the eyes of some [female] readers, that the writer was censured because, when arranging the fates of the characters of the drama, he had not assigned the hand of Wilfred to Rebecca, rather than the less interesting Rowena. But, not to mention that the prejudices of the age rendered such a union almost impossible, the Author may, in passing, observe that he thinks a character of [such] a highly virtuous and lofty stamp is degraded rather than exalted by an attempt to reward virtue with temporal prosperity.... A glance on the great picture of life will show that the duties of self-denial, and the sacrifice of passion to principle, are seldom thus remunerated [*Ivanhoe*, pp. xiii–xiv].

It is interesting to see what kind of prejudice against Jews Scott thought his characters and readers had. As we have already noticed, he reserves the appearance of Rebecca until the middle of the book. Even then, her identity as a Jewess is hidden from the hero until she declares herself. At first, recuperating from wounds after the battle with the Templars, awaking from sleep, Wilfred looks upon the figure who attends his sick-bed as a dream from Palestine, a "fair apparition" of Eastern exoticism:

> To his great surprise, he found himself in a room magnificently furnished, but having cushions instead of chairs to rest upon, and in other respects partaking so much of Oriental costume that he began to doubt whether he had not, during his sleep, been transported back again to the land of Palestine. The impression was increased when, the tapestry being drawn aside, a female form, dressed in a rich habit, which partook more of the Eastern taste than that of Europe, glided through the door, which it concealed, and was followed by a swarthy domestic.... She performed her task with a graceful and dignified simplicity and modesty, which might, even in more civilised days, have served to redeem it from whatever might seem repugnant to female delicacy. The idea of so young and beautiful a person engaged in attendance on a sick-bed, or in dressing the wound of one of a different sex, was melted away and lost in that of a beneficent being contributing her effectual aid to relieve pain, and to avert the stroke of death [pp. 247–48].

Wilfred goes so far as to call Rebecca "noble damsel" in Arabic before she dispels his illusions and explains that she is Jewish:

> "Bestow not on me, Sir Knight," she said, "the epithet of noble. It is well you should speedily know that your handmaiden is a poor Jewess, the daughter of that Isaac of York to whom you were so lately a good and kind lord."

Now the scales fall from Wilfred's eyes. At the mere word "Jewess," all his prejudices come tumbling out:

> Ivanhoe was too good a Catholic to retain the same class of feelings towards a Jewess. This Rebecca had foreseen, and for this very purpose she had hastened to mention her father's name and lineage; yet—for the fair and wise daughter of Isaac was not without a touch of female weakness—she could not but sigh internally when the glance of respectful admiration, not altogether unmixed with tenderness, with which Ivanhoe had hitherto regarded his unknown benefactress, was exchanged at once for a manner cold, composed, and collected, and fraught with no deeper feeling than that which expressed a grateful sense of courtesy received from an unexpected quarter, and from one of an inferior race. It was not that Ivanhoe's former carriage expressed more than that general devotional homage which youth always pays to beauty; yet it was mortifying that one word should operate as a spell to remove poor Rebecca, who could not be supposed altogether ignorant of her title to such homage, into a degraded class, to whom it could not be honourably rendered.

In this confrontation between ethnic types, Scott strikes the emotional quick with his choice of words: epithet, class, race, title, respect, inferiority, degradation. That his descriptions of Ivanhoe and Rebecca were intended for modern readers (and indeed for all time) is evident from his ironic remark about "more civilized days."

Let us glance briefly at Scott's portrayal of Templars, another theme of *When Scotland Was Jewish*, before drawing some conclusions about his notion of British history and Judaism. These characters tend to fall either into the "good Templar" or "bad Templar" mold, with a few tortured souls in between. The Grand Master Lucas Beaumanoir, for instance, is described as an "ascetic bigot" (p. 325). Front-de-Bœuf is a man "more willing to swallow three manors ... than disgorge one of them" (p. 117). He tortures Isaac with all the grisly instruments of the Inquisition, attended by "black slaves ... stripped of their gorgeous apparel, and attired in jerkins and trowsers of coarse linen, their sleeves being tucked up above the elbow, like those of butchers when about to exercise their function in the slaughter-house" (pp. 187–88). He utters speeches like this (p. 193)—

> "Dog of an infidel," said Front-de-Bœuf, with sparkling eyes, and not sorry, perhaps, to seize a pretext for working himself into a passion, "blaspheme not the Holy Order of the Temple of Zion, but take thought instead to pay me the ransom thou hast promised, or woe betide thy Jewish throat!"

—only to meet his just deserts, on page 274, when he is sealed into a fiery tomb by Ulrica the witch and dragged off to hell.

Bois-Guilbert, Rebecca's captor, alone has any redeeming qualities. Yielding to her sophisticated arguments, which are based on subtleties in the Templar rule and the Latin law of the land as well as the Cabala, alchemy, and Muslim logicians, he does not rape her. Instead, he straps her across his horse and takes her to Templestow, where he continues to woo her:

> "Listen to me, Rebecca," he said, again softening his tone; "England—Europe—is not the world. There are spheres in which we may act, ample anought even for my ambition. We will go to Palestine ... and league ourselves [rather with Islam] than endure the scorn of the bigots whom we condemn ... thou shalt be a queen, Rebecca: on Mount Carmel shall we pitch the throne which my valour will gain for you [p. 368].

Her Christian lover, of course, attempts to convert her, but Rebecca insists with pride on the glory and grandeur of her people:

> "Thou hast spoken the Jew [sic]," said Rebecca, "as the persecution of such as thou art has made him. Heaven in ire has driven him from his country, but industry has opened to him the only road to power and to influence, which oppression has left unbarred. Read the ancient history of the people of God, and tell me if those by whom Jehovah wrought such marvels among the nations were then a people of misers and of usurers! And know, proud knight, we number names amongst us to which boasted northern nobility is as the gourd compared with the cedar — names that ascend far back to those high times when the Divine Presence shook the mercy-seat between the cherubim, and which derive their splendour from no earthly prince, but from the awful Voice which bade their fathers be nearest of the congregation to the Vision. Such were the princes of the House of Jacob" [pp. 369–70].

We have quoted Rebecca's apologia at length in order to capture some of its double meanings. It cannot have been lost on Scott's readers that the children of Israel described in her passionate apologia bore the same name as the Jacobites of popular parlance, the Scots, with their Davidic kings, the Stuarts. "Sons of Jacob" thus reinforces the novel's subtext valorizing Scots nationality.

The climax of the tale unwinds as Rebecca is condemned to be burnt at the stake as a witch. Rebecca's response to the Grand Master's question, "Who will be the champion of a Jewess?," is ironic:

> "It cannot be that in merry England, the hospitable, the generous, the free, where so many are ready to peril their lives for honour, there will not be found one to fight for justice" [p. 423–24].

Then it is that the wounded Ivanhoe finds a horse, rides to the lists and becomes her champion. His adversary Bois-Guilbert dies a "victim of his own contending passions"; Ivanhoe is excused from killing him, thus preserving the moral integrity of both men, and King Richard comes on stage as the Black Knight and restores order out of chaos. All is right with the world. Right?

Wrong. Rowena, now "The Lady of Ivanhoe," receives a visit from Rebecca, who kisses the hem of her gown and offers thanks for her champion. She blesses the marriage of Rowena and Wilfred. But when she says, in effect, "I'll be going now," Rowena attempts to change her mind. Rowena tells Rebecca how well protected her people are in England.

> "Lady," said Rebecca, "I doubt it not; but the people of England are a fierce race, quarrelling ever with their neighbours or among themselves, and ready to plunge the sword into the bowels of each other. Such is no safe abode for the children of my people."

Rowena then tries to tempt the Jewess to conversion, but Rebecca answers that she "may not change the faith of my fathers like a garment unsuited to the climate in which I seek to dwell; and unhappy, lady, I will not be" (p. 431). Rebecca then departs, nearly missing the boat that conveys her to relatives in Moorish Spain. Ivanhoe and his lady live happily ever after, though "it would be inquiring too curiously to ask whether the recollection of Rebecca's beauty and magnanimity did not recur to his mind more frequently than the fair descendant of Alfred [Rowena] might altogether have approved" (p. 432).

We see that the figure of Rebecca the Jewess corresponds to an element of resolution in the ethnic conflict of the novel. "Scott's history of happily mixed racial origins [cannot] be entirely congenial, if English Jews such as Rebecca and her father are left out of the game of national belonging" (Wee 1997, p. 203). Jewish culture (not necessarily the same as the religion) is thus presented as Britain's secret gift; it is also the country's secret shame, its national guilt.

As for the Jewish characters, Isaac teeters between love of his shekels and love of his daughter; he is a latter-day Shylock. We have already noted how Rebecca is the surprise heroine. She heals Ivanhoe, brings peace, and even softens the hard heart of a proud Templar. But she cannot prevail as long as the "one word" clings to her. In the reading of critics, Scott raises "the Jewish question" as one of conversion and resistance to conversion. "The trope of conversion becomes a crucial figure used by writers of English history to construct, regulate, maintain, and erase different racial and national identities" (Ragussis 1995, p. 93). In the rhetoric of Imperial England over the course of the nineteenth century, it was to become an absorbing and ultimately futile mission.

Closing Thoughts

Too often, it seems, the story of the Jews has been told solely in terms of their persecution. From this myopic perspective, Jewish history becomes nothing more than the barren chronicle of anti–Semitism (a word only invented in Victorian times). Following the extermination of German Jewry under Hitler, there was a rush to demonstrate that this or that British author — Matthew Arnold, Shakespeare, Dickens, Joyce, Eliot, even Chaucer — was anti–Semitic. A spate of academic articles took up the hue and cry, and the poor figure of Shylock was hounded through the canon of English and American literature. Disagreements became rancorous. Some claimed Eliot was more anti–Semitic than Pound; others the opposite. An apt parallel is Native American studies, where the plight of the Indian is the central issue. The main events in the background are a series of treaties, removals, and extinctions. The subject is treated more like an involved legal docket than the biography of a people.

If Judaic studies have turned into the nearly exclusive preserve of what Scott once called the Reverend Dr. Dryasdusts, it is not surprising that "no one noticed" Scots Jews. They weren't on the cultural agenda. In the past 1,500 years, the only religious conflicts in Scotland have been between Christians. Anti-Semitism is not to be found in either Scots history or literature. On the contrary, philo–Semitism is a strong theme, as we have seen in Ivanhoe— its characters are a sublimated vision of the national pedigree.

As recent anthropological studies remind us in the case of the Jewish African Lemba tribe and other "rediscovered" ancestries (Hall and du Gay 1996, Brodwin 2002, Elliott and Brodwin 2002), ethnic identity in public discourse often provokes a debate between the essentialists and the existentialists— between those who believe that ethnicity is a fixed attribute largely deterministic of our behavior and our predispositions, on the one hand, and those who would argue that it derives rather from individuals' crafting of their own identity through social performance, from group belonging, and from the political and economic struggle of classes. Emerging knowledge of a people's roots can cut both ways, just as tracing genetic identity can lead to more problems than it solves (Elliott and

Brodwin). It can confirm or dispel differences, unite and divide. One controversy turns on the question of who gets to decide who is Jewish, who is African, who is Native American, and for what purposes? Who gets to determine new claims of nationality or ethnicity? How authoritative is the voice of science, and how binding are government rules or religious guidelines? What are the stakes and vested interests involved, and who benefits from the decisions?

Without siding with either the essentialists or existentialists, we believe that Scott wove such questions into the subplot of *Ivanhoe*. His reinvention of British ethnicity did occur at a fortuitous time, nor was it without relevance for him to include the Jewish people in the British national consciousness. It was a moment in history when Crypto-Jewish families and individuals, long hidden, could crystallize into what they truly were. Lord Gordon, for instance, chose solidarity with other Jews, while others opted to assimilate into a sort of studied conformity, blend into society, sublimate, or adopt any number of stances and custom identities, including ambiguity and anonymity.

With many Scottish Jews, this novel social opportunity must have been confusing. "Some Jews," we read, "ceased to practice the rites of Judaism altogether, without necessarily abandoning their identity as Jews— that is, without converting or intermarrying, and without developing an intellectual justification for their break with the past. Many others came to adopt an attitude toward the *mitzvot* that was casual and selective, continuing to observe some *mitzvot* and ignoring others. An individual might close his business on the Sabbath, but eat nonkosher food when visiting Christian friends. He might attend synagogue on one Sabbath and stay at home on the next. No doubt the vagaries of personality ... were among the decisive factors in each case" (Endelman 1979, p. 132). The case of a Scottish butcher in London is particularly poignant:

> In 1783, John Watson, a Jewish butcher, astonished an English judge by being sworn on a New Testament and then, when resworn on a Hebrew Bible, by not covering his head. The judge found his behavior incomprehensible, as the following exchange reveals:
>
> **Court:** What do you mean by taking the oath as you did?
> **J.W.:** I never took an oath in my life ...
> **Court:** Pray friend, do not you know when people of your profession take an oath they always put on their hats?
> **J.W.:** I work among Englishmen, and I was always among Christians.
> **Court:** Do you mean to take the oath as a Jew or as a Christian?
> **J.W.:** I can call myself a Christian, because I am never among the Jews.
> **Court:** What do you call yourself, are you Jew or Christian?
> **J.W.:** I do not know, please your honour; whatever you please to call me.
> **Court:** I wish you would understand that it is an exceeding indecent thing in you, or any man, to come here to trifle with any religion in the sort of way you do.
> **J.W.:** I follow more the Christian ways, than I do the Jews.
> **Court:** You are a good-for-nothing fellow, I dare say, whatever you are. Stand down [Endelman 1979, pp. 141–42].

If religious identities were confusing to individuals themselves, and if even contemporary judicial officers could not determine the affiliation of a Crypto-Jew, as Watson certainly appears to have been, how are we to decide at a remove of hundreds of years?

The answer lies in assembling and evaluating all the evidence, including genetic clues, as well as crediting vestiges of living traditions that do survive, however underground. "The rediscovery of the breadth and depth of the English interest in the Jews is now generating a rewriting of English literary and cultural history from the early modern period through the beginning of the twentieth century," says one critic (Ragussis 1997, p. 289). "This rediscovery is first and foremost an act of recovery — that is, an archival recovery of documents and events that have been neglected in understanding the development of English history, culture, and literature." We hope that our book has contributed to this recovery and rediscovery for Scotland and her Jews.

Raw Scores for Participants in Melungeon DNA Surname Project

Control No.	Surname	393	390	394|19	391	385a	385b	426	388	439	389|1	392	389|2	Hg	Remarks
1. 6659	Gordon I	12	23	14	10	13	17	11	15	11	13	11	30	J2	Russ. Kohan
2. 6546	Gordon II	12	23	14	10	13	18	11	16	11	13	11	31	J	Russ. Kohan
3. 6532	Bowles	12	24	15	11	15	17	11	15	11	12	11	28	J2	Scots Cherokee
4. 5012	Grimwood	12	25	14	13	11	14	12	12	13	13	13	29	R1b	Liverpool
5. 11280	Collins	13	21	15	10	16	20	11	12	11	13	11	31	E3a	Portuguese
6. 1885	Locklear	13	22	14	10	13	14	11	14	11	12	11	28	I	Lumbee, Viking
7. 13253	Baggett	13	22	14	10	13	14	11	14	11	12	11	29	I1a1	Rare Viking type
8. 2220	Sizemore	13	23	13	10	14	16	12	12	11	13	14	30	Q3	Native American
9. 1814	Blevins I	13	23	13	10	17	18	11	12	12	13	11	30	E3b	Welsh, Levite
10. 1815	Blevins II	13	23	13	10	17	18	11	12	12	13	11	30	E3b	Welsh, Levite
11. 10005	Adkins	13	23	14	10	10	14	12	12	13	13	13	29	R1b	"fr. Aachen/Aix"
12. 3085	Gordon III	13	23	14	10	11	14	12	12	12	13	13	29	R1b	Clan, Davidic
13. 2989	Carter	13	23	14	10	11	15	12	12	12	13	13	29	R1b	Norman
14. 5011	Newberry	13	23	14	10	12	14	11	14	9	12	11	28	I	Lumbee, Norman
15. 10113	Tankersley	13	23	14	10	14	15	11	15	11	12	13	28	I	Viking, Cherokee
16. 3015	Bruce I	13	23	14	11	11	12	12	12	11	14	13	31	R1b	Scottish Clan
17. 3035	Bruce II	13	23	14	11	11	14	12	12	11	13	13	30	R1b	Scottish Clan
18. 1843	Chaffin	13	23	14	11	11	14	12	12	12	13	13	29	R1b	Fr. (Lavender)
19. 2258	Wallen	13	23	14	11	11	15	12	12	11	13	13	29	R1b	Longhunter name
20. 3059	Alexander I	13	23	14	11	11	15	12	12	12	14	13	31	R1b	Clan Macalister
21. 13029	Coslow	13	23	14	11	13	14	11	14	11	12	11	28	I	Viking

	Control No.	Surname	393	390	394|19	391	385a	385b	426	388	439	389|1	392	389|2	Hg	Remarks
22.	7802	Vaughan	13	23	14	12	10	13	12	12	11	13	13	30	R1b	Native American
23.	9935	Chase	13	23	14	12	11	15	12	12	10	13	13	29	R1b	
24.	2134	Skeen	13	23	15	10	12	12	12	12	11	13	13	29	R1b	Clan Skene
25.	6009	Reed	13	23	15	10	15	16	11	13	13	13	12	30	I	formerly G
26.	1779	Moore	13	24	13	10	11	14	12	12	11	13	13	29	R1b	
27.	6929	Ney	13	24	13	10	17	18	11	12	12	13	11	31	E3	Ashkenazi Levite
28.	1813	Wolf	13	24	13	10	17	18	11	12	13	13	11	30	E3b	Ashkenazi Levite
29.	3036	Campbell	13	24	14	10	11	15	12	12	13	13	13	30	R1b	Scottish Clan
30.	6870	Kennedy II	13	24	14	10	12	14	12	12	11	15	13	32	R1b	France, Turkish
31.	3268	Douglas I	13	24	14	10	12	14	12	12	12	12	13	29	R1b	Scottish Clan
32.	4176	Givens	13	24	14	11	11	11	12	12	11	13	13	29	R1b	Longhunter name
33.	2823	Boone	13	24	14	11	11	13	12	12	11	13	13	29	R1b	Longhunter name
34.	3037	Forbes I	13	24	14	11	11	14	12	12	11	14	13	30	R1b	Scottish Clan
35.	1930	Wampler	13	24	14	11	11	14	12	12	12	12	13	29	R1b	Levite
36.	1110	Caldwell	13	24	14	11	11	14	12	12	12	13	13	29	R1b	No. Italy, Levite
37.	1780	Cooper*	13	24	14	11	11	14	12	12	12	13	13	29	R1b	France, Levite
38.	1781	Ramey	13	24	14	11	11	14	12	12	12	13	13	29	R1b	France/Spain, Levite
39.	2679	Saylor	13	24	14	11	11	14	12	12	12	13	13	29	R1b	Germany, Levite
40.	4892	Harry	13	24	14	11	11	14	12	12	12	13	13	29	R1b	France, Levite
41.	6011	Woods	13	24	14	11	11	14	12	12	12	13	13	29	R1b	
42.	3214	Stewart I	13	24	14	11	11	14	12	12	12	13	13	29	R1b	Royal
43.	3051	Stewart II	13	24	14	11	11	14	12	12	12	13	13	30	R1b	Royal
44.	1609	Leslie	13	24	14	11	11	14	12	12	14	13	13	29	R1b	Clan, Hungary
45.	8391	Johnson	13	24	14	11	11	14	12	12	14	13	13	29	R1b	Matched Leslie
46.	1798	Berry	13	24	14	11	11	15	12	12	12	13	12	30	R1b	assoc. Clan Forbes
47.	158	Kennedy I	13	24	14	11	11	15	12	12	12	13	13	29	R1b	Matched Gordon IV
48.	3071	Gordon IV	13	24	14	11	11	15	12	12	12	13	13	29	R1b	Scottish Clan, Levite
49.	3355	Douglas II	13	24	14	11	14	14	12	12	12	13	13	29	R1b	Scottish Clan
50.	3245	Alexander II	13	24	15	10	11	14	12	12	12	13	13	29	R1b	Macalister Clan
51.	7813	Conk	13	24	15	10	11	15	12	12	12	13	12	29	R1b	
52.	2524	Christy	13	24	15	10	11	15	12	12	12	13	13	29	R1b	assoc. Farquharson
53.	9444	Shelton	13	24	15	11	9	14	12	12	12	14	13	30	R1b	English gentry
54.	3039	Forbes II	13	24	15	11	11	13	12	12	13	13	13	29	R1b	Scottish Clan
55.	1783	Yates*	13	24	15	11	11	14	12	12	11	13	13	29	R1b	Israelite, France

*Yates was previously misreported as Cooper (and vice versa). Because of an undetected error at the original lab, Yates was retested a number of times and his scores confirmed by three other laboratories. It was also the only sample that was actually SNP tested, being reported as R by Trace Genetics. In the YHRD, Yates had 5 exact matches, with Switzerland being the modal response (2— the others were Ireland, Central Portugal and Greenland). At Ysearch, Yates produced an 18/25 marker match with a descendant of Henry Whitney (1621–1673, England).

	Control No.	Surname	393	390	394|19	391	385a	385b	426	388	439	389|1	392	389|2	Hg	Remarks
56.	2204	Hale	13	25	16	11	12	16	11	13	11	13	12	30	I1b	So. Viking, Moorish
57.	1773	Morrison	13	26	15	10	11	16	11	13	11	13	11	32	?	Scottish Clan, Ire.
58.	1897	Perry	14	22	15	11	14	15	11	13	11	12	11	28	G2	Romani?
59.	6922	McAbee	14	22	16	10	16	18	11	15	11	14	13	30	?	Hasmonaean?
60.	6923	Flores	14	24	14	10	11	14	12	12	11	13	14	29	R1b	Portuguese Jewish
61.	6514	Rogers	14	24	14	11	11	14	12	12	12	13	13	29	R1b	Norman
62.	6010	Blizzard	15	23	15	11	14	15	11	13	11	14	12	32	I	Viking

Source: Family Tree DNA, Houston, Texas. Note that the markers labeled 385a, 385b and 439 are considered fast-mutating. Matching on these sites is not essential and close matches may indicate branches of the same family, all other things being equal. Shaded portion shows one-off and two-off matches with Caldwell-Cooper-Ramey-Stewart haplotype (R1b), thought to be originally southern French/northern Spanish. Nos. 36–42 are exact matches to each other.

Naming and Jewish Priest-Kings

When Bernard of Clairvaux integrated the Celtic church into the Cistercian order and Scotland got its first Templar king, David I (1124–1153), a peculiar tradition became fixed in the royal genealogies: the eldest son was invariably named after his grandfather. The pattern can also be seen in the house of William the Conqueror, where Robert and William alternate in the lineage of the dukes of Normandy. By alternating Malcolms and Davids, David of Scotland clearly wanted to put the stamp of a dynasty on his house.

David's first-born, Malcolm, was murdered, and his second son, Henry, died before he could assume the throne. Thus Henry's son Malcolm (known as "the Maiden") became king at the age of eleven. That preserved the rules of primogeniture and also ensured the succession of a prince with the right name.

With the Stewarts we see a careful preservation of this tradition, all the way down to King James I of England, who named his heir-apparent, Henry, after his father, Henry Stewart, Lord Darnley, husband of Mary Queen of Scots (the name Frederick came from Henry's other grandfather, Frederick II of Denmark):

Family Tree of James VI King of Scotland (James I King of England)

1. James I d. 1437
. **2.** James II d. 1460
.... **3.** James III d. 1488
.... **4.** James IV d. 1513
.... **5.** James V d. 1542
.... **6.** Mary Queen of Scots d. 1587
.... +Henry Stewart Lord Darnley
.... **7.** James VI (James I of England) d. 1625
.... **8.** Henry Frederick Prince of Wales
Note: Died of typhoid 1612

This pattern had been established before the Stewarts had come to Scotland, when they were known as Stewards (Lat. *Dapifer*, Flemish *Flaald*) of Dol in Brittany. For centuries we can trace the alternation of Walters and Alans, Fitz-Walters and Fitz-Alans, until King Robert II Stewart, 7th High Steward of Scotland, grandson of Robert I Bruce, founded the royal House of Stewart with his coronation in Scone Abbey in 1371.

The High Stewards of Scotland

1. Walter Thane of Lochaber, b. ca. 1045
. 2. Alan of Lochaber, ca. 1088–1153
.... 3. Walter Fitz Alan, 1st High Steward of Scotland, d. 1177
.... 4. Alan Fitz Walter, 2nd High Steward of Scotland, d. 1204
.... 5. Walter Stewart, 3rd High Steward of Scotland, d. 1214

The practice of alternating names goes back to the ancient Jewish custom of the high-priestly family of Zadok in Jerusalem, whose members were named alternately Onias and Simon from 332 to 165 b.c.e. This signature of spiritual sovereignty was imitated by the Hasmonaean rulers that followed them, as well as by the heirs of Herod (37–4 b.c.e.). Later, it was used by the Hillelites, with the names Gamaliel and Judah succeeding each other (with an occasional occurrence of Simon and Hillel [Jacobs 1906–1911]). About this time, the practice of double names for the same person began to be adopted, another Jewish trait revived by the Stewarts (e.g. "James Edward Stuart").

Thus the "stewards" of an obscure fiefdom in Brittany began to see themselves as stewards of the kingdom of heaven on earth. By virtue of their Templar heritage, moreover, "the Scots royal line comprised not only Priest Kings but Knight Priest Kings" (Gardiner 2001, p. 226).

APPENDIX C

Early Jewish Names in France and England

According to Eleazar ha-Levi,[*] three rules were applied in naming Jewish children throughout the medieval period and, even, up to the present time: the Talmud, *kinnui* (secular) versus *shem ha kadosh* (sacred) names, and the role of the female in Jewish ritual practice.

He goes on to list the basic progression of a Jewish name:

Joseph ben (son of) Simon
Joseph ben Simon ben Moshe
Joseph ben Simon ben Moshe of London
Joseph ben Simon ben Moshe the Kohane (priestly family) of London

According to Jacobs (1893), the most frequent male names are Isaac (59 men), Joseph (55), Abraham (49), Berachiyah and its Latinized form Benedict (45), Jacob (40), Moses (38), Samuel (37), Hayyim and its Latin equivalent Vives (23), Elias (19), Aaron (18), Deulecresse (Solomon or Gedaliah) (17), Manesser (17), Samson (16), and Solomon (15). Place-names appear in the records to be the most common descriptions and were used alone (e.g., Joseph of London) about as often as "son" or "daughter" of. Some forty-eight separate towns are included in the "master lists" in *The Jews of Angevin England*, with London (110 names), Lincoln (82), Norwich (42), Gloucester (40), Northampton (39), Winchester (36), Cambridge (32), Oxford (22), Bristol (18), Colchester (16), Chichester (14) Bedford and York (13 each), Canterbury and Worcester (12 each), and Hertford (11) all having ten or more entries.

In some cases, a male is listed with his mother's rather than his father's name; e.g. Moysses fil Sarae (Moses ben Sarah). The most likely explanation is that the mother was simply better known. As is well known, Jewish women were allowed to own property and enter into business on their own. Several became well-known financiers, such as Licoricia, widow of Isaac of York, who maintained the business after his death, and Mildegod of Oxford, who was a prominent innkeeper (ha–Levi).

---

[*] *"Jewish Naming Convention in Angevin England," Society for Creative Anachronism, <http://www.sca. org/heraldry/laurel/names/jewish.html.>*

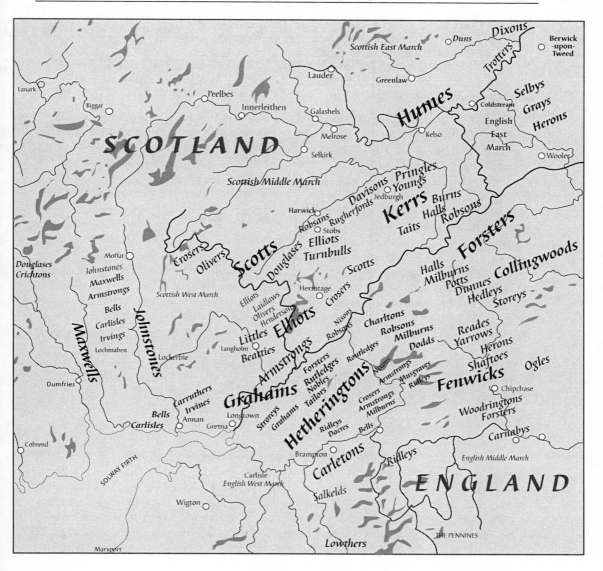

Scottish Borders area exhibiting high modern-day levels of Mediterranean and Semitic DNA halotypes. Map by Donald N. Yates.

As evidenced in Roth (1937), two other descriptors used by medieval (and modern) Jews are ha–Levi and ha–Kohane, denoting descent from the class of Levites and priestly caste of the ancient Hebrews.

Since the word rabbi means "teacher," it was sometimes translated as Magister or Master. "Cantor" may appear as *le Prestre* (the priest). Parnas, the head of the synagogue or of the community, and *gabbai*, synagogue (or community) treasurer are also found. Throughout much of medieval Europe, the Jews had a great deal of autonomy over their own affairs, even to having their own local courts of Jewish law. Jacobs (1893) explains the descriptor Episcopi ("of the bishop") which occurs several times as referring to the judge of one of these courts. The Hebrew term is *dyan,* which has become a modern Jewish family name.

Several kings, starting with Richard I, appointed what amounted to a "King's Minister or Liaison for Jewish Affairs," a prominent member of the community and often a rabbi; these are remembered as the *Judeus Presbyter.* The term was first translated as a sort of high priest, although the role was secular. The term "presbyter" appears several times on the [Roth] list and may well refer to these men (there were about a half dozen). One of the assistants, the chirographer [scribe, or clerk], is also mentioned on the list [ha–Levi].

Other descriptors referring to professions are aurifaber (goldsmith), medicus (physician), and miles (soldier, or perhaps, knight). The Hebrew translation of medicus was *ha-rophe* which can mean both "the physician" and "the leach." A "furmager" or "fermager" is a tax "farmer," paying the king a fee for the right to collect the tax in a given area. He kept the taxes for himself with all monies above the original fee being his profit for the venture. "Scriptor," scribe, generally referred to a *sophar,* a writer of religious texts, a busy man in a community whose religion emphasized literacy. "The Pointer" refers to two grammarians, students of the Hebrew language.

Jewish custom calls for the use of two separate names. The *shem ha-kodesh* or religious name is used during Jewish ritual such when one is being called up to read a portion of the Torah. The common name, *kinnui,* was used in everyday affairs. It could be formed in several ways: (1) the *shem ha-kodesh* could be translated into the vernacular. Thus, Berichiyah, "blessing," becomes Benedict; Obediah, "servant of G-d," Norman French Serfdieu. (2) A name similar in sound to—or using some of the letters in—the *shem ha-kodesh* could be used; thus, Robert for Reuben, George for Gershom. (3) A nickname could be made from the *shem ha-kodesh.*

Hebrew nicknames go back to the days of the Bible. Numbers 13:4–15 lists the names of the spies Moses sent into the land of Canaan, giving several with a nickname as well. Josce, Hok, and Copin were common period English nicknames for Joseph [Isaac, and Jacob] (Heb *Yos-eph, Ytz-hok* and *Ya-a-kov,* respectively). Biket was used for Rebeccah. Even *kinnui* were not exempt. Deulecresse, the translation given for both Gadaliah and Solomon, is often abbreviated to Crease.

Sometimes, a name that in some way referred to *shem ha-kodesh* (or the individual) could be used. A common practice was to take the references made by Jacob on his deathbed (Genesis 49) or Moses in his final oration to the Children of Israel (Deuteronomy 33). Thus, Judah became Leon ('Judah is a lion's whelp,' Genesis 49.9). Other times, a more obscure reference was used. Jacobs suggests that Jornet, coming from the word 'jerkin' (jacket) was a *kinnui* for Joseph. And, in what seems to be a rare instance, the name Belaset was derived from *bella assez* (fair to look upon) and applied to Rachel (Genesis 29:17, 'Rachel was fair to look upon') Bonevent (good day) referred to a child born on a holiday, especially Passover (ha–Levi) ....

Parents of Jewish girls, says ha–Levi, had more leeway in naming them. Some Biblical or Hebrew names were used—Abigail, Zipporah, Esther, Anna or Hanna, Judith, Miriam and Sarah. More common, however, were vernacular names: flowers (Fleur de liz, Fleur, Rose); things of value (Almonda, Chera (Greek: *Iekara,* precious stone), Licoricia); desirable traits: Bona (good), Belia (pretty), Genta (gentle), or terms of endearment: Columbia (dove), Comitessa (countess), Pucella (little girl); or simply the names their neighbors used (Elfid, Auntera, Margaret, Sweetecote).

Female and Male Jewish Names from Medieval England

Name	Variant(s)	Sex	Origin
—de domo—	(name) of the house of (name)	Both	
—de (place)	(name) of (placename)	Both	

Name	Variant(s)	Sex	Origin
—fil—	(name) son or daughter of (name)	Both	"ben" or "bas" (name)
—mater—	(name) mother of (name)	Female	
—uxor—	(name) wife of (name)	Female	
—vidua—	(name) widow of (name)	Female	
Aurifaber		Male	goldsmith (?)
bandylegged	given as "cum pedibus tortis"	Male	
Cyrograparius	assistant to King's minister for Jews	Male	
Episcopus	"Bishop" (judge of local Jewish court)	Male	
Furmager	fermager	Male	tax "farmer"
Gabbai		Male	synagogue treasurer
Ha-Nakdan	the Pointer, the Punctuator, le Pointur	Male	grammarion
le Blund	Blund	Male	Ha-Levi misspelled
le Evesq	Evesk, Evesque, le Vesq, Levesq	Male	Fr. for ha-Kohane
le Gros	Grassus	Male	"big," "fat"
le Prestre	the priest (cantor[?])	Male	
le prestre	the priest	Male	cantor
Lengus	Le Lung	Male	"long" or "tall"
Medicus	ha–Rophe, the physician, the "leach"	Male	
Militis		Male	knight (?), soldier
Naso		Male	"nosey," "big nosed"
Parnas	Parnaz	Male	synagogue leader
Parvus		Male	"small"
Parvus		Male	"little" (Latin)
Rabbi	Magister, Master (before or after name)	Male	
Scriptor	ha–Sophar, the Scribe (of Jewish texts)	Male	
—frater—	(name) brother of (name)	Male	
—gener—	(name) son-in-law of (name)	Male	
—juvenis	(name) the younger	Male	
—nepos—	(name) nephew of (name)	Male	
—neptis—	(name) grandson or nephew of (name)	Male	
—senex	(name) the older	Male	
—sorori—	(name) brother-in-law of (name)	Male	
Abigail	Auigai, Avagaye, Avigay, Avigai	Female	English equivalent
Alemandrina	(from Alexandria?)	Female	English equivalent
Alfid		Female	Uncertain
Almonda		Female	English
Anna	(from Hanna)	Female	English equivalent
Auntera	Anteria, Antera	Female	Uncertain
Belaset	Belasset, Belassez, Bella Assez, (=Rachel)	Female	Norman French transl.
Belia	Belina	Female	Uncertain
Bona	Bone	Female	English equivalent
Chera	Chere ("Iekara" = precious stone)	Female	Greek?
Chipora	Cypora, Zippora	Female	English equivalent

Name	Variant(s)	Sex	Origin
Clarice		Female	Uncertain
Columbia		Female	Latin
Comitessa	Comitesse, Comitissa	Female	Norman French
Cuntasse		Female	Uncertain
Drua		Female	Uncertain
Esther	Ester	Female	English equivalent
Fleur de Liz		Female	Norman French
Flora	Floria, Fluria, Flurie	Female	Uncertain
Genta	Gentil, Gentilia	Female	Uncertain (French?)
Hanna	Hana, Hannah, Henna	Female	English equivalent
Jessica		Female	Uncertain
Joie	Joia, Joiette, Joya	Female	Norman French
Judith		Female	English equivalent
Juetta	Juette	Female	Uncertain
Lia	Leah	Female	Uncertain
Licoricia		Female	Uncertain
Margaret	Margarede, Margalicia	Female	Uncertain
Melka		Female	Uncertain
Mildegod		Female	Uncertain
Mirabel	Mirabella	Female	Uncertain
Miriam	Maria, Miriana	Female	English equivalent
Muriel		Female	Uncertain
Pucella	Pucellae, Pucelle	Female	(Latin = "girl")
Pya		Female	Uncertain
Rachel	(see Belaset)	Female	English equivalent
Rane		Female	Uncertain
Rebecca	Biket	Female	English equivalent
Regina		Female	Latin
Rose		Female	English
Samulina	Slema (?)	Female	(from Samuel)
Sarah	Sare, Sarra, Sera	Female	English equivalent
Swetcote		Female	Uncertain
Zeuna		Female	Uncertain
Aaron	Aharon	Male	English equivalent
Abraham	Abbe, Abrahe, Abram	Male	English equivalent
Akelin		Male	Uncertain
Alexandrini	Alexandrinus	Male	English equivalent
Amiot		Male	Norman French
Asher	Aser, Asser	Male	English equivalent
Baruch (1 of 2)	Barchyah, Barechiah, Baruchiya	Male	Hebrew
Baruch (2 of 2)	Bendit, Benedict, Bencit, Beneyt	Male	English equivalent
Bateman	Pateman	Male	Uncertain
Benjamin	Benami (See Also Bonami, Bonefaund)	Male	English equivalent

Name	Variant(s)	Sex	Origin
Benleveng		Male	Uncertain
Bonafy (1 of 2)	Bonavie, Bonavy, Bonefei, Bonavy	Male	Norman French
Bonafy (2 of 2)	Bonevie, Bonevy, Bonfey, Biniface	Male	Norman French
Bonami	Bonamy (see Benjamin)	Male	Norman French
Bonel		Male	Uncertain
Bonenfaud	Bonenfaunt, Bonesaut, Bonenfant	Male	Norman French
Brin	Brun	Male	Norman French
Calamond		Male	Uncertain
Chermin		Male	Uncertain
Cok (1 of 2)	Coket, Hake, Hakelin (fm Ytzchak = Isaac	Male	English nickname
Cok (2 of 2)	Hakelot, Kok	Male	English nickname
Copin	Copyn, Jopin; from Jacob	Male	English nickname
Cresse	Cresselin; (see Deulecresse)	Male	Norman French
Crispia	Crispin	Male	Uncertain
David		Male	English equivalent
Deodone	Deodon ("gift of G-d" = Nathah; Jonathan)	Male	Norman French
Deotatus	Deodata (=Nathan or Elchanan)	Male	Norman French
Deuaie	Deusaie, Diaia, Diaie (=Eleazar)	Male	Norman French
Deulasalt	Deulesaut (=Joshua)	Male	Norman French
Deulecress	Deulecresse, Deulecret (Given from G-d)	Male	Norman French
Deulegard	(??? of G-d = ???) [God guard him]	Male	Norman French
Elchanan	Elhanan	Male	English equivalent
Eleasar	Elie, Eliezar	Male	English equivalent
Eliab		Male	English equivalent
Elijah	Elekin, Elias, Elaya, Eligai, Elyas	Male	English equivalent
Eudon		Male	Uncertain
Ezra		Male	English equivalent
Flameng	Flamengi	Male	Uncertain
Gamaliel		Male	English equivalent
Gershom	Garsie, Kershun	Male	English equivalent
Haggai		Male	English equivalent
Hamo		Male	Uncertain
Hamyot		Male	Uncertain
Hanechin	Hanuchin	Male	English equivalent
Hayyim (1 of 2)	Chaim, Hagin, Haim; see Vives (="life") [may you live]	Male	English equivalent
Hayyim (2 of 2)	Hakin, Haim	Male	English equivalent
Helye	Uncertain	Male	English equivalent
Hose	(Hosea?)	Male	English equivalent
Isaac	Isaac (3 syllables), Ysaac	Male	English equivalent
Jacob	Jacobus (See also: Copin)	Male	English equivalent
Jagunce		Male	Uncertain
Janem		Male	Uncertain
Jechiel		Male	English equivalent

Name	Variant(s)	Sex	Origin
Jedidiah		Male	English equivalent
Jehoizadak		Male	English equivalent
Jehosua	Joshua, Oshaya	Male	English equivalent
Jekuthiel	Jekutiel, Yekuthiel, Yekutiel	Male	English equivalent
Jeremias	Jheremias	Male	English equivalent
Jezreel		Male	English equivalent
Jornet (1 of 2)	may be from "coat (of colors)" = Joseph	Male	Hebrew nickname?
Jornet (2 of 2)	Jurnin, Jurnet	Male	Hebrew nickname?
Joseph (1 of 2)	Gosee, Gotsche, Joce, Jocepin, Joppin	Male	English equivalent
Joseph (2 of 2)	Josce, Joscej, Joscepin, Josepin	Male	English equivalent
Judah	Jehudah, Judelin	Male	English equivalent
Kanonimos	(from Kalonymos = "Shem Tov" = Good Name)	Male	English equivalent
Leo	Leon, Leonis, Leun (=Judah)	Male	English nickname
Levi		Male	English equivalent
Liun		Male	Uncertain
Lumbard		Male	Placenames
Magni		Male	Latin
Makir		Male	English equivalent
Manassah (1 of 2)	Manaser, Manasser, Manasseri, Manasses,	Male	English equivalent
Manassah (2 of 2)	Manser	Male	English equivalent
Martiri		Male	Uncertain
Matathias	Matatias	Male	English equivalent
Mehy		Male	Uncertain
Meir	Melin, Melinus, Merin, Merinus, Meyer	Male	English equivalent
Menachem	Menahem	Male	English equivalent
Meshullam		Male	English equivalent
Meus	[from Meir: Jacobs]	Male	Uncertain
Mileon	Miles, Milo (from Meir)	Male	Uncertain
Mordechai		Male	English equivalent
Morell		Male	English equivalent
Moses	Mosey, Moss, Mosse, Mosseus, Mossy, Moyses	Male	English equivalent
Natroni	Natronai	Male	Uncertain
Nahemiah	Naemia	Male	English equivalent
Nichol		Male	Uncertain
Obediah	(trans to French "Serfdeu")	Male	English equivalent
Peitevin	Peytevin, Pictavin [Picard]	Male	French placename
Peretz	Perez	Male	Uncertain
Peter	Petri, Piers	Male	Greek
Potelin		Male	Uncertain
Pucel		Male	Uncertain
Rahama	[caravan merchant?]	Male	Uncertain
Sabecoe	(from Sabbattai?)	Male	Uncertain
Sadekin	Sadiken	Male	Uncertain

Name	Variant(s)	Sex	Origin
Samarias		Male	English equivalent
Samson	Sampson	Male	English equivalent
Samuel	Mullin (diminutive?)	Male	English equivalent
Sancto		Male	Uncertain
Sandin		Male	Uncertain
Seignuret		Male	Norman French?
Simeon	Simon, Simund	Male	English equivalent
Solomon	Salamon, Salemun, Salle, Salom, Saloman	Male	English equivalent
Strabman		Male	Uncertain
Sweteman	(from Asher)	Male	Uncertain
Ursel	Ursell (=Joshua)	Male	Germanic
Vives	Vivard, Vivelot, Vivo, Vivus (see Hayyim)	Male	English equivalent
Yom Tov	Yom Tob (or either spelled as one word)	Male	English equivalent
Yvo	Yvelin, Yveliny, Yvoliny, Yuo	Male	Uncertain
Zerach		Male	English equivalent

Sources: Jacobs, ha–Levi, Roth.

Names of Jews on the 1292 Paris Census

In 1292, just two years after the expulsion of the Jews from Angevin England, and shortly before their banishment from the Île de France and French-ruled areas, a census was made by the royal authorities in Paris. Jews were marked with the letter J. These entries are shown below, with our comments.

Name	Comment
Baru le mestre	Baruchiah, a teacher/professor or master craftsman
Bèle [une] fame	"Pretty" woman
Bèle-Assez de Gonesse, veuve	"Very Pretty" widow, from Ghent (?)
Assez-Bèle de Breban	From Brabant (town in Flanders)
Belle Assez la veuve	Widow
Bien-le-Viengne le Prestre	"Well come," priest (Cohen), perhaps Benveniste
Bonefoy l'Anglois	Good faith, English
Bone-Vie de Chartres [un mari]	From Chartres, a university town, husband
Bonne Bourbote de Compingne [veuve]	From Compiègne
Bonne-Pille [une] fame	Married woman
Bonoque [une] fille	Unmarried daughter
Chière [une] seur	Sister
Copin le mire	=Jacob, a tradesman ("lord")
Cressant [un mari]	
Cressin qui porte les chaperons	He who carries around cloaks (old clothes peddler)
Dieu-le-Croisse Cohen	Priest (Cohen)
Florion [une] fille	
Haguin Landenaise	Hagin the Londoner

Name	Comment
Hanna [une] fille	
Haquin Cohen	
Hava [une] fame	
Helie Doucet	
Hermineite [une] fame	
Hétouyn le bouchier	Edwin (?) the Butcher, perhaps a ritual slaughterer
Honot de Gonnesse	From Ghent, town in Flanders (?)
Jivete [une] fille	
Jococ le mari Maronne	Marrano: Jew from Arab lands
Joie la farnière, veuve	Flour merchant, widow
Jorin l'Englois	Englishman
Josse Poulain le jenne	
Josson Pate et sa fame	
Léal [une] fame	
Lion d'Acre	Lion of St.-Jean-d'Acre, Crusader town in Palestine
Lyon d'Acre, [un] mire	
Maronne [une fame]	Marrano woman: Jewess from Arab lands
Mique [une] dame	Wife of tradesman, "lady"
Moreau [un] fuiz	Silk or paper maker (?), son
Mosse l'Englois	Englishman
Mousse de Dreues	From Trier, town on the Moselle E of Paris
Parise [une] fame	
Pricion	
Quabin	Rabbin (?)
Rauve de Miauz, veuve	From Meaux (town N of Paris)
Rose l'Englesche	Englishwoman
Salemon [un] fuiz	
Samuel [un mari]	
Sarre la Bocacharde	Sarah the glover (?)
Senior du Pont	Seneor from Brugges (town in Flanders)
Souni [un] fuiz	
Viau de Brebon	From Brabant
Vivant Caro [un mari]	Hayim Karo, of Davidic/gaonic Karo family
Ysaac de Sesanne	From Soissons (town NW of Paris)?

Source: Lord Colm Dubh, extracted by Henry MacQueen and Judy Gerjuoy, http://www.sca.org/heraldry/laurel/names/paris.html.

At the time this list was made, France was at war with England (and would be for another hundred years). Many Jews in Paris were clearly regarded as ex-nationals of England. Their association with Jews from Brabant, Brugges, Ghent, Soissons and Meux can be read as a sign that some Jews expelled by Edward I took refuge with Flemish relatives and business partners, likely retracing their steps in coming to England with the Normans. Here they also mingled with Jews from the Rhineland, Iberia and southern France, Prague, Palestine and Babylon.

APPENDIX D

Davidic Jewish Genealogies

Arthur Benveniste is one of the founders of America's Society for Crypto-Judaic Studies. He traces his Ladino family back to twelfth century Catalonia and Narbonne and ties it to the Shealtiel, Gracian and Luna families of Sephardic Spain, all of whom claim Davidic descent. Of the name itself, he writes that it belongs to "an old, rich, and scholarly family of Narbonne, the numerous branches of which were found all over Spain and the Provence, as well as at various places in the Orient." It is still borne, he notes, by certain families in Bulgaria, Serbia, and Vienna, and until World War II it was also found in Salonika, Izmir and Rhodes. His sketch of family history includes extensive biographical notes on leading related rabbinical families through the ages.[*]

In an online article titled "Can We Claim Descent from David?" Moshe Shaltiel-Gracian discusses Shealtiel Family Davidic Descent.[†] He responds to the article "Can We Prove Descent from King David?" by David Einsiedler, who points out that whereas a great many families claim descent legitimately from Rashi, the most famous Talmudic scholar, others have gone farther and claimed descent through Rashi to King David.[‡] According to these authors, one of the earliest claims to descent from King David is found in the genealogy *Mishpachat Luria*, discussed by Abraham Epstein (Vienna, 1901). This source states that before his death, Yehiel Luria told his nephew, Moses Enosh, that he had a *yichus* brief (pedigree scroll) going back to Johanan Ha-Sandlar. Johanan Ha-Sandlar lived in the second century c.e., was a Tannah (sage) of the Mishnah, and was considered a descendant of King David. According to Epstein, this record "was lost in the Swiss War, and Johanan Luria mourned the loss of his yichus brief more than the material goods he was robbed of." Einsiedler notes, moreover,

In *Seder Ha-Dorot* (The Order of Generations) (Zhitomir, 1867), R. Jehiel Heilprin claims descent from Jehiel, the father of Solomon Luria (MaHaRaSHaL),[§] from Rashi, and from the Tannah Johanan Ha-Sandlar. This claim is made on the title page; in Part II, page 201, under the entry "Rabbi Johanan Ha-Sandlar" and again in the section on books under "Lulaot Ha-Shir" (page 60). He gives no details. More detailed references are found in *Maalot Ha-Yuchsin* (Degrees of Descent), by R. Ephraim Zalman Margolioth of Brody (Lemberg, 1900). It includes a fractional genealogy "from the Tannah Johanan Ha-Sandlar to Rashi to

---

[*]*Arthur Benveniste, http://home.earthlink.net/~benven/.*
[†]*<http://www.shealtiel.org/david.html (accessed 12 March 2003), cf. Shaltiel-Gracian Feb 2003.*
[‡]*Rabbine Special Interest Group Online Journal, http://www.jewishgen.org/Rabbinic/journal/descent.htm.*
[§]*Perhaps the origin of the surname Marshall.*

Rabbi Solomon Luria to the author of *Seder Ha-Dorot*." (Heilprin) The part relevant to this article shows a succession of about a dozen generations from Johanan Ha-Sandlar to Rashi with a few gaps between them. (See *Avotaynu*, Vol. VII, No. 2, page 20.)

Both authors cast doubt on these genealogies, however, because of a gap of about 900 years. As they point out, moreover, in none of his writings did Rashi mention anything about descent from King David or from the Tannah Johanan Ha-Sandlar, the claimed link. Einsiedler maintains that similar arguments from the Karo and Yahia-Charlap families can also be dismissed, though Shaltiel is not so sure.

Sassoon and Abravanel

The Sassoon family is often also referred to as being of Davidic descent. In *The Sassoons* (New York, 1968) Stanley Jackson writes:

> Small colonies (of Jews) have settled from antiquity in India and China, but Baghdad remained the nerve center of the exiled. Over 40,000 were living in the city by the 12th century, and the Sassoons were among an elite who claimed their pedigree from King David himself.... Among their ancestors were the Ibn Shoshans, princes of the community in Toledo, Spain.... As early as the 17th century, a scholar and mystic of Venice, Abraham Sason, proudly claimed descent from Shephatiah, the fifth son of King David.... The first member of the family of whom there is any significant documentary evidence was Sason ben Saleh, born in Baghdad in 1750, who was the Chief Banker and had the honorary title of Sheikh, and became in 1778 Nassi (Prince of the Captivity) of the Jewish community.

However, as Einsiedler remarks (qtd. in Shaltiel), Davidic descent is not mentioned in either Chaim Bermant's *The Cousinhood* (MC, 1972) or Cecil Roth's *The Sassoon Dynasty* (London, 1941).

The Abravanel/Abarbanel family of Spain is frequently characterized as of Davidic descent. The *Encyclopaedia Judaica* (Jerusalem, 1972) reports that

> the family, first mentioned in 1300, attained distinction in Spain in the 15th century.... Don Isaac Abravanel (1437–1509), finance minister to the Kings of Portugal, then Spain, then Naples, wrote in his memoirs: "All my forebears, descended from King David, son of Jesse of Bethlehem, were worthy leaders of our people" [Volume II, page 102].

But Shaltiel quotes Einsiedler as rejecting these claims, for the latter says, "I have not found sources going far enough back to support the claim of Davidic descent." Shaltiel concludes,

> The bottom line is: King David had a number of wives and concubines, and about two dozen children are mentioned in the Bible. King Solomon "had seven hundred royal wives and three hundred concubines" (I Kings 11:3). One can only imagine how many children he had. After nearly 3,000 years, there may be an untold number of their descendants. There is a fair possibility that you and I may be among them. All we need is good evidence and records that go back that far and [to] give convincing proof of our claim. So far, available records cannot do it. Some individuals rely on tradition and faith to back their claim. More power to them. The rest of us may have to wait for that promised descendant — the Messiah.

We agree with this rebuttal and propose that these Sephardic families very likely *converted* to Judaism around 750–900 c.e. in France, together with several families who subsequently moved to Scotland (e.g., the Stewarts, Davidsons). In all these cases, we suggest that because they were converted *by* a Davidic descendant at the Jewish Academy in Narbonne, they came to believe that they therefore descended from King David themselves, in accordance with the generational myth-making process described by Zerubavel (2003). Note that virtually all these "Davidic pedigrees" begin around 900–1100.

Notably also, DNA from over 10 descendants of the Sisson family in the United States matched the Caldwell-Yates-Ramey-Stewart haplotype and is R1b Sephardic, but not Semitic.

APPENDIX E

Border Reiver DNA

Since completing *When Scotland Was Jewish*, the authors became aware of a large collaborative project called Border Reiver Families DNA Study (available at http://freepages. genealogy.rootsweb.com/~donegalstrongs/reiver_families. htm). The Borderlands separating England from Scotland are notable as the traditional stronghold of several important Scottish clans and septs, including Scott, Burns, Tait/Tate, Forster, Beatty, Rutledge, Graham, Armstrong, Elliot, Johnston, Kerr, Kay, Gray, Hume, Bell, Davidson, Storey, Robinson, Crow, Langley, Heron, Hunt, Lindsay, Jackson, Taggart, Bold, Reade, Young, Oliver, Brown, Watts, Turner, Taylor, Chamberlain, and Maxwell. Members of these families emigrated in high numbers to America during the Scots-Irish migration of the eighteenth century and crop up among the Melungeons.

The interpretive results of this study will be years in coming, but it is evident at a glance that the leading families who controlled this region have a similar mixture of DNA lines as the Scots investigated in our book, with Iberian-centered R1b forming the overwhelming majority of male lineages. Some surprises that tend to corroborate our thesis include Hall, Moorish (E); Liddell and Armstrong (J2); numerous Hungarian names*; and Elliott (C).†

---

*Tentatively, we note Carruthers, Carr/Kerr (swordsman), Carnaby, Darby (D'Arby), Armstrong, Strange, Strong, Brown (through translations of Hungarian words like kar, nagy and barna), Bell (Bela?), Selby (csel "deceive"), Taggart (member) and perhaps Heron (white, blonde), Irvin/Erwin and Beatty (fearless). Carnegie ("big czar") has already been discussed.

†About this lineage, the author of the Clan Elliott subsheet speculates: "The top five hits in YHRD fell in Gotland, China, Iran, Spain, Venice and among the Iraqi Kurds.... this haplotype may be Hunnish or Indo-Iranian in origin, and could have come to Britain with the Sarmatians in the Roman Army, or with Norman invaders of Alanic or Visigothic [emphasis added] descent.... these Elliotts (or Eliots) were reputedly descended from a Norman knight surnamed 'Aliot.'" We have suggested above that Elliot comes from Judeo-Arabic and means "those who go up" (i.e., who are called up for service, or make an aliyah, who become distinguished). The famous poet and man of letters, Thomas Stearns Eliot (1888–1965), has Anglo-French Jewish ancestry in both his maternal and paternal lines, a fact which sheds light on his efforts to help Jewish refuges and alleged anti–Semitism; see R.F. Fleissner, "T.S. Eliot and Anti-Semitism," Contemporary Review (Dec. 1999).

Chapter Notes

Chapter 1

1. Scotland even lacks an agreed-upon history of its place-names. As has been pointed out, its landscape, glacial and volcanic at once, with marine fossils in the Grampian Mountains, and some of the deepest lakes in the world, was so bewildering that the modern science of geology had to be created to explain it (by James Hutton and Sir Charles Lyell; see Magnusson 2000, pp. 2–3). Two archeological marvels are distinctively Scottish, the brochs (stone towers) and crannogs (lake fortresses), while all Scotland's major rivers and firths show evidence of having been bridged with a network of highways prior to the Roman arrival. Modern-day attempts to etymologize many of Scotland's oldest place-names, however, are conflicting because no consensus has emerged on the country's underlying chronology of settlement. Does the name Douglas derive from "dark stranger," "black water," or "one from Gaul"? It depends on what you believe was the original language— Scottish Gaelic, some other Gaelic: English, or French. Does the name for Tiree, one of the islands of the Inner Hebrides, come from Gaelic *Tir-iodh* "Land of Corn," or *Tir fo Thuinn* "Land Below the Waves"? Or was the original name something else, in a different language? Curiously, most of Scotland's islands bear names that were apparently given in the Greek language: Hebrides = Hebrew Islands; Orkneys = Islands of the Whales; Skye = Island of the Scythians; Iona = Jonah's Island; Tiree = Island of the Phoenician Sea Goddess Tyre; Mull = Island of Black Lead (Greek μόλυβδος). Yet no Greek-speaking inhabitants have ever been documented, much less proposed, in Scotland's entire history.

2. "Picts" ("painted people") was the name given by Romans to the indigenous people they found when they conquered Britain in the first century. Their language is presumed to have been Celtic, a distant cousin of Latin and major branch of the Indo-European language group. In the 18th century, historians discovered evidence of a link between Celtic and Phoenician, the Semitic language of ancient Carthage. Among the plays of the Roman author Plautus (died 184 B.C.E.) is a work called *Penulus* (Phoenician) in which the dramatist placed a specimen of then-current Phoenician into the mouth of one of his characters. The similarity between the Phoenician of Plautus and early Irish-Celtic was first proposed by Thomas Moore in his *History of Ireland* and accepted by scholars such as Charles Vallancy, Lord Rosse, and Sir William Betham (Brooks 2001). Modern language scholars have confirmed the link, which tends to support an early settlement of England, Scotland, Wales and Ireland by a Mediterranean and Semitic-Hamitic people, the "Phoenicians." "Therefore we can say that in ... a multitude ... of ways, the Celts and Hebrews bear a remarkable relationship. Since the Celts were spread over most of Europe, the cultural, historical, and [religious] implications ... are immensely significant" (Brooks 2001, p. 90).

3. While stereotypes are often exaggerations or untruths, they do have value as social constructs, playing as legitimate a part in the study and writing of history as in the practice of marketing, anthropology, and government.

4. Melungeons are sometimes also referred to as Black Dutch. On the beginnings of the use of this term in U.S. history to refer to Hollanders of dark appearance (with mention neither of Melungeons nor Jews), see Mary Bondurant Warren, editor, *Family Puzzlers* (July 22, 1976, No. 457; reproduced on USGenNet, <http://www.tngenweb.org/cherokee _by_blood/dutch.htm>). Warren is a reputable source, as she served as historian of the state of Georgia. The same people were often called Portuguese in colonial Virginia and Carolina records (Gallegos 1997). A connection between the two lies in the Sephardic Jewish merchants who settled in the Dutch Republic following its independence from Spain, who called themselves, ambiguously, *gente del linaje*, or *homens da naçāo*, or "Hebrews of the Portuguese Nation" (on which, Bodian 1997, without reference to Melungeons). They streamed into Britain, and thence to America, beginning with the mission of

Amsterdam chief rabbi Menasseh Ben Israel to readmit Jews to England under Cromwell (Wall 1987). The first known use of the word Melungeon in U.S. records ("Melungin") occurs in the minutes of the Primitive Baptist Church of Stony Creek, Tennessee, in 1813 (Goins 2000, p. 9), where it is applied to certain "irregular" members with the surnames Minor, Gibson, and Collins who fraternized with the Sizemores (Cismar), a mixed Portuguese Jewish and American Indian family, on Blackwater Creek (see Horton n.d.; appendix A for Sizemore DNA). Mere knowledge of such a rare term, thought to be Arabic ("cursed souls"), must have come from the Collinses, Goinses, Sizemores, and others, who moved in a Caribbean and Spanish-Portuguese orbit. Many years later, these and other families who clustered on Newmans Ridge were labeled as Melungeon by a Nashville journalist named Drumgoole (1890), and the term has stuck. She was a descendant of Alexander Drumgoole (d. 1837), a Scots trader among the Cherokee, whose mixed-blood daughter Nannie married Cherokee chief Doublehead (d. Aug. 9, 1807). This journalist is credited with popularizing many elements of the Melungeon legend at a time when her cohorts among New York travel writers were inventing "hillbillies" (Benjamin Albert Botkin, *A Treasury of Southern Folklore* [New York: Crown Publishers, 1949], pp. 85–86). The term Melungeon is also used in Brazilian history to refer to settlements by Portuguese Jews and Moorish adventurers among Amerindians of the Wild Coast (the great bulk of Brazil's African slaves came from Angola and were Malungin-speaking). Obviously, it is not restricted to people of Newmans Ridge and surrounding area, any more than the term Black Dutch is confined to Virginians or North Carolinians.

5. A Scots presence among Melungeons must be seen in the larger context of Scottish mercantilism, exploration, colonization, and emigration. Scots clearly preceded English, and Spanish, and French to North America (Thompson 1994, pp. 303–31). Parts of the New World were known throughout the Middle Ages as Albany, the traditional designation for the realm of Scotland and the British Isles (in Norse, Vitramannaland, or "Glass-man Country," perhaps a rendering of Glasvegiana "New Glasgow"). Viking colonists used Scotsmen as guides and interpreters, as did also the Spanish conquistadors. Thorfinn Karlsefni, who established the first settlement in Vinland after explorations by Eric the Red and Leif Ericsson around the year 1000 C.E., put two Scots ashore in the new land, probably the southern coast of Labrador, with instructions to explore the countryside, and they returned with cranberries and an ear of wild barley (Mallery and Harrison 1979, pp. 75, 80, 124). At this time, the Orkneys were ruled by the Thorfinn dynasty, which owed allegiance to the Norwegian Crown (see MS p. 10 above). The name, however, came from France, and with the widow of the last Orkney ruler the line merged with Scotland's. In 1398, Templars under Henry Sinclair, Earl of the Orkneys, mounted an expedition to Greenland and beyond, one of his men dying on the voyage and being entombed in the future state of Massachusetts (Thompson 1994, p. 302). Tam Blake (Tamas Blaque) was a subject of King James V, the son of William Blake and Agnes Mowat, who joined the Coronado Expedition in 1540 to explore what is now Arizona and New Mexico (Hewitson 1993, pp. 11–13).

6. The sandstone trophy that was "returned" to Scotland by the English amid much fanfare in 1996 (Ascherson 2002, pp. 1–24) is held by many not to be the real Stone of Destiny (Saxum Fatale) but a decoy that was allowed to go to England with the armies of Edward I in 1296 (see, for instance, Gardiner 2001, pp. 246–48). The original ancient symbol of Scottish nationality is thought to have been smaller and of basalt.

7. Perhaps Chaldees, Babylonians?

8. The name has been traced to Béthune, the town in Flanders, but perhaps the town was named for "Beatons," not vice versa.

9. The Scottish bagpipe is attested as early as the 5th century. Of the Old Irish bagpipe, "very little is known of this instrument," although "there is reason to believe that the origin of the bag-pipe must be sought in remote antiquity. No instrument in any degree similar to it is represented on any of the monuments of Egypt or Assyria known at the present day; we are, nevertheless, able to trace it in ancient Persia and by inference in Egypt, in Chaldaea and in ancient Greece" (*Encyclopaedia Britannica* 1911).

10. It is interesting to note that when Charlemagne gathered about him a select academy of bards and scholars at his capital Aachen, he chose the secret name King David (Einhard, *Vita Karoli*). His features were used in Carolingian illuminated psalters for the portrait of King David, believed at that time to be the author of the Psalms.

11. The founder of the order was Bernard of Clairvaux (1090–1153), the son of Tescelin Sorrel and Aleth, the daughter of the Lord of Montbard. Born on the family estates of Fontaines de Dijon, Burgundy, he became the instigator of the Second Crusade, a revered figure in the Templar Order, and target of one of the major masterpieces of medieval literature, *Isengrimus*. This long satire written about 1150 is attributed to a figure known as Simon of Ghent, who wove Hebrew and Arabic fables into his analysis of contemporary events and may have been a Jewish convert (Yates 1979).

12. Nearly all Western European manuscript illumination (painting on parchment leaves of books) during the period 500–800 C.E. came from Ireland, Scotland or scriptoria (writing schools in monasteries) founded by Irish and Scottish monks, such as Dublin, Iona, Jarrow, Wearmouth, Bobbio, Fulda, Würzburg or Luxeuil. The only other regions where sumptuous books were still produced after the fall of Rome were Byzantium, Egypt, the Middle East, and to a small degree, isolated monasteries in Visigothic Spain and Southern Italy.

13. At the end of the fifteenth century there may have been up to 300,000 *conversos* in Spain and Portugal. They constituted the educated urban bourgeoisie of Spain, and the richer families frequently intermarried with the Spanish aristocracy and even transmitted their bloodlines to the royal family itself.

14. The authors are aware of the controversy and even dismissal that first greeted Stewart's claims.

However, his assertions about Scottish history and Stewart genealogy, they maintain, should be judged on their own merits.

15. For the line of succession of the High Stewards of Scotland, see appendix B.

16. Note that this is analogous to the Jewish hereditary priesthood, the Kohanim or Cohens; see appendix B.

17. We propose *sheriff* to be derived from Arabic *sharif*, meaning "leader," "master," or "chief," rather than from the Anglo-Saxon words "shire" and "reeve" (as, for instance, Bruce 1999, p. 14). *Sharif* in turn comes from *shari'a* "body of law." On its use in the Arabic world to distinguish leaders who based their claim to authority on descent from the Prophet, see Hourani 1991, p. 115. Before the arrival of the Normans in the British Isles, the equivalent term for "sheriff" was "thane." "Shire Reeve" is not found before the reign of Athelred, whose consort and regent was the Norman princess Emma (Bruce, p. 14). We believe the system of "*sharif*-doms" introduced subsequently by the Normans came directly from Moorish-Judaic traditions in Spain. If we are right, this key institution in the civil justice of English-speaking countries should be attributed to Islamic influence, like the Exchequer (chessboard-like accounting method), *starr* (record of debt in Hebrew) and other "innovations" of the Norman system of administration. The Exchequer entered England with the Dukes of Normandy, who copied it from the Counts of Flanders. It came to Scotland with the Stewarts, whose badge of office became the "Fess Chequey" (for an illustration, see Gardiner 2001, p. 229; cf. the photo of the Queen's Remembrancer in Bruce, p. 214). Ceremonial offices in Britain and Scotland that apparently owe a debt to Judeo-Arabic protocol are: Marshall, Lord High Chancellor of the Exchequer, Master of the Mint, Keeper of the Great Seal (Lord Ashley under Charles II), Groom of the Bedchamber (held by Robert Cooper under Henry V), Lyon King of Arms, Lord High Constable of Scotland, and King's Remembrancer (instituted by Henry II). "Bailiff" is popularly explained as coming from Lat. *baiulare* "to fetch" but its true origin may lie in Arabic *bay'a* "investiture" (see Hourani 1991, p. 136). The following Norman surnames seem to be formed from Arabic practices: Cate/Katy/Cade from *quadi* "judge," *Day/Dey* from dey "leader," Due from *du'a* "prayer," Mustain(g) from "Allah's assistance is sought, cared for by God" an Ottoman dynastic name related to *musteño* "mustang," Haley from *ali* "man," Shaw from *shah* "emperor," Wallace/ Walys from *wali* "friend, saint," Mofatt/Mowat/Mouawad/Muffat/ Muphat from *mufti* "jurisconsult, barrister, attorney," Payne/Paine from *payin* "infidel," Elliot/Eliot from *eyelet* "administrative province, tax farmer" (cf. Hebrew *aliyah*, pl. *aliyot* "rising, going up, honor").

18. See appendix B, "Naming and Jewish Priest-Kings."

19. We can add a second Scottish Jew, Fogo, the name of one of the Scots bishops in the 1600s. The family name derives from a mountain in the Cape Verde Islands off the coast of Africa, settled by the Portuguese in the 1500s.

Chapter 2

1. The clash between Jewish groups about their identity in America has been described in a recent bestseller titled *Jew vs. Jew: The Struggle for the Soul of American Jewry* (Freedman 2000).

2. Of the three "castes" or divisions, around 90 percent of Jews belong to the lineage known as Israelites; the other two lineages, Cohanim and Levites, are specifically recognized as Semitic (Thomas et al. 2000, p. 676). In Passover liturgies, the same division is mentioned, with the Israelites identified with the non–Hebrew "multitudes" that came out of Egypt in the Exodus.

3. In Spanish and Netherlands history, a Marrano was a Jew who converted to the Christian faith to escape persecution, but who continued to practice Judaism secretly. It was a term of abuse and was also applied to any descendants of Marranos. The origin is uncertain (but see chapter 6).

4. Subsequent work has confirmed the original study (Semino et al. 2004; Nebel et al. 2003; Hammer et al. 2000; Thomas et al. 2000). The Lemba "Black Jews" of southern Africa, for instance, were shown to have a high frequency of the CMH, while the haplotype was absent in the neighboring Bantu populations, thus supporting Lemba claims of paternal Judaic ancestry (Thomas et al. 2000).

5. The rationale, method and technical details for our genealogical use of the YHRD are described in Yates and Hirschman (2006). Another introductory essay is Shriver, M.D. and R.A. Kittles, "Genetic ancestry and the search for personalized genetic histories," *Nature Rev. Genet.* 5:611–618 (2004). It should be noted that FTDNA includes "blind" (anonymous) samples representing persons of self-identifying Jewish religious affiliation, usually described as "Ashkenazi" (a study of Spanish exiles or Sephardi Jews is hoped to be added).

6. We had two Alexander donors, following our protocol, but the other sample matched with three persons having another surname, seeming to point to a "non-paternity event," and was accordingly not used in the present study.

7. One might argue that the YHRD sample is skewed since several of the contributing studies come from Iberia (though more come from Germany), or that the Iberian pattern represents the deep history of the expansion of human settlements and repopulation of Europe after the Ice Age. But the fact remains that there is a very high percentage of males in Spain and Portugal exhibiting the same haplotype as our Scots-Melungeon Alexander. If Alexanders were Gaelic or Celtic, these Spanish and Portuguese cousins would be hard to account for. In historical times, Scotland did not send any colonists to the Iberian peninsula. However, as we will demonstrate, Iberia did send colonists, in several stages, to Scotland.

8. <http://www.familytreedna.com/public/forbes/>. As of this writing, there were nine donors and only two participants matched each other exactly.

9. A search for the "extended" haplotype, adding markers DYS438 and DYS439, yielded one match in Northern Portugal, seeming to indicate that this was

the homeland of Forbes I. It should be pointed out, however, that currently only about 22 percent of all YHRD samples are extended by these two loci, so any results are likely to be incomplete.

10. A tradition apparently as old as the Elizabethan privateer Martin Frobisher and continued by America's entrepreneurial publisher Malcolm S. Forbes, Sr. (died 1990). The most recent study of Frobisher notes that the trail of his genealogy leads to John Frobisher, a Scot born circa 1260 who served under Edward I, in other words, during the generation that saw many English Jews go underground (McDermott 2001, p. 8). Frobisher's career on the high seas blossomed with the influence of Raleigh, Grenville, merchant-banker Michael Lok, and others of the same background whose true colors can be seen, we suggest, in the names of their ships, sometimes obviously (French) Jewish: Ark Royale, Denys, Emanuel of Bridgewater, Emanuel of Exeter, Gabriel, Isaac, Judith, Michael, Salomon, Sampson, Samson, and Argo (pp. 505–7). Given that Forbush was a common form of the name in Scotland, it is an easy step to Forbusher (1578) and then Frobisher. Significantly, Frobisher is said to have had "contacts in Germany (probably Hamburg), Ireland and Scotland" (p. 111), to have derived knowledge of the sailing directions and the shoreline of North America from a map associated with the Sinclair family and the Orkneys, and even to have had a German prospector with a Jewish name on board for his 1577 voyage of discovery to the land of the Inuits (p. 175). A contemporary portrait of Frobisher shows him to have a dark complexion, bony frame, and green eyes.

Robert (Bertie) Charles Forbes was a journalist and financier who lived from 1880 to 1954. Forbes was born in New Deer (Aberdeenshire) and emigrated to the U.S. in 1906, settling in New York, and founding the business review *Forbes* magazine in 1917.

11. The following Forbes family trees have been published on the Internet at Stirnet Genealogy (<http://www.stirnet.com/HTML/genie/british/ff/bindff.htm>): Forbes of Forbes, Forbes of Pitsligo, Forbes of Rires, Forbes of Tolquhorn, Forbes-Leith of Whitehaugh, Forbes of Corse, Forbes of Craigievar, Forbes of Granard, Forbes-Mitchell of Thainstone, Forbes of Corsindae, Forbes of Monymusk, Forbes of Culloden, Forbes of Pittencrieff, Forbes of Brux, and Forbes of Echt.

12. A second Bruce differed in several loci, indicating probably a separate branch of the family, but did not sign a release form. His DNA produced no matches in the YHRD.

13. The name Muse, spelled in early English documents Meus, is a Hebrew given name, equivalent to Meir. For instance, Jacob, "the Rothschild of English Jewry" and wealthiest man in Norman Canterbury, had sons named Samuel and Aaron, a son-in-law Meus (Meir), and Simon, a nephew (Adler 1939, p. 59). The name was also rendered as Miles and Milo (p. 135, n. 4). Musa, notably, also is Arabic for Moses.

14. See Charles H. Lippy, *Bibliography of Religion in the South* (Macon, Ga.: Mercer University Press, 1985).

15. Information of Dr. Kathy Ryder of Tampa, Florida, whose family (Henriques and Franks) were early Jewish Jamaican merchants.

16. One of the Campbells in our family was Salathiel Campbell, a wealthy medical doctor who was born in Tennessee and lived in Arkansas (1810–1903). Salathiel ("God is asked") is a name that is exclusively Jewish; it is a variant of Shealtiel, the son of Zerubbabel. His Campbells are traced to Robert Campbell, born 1700 in Edinburgh.

17. Jacobs 1906–1911.

18. <http://jordannctoal.homestead.com>.

19. Byron created a sensation with the publication in 1815 of "Hebrew Melodies," poems which were set to traditional Hebrew music by I. Nathan. His mother was Catherine Gordon of Gight, and his uncle and predecessor in the baronetcy was Lord George Gordon (1751–1793), who publicly "converted" (more likely returned) to Judaism in 1787 and wrote tracts against Jewish assimilation into English society (Endelman 1979, p. 122).

20. On Benedict Arnold and his relations with the Jewish Franks family, see Lebeson (1950), pp. 134, 137. Abraham Arnold was a Jewish member of the Republican Committee under Abraham Lincoln (p. 287).

21. "The whole business of 'Jewish' names is quite confusing. There was a definite tendency on the part of the immigrant Jews in those days to drop their Spanish and their German Jewish names as they passed through England, and to appropriate English names. Thus it is that we find them in the seventeenth and eighteenth centuries with such names as Phillips, Brown, Rice, Hays, Henry, Laney, Simson, Jones, and the like" (Marcus 1973, vol. II, p. 249). "Saul Pardo ('brown') blossomed forth as Saul Brown" (vol. I, p. 35).

22. Jacobs 1906–1911.

23. *Ibid.*

24. *Ibid.*

25. Probably formed from Germanic Schellmann, "pilgrim, wanderer."

26. <http://www.angelfire.com/nb/stewart dna/>.

27. Robert James Andrews, <http://www.thefrasers.com/fraserdna.html>.

28. Way and Squire 1999, pp. 142–45.

29. Project Manager, Laura Cowan Cooper, Kodak, Tennessee, e-mail address: dacooper@usit.net.

30. This is evidently a Celticized rendering of Cowan, perhaps the same as MacKuen. The Scotsman James MacQueen (1683–1811) was the grandfather of the Native American chiefs Tecumseh (b. 1768) and Osceola. He jumped ship in Pensacola harbor in 1718 and established a trading post in Creek country at Tallassee, near present-day Montgomery, Alabama, where he married into the Tuckabatchee hierarchy. His son Peter MacQueen married a French Indian Jew, Betsy Durant.

31. The Seneor family held the post of chief tax collector for the Spanish Crown for three generations over the course of the fifteenth century (Gitlitz 1996, p. 17).

32. Koontz/Kuntz is a Hebrew name formed from the letters K-N-TZ, meaning Kohan Tzadik, or "righteous Priest" (Jacobs 1906–1911).

33. Statistically, the size of a valid random sam-

ple required for a population of 6 million is 384 (with a confidence level of 95 percent and confidence interval of 5 points). With 520 we have exceeded this minimum and raised the confidence level to 98 percent. This presupposes the data were reported from a single one-time randomized selection of all eligible Scots. In actuality, the sample is biased owing to a number of unknown factors, such as timing, self-selection, degree of relatedness, geographical spread, age of the participants, affordability spread, and purposive sampling (e.g., for medical testing), depending on the contributory studies. Any nonrandom circumstances render the results, and interpretations based on them, less "robust." It should be noted most national polls use the "magic number" of 384.

34. Chapters 3 through 6 will elaborate on a population movement from southern France to the Rhineland, Flanders and Normandy during the period of 500–800, when a new order was established in the western lands of Europe.

Chapter 3

1. The Saint Clair (Sancto Claro = Sacred Light) family is closely associated with the Templars and Cabalistic Judaism. They will be discussed in chapter 8.

2. Perhaps connected with the Jewish name Tamaris "palm tree" (Hebrew *Tamar*, Greek *Tamaris*, French *Demaris, Demarice*).

3. Accounts differ on this; see Gardner 2001, p. 245; Brown 1998.

4. The names Isaac, Isaacs, Kissack, Kissock, and McKessack are all derivatives of the Hebrew surname Isaac. Barnett/Burnett and Harris are leading surnames in Jacobs' list of Jewish philanthropists in 19th century England, mentioned above. Orr and Ure mean "gold," and Tawes, McTause, McTavish and Taweson are taken from the Hebrew/Greek letter Taw. As will be demonstrated in chapter 7, the Tau/Thow/ Tough symbol is an X, not a Christian cross. It has Cabalistic links and is found in the Templar effigies showing knights with crossed legs, in the Scottish Saltire flag and in the Freemasons' skull and crossed shin bones image.

5. Other forms apparently are Fordyce, Fordice, Forbush, Forbish, Fobes, Forbess and Faubus. The name may be Greek in origin, seeming to go back to Phoebus, a divine appellation for Apollo as the Sun God. Both Phoebus and Apollo were common names adopted by Hellenizing and Roman Jews (Jacobs 1906–1911). This was a particular trend during the spread of Mithraism, an ancient Iranian religion that, before its eclipse by Christianity, was the most popular cult in the Roman Empire of the second and third centuries C.E., particularly among soldiers and the federated Germanic tribes on the Rhine, Danube and Dnieper (*Oxford Classical Dictionary*, s.v. "Mithraism"). In Visigothic Spain, Phoebus became Febos, a Marrano name amply attested in the records of the Inquisition. It was corrupted to Feibus and after several generations in Salonica and Izmir, followed by a migration to Vienna, to Federbusch

("feather bush"). It also seems likely that Martin Frobisher, Elizabethan explorer, came was of this ilk (on whom, see chapter 2).

6. Perriman and Rediat are Sephardic Jewish surnames in the records of Bevis Marks Synagogue, London; both Rebecca and Deborah are Hebrew given names.

7. The Cherokee Stand Watie (1806–1871) is remembered as the last Confederate general to surrender in the War Between the States. With his cousin Maj. John Ridge and brother Buck Watie (who changed his name to Elias Boudinot after the French Jewish statesman from New Jersey and became the first editor of the Cherokee newspaper, *The Phoenix*), he was a leader of the Removal, or Treaty, Party (those who collaborated with the federal government in removing the Cherokee west of the Mississippi) and the Knights of the Golden Circle, a Masonic organization that resisted Christian missionary activity in the Cherokee Nation. Watie was rendered Oowatie in Cherokee, but has no meaning in the Cherokee language. The family acknowledged descent from a "Dutch" Cherokee. Intermarriages occurred between Waties and persons named Field, Gist (da Costa, Κώστας, גוסטא), Looney (de Luna), Miller, Bell (*Belle*), Reece (Rice), Gold (almost invariably Jewish), Wheeler, Smith and Candy (Kennedy; see chapter 2), suggesting a Crypto-Jewish background for them. One of Gen. Watie's sons was named Saladin Watie. On the Watie party, see William G. McLoughlin 1991, *After the Trail of Tears* (Chapel Hill, N.C., and London). Watts and Waters are also frequent surnames in this family tree.

8. Saltoun = Sultan, meaning a prince or ruler in Arabic.

9. Lovat comes from Levy, a Hebrew tribal name. On a Lovatt match with Caldwell-Stewart, see chapter 2.

10. We should perhaps note that Panton, Leslie's trade differed from that of many merchants and brokers not only in taking on a truly international dimension, but also embracing all manner of merchandise, including staple foodstuffs (which were often denied to Jewish firms) and metal, coin and specie (normally a privilege controlled by the Crown). When the firm was dissolved, all interested parties wanted to know where the money went. The answers lie in the papers of Panton, Leslie and Co., which occupy some 150 shelf-feet, now divided between the University of West Florida and heirs and descendants in Mobile, New Orleans and elsewhere. But since the founding principle of the enterprise was barter, it is doubtful whether any great fortune was banked. The demise of this great Sephardic-Scots trading firm had the unusual side-effect of giving birth, posthumously, to an American Indian tribe: the Poarch Band of Creek Indians was recognized by the federal government of the United States in 1986 under a charter granted to Panton, Leslie in the last days of the royal Spanish superintendency (Sutton 1991).

11. *Dubhglas, Dubhgal* (pronounced Doov-GLAS and Doov-GALL). *Dubh* does mean black, but we have not found that *gall* or *glas* means "stranger" in the Gaelic language. *Glas* is normally translated as "gray." The element *-gall* is probably better rendered

as a patronymic "from Gaul." Both MacDougall and Douglas arms show ships arriving from foreign lands, and lions, usually an association with the East.

12. The etymologies of the name are contradictory, some taking it back to the Pontic king Gordius and the Gordian knot famously cut by Alexander the Great (Graves 1996, pp. 263–64), others to the river Jordan, often adopted as a surname by Jews in exile. Perhaps significant is the fact that the best-known chronicler of the origins and deeds of the Goths, around 550 C.E., was Jordanes, or Jornandes, an Arian Scythian of a foreign family of court officials who adopted his name in honor of the river Jordan when he converted to Christianity (Hodgkin 2000, pp. 577–583). He may have been Jewish by origin. In France, the name seems to have become confused with Jarden ("garden"), based on the root *gards, a Visigothic word for "yard," also a term for territory and administrative units. In Spanish, G and J have the same value, and Jordan became a common name for medieval Jews and later Crypto-Jews. In Italian, the name also starts with a G, i.e. Giordano.

13. Available at <http://www.tartans.com>.

14. In addition to Lombard Hall, there was also a Jacob Hall and a Moses Hall. The Jewish mercantile quarter in Philadelphia was also named Lombard Street. The Lumbee Tribe of American Indians was named after the town in Robeson County, N.C., that was their center, now Lumberton, perhaps originally Lumbard-ton. This county today is about one-third Indian in its population. It received its name from the Scots Robinson ("son of Rueben") family that also produced Maj. James Robertson, a trustee of the Watauga Association and founder of Nashville in Tennessee (1742–1814). Locklear and Newberry are Lumbee names (see appendix A).

15. See also appendix B, "Naming and Jewish Priest-Kings."

16. The utter silence about Jews in the records of Henry I is strange (Tovey 1738, pp. 10–11). There seems to have been an official *obliteratio memoriae* in his reign. His brother and predecessor William Rufus "was said to have set up a debate between the scholars of the London Jewry and his bishops, and joked that if the Jews had the better of the argument, he would convert" (Crouch 2002, p. 139).

17. Douai, a medieval capital of Flanders, may be a locative form of "David" ("David's Town").

Chapter 4

1. The authors of this account "telescope" history and confuse the Albigensian and Waldensian sects which were prominent in the 13th and 14th centuries with the Protestant Reformation, which did not begin until the 1400s. Communities of French Jews were established in Piedmont 1390–1430, joining Jews from Rome (Barnavi 1992, p. 126).

2. This portion of the story is difficult to understand, as returning to Spain in the midst of the Inquisition would have meant death for Jews, Protestant "heretics," or Muslims. Perhaps the Caldwells were granted special status as foreigners. There were windows of opportunity for Jews from Spain and Portugal. For instance, Henri II issued letters patent in August 1550 for Portuguese New Christians to settle in France (renewed in 1574 by Henri III). And Charles V, who ruled both Spain and the Holy Roman Empire, granted the "Great Privilege" to the Jews of the German Empire in 1544. Between 1506 and 1531 there was a "period of grace" during which New Christians were allowed to leave Portugal and many immigrants chose to resettle in the Ottoman Empire (Barnavi 1992).

3. "Origin of the Caldwell Name," <http://www.geocities.com/Heartland/Estates/6455/history.html>.

4. The name of a synagogue in Wolhynia, Kahwel (in the Ukraine), appears on a metal Jewish collection vessel which Joseph, son of the Paris rabbi Jechiel, offered to a Zionist movement in 12th century England (Tovey 1738, pp. 248–51). "The famous Bodleian Bowl found in a Norfolk marsh [about 1698], with a long Hebrew inscription, was probably the gift of R. Joseph b. Yechiel, who had intended to emigrate to Palestine, but, on his appointment in 1209 as Archpresbyter of the English Jews, had to abandon his intention. The purpose of the bowl was probably for the collection of subscriptions for the pilgrims. The pilgrimage may have been inspired by the messianic hopes of the Jews of the time, who, by a calculation based on Daniel, had been led to expect the advent of the Messiah in 1211 or 1216. Of the three hundred pilgrims, many settled in Palestine, and we meet with their descendants for generations later" (Adler 1987, p. xv). This may be the source of the Caldwell name and a record of the previous emigrations of this family. If so Caldwell has nothing to do with Cold Well, as suggested by some, and was not English in its origin, but ultimately derives from Kahwel. Going further, the origin of the Albigensian and Waldensian communities in northern Italy lay among the Cathars and Bulgarians, leading us, again, to the Eastern Visigothic cultural area. Thus, the German word for "heretic" is *kertzer* "Khazar." The Khazars were a large, central Asian convert population that significantly swelled the numbers of Ashkenazic Jews from the 12th century onward.

5. "Comunità Ebraica di Casale Monferrato," <http://www.menorah.it/qqcasale/indice.htm>.

6. Perhaps originally Casale (an important Piedmontese Jewish community), filtered through French.

7. There is a Portuguese Jewish merchant family by this name in Colombo, Sri Lanka (Orizio 2000, p. 32).

8. <http://home.talkcity.com/DeckDr/big-james7/irishhuganoautimigration.html>.

9. See also the discussion in chapter 2.

10. Extracted from the Alexander GenForum online.

11. See Donald N. Panther-Yates, "You Will Never Find the Truth," online article archived at Melungeons.com, <http://www.melungeons.com/articles/march2003a.htm>.

12. And perhaps even Anders and Andrews.

13. The term was used of the Temple Sisterhood in Primitive Baptist Churches of the Holston Association in Tennessee (Denton n.d., p. 51).

14. On which, see chapter 2.

Chapter 5

1. E.g., "There is ... no doubt whatsoever that William I was responsible for the influx of a large crowd of Jews into England. They came from Rouen." (Ludovici 1938). Cf. Tovey 1967; Jacobs s.v. "England" in the Jewish Encyclopedia (1906–1911).

2. "Il y eut sans doute, en Gaule, des émigrés juifs qui remontèrent le Rhône et la Saône, et servirent en quelque sorte de levain; mais il y eut aussi une foule de gens qui se rattachèrent au judaïsme par conversion et qui n'avaient pas un seul ancêtre en Palestine. Et quand on pense que les juiveries d'Allemagne et d'Angleterre son venues de France, on se prend à regretter de n'avoir pas plus de données sur les origines du judaïsme dans notre pays. On verrait probablement que le Juif des Gaules du temps de Gontran et de Chilpéric n'était, le plus souvent, qu'un Gaulois professant la religion israélite." ("... there was a mass of people who embraced Judaism through conversion and who didn't have a single ancestor in Palestine.... probably the Jew of the Gauls of the time period of Gontrand and Childeric, in most cases, was nothing more than a Gaul professing the religion of Israel.")

3. Compare the description in Cunliffe of the trade routes across the "neck" of southern France from Narbonne to Bordeaux and of the Roman roads and river routes branching from southern France into the Rhineland and to L'Havre at the mouth of the Seine and the coast of Boulogne in Flanders (pp. 303, 398).

4. This will be discussed at length in chapter 9.

5. When we arrive in Scotland we will find Nimmo ("from Nîmes") to be a common surname.

6. Ibn Daud means Son of David or Davidson.

7. Interestingly, this is the strict maternal (mitochondrial DNA) line of Marie Antoinette, queen of France, who traced her female ancestry back to the 12th century figure Bertha von Putelendorf (Jehaes et al. 1998). Although most royal genealogies stop with Bertha, we have found one authority who gives her great-great grandmother as Judith of Schweinfurt (Dr. Hans Peter Stamp, "Die Ahnenliste des bayerischen Königs Ludwig II entspricht...," <http://www .drstamp.de/start/a1613.html>). Furthermore, Judith's mother was a descendant of Frederuna of France, consort of Charles the Simple, and Frederuna herself was a daughter of Count Theodoricus, an illegitimate younger son of Charlemagne by his concubine Ethelind/Adelheid. Thus Marie Antoinette's female heritage (and that of most of the queens of France) goes back to the wife or concubine of Theodoricus (French "Thiérry"), who according to Einhard's Life of Charlemagne was imprisoned in a monastery by his half-brother the emperor Louis the Pious (Gertjan Broekhoven, "Achternamenlist," <http:// home.zonnet.nl/broek hoven2/Broekhoven/ surnlist.htm>).

8. Since formulating the Machir-Stewart theory presented above, we were pleasantly surprised to encounter a Web page titled "The House of David, Evidence of the Davidic Dynasty." Darren Michael not only traces his maternal line back to Machir and the line of Davidic princes in Narbonne, but links them explicitly with his father's royal Scottish line (<http://www.scotlandroyalty.org/house-of-david. html>). We reproduce his Babylonian-French genealogy of the so-called Nasi below:

The Resh Galuta — Princes of the Dispersion

	Began	Ended
BABYLON		
Nahum	c. 140	c. 170
Huna I ben Nahum	c. 170	c. 210
Mar Ukba I ben Nahum	c. 210	c. 240
Huna II ben Ukba	c. 240	c. 260
Nathan I ben Huna	c. 260	c. 270
Nehemiah ben Nathan	c. 270	313
Mar Ukba II ben Nehemiah	313	337
Huna III ben Nehemiah	337	c. 350
Abba ben Ukba	c. 350	c. 370
Nathan II ben Abba	c. 370	c. 400
Kahana I ben Abba	c. 400	415
Huna IV ben Kahana	415	442
Mar Zutra I ben Kahana	442	455
Kahana II ben Zutra	455	465
Huna V ben Zutra	465	470
vacant	470	484
Huna VI ben Kahana	484	508
Mar Zutra II*	(508)	510–520
Ahunai	520?	531 (to c. 560)
Hofnai	c. 560	c. 560
Haninai	c. 580	c. 590
BAGHDAD ERA		
Bustanai ben Haninai	?	670
Hisdai I ben Bustanai	670	?
Bar Adai ben Bustanai	?	?
Hisdai II ben Bar Adai	?	733
Isaac Iskoy ben Solomon	?	?
Hananiah ben David	fl. c. 760	?
Zakkai Judah ben Ahunai	?	d. before 771
Makhir Natronai ben Habibi†	771	?
Zakkai	c. 772	775
Moses	?	?
Isaac Iskoy II ben Moses	fl. c. 800	?
David I ben Judah	820	857
Judah I ben David	fl. c. 857	?
Natronai	fl. c. 860	?
Hisdai III ben Natronai	?	?
Ukba	c.900	915
David II ben Zakkai	918	930
Hasan ben Zakkai	930	933
?	?	?
Judah II ben David	940	?
?	?	?
Solomon ben Hasan	951	953
Azariah ben Solomon	?	?
Hezekiah I (ben Judah?)	?	?
David III ben Hezekiah	?	?

*Mar Zutra established a rebel state in the Lower Euphrates in opposition to the anti–Semitic Shah Kobad. Relations were again normalized upon the ascension of Shah Khusrau the Just in 531.

†Makhir Natronai was sent to Pepin of the Franks, and soon thereafter established the reign of the Resh Galuta in Narbonne, after it had become its own principality under Jewish rule.

	Began	*Ended*
Hezekiah II ben David	1021	1058
David IV ben Hezekiah	1058	?
Hezekiah III	?	1090
David V ben Hezekiah	?	?
Hisdai IV ben David	?	d. 1134
?	?	?
Daniel I ben Hisdai	1150	1174
Samuel I ha-Mosuli	1174	1195
David ben Samuel	?	d. after 1201
Daniel II	?	?
Samuel II ben Azariah	1240	1270

Chapter 6

1. Race Archives.

2. The Jewish contribution to the Conqueror's line may have been closer to home than the remote Carolingians. The name and identity of William's mother are disputed. She is given, variously, as Herleve de Falaise, also spelled Harlette and Arlette, or Arlotta, perhaps a rendering of the word "harlot" and therefore not a proper name at all but a sobriquet. Contemporary sources state that she was Duke Robert's mistress, a Rouen tanner's daughter. She married a Norman nobleman after Robert's death and helped save her son's dukedom by this marriage. According to Barnavi (1992, p. 71) the occupation of tanner was dominated by Jewish artisans, particularly in Constantinople and other trading centers. Tanner, Ledermann and similar names in all European languages are common Jewish surnames even today.

3. Recall the Béthune/Beaton family, which was a hereditary dynasty of physicians serving the kings of Scotland.

4. For example, from examining the family genealogy we believe that the ancestors of Sir Walter Raleigh were likely originally Jewish and then converted to Christianity (remaining secretly Jewish). Raleigh established the first English colony in America in 1587 near Roanoke, Virginia. DNA analysis of these colonists' descendants, as well as genealogical and historical documents, suggest that they were Sephardic Jews (Hirschman 2005).

5. Though Ludovici was a reactionary, and rather obviously anti–Semitic, he was fastidious in his scholarship. He left his fortune to the University of Edinburgh to study "miscegenation." Edinburgh refused the gift.

6. We assume the private ones were destroyed.

7. The DNA of William's descendants is different from all but one of the participants in the online Cooper Surname DNA Project. Our specimen comes from a male cousin of both our mothers (each descended from William Cooper, the guide for Daniel Boone). William's father is thought to be James Cooper, a James River plantation owner who died in Southwark, Surry County, Virginia, in 1734. James's father, in turn, is held to be Reuben Cooper, identified as Robert Cooper, a London goldsmith, later a ship's surgeon, who married Elizabeth Gislingham in London in 1674 and died at sea in 1691,

leaving two orphans. Rueben/Robert's father was another Robert Cooper, a merchant of Yarmouth in Norfolk, possibly born in Stratford on Avon, Warwickshire. Connections with the family of Shaftesbury and Jewish mercantile houses are borne out by the names Ayliffe (Alef, of Amsterdam), Astley, Rousse/Ross, Gist, Looney/Luna, Howard, Harrison, Currer, Gilbert, Phillips, Massey, Cotton, Clark, Hart, Anthony, Boleyn/Bollin, Andrews, Arnold, Jones, Gold and Lawrence.

8. The tens of thousands of documented living descendants of Pocahontas, daughter of Chief Wahunsonacock of the Powhatan Indian Confederacy, who according to legend helped save the English settlers at Jamestown (d. March 21, 1616/17), all trace their genealogy through Pocahontas' only granddaughter, Jane Rolfe, who married Col. Robert Bollin(g) of the English Boleyn family, maternal line of Queen Elizabeth I (perhaps originally the Hebrew surname Balin "ritual bath keeper"). See Pocahontas Foundation; cf. Rountree 1996. Names covered include Armistead, Archer, Bentley, Bernard, Black Fox, Blair, Bland, Blevins, Bolling, Branch, Byrd, Cabell, Catlett, Cary, Clark, Cooper, Dandridge, Dixon, Douglas, Duval, Eldridge, Ferguson, Field, Fleming, Gay, Gordon, Griffin, Grayson, Harrison, Hubbard, Jefferson, Johnson, Kennon, Lewis, Logan, Markham, Maxey, Meade, McRae, Murray, Page, Payne, Poythress, Rabun, Randolph, Redwine, Robertson, Sizemore, Skipwith, Stanard, Tazewell, Walker, Ward, Watson, West, and Whittle.

9. Gilbert Burnet, *History of His Own Times,* vol. I, bk. I, sec. 96, footnote by Onslow.

10. *Converso* is another term for a Jew who had publicly accepted Christianity, but who privately remained Jewish.

11. And we encounter yet another likely Crypto-Jew: letters of Lady Jane Grey, "the Nine Days Queen" (1536–54), contain three (beautifully executed) Hebrew words: Lady Jane Grey to Bullinger, 12 July 1551: Zurich, Zentralbibliothek, MS RP 17; same to same, 7 July 1552: MS RP 18; same to same, before June 1553: MS RP 19. These letters are printed as nos. IV–VI in *Original Letters Relative to the English Reformation,* ed. H. Robinson (Cambridge: Parker Soc., 1846/7), i. 4–7, 7–8, 9–11. On 29 May 1551 John Ab Ulmis even suggested to Conrad Pellican that he should "honourably consecrate to her name your Latin translation of the Jewish Talmud" (*ibid.,* ii. 432). See also the three letters from Ulmis to Bullinger between Nov. 1551 and July 1552 (*ibid.,* 437, 451–2, 452–3).

12. As frequently noted by students of Judaica, none of the explanations suggested for the origin of Marrano seems very compelling, least of all the suggestion that the word is derived from Spanish *marrano* "wild pig." Rather too ingenious, to our mind, is one author's claim that the word comes from "a haplologic contraction of the Hebrew *mumar-anus* (which caused the omission of the first syllable), effecting the transformation: mumaranus, maranus, marano, marrano" (Netanyahu 1999, p. 59). In both the civil jurisprudence and canonical law of the period, as well as in popular currency, the sense of *maranus* (Lat.) is "privileged Jewish administrator

who feigns to be Christian." We propose here a radically different origin, the Mariannu mentioned in Egyptian annals. They were Ramses III's "only trustworthy allies" against invading Persians, according to the Elephantine Papyri. The word was introduced into the Egyptian language from the Aramaic Mareinu, meaning "noblemen," and applied to the Semitic "princes" who garrisoned a Jewish military town in Elephantine, an island in the Nile opposite Aswan. This important colony maintained several synagogues, along with a "temple in exile" that substituted for the Temple of David in Jerusalem destroyed by the Assyrians. "The very first words ... are *el-maran*, which means 'to the sir,' and the word *maran* is repeated again and again in this and in others of the Elephantine papyri [dated to the 5th to 4th centuries]. The word *maran* or *marenu* ('our sir') was put before the name of the satrap [provincial governor] in Jerusalem when the chiefs of the colony wrote to him; they themselves were addressed as *mareinu* ('our sirs') by the ordinary members of the colony in their letters. The singular and plural possessive forms, *marenu* and *mareinu*, are used profusely in the papyri of Elephantine" (Velikovsky 1977, pp. 62–65). We believe the Egyptian word *maran*, carried by the conquering Arabs to Spain and retained in their civil administration, gave birth to Spanish *marrano* and survived in the surname Moran, Morene, Moreno and their many variants.

13. William was descended from the house of Nassau in Germany and was the great-grandson of William the Silent, Prince of Orange (in southern central France). His mother was Maria Henrietta, the daughter of Charles I of England and Scotland. He married his first cousin, James's daughter Mary, which would have provided their children with a fully Davidic lineage, according to their presumption of ancestry from King David.

14. [John Toland], *Reasons for Naturalizing the Jews in Great Britain and Ireland, On the Same Foot with All Other Nations* (London, 1714). It must have been published between 18 Oct 1714 and 1 Dec. 1714, because a reply appeared at that time: Anon., *Confutation of the Reasons for Naturalizing the Jews* (London, 1715). Cf. *Monthly Catalogue*, 1/8 (1714), 53. The two copies are at the Jewish Theological Seminary, New York City; and Trinity College, Dublin. A reprint can be found in *Pamphlets Relating to the Jews in England in the Seventeenth and Eighteenth Centuries*, ed. P. Radin (San Francisco: California State Library, Sutro Branch, 1939).

Chapter 7

1. Most of Scotland's public civil records prior to 1340 were destroyed by the English during the military campaigns of the Lancastrian kings, if indeed any escaped the ravages of Edward I.

2. And who was likely a Jew, given his Hebrew first name.

3. Significantly, a Sinclair was among the original committee members of the Glasgow Hebrew Burial Society (Collins 1987, p. 87).

4. As will be shown in chapter 8, the pyramid shape is indicative of Scottish Rite Masonic affiliation, not Christianity.

5. Ayrshire was the historical dwelling place of the Kennedys and Caldwells when they arrived in Scotland.

6. Perhaps a shortening of Modern Greek Βασιλεΰς "King," (b-sounds being pronounced as v). In 1519, the Marrano Adam Vas was arrested in Catholic Antwerp (Belgium) on grounds of Judaizing and corresponding with heretics (Goris 1925, p. 651). Portuguese Jews spread to Antwerp from Bruges and Brabant, bringing with them the metal commodities exchange, chemical and pharmaceutical dealing, coin minting, and the diamond cartel (pp. 37, 259). Basileus, in turn, was, in some instances, a translation of Turkic Beg, the Khazar clan that converted to Judaism (Golb and Pritsak 1982).

7. Solomon Luria (1510–1573) was the first great Talmudic scholar in Lithuania. Rabbi Isaac Luria Ashkenazi was the leader of the kabbalists of Safed in the land of Israel about 1570.

8. The usual form in German-speaking lands was Goetz, Götz, or Getz, which has the same pronunciation in English as Yates/Gates. Other forms, all duly listed by the Mormon genealogists in their guides to surnames, are Oetz, Utz, Aytes, Jetts, Jeter, Gater and Jett. The line of Yateses of one of the authors is clearly tied to Poland/Ukraine and has been recorded as an old Ashkenazi family. According to Stern (2003), Eliakim Goetz, of Strelitz, near Danzig, was the father of Rabbi Benjamin Yates, head of the Liverpool (England) Jewish community, and Samuel Yates (1757–1825), who married an Abraham woman and became the founder of a long line (Stern 1991, p. 220, based on the records of Shearith Israel in New York). How do we get from Goetz, apparently a German name, to Yates? Jacobs (1906–1911) compares Yates to Katz, the most common Jewish surname of all. While Katz is an anagram meaning "righteous priest," Yates is a contraction formed from the first letters of the Hebrew words Ger ("convert") and Tzadik ("righteous"). It is evident, then, that the founder of this large family was a non–Semitic male, probably of the local majority population, who converted to Judaism, perhaps as early as the 9th or 10th century, when such anagrams began to be popular among Jewish fraternal orders at Speyer, Mainz and Augsburg. Of course, Rhineland Jewry goes back to Roman times and makes up the core of what we know today as the Ashkenazi Jews (Biale 2001, pp. 449–518). The Hebrew anagram is ג צ (which appears on a very old cattle brand brought by author Donald Yates's family from Virginia to colonial Georgia, now in the possession of Ruth Yates Spence of the Osceola County Historical Society). The earliest mention in the British Isles is on a rent roll of the 11th century, Adam de Jett. Note the Hebrew given name Adam, which was almost exclusively borne by Jews at the time.

9. Andrée Aelion Brooks, *The Woman Who Defied Kings: The Life and Times of Dona Gracia Nasi* (Paragon 2002). Her husband, Francisco Mendes, and brother-in-law, Diogo Mendes, were very successful bankers allied with the Spanish-Portuguese de Luna family, which the De Medicis later brought to

Florence. Another branch settled in Ballagilley on the Isle of Man and emigrated to Virginia, where they became prominent in frontier affairs, producing, for instance, Capt. John Looney (1744–1819) and Cherokee Chief John Looney (1776–1846). A thorough book on the Looneys of America is Madge Looney Crane and Philip L. Crane's *Most Distinguished Characters on the American Frontier. Robert Looney (b. 1692–1702, d. 1770) of Augusta (now Botetourt) County, Virginia, and Some of his Descendants, with Histories of the Great Road, Looney's Ferry, Crow's Ferry, Anderson's Ferry, Boyd's Ferry & Beale's Bridge*, vol. I (Apollo, Pa.: Closson Press, 1998).

10. "Gervase Ridale was a witness to a charter of David I in 1116.... Sir John Riddell was created a Baronet of Nova Scotia ... [and] his third son, William, was knighted by Charles I and later served in the wars in the Netherlands.... John Riddel, a prominent seventeenth-century Edinburgh merchant, claimed descent from Galfridus de Ridel. He amassed great wealth from the trade across the Baltic, particularly with Poland.... he is said to have intrigued with the forces of Oliver Cromwell, becoming a close friend of General Monck" (Way and Squire 1999, pp. 451–2).

11. The Scrymgeours were hereditary standard bearers of the Scottish kingdom, officially holding the Honourable Office of Bearer for the Sovereign of the Royal Banner of Scotland; their arms show a scimitar, lion and royal purple.

12. Notably, one James Mossman/Mosman ("Moses") and his father John were officials of the Royal Scottish Mint, and also treasurers to the Stewart monarchs. The goldsmiths in Edinburgh worshiped at St. Giles Church where they had set up a special altar to "St. Eloi," one of the Hebrew names for God. Mosman also created the Royal Stewart crown.

13. "Moors' Church."

14. We argue in chapter 10 that the Presbyterian Church in Scotland originated with Crypto-Jews.

15. "Prior," an office of the Templars; see chapter 8.

16. "Son of Kay," used, we suggest, as a patronymic for the family of any Scotsman adopting the letter K for his original name, including Kohanes; cf. Mackay, Mackey.

17. From Arabic *waqf* "benefice, tax district."

18. From Barthenia, a popular medieval French given name patterned on Parthenia, a name for the "maiden" goddess Minerva.

19. Hyssop was a bitter herb used in the purificatory rites, especially at Passover, by the ancient Jews.

20. Hebrew; cf. Tarbell.

21. From "Cossack."

22. Geddes is an early spelling for Cadiz, the primary seaport in southern Spain (Latin *Gades*).

23. A Flemish Jewish surname; cf. Epstein.

24. Zorababel.

25. Sometimes spelled Sample(s), evidently from Sampson + *-el*.

26. Cf. Maxey, Maximii. The Emperor Maximius was a patron of the Gothic tribes.

27. Pl. of *starr*, a record of a debt.

28. German *Rind* "beef, bull."

29. From French Reine, as in the part of Queen Esther played by prominent male members of the community in Purim plays (Jacobs).

30. Possibly from Hebrew *kos* "cup," hence "cup bearer or maker."

31. "Little Moses."

32. "Clockstone."

33. "Man from Hainaut."

34. = Haag, "one from the Hague."

35. =de Yet, "Yates."

36. = "Baker" in Yiddish.

37. Greek "treasure ship."

38. Diana Connell (n.d.), The Glass Workers of Scotland.

39. This and Tullas refer to the kingdom of Toulose in southern France.

Chapter 8

1. Which we take as implying they were Jews or Muslims from the Holy Land.

2. And who, according to the genealogy discussed in chapter 3, was of Davidic Jewish descent.

3. Patrick Payne started an ambitious, and exemplary, Payne Family DNA Project in 2002, eventually enrolling 23 members; available at <http://home. earthlink.net/~ppayne1203/>. Painstaking investigation of allele mutations in the multiple, mostly mercantile lines that entered the American colonies around 1650 revealed that the Paynes of the British Isles, Channel Islands and France seem to form a single, though ancient lineage, somewhat in the same mold as a Scottish clan. On the face of it, the surname itself, a form of *payin* ("pagan") suggests a distinctly foreign and eastern origin. In a separate project, Marshall Payn of Sarasota, Fla., a descendent of the Payne family of Long Island that produced John Howard Payne, was found to match an individual in Tibet. Payne (1791–1852) was the son of Sarah Isaacs, of a prominent New York and Newport Sephardic family (Stern 1991, p. 92). He is remembered as an indefatigable tract writer and author of "Home Sweet Home" (Marcus 1973, vol. I, p. 93). He was also an adopted Cherokee tribe member and perhaps the foremost early defender of Native American rights. Payne served as the American consul to Tunis in the latter years of his life.

4. Note that Noor/Norrie is a surname we frequently found in Scotland.

5. "There were also several smaller administrations established ... for the management of the farms and lands, and the collection of rent and tithes. Among these were Liddele and Quiely in the diocese of Chichester; Eken in the diocese of Lincoln; Adingdon, Wesdall, Aupledina, Cotona, etc. The different preceptors of the Temple in England had under their management lands and property in every county of the realm.

"In Leicestershire the Templars possessed the town and the soke of Rotheley; the manors of Rolle, Babbegrave, Gaddesby, Stonesby, and Melton; Rothely wood, near Leicester; the villages of Beaumont, Baresby, Dalby, North and South Mardefeld, Saxby,

Stonesby, and Waldon, with land in above *eighty* others! They had also the churches of Rotheley, Babbegrave, and Rolle; and the chapels of Gaddesby, Grimston, Wartnaby, Cawdwell, and Wykeham.

"In Hertfordshire they possessed the town and forest of Broxbourne, the manor of Chelsin Templars, (*Chelsin Templariorum,*) and the manors of Laugenok, Broxbourne, Letchworth, and Temple Dynnesley; demesne lands at Stanho, Preston, Charlton, Walden, Hiche, Chelles, Levecamp, and Benigho; the church of Broxbourne, two watermills, and a lock on the river Lea; also property at Hichen, Pyrton, Ickilford, Offeley Magna, Offeley Parva, Walden Regis, Furnivale, Ipolitz, Wandsmyll, Watton, Therleton, Weston, Gravele, Wilien, Leccheworth, Baldock, Datheworth, Russenden, Codpeth, Sumershale, Buntynford, etc., and the church of Weston.

"In the county of Essex they had the manors of Temple Cressynge, Temple Roydon, Temple Sutton, Odewell, Chingelford, Lideleye, Quarsing, Berwick, and Witham; the church of Roydon, and houses, lands, and farms, both at Roydon, at Rivenhall, and in the parishes of Prittlewall and Great and Little Sutton; an old mansion-house and chapel at Sutton, and an estate called Finchinfelde in the hundred of Hinckford.

"In Lincolnshire the Templars possessed the manors of La Bruere, Roston, Kirkeby, Brauncewell, Carleton, Akele, with the soke of Lynderby Aslakeby, and the churches of Bruere, Asheby, Akele, Aslakeby, Donington, Ele, Swinderby, Skarle, etc. There were upwards of thirty churches in the county which made annual payments to the order of the Temple, and about forty windmills. The order likewise received rents in respect of lands at Bracebrig, Brancetone, Scapwic, Timberland, Weleburne, Diringhton, and a hundred other places; and some of the land in the county was charged with the annual payment of sums of money towards the keeping of the lights eternally burning on the altars of the Temple church....

"In Yorkshire the Templars possessed the manors of Temple Warreby, Flaxflete, Etton, South Cave, etc.; the churches of Whitecherche, Kelintune, etc.; numerous windmills and lands and rents at Nehus, Skelture, Pennel, and more than sixty other places besides.

"In Warwickshire they possessed the manors of Barston, Shirburne, Balshale, Wolfhey, Cherlecote, Herbebure, Stodleye, Fechehampstead, Cobington, Tysho and Warwick; lands at Chelverscoton, Herdwicke, Morton, Warwick, Hetherburn, Chesterton, Aven, Derset, Stodley, Napton, and more than thirty other places, the several donors whereof are specified in Dugdale's history of Warwickshire; also the churches of Sireburne, Cardinton, etc., and more than thirteen windmills.

"In Kent they had the manors of Lilleston, Hechewayton, Saunford, Sutton, Dart ford, Hal gel, Jewell, Cockles comb, Strode, Winfield Manes, West Greenwich, and the manor of Lynden, which now belongs to the archbishop of Canterbury; the advowsons of the churches of West Greenwich and Kingeswode juxta Waltham; extensive tracts of land in Romney marsh, and farms and assize rents in all parts of the county. In Surrey they had the manor farm of Temple Elfand or Elfante, and an estate at Merrow in the hundred of Woking.

"In Gloucestershire, the manors of Lower Dowdeswell, Pegsworth, Amford, Nishange, and five others which belonged to them wholly or in part, the church of Down Ammey, and lands in Framton, Temple Guting, and Little Rissington. In Worcestershire, the manor of Templars Lawern, and lands in Flavel, Temple Broughton, and Hanbury.

"In Northamptonshire, the manors of Asheby, Thorp, Watervill, etc. etc.; they had the advowson of the church of the manor of Hardwicke in Orlington hundred, and we find that 'Robert Saunford, Master of the soldiery of the Temple in England,' presented to it in the year 1238.

"In Nottinghamshire, the Templars possessed the church of Marnham, lands and rents at Gretton and North Carleton; in Westmoreland, the manor of Temple Sowerby; in the Isle of Wight, the manor of Uggeton, and lands in Kerne."

6. Formerly Marischall (French).

7. The Rosses were multiply intermarried and allied in business with the Cooper/Cowper family.

8. Warwickshire was awarded to the earls of the Newburgh/Newberry family in the apportionment of Britain by William the Conqueror.

9. Recall the photographs and commentary on Cowane's Hospital for Guild Brothers in Stirling.

10. As discussed in chapter 1, the Beaton family of Scotland, physicians to the Dalriadic and Stewart kings, had copies of Avicenna's writings.

11. "Tree" in Hebrew is עץ (etz), which may be alluded to in the surnames Oetz, Uetz and Etz.

Chapter 9

1. Thus Aberdeen continued an ancient toleration of the "three faiths of the Book," Islam, Judaism, and Christianity.

2. A famous bearer of the name was Nikola Mencetich (de Menze), a Ragusan Jew who came to England in 1592 to work for Nicholas Gozzi/Costa/Gist (Eterovich 2003, p. 70).

3. *Elgin* is not a Gaelic word. We believe it comes from Aramaic *El* ("God") + *gin/jin* ("spirit").

4. There was a famous Karaite rabbi named Anan ben David from the 1200s.

5. The Ladino Haim family was connected with the Lunas, Benvenistes, Feboses (Forbeses) and Gracias (Shaltiel-Gracian, February 2002; Benveniste Web site). They fled the Peninsula around 1492, and the main branch went to Turkey, where they served as tax farmers for the Sublime Porte. After Joseph II's emancipation of Jews in the Austro-Hungarian Empire, one line came to Vienna via Ottoman Romania with the stockbroker and *Hofrat* (court advisor) Johannes Haim, remarrying into the Ladino Melamud and Febos (Forbes) families (author's family information).

6. Perhaps formed on Arabic *qodi* ("judge") + *El*.

7. Brody is a widely recognized Ashkenazic surname, e.g., actor Adrian Brody, recent Academy Award winner (*The Pianist*).

8. For Murray, see note in chapter 7.

9. Lat. *procurator*, "administrator."

10. French Bonhomme, Bonham, English Goodman, German Gutmann.

11. Also Lurie. Sephardic: Luria, a rabbinical family. The same as Lowrey.

12. "One from Lobbes," an important mercantile city.

13. Perhaps from *Khar Nagi*, Hungarian and Ottoman Turkish for "Great Ruler."

14. "One from Castile," Spain.

15. =Heb. *Barak*, "lightning," cognate with *baruch* "blessing," also "baroque," a type of pearl whose trade was dominated by Jews and thus so-named, becoming synonymous with an extravagant style of architecture.

16. Legend declares the high priest in Jerusalem promised Alexander the Great that all the children of priestly families following his visit would be named Alexander, after him; the name has been favored by Jews throughout the ages. As a surname it was often rendered Sand, Sander, Zander, Sanders, Saunders, Sandison, Sandford and the like.

17. "One from Brabant," a medieval Flemish duchy that spanned most of eastern Belgium and bordered on Normandy, with important ties to the cloth, weaving and woolen, and banking industries of Lombardy. Before the mid-sixteenth century, when it was replaced by Antwerp, it was also the center of the diamond trade. A 1292 census of Paris by Lord Colm Dubh lists numerous wealthy Jews from Brabant (*de Brabant, Brebois*) (<http://www.sca.org/heraldry/laurel/names/paris.html>). Bradby, a family that supplied multiple chiefs to the Pamunkey Indians of Virginia, is probably a corruption. A photograph of Chief William Bradby, 1899, appears in Kennedy 2000, p. 159.

18. Priscilla is a Roman name favored by the Jews of antiquity (Jacobs 1911). "Reva" is Heb. for "Rebecca."

19. The earliest form of this surname was probably Old French *Coupard*, a common Ashkenazic name meaning "copper-worker" or "cup person." The occupation was a loftier one than barrel maker (*tonnelier*) and was at times a title (Lat. *cupifer*) signifying, variously, "minter," "locksmith," or "ark keeper/bearer." The earliest Jewish Cooper can probably be placed in Carolingian times, if not earlier. The trail leads to Speyer, as some Cooper families, both in England and Russia, have the surname Shapiro ("from Speyer" [Daitch-Mokotoff Soundex System]). The surname evidently came over to England from Rouen in the train of William the Conqueror and branches of it continued to practice Judaism in an underground fashion with the expulsion of the Jews by Edward I in 1290. Both authors are descended from Isaac Cooper of Granger Co. (Tenn./Wayne Co., Ky.; abt. 1770–aft. 1838), a grandson of William Cooper the scout, who married a daughter of Cherokee Chief Black Fox (d. 1811) and acted as a *hazzan* (functionary for life-change events like weddings and funerals) in the Watauga Country. See Panther-Yates (June 2002).

20. Beginning in the late 12th century (although the roots of this belief are earlier), Jews were popularly blamed for the death of Jesus and forced, by law, to wear various emblems of "shame," the best-known being probably a yellow star sewn on their clothing.

21. It is well known that Jews were identified with the glass, crystal and mirror trade: the night when Nazis smashed Jewish storekeepers' windows in Germany and began to deport Jews to concentration camps is commemorated as *Kristallnacht*.

22. "Merchant vessel of the largest size, especially one from Ragusa-Dubrovnik, whence the name" (Eterovich 2003, p. 75). Many of the seamen and most of the Ottoman admirals came from Croatia (p. 29). "In the years 1544 to 1612, nine grand viziers came from Bosnia, and Bosnia gave to the Empire most of the twenty-four grand viziers of Croatian ancestry in addition to many pashas, sandiak-begs, beger-begs, and other dignitaries" (p. 23). Moreover, "[A] majority of the mariners and pilots on the [English] king's ships at this period were foreigners—Ragusans (listed first), Venetians, Genovese, Normans and Bretons ... [as] noted by French Ambassador Marillac, writing in 1540" (p. 62). Many of the ship's captains were also Jewish, e.g. Nikola Gucetich (Gozzi, Gast, Gass, Goss, Gist, Guest, and Guess in English [Daitch-Mokotoff s.v.]), who came from the Sephardic Da Costa family and lived in Tower Ward, later the home of Samuel Gist, the business partner of George Washington.

23. Gaelic *kynochs* "dark."

24. Jews were often selected as heralds because of their literacy and foreign language abilities.

25. "For the king [sc. Solomon] had a Tarshish fleet on the sea, along with Hiram's fleet. Once every three years, the Tarshish fleet came in, bearing gold and silver, ivory, apes, and peacocks" (I Kings 10:22).

26. The Spanish called the Greek-speaking Byzantine Jews (Romaniots) *Gregos*, which apparently gives us the surnames Greig and Gregg. But the name could also be interpreted to mean "Gray," and perhaps was understood this way. Beginning in the eleventh century, residence of Jews in Christian Byzantium was restricted to Constantinople and Salonika. Spanish Jews settled in Constantinople in the late fourteenth century, heavily so after 1492, and Ottoman-ruled Salonika developed one of the greatest centers of Jewish learning in the East (Barnavi 1992, p. 70).

27. Jewish families teased this name into a hundred fanciful forms. A sampling of girls' names from the authors' own family histories includes Lovina, Louisa, Luetta, Luida, Louhanna, Lovida, Lovisa, Louah, Ludella, Luverna, Lavona, LaVera, Lutilla, Lula, Louina, Levicy, Vicy, and Viny. Lovie was further turned into Dovie and Dicy, especially in the American South. It was said that any name beginning with Lu- or Lou- was acknowledgment of the family's origin as "Lusitanians," i.e. Portuguese. Male equivalents were Lewis, Lodovic, Lawson, Lovis, Lovice, etc. Lovice Looney, for instance, was born about 1743 in Virginia and came from the De Luna family of Spain and Portugal, via the Isle of

Man and port of Philadelphia. On the Looney/Lunas, see Panther-Yates 2000.

28. Anglo-Jewish: Adler 1939, p. 22 *et saepe*.

29. Κάλλας, "beautiful" or else Hebrew "bride."

30. Jacobs 1911. One of the top 10 Anglo-Jewish surnames.

31. We count in this 50 percent the "dark color" surnames such as Black, Brown and Gray, as these were commonly used in the North to refer to the skin/hair/complexion of the peoples of the Mediterranean and South. Brown has a further meaning of a reference to Rabbi Nachman among the descendants of the Jewish community at Speyer. One must bear in mind that, like Y-chromosome testing, salient surnames recorded in archives and cemeteries represent only the male line of any geopolitical group. In the nature of things, there is a bias toward the upper echelons of society. Accordingly, care must be taken in projecting these figures to the general population.

32. "Lista de Apellidos Judios segun noto de Pere Bonnin," <http://www.personaes.com/ colombia>. This Colombian surname list was based on Pere Bonnin, a Barcelona writer, who wrote *Sangre Judia*, or *Jewish Blood*, in which he compiled a list of 3,500 surnames of Jewish origin, using documents found in old Jewish neighborhoods and Inquisition archives. The following prominent Italian Jewish surnames may also be compared, taken from Shlomo Simonsohn, *The Jews in the Duchy of Milan* (Jerusalem, The Israel Academy of Sciences and Humanities, 1986): Abramo, Anna, Aron, Bella, Bona, Cervio, Cervo, David, Davit, Falcone, Gabriele, Gaio, Gavo, Manno, Michele, Moise, Moses, Moyse, Salomon, Salomone, Samuel, Sansone, Sarra, Simon, Simone, Solomon, Tarsia, Vita, Vitale, Vitta, Bolanis, Bollano, Boscho, Grassis, Rippa (It. for "coast," Sp. *Da Costa*, Ger. *Kist*). There is a complete index on pp. 3017–3082.

33. There are three explanations for this common surname, which also appears as Atkin, Aitken and Akin (and possibly Adkins). One theory derives it from the French city of Agincourt, another from the Berber clan Agoun, and a third from Charlemagne's capital at Aix/Aachen (or the similarly named city Aix-en-Provence in the South of France).

34. Rochus Bastardus was a prominent Marrano merchant who lived, variously, in Rouen, Amsterdam and other places of refuge for Sephardic Jews.

35. Jacobs (1911) maintains that Morrell comes from Samuel.

36. Jewish surnames such as Prince/Printz, Noble/Nobel, Duke/Duque, King/Konig and Pape/Pope are believed to derive from their bearers' being in the service of these functionaries (Stern 1950). This also may be the root of the name Raney, French *Reine*, as well as Ray/Reyes.

37. Jacobs 1911.

38. Jacobs 1911; cf. French Mercer, German Kaufmann.

39. Aramaic "palm tree" (with its sweet fruit); the French form is Demarice.

40. As we saw in chapter 2, Perthshire contains the densest concentration of haplotype J in the British Isles.

Chapter 10

1. A convenient and reliable summary of the mission of Columba to Scotland may be found in McNeill (1974).

2. A further peculiarity that deserves investigation is the apparent observance of *kashrut* by the early Scots. A document dating to the time of Columba, the *Canones Adomnani*, is notable for its unusual lists of clean and unclean meats, drawn not only from the Torah but apparently also from Talmudic law (McNeill 1974, p. 100). Western and northern clerics refused to eat at the table of their eastern counterparts, perhaps because the Roman-styled churches in England did not keep kosher (Deansely 1963, p. 85).

3. It is hard not to believe that this word comes from Chaldea, the ancient name for Babylonia, to which the Jews were exiled in Biblical times, though Howie derives it from *Cultores Dei* "worshipers of God" (1981, p. 4).

4. Alexander Spottswood was born in 1676 at Tangier, then an English colony, his father being the resident surgeon. He was a thoroughly trained soldier, serving on the continent under the Duke of Marlborough. He was dangerously wounded at the battle of Blenheim in 1704, while serving as quartermaster-general with the rank of colonel. He arrived in Virginia in 1710 as lieutenant-governor under George Hamilton, the Earl of Orkney, and his administration became remembered as the most able of all the Colonial rulers. He was connected with Robert Carry of England and established the first iron furnace in North America. In 1730, he was deputy Postmaster-General for the American Colonies, and it was he who promoted Benjamin Franklin to the position of postmaster for the province of Pennsylvania. He rose to the rank of major-general and on the eve of embarking with troops destined for Carthagena, died at Annapolis, Maryland, on June 7, 1740. He owned the house in which Lord Cornwallis afterward signed the articles of capitulation at Yorktown ("Appalachian Mountain Families," <http://freepages.genealogy.rootsweb.com/~appalachian/History/Alexander_Spottswood/alexander_spottswood.html>).

5. See chapter 1.

6. These letters spell the Jewish name for God, as already noted in chapter 7: they were the central meditative device in a Cabalistic tradition that was present contemporaneously in southern France.

7. Cop, also rendered Cope, should probably be viewed as another one of those British surnames we catalogued in Chapters 8 and 9 that are based on Hebrew letters, in this case *Kaf* כ.

8. An Italo-Arabic surname.

9. A Sephardic French surname.

10. Sects highly monotheistic and consequently quite compatible, theologically, with Judaism.

11. Goris (1925) gives lists of Marranos arrested 1519–1570, some accused of Judaizing, others of Calvinism; one, Marcus Perez, was banished, and Alfonso Rubero fled to England in 1540 (pp. 651–654).

12. Howie states that Knox was sent to St. Andrews

to study under John Mair or Major, and M'Gavin in his note attempts to reconcile this fact with a record at Glasgow of 1520.

13. We have seen above how consistent this vision is to the Jewish ideal of Zedakah.

14. Compare the description of Marrano attitudes toward Mary in Gitlitz (2002), pp. 142–144. Often couched in mock theological arguments or told in the style of ribald miracle stories, this Marrano trait might be termed "Marioclasm," the angry ridicule of Mariology and all Catholic superstition connected with it.

15. In the absence of Marrano ancestry, Knox's antipathy toward Spain is virtually inexplicable. No histories of his life mention his traveling to Spain or even actually known any Spaniards. Thus there do not seem to be any negative personal experiences to account for his hatred of Spain.

16. With Margaret, Knox had three daughters, Martha, Margaret and Elizabeth; again, all Biblical names. Martha married Alexander Fairlie/Fairleigh; Margaret married Alexander Fairlie/Fairleigh; Margaret married Zachary (du) Pont; and Elizabeth married John Welsh.

Chapter 11

1. The first synagogue was established in Scotland in 1816, but it was of the Ashkenazic rite and records were kept in Yiddish (Phillips 1979, p. 10). It is interesting, however, to note the French and Flemish Sephardic names associated with the Braid Place cemetery and early Richmond Court synagogue, including Lyon, Davis, Symons, David, Mosely, Chalmers, Laurier, Prince, Hart, and Vallery (pp. 4–9). Also, the first Scotsman to be circumcised in Glasgow, in 1824, was Edward Davis, son of David Davis, a name, as we have seen, often borne by French Crypto-Jews in Scotland (Lionel Levy n.d., pp. 12–13). Among the dead in the Glaswegian Necropolis we find (Semion Philippa) Burns, Frazer, Davi(e)s, Michael, and Rubens (pp. 28–30). Its gates were inscribed with twelve lines of poetry by Byron, followed by the initials M.K.B.I. (מכבי), standing for the Hebrew prayer "Who among the Mighty is like unto thee, Jehovah" (*Mi cha-mo-cha ba-ei-lim, A-do-nai*), which Blair, the cemetery's historian, explains as the origin of the name Maccabeus,

the equivalent of MacBeth, a founder of Scotland (pp. 25–26).

2. Scott earned close to ten thousand pounds a year in royalties and advances in his heyday (Herman 2001, p. 309).

3. This rabbinical family traces its ancestry to Rabbi Zev Wolf. The reigning matriarch in living memory was Mrs. Godfrey S. (Helen Gratz) Rockefeller (Birmingham 1971, pp. 162–63).

4. Not many of his readers noticed, but in his first Waverley novel Scott made its hero an Englishman, not a Scot at all, but an officer in the British army who is garrisoned in Scotland on the eve of the doomed Stuart comeback under Bonnie Prince Charles in 1745.

5. Although the figure of Robin Hood in English literature and history is a problematical and much debated subject, the weight of historical evidence now inclines to identify the first personification of the outlaw from the north with Robin Deakyne, a Norman from York, son of William, ca. 1175 (History Channel TV special 1999; see Deakyne Family Genealogy Forum, <http://genforum.genealogy.com>.) A contender for the title remains David, Earl of Huntingdon (1152–1219), the nephew of William the Lyon, King of Scotland ("The Search for the Real Robin Hood," <http://www.geocities.com/ puckrobin/rh/realrob2.html>; K.J. Stringer, *Earl David of Huntingdon*, Edinburgh University Press, 1985). We have studied the earl's genealogy and note that his daughter Isabella married Robert Bruce, ancestor of Robert I the Bruce. The name Deakyne (also rendered Deakin) comes from "of Aix/Aachen" (Charlemagne's capital). The family originated in Flanders, as did the Bruces and Stewarts. Deakynes immigrated to Maryland and at least one branch today continues to be Jewish. Robin derives from the Hebrew Rueben.

6. Interestingly, the "Saxe" part of this once obscure Luxemburgish line, which occupied virtually every throne in Europe during the nineteenth century, came from the Spanish-Portuguese Jewish Seixas family (Birmingham 1971, pp. 29–32). It is the same name found in the New York department store Saks Fifth Avenue.

7. Something conveniently happens to Athelstane to remove him: "he was a cock that would not fight" (p. 428).

Bibliography

Addington, Arthur Charles (1969). *The Royal House of Stuart: the Descendants of King James VI of Scotland, James I of England.* London: Skilton.

Addison, Charles G. (1892). *The History of the Knights Templars.* Reprint 1997. Kempton: Adventures Unlimited.

Adler, Michael (1939). *Jews of Medieval England.* London: Jewish Historical Society of England.

Adath Yisroel (n.d.). Cheshunt Cemetery — Adath Yisroel Burial Society Records. <http://www.jgsgb.org.uk/bury01.htm>.

Alden, John Richard (1985). *The South in the Revolution 1763–1789. A History of the South,* vol. III. Ed. W.H. Stephenson and E.M. Coulter. Baton Rouge: Louisiana State University Press.

Americanization of Portuguese Names (n.d.). "Americanization of Portuguese Names from California circa early 1900s." E-mail discussion group posting. <sephardicforum@yahoogroups.com>.

Angel, Marc D. (1978). *The Jews of Rhodes: The History of a Sephardic Community.* New York: Sepher-Hermon.

Ascherson, Neal (2002). *Stone Voices: The Search for Scotland.* New York: Hill and Wang.

Atherton, Mark (2002). *Celts and Christianity.* Cardiff: University of Wales.

Ball, Bonnie (1984). *The Melungeons.* Eighth edition. Privately published.

Barnavi, Eli, gen. ed. (1992). *A Historical Atlas of the Jewish People from the Time of the Patriarchs to the Present.* New York: Schocken.

Barnett, Richard D. (1959). "Tombstones in Barbados." *Tesora de los Judios Sefardies* (Jerusalem) 2:XLV–XLVI.

Behar, Doron M. *et al.* (2003). "Multiple Origins of Ashkenazi Levites: Y Chromosome Evidence for Both Near Eastern and European Ancestries." *American Journal of Human Genetics* 73/4:768–79.

Benbassa, Esther (1999). *The Jews of France.* Princeton, N.J.: Princeton University.

Benbassa, Esther and Aron Rodrique (1995). *Sephardi Jewry.* Berkeley: University of California.

Beresniak, Daniel and Haziz Hamani (2000). *Symbols of Freemasonry.* New York: Aspouline.

Bergsson, Snorri G. (2002). "Iceland and the 'Jewish Question.'" English translation of Icelandic masters thesis. <http://notendur.centrum.is/~snorrigb/holoc.htm>.

Bernstein, Henrietta (1984). *Cabalah Primer: Introduction to the English/Hebrew Cabalah.* Marina del Rey: Schocken.

Biale, David (2002). *Cultures of the Jews. A New History.* New York: Schocken.

Bible, Jean Patterson (1975). *Melungeons: Yesterday and Today.* Signal Mountain: Mountain Press.

Birmingham, Stephen (1971). *The Grandees. America's Sephardic Elite.* New York: Harper & Row.

Bodian, Miriam (1997). *Hebrews of the Portuguese Nation: Conversos and Community in Early Modern Amsterdam.* Bloomington: Indiana University Press.

Bourdieu, Pierre (1993). *The Field of Cultural Production.* New York: Columbia.

Bosch, Elena *et al.* (2001). "High-resolution Analysis of Human Y-Chromosome Variation Shows a Sharp Discontinuity and Limited Gene Flow between Northwestern Africa and the Iberia Peninsula." *American Journal of Human Genetics* 68:1019– 1029.

Braund, Kathryn E. Holland (1993). *Deerskins and Duffels: The Creek Indian Trade with Anglo-America 1685–1815.* Lincoln and London: University of Nebraska.

Brett, Michael and Elizabeth Fentress (1996). *The Berbers.* Oxford: Blackwell.

Brodwin, Paul (2002). "Genetics, Identity, and the

Anthropology of Essentialism." *Anthropological Quarterly* 75/2:323–330.

Brooks, Jory S. (2001). "The Hebrew-Celtic Connection: Language, Cultural and Religious Ties." *Midwestern Epigraphic Journal* 15:88–90.

Brown, J. Wood (1897). *An Enquiry into the Life and Legend of Michael Scot.* Edinburgh: Douglas.

Brown, Michael (1998). *The Black Douglases.* East Lothian: Tuckwell.

Bruce, Alastair (1999). *Keepers of the Kingdom: The Ancient Offices of Britain.* Photographs by Julian Calder and Mark Cator. New York: Vendome.

Burke's Peerage and Baronetage (1999). 2 vols. Brian Morris, publisher. 106th edition. Oxford: Boydell and Brewer.

Burnet, Gilbert (1922). *An Abridgment of Bishop Burnet's History of His Own Times*, ed. Thomas Stackhouse. London: Dent.

Carvajal-Carmona, Luis G. *et al.* (2000). "Strong Amerind/White Sex Bias and a Possible Sephardic Contribution among the Founders of a Population in Northwest Colombia." *American Journal of Human Genetics* 67:1287–1295.

Casson, Lionel (1971). *Ships and Seamanship in the Ancient World.* Princeton: Princeton University Press.

Cesarini, David (2004). *Port Jews: Jewish Communities in Cosmopolitan Maritime Trading Centres, 1550–1950.* London: Frank Cass.

Christie, Neil (1998*). The Lombards.* Oxford: Blackwell.

Coker, William S. (1986). *Indian Traders of the Southeastern Spanish Borderlands.* Panton: Leslie and Company and John Forbes and Company, 1783–1847.

Collins, Kenneth E. (1990). *Second City Jewry: The Jews of Glasgow in the Age of Expansion 1790–1919.* Glasgow: Scottish Jewish Archives.

Collins, Kenneth, ed. (1987). *Aspects of Scottish Jewry.* Glasgow: Glasgow Jewish Representative Council.

Connell, Diana (2001). *The Glass Workers of Scotland.* Glasgow: FHS.

Cooper, William Ross (1932). *History of the Cooper and Ross Families of England, Scotland, Ulster and America.* Privately printed.

Crouch, David (2002). *The Normans: The History of a Dynasty.* London and New York: Hambledon and London.

Cunliffe, Barry (2001). *Facing the Ocean: The Atlantic and Its Peoples.* Oxford: Oxford University Press.

Daitch-Mokotoff Soundex System. <http://www.jewishgen.org>.

Dixon, Max (1976). *The Wataugans.* Johnson City, Tenn.: Overmountain.

Deanesly, Margaret (1963). *The Pre-Conquest Church in England.* London: Adam and Charles Black.

Denton, John H. (n.d. but ca. 1969). *A Brief Historical Background and History of Gardiner's Chapel Primitive Baptist Church.* N.p. Kingsport (Tenn.) Public Library.

Devine, T. (2006). *The Scottish Nation.* London: Penguin.

Dobson, David (1998). *The Mariners of the Clyde and Western Scotland: 1600–1800.* Willow Bend.

Dolan, J.R. (1972). *English Ancestral Names — The Evolution of the Surname from Medieval Occupations.* New York: Potter.

Douglas, David C. (2002). *The Normans.* London: Folio Society.

_____ (1964). *William the Conqueror.* Berkeley: University of California.

Drake, Richard B. (2001). *A History of Appalachia.* University Press of Kentucky.

Dromgoole, Will Allen (1891). "The Melungeons," *Arena*, March 1891: 470–479.

Einhard (1997). *Charlemagne's Courtier: The Complete Einhard.* Ed. Paul Dutton. New York: Broadview.

Elder, Pat Spurlock (1999). *Melungeons: Examining an Appalachian Legend.* Blountville: Continuity.

Elliott, Carl and Paul Brodwin (2002). "Identity and Genetic Ancestry Tracing." *BMJ* 325 (7378):1469–1471.

Encyclopedia of Southern Culture (1989). Charles Reagan Wilson and William Ferris, coeditors; Ann J. Abadie and Mary L. Hart, associate editors. Chapel Hill and London: University of North Carolina.

Endelman, Todd M. (1979). *The Jews of Georgian England 1714–1830.* Philadelphia: Jewish Publication Society of America.

Esposity, John L. (1999). *The Oxford History of Islam.* Oxford: Oxford University Press.

Eterovich, Adam S. (2003). *Croatia and Croatians and the Lost Colony 1585–1590.* San Carlos: Ragusan.

Finn, James (1841). *Sephardim: Or the History of Jews in Spain and Portugal.* London: Rivington.

Fletcher, Richard (1992). *Moorish Spain.* Berkeley: U of California P.

Franklin, Dexter Z. (1998). *Paternity — Disputed, Typing, PCR and DNA Tests: Index of New Information.* Washington: Abbe Publishing.

Fraser, Flora Marjory (1997). *Clan Fraser.* Edinburgh: Scottish Cultural Press.

Freedman, Samuel G. (2000). *Jew vs. Jew: The Struggle for the Soul of American Jewry.* New York: Simon and Schuster.

French Sephardim (n.d.). "Sephardic and Jewish Surname List." <http://www.geocities.com/sephardim2003/surnamesA.html>.

Gallegos, Eloy J. (1997). *The Melungeons: The Pioneers of the Interior Southeastern United States 1526–1997.* Knoxville: Villagra.

Gardiner, Laurence (2001). *Bloodline of the Holy Grail.* Gloucester: Fair Winds.

Gibbon, Edward (n.d.). *The Decline and Fall of the Roman Empire*. 3 vols. London: Frederick Warne.

Gitlitz, David M. (2002). *Secrecy and Deceit: The Religion of the Crypto-Jews*. Introduction by Ilan Stavans. Albuquerque: University of New Mexico.

Goins, Jack H. (2000). *Melungeons: and Other Pioneer Families*. N.p.

Golb, Norman (1998) *The Jews in Medieval Normandy: A Social and Intellectual History*. Cambridge: Cambridge University Press.

Golb, Norman (1998). *The Jews in Medieval Normandy*. New York: Cambridge University Press.

Golb, Norman and Omeljan Pritsak (1982). *Khazarian Hebrew Documents of the Tenth Century*. Ithaca: Cornell University Press.

Gordon, Cyrus (1971). *Before Columbus*. New York: Crown.

Goris, J.A. (1925). *Etude sur les colonies marchandes méridionales (Portugais, Espagnols, Italiens) à Anvers de 1488 à 1567*. Louvain: Librarie Universitaire.

Graves, Robert (1975). *The White Goddess*. New York: Farrar, Straus and Giroux.

Graves, Robert (1996). *The Greek Myths*. London: Folio Society.

Gusmao, L. *et al*. (2003). "Grouping of Y-STR haplotypes discloses European geographic clines." *Forensic Science International* 134:172–179.

Ha-Levi, Eleazar (n.d.). "Jewish Naming Convention in Angevin England," an article available on the website of the Society for Creative Anachronism, at http://www.sca.org/heraldry/laurel/names/jewish.html.

Haliczer, Stephen, ed. (1987). *Inquisition and Society in Early Modern Europe*. Totowa: Barnes & Noble.

Hall, Stuart and Paul du Gay, eds. (1996). *Questions of Cultural Identity*. London: Sage.

Hammer, M.F. *et al*. (2000). "Jewish and Middle Eastern non–Jewish populations share a common pool of Y-chromosome biallelic haplotypes." *PNAS* 97/12:6769–74.

Haskins, Charles Homer (1957). *The Renaissance of the Twelfth Century*. Cambridge: Harvard University Press.

Helgason *et al*. (2000). "mtDNA and the Origin of Icelands." *American Journal of Human Genetics* 67:697–717.

Herman, Arthur (2001). *How the Scots Invented the Modern World*. New York: Three Rivers.

Hernandez, Frances (1993). "The Secret Jews of the Southwest." In *Sephardim in the Americas*, by Martin A. Cohen and Abraham J. Peck. London and Tuscaloosa: American Jewish Archives and University of Alabama.

Hewitson, Jim (1993). *Tam Blake and Co.: The Story of the Scots in America*. Edinburgh: Canongate.

Heyer, E., J. Puymirat, P. Dieltjes, E. Bakker, and P. de Knijff (1997). "Estimating Y chromosome specific microsatellite mutation frequencies using deep rooting pedigrees." *Human Molecular Genetics* 6(5):799–803.

Hirschman, Elizabeth C. (2005). *Melungeons: The Last Lost Tribe in America*. Macon: Mercer University Press.

Hodges, Miles H. (2000). "Biography of John Knox." <www.newgenevacenter.org/biography/knox2.htm>.

Hodges, Miles H. (2000). "Biography of John Calvin," <www.newgenevacenter.org/biography/calvin2.htm>.

Hodgkin, Thomas (2000). *The Visigothic Invasion*. London: Folio Society.

Horton, Jean K. (n.d.). *Minutes of the Blackwater Church (on Blackwater Creek), Hawkins (now Hancock) County, Tennessee (1816–1837), Transcribed from the Original*. Kingsport (Tenn.) Public Library.

Hourani, Albert Habib (1991). *A History of the Arab Peoples*. Cambridge: Harvard University Press.

Howie, John (1981). *Lives of the Scottish Covenanters*. Greenville: A Press. Repr. of Glasgow ed. of 1858, rev. by William M'Gavin.

Hyamson, A. M. (1908). *History of the Jews in England*. London: n.p.

Jacobs, Joseph (1901–1906). "Personal Names." In *The Jewish Encyclopedia: A Descriptive Record of the History, Religion, Literature, and Customs of the Jewish People from the Earliest Times to the Present Day*. Pub. by Isidore Singer and ed. by Cyrus Adler. Orig. published in London. Reprint by KTAV, 1980. <http://www.Jewish Enclo pedia.com/>.

Jacobs, Joseph (1893). *The Jews of Angevin England*. New York: Putnam's Sons.

Jehaes, E. *et al*. (1998). "Mitochondrial DNA analysis on remains of a putative son of Louis XVI, King of France and Marie-Antoinette." *Eur. J. Hum. Genet*. 6/4:383–95.

Jobling, Mark A. (June 2001). "In the Name of the Father: Surnames and Genetics." *Trends in Genetics* 17/6:353–357.

Jobling, M. A. and Tyler-Smith, C. (2003). "The human Y chromosome: an evolutionary marker comes of age." *Nature Reviews Genetics* 4:598–612.

Jones, Prudence and Nigel Pennick (1995). *A History of Pagan Europe*. New York: Barnes and Noble.

Katz, David S. (1996). *The Jews in the History of England*. Oxford: Clarendon.

Katz, Solomon (1937). *The Jews in the Visigothic and Frankish Kingdoms of Spain and Gaul*. Boston: Mediaeval Academy of America.

Keith, Alexander (1988). *A Thousand Years of Aberdeen*. Aberdeen: Aberdeen University.

Kennedy, Ludovic (1995). *In Bed with an Elephant.* London: Bantam.

Kennedy, N. Brent (2000). *The Melungeons: The Resurrection of a Proud People.* Macon: Mercer University Press.

Kleiforth, Alexander Leslie (1993). *Grip Fast: The Leslies in History.* Chichester: Phillimore.

Kleiman, Rabbi Yaakov (2001). "The Cohanim/DNA Connection." Aish HaTorah (aish.com) Society Today. <http://www.aish.com/society-Work/sciencenature/The_Cohanim_-_DNA_Connection.asp>.

Laistner, M.L.W. (1966). *Thought and Letters in Western Europe, a.d. 500–900.* New, rev. ed. Ithaca: Cornell.

Lavender, Abraham D. (2003). "DNA and the Sephardic Diaspora: Spanish and Portuguese Jews in Europe." *HaLAPID* 10/1:1–7.

Lawson, Bill (1994). *Croft History, Isle of Harris.* Volume 7. Isle of Harris: Bill Lawson.

_____ (1998). *Index to Marriages in the Parish of North Uist 1820—1855.* Isle of Harris: Bill Lawson.

_____ (1995). *Index to Marriages in the Parish of South Uist: 1820—1855.* Isle of Harris: Bill Lawson.

Lebeson, Anita Libman (1950). *Pilgrim People.* New York: Harper.

Levy, A. (1949*). The Origins of Glasgow Jewry 1812–1895.* Glasgow: A.J. MacFarlane.

Levy, Lionel (n.d.). "Commentary on Paul Sebag: *Les Noms des Juifs de Tunisie* (Appendix 'Les noms des Livournais.'" <http://www.orthohelp.com/geneal/levyseba2. htm>.

Lippy, Charles H. (1985). *Bibliography of Religion in the South.* Macon, Ga.: Mercer University Press.

"Lista de Apellidos Judios segun noto de Pere Bonnin [*Sangre Judia*]." <http://www.personaes.com/colombia>.

Ludovici, Anthony (1938). *The Jews, and the Jews in England.* London: Boswell. Part 3. <http://www.revilo-oliver.com/Writers/Ludovici/The_Jews_in_England_part3. html>.

Mackay, Charles (1989). *Extraordinary Popular Delusions and the Madness of Crowds.* With a foreword by Bernard M. Baruch. New York: Barnes and Noble.

Mallery, Arlington and Mary Roberts Harrison (1979). *The Rediscovery of Lost America.* New York: E.P. Dutton.

MacLeod, John (1999). *Dynasty: The Stuarts 1560–1807.* New York: St. Martin's.

Marcus, Jacob Rader (1973). *Early American Jewry.* Vol. I: *The Jews of New York, New England and Canada 1649–1794.* Vol. 2: *The Jews of Pennsylvania and the South 1655–1790.* New York: KTAV.

Marshall, Rosalind (2000). *Mary of Guise.* Edinburgh: National Museums of Scotland.

McCartney, D.J. (1997). *The Ulster Jacksons from Cumbria to the White House, Shenandoah and Australia.* Belfast: Carrickfergus Borough Council.

McDermott, James (2001). *Martin Frobisher, Elizabethan Privateer.* New Haven: Yale University.

McDonnell, Francis J. (1998). *Roll of Apprentices, Burgh of Aberdeen 1751–1796.* St. Andrews.

McNeill, John T. (1974). *The Celtic Churches: A History a.d. 200 to 1200.* Chicago: University of Chicago.

Meek, Donald E. (2000). *The Quest for Celtic Christianity.* Edinburgh: Handsel.

Mira, Manuel (1998). *The Portuguese Making of America : Melungeons and Early Settlers of America.* N.p.: P.A.H.R. Foundation.

Moffat, Alistair (2002). *The Borders: A History of the Borders from Earliest Times.* Selkirk: Deerpark.

Morgan, Diane (2000). *Old Aberdeen (Villages of Aberdeen S.).* Aberdeen: Denburn.

Morris, David B. (1919). *The Stirling Merchant Guild and Life of John Cowane.* Stirling: Jamieson and Munro.

Moss, H. St. L.B. (1998). *The Birth of the Middle Ages 395–814.* London: Folio Society.

Nebel , A. *et al.* (2003). "Y chromosome evidence for a founder effect in Ashkenazi Jews." *European Journal of Human Genetics* 13/3 (2005): 388–391.

Netanyahu, B. (1999). *The Marranos of Spain from the Late 14th to the Early 16th Century, According to Contemporary Hebrew Sources.* Third Edition, updated and expanded. Ithaca and London: Cornell.

Olson, Steve (2002). *Mapping Human History.* Boston: Houghton Mifflin.

Oram, Richard (2002). *The House of Stewart.* Stroud: Tempus.

Orizio, Riccardo (2000). *Lost White Tribes : The End of Privilege and the Last Colonials in Sri Lanka, Jamaica, Brazil, Haiti, Namibia, and Guadeloupe.* New York: Free Press.

Panther-Yates, Donald N. (2002). "The Influence of Sephardic Jews and Moors on Southeastern American Indian Cultures." Address at Annual Conference of the Institute for the Study of American Cultures and Epigraphic Society, Columbus, Ga., October 25–27, 2002.

_____ (June 2002). "Shalom and Hey, Y'all: Jewish-American Indian Chiefs in the Old South." *Appalachian Quarterly* 7/2:80–89.

Parry, J.H. (1966). *The Spanish Seaborne Empire.* Berkeley: University of California.

Phillips, Abel (1979). *A History of the Origins of the First Jewish Community in Scotland — Edinburgh 1816.* Edinburgh: John Donald.

Pocahontas Foundation (1994–1997). *Pocahontas' Descendants*, 3 vols. Baltimore: Genealogical Publishing.

Pontikos, Dienekes (2003). *Dienekes' Anthropology Blog.* <http://www.dienekes.com/blog/archives/000212.html>.

Portuguese Translation (n.d.). "Portuguese Translation of Names from Sephardim List." E-mail discussion group postings. <sephardic-forum@yahoogroups.com>.

Ragussis, Michael (1995). *Figures of Conversion: "The Jewish Question" and English National Identity.* Durham: Duke University Press.

_____ (1997). "The 'Secret' of Anglish Anti-Semitism: Anglo-Jewish Studies and Victorian Studies." *Victorian Studies: A Journal of the Humanities, Arts and Sciences* 40/2:295–307.

_____ (2000). "Jews and Other 'Outlandish Englishmen': Ethnic Performance and the Invention of British Identity under the Georges." *Critical Inquiry* 26/4:773–97.

Renan, Ernest (1943). *Le Judaïsme comme race et comme religion.* New York: Rand School of Social Science.

Rite, U., E. Neufeld, M. Broit, D. Shavit, and U. Motra (1993). "The Differences Among Jewish Communities— Maternal and Paternal Contributions." *Journal of Molecular Evolution* 37: 435–43.

Roberts, Allen E. (1985). *Freemasonry in American History.* Richmond: McCoy.

Robinson, John J. (1989). *Born in the Blood: The Lost Secrets of Freemasonry.* New York: M. Evans.

Rogers, Edward Andrew and Mary Evelyn Rogers (1986 and 1988). *A Brief History of the Cherokees 1540–1906.* E-book. <http://www.innernet.org/tsalagi/index.html>.

Ross, James R. (2000). *Fragile Branches.* New York: Riverhead.

Roth, Cecil (1937). *The Spanish Inquisition.* New York: W.W. Norton.

Rountree, Helen C. (1996). *Pocahontas's People: The Powhatan Indians of Virginia Through Four Centuries.* University of Oklahoma.

Royster, Charles (1999). *The Fabulous History of the Dismal Swamp Company.* New York: Knopf.

Rubinstein, W. D. (1996). *A History of the Jews in the English-speaking World: Great Britain.* London: Macmillan.

Santos, Richard G. (2000). *Silent Heritage. The Sephardim and the Colonization of the Spanish North American Frontier.* San Antonio: New Sepharad.

Scott, Sir Walter (1988). *Ivanhoe.* New York: Bantam.

Selwood, Dominic (1999). *Knights of the Cloister.* Rochester, N.Y.: Boydell.

Semino, O. *et al.* (2004). "Origin, diffusion, and differentiation of Y-chromosome haplogroups E and J: inferences on the neolithization of Europe and later migratory events in the Mediterranean area." *Am. J. Hum. Genet.* 74(5): 1023–34.

Sephardim.com. "Namelist." Search available online at <http://www.sephardim.com/namelist.shtml>.

_____. "Sephardic Names Translated into English from Arabic (A), Aramaic (AR)...." Available online at <http://www.sephardim.com/html/translated_names.html>.

Shackel, Paul A. (2001). "Public Memory and the Search for Power in American Historical Archaeology." *American Anthropologist* 103/3: 655–670.

Shaltiel-Gracian, Moshe (February 2002). "Tracing a Davidic Line from Babylon to the Modern World." *Sharsheret Hadorot. Journal of Jewish Genealogy* 16.2 (2002): ii–x.

Sinclair, Andrew (1992). *The Sword and the Grail.* New York: Birlinn.

Simonsohn, Shlomo (1986). *The Jews in the Duchy of Milan.* 4 vols. Jerusalem: Israel Academy of Sciences and Humanities.

Skorecki, K., S. Selig, S. Blazer, R. Bradman, N. Bradman, P.J. Waburton, M. Ismajlowicz, M.F. Hammer (Jan. 1997)."Y chromosomes of Jewish priests." *Nature* 2.385 (6611):32.

Smout, T.C. (1969/1998). *A History of the Scottish People: 1560–1830.* London: Harper Collins.

Southern, R.W. (1961) *The Making of the Middle Ages.* New Haven: Yale.

Stern, Malcolm H. (1991). *First American Jewish Families.* Third edition. Baltimore: Ottenheimer.

Stern, Selma (1950). *The Court Jew: A Contribution to the History of Absolutism in Central Europe.* Trans. by Ralph Weiman. Philadelphia: Transaction.

Stewart, Michael (1999). *The Forgotten Monarchy of Scotland: The True Story of the Royal House of Stewart and the Hidden Lineage of the Kings and Queens of Scots.* New York: Element.

Stirling's Talking Stones (2002). Stirling: Stirling Council Libraries.

Sutton, Leora M. (1991). *Success beyond Expectations: Panton Leslie Co. at Pensacola.* Pensacola: L.M. Sutton.

Sykes, Bryan and Catherine Irven (2000). "Surnames and the Y Chromosome." *American Journal of Human Genetics* 66:1417–1419.

Teresi, Dick (2002). *Lost Discoveries: The Ancient Roots of Modern Science — from the Babylonians to the Maya.* New York: Simon and Schuster.

Thomas, M.G. *et al.* (July 1998). "Origins of Old Testament priests." *Nature* 9;394(6689):138–40.

Thomas, M.B. *et al.* (2000). "Y Chromosomes Traveling South: The Cohen Modal Haplotype and the Origins of the Lemba the 'Black Jews of Southern Africa.'" *American Journal of Human Genetics* 66:674–686.

Thompson, Gunnar (1994). *American Discovery.* Seattle: Argonauts Misty Isle.

Tovey, D'Blossiers (1738/1967). *Anglia Judaica, or the History and Antiquities of the Jews in England.* Oxford: At the Theatre; repr. New York: Burt Franklin.

Velikovsky, Immanuel (1977). *Peoples of the Sea: A Reconstruction of Ancient History.* New York: Doubleday.

Wall, Moses (1987). *Menasseh ben Israel, The Hope of Israel. The English Translation by Moses Wall, 1652.* Edited with an introduction and notes by Henry Méchoulan and Gérard Nahon. Oxford: Oxford University Press.

Way of Plean, George, and Romilly Squire (1999). *Scottish Clan and Family Encyclopedia.* New York: Barnes and Noble.

Wee, C.J.W.L. (1997). "Jewishness and Race, Gender and Class in the English Novel." *College Literature* 24/2:202–210.

Weiss, Walter M. (2000). *Islam: An Illustrated Historical Overview.* Hauppauge: Barnes.

Whiznitzer, Arnold (1960). *Jews in Colonial Brazil.* New York: Columbia University Press.

Wilkins, Frances (1995). *The Smuggling Story of the Northern Shores: Oban to Montrose.* Kidderminster: Wyre Forrest.

Williams, Ronald (1983/1997). *The Lords of the Isles.* Argyll: House of Lochar.

Williams, Thomas (2003). *The Cambridge Companion to Duns Scotus.* Cambridge: Cambridge University Press.

Willuweit, Sascha *et al.* (2006). "Y-STR Haplotype Reference Database, created by Sascha Willuweit and Lutz Roewer, Institute of Legal Medicine, Humboldt-Universität Berlin, Germany in cooperation with Michael Krawczak (Kiel), Manfred Kayser (Leipzig) and Peter de Knijff (Leiden), based on the continuous submission of Y-STR haplotypes by the International Forensic Y-User Group." Release 19 from August 1, 2006. Database consists of 41,965 haplotypes in 357populations. A subset of 35 percent has been analyzed for the loci DYS438 and DYS439. Available online at *http://www.yhrd.org.*

Wilson, James F. *et al.* (2001). "Genetic Evidence for Different Male and Female Roles During Cultural Transitions in the British Isles." *Publications of the National Academy of the Sciences* 98/9:5078–5083.

Wolfram, Herwig (1988). *History of the Goths.* Berkeley: University of California.

Wright, Philip (1976). *Jewish Tombstone Inscriptions.* Kingston: Privately printed.

Yates, Donald N. (1981) "Isengrimus à clef." *Third International Beast-Epic, Fable and Fabliau Colloquium, Münster 1979, Proceedings.* Ed. Jan Goossens and Timothy Sodmann. Niederdeutsche Studien: Cologne, 1981. Pp. 517–536.

Yogev, Gedalia (1978). *Diamonds and Coral: Anglo Dutch Jews and Eighteenth-century Trade.* Leicester: Leicester University Press.

Zerubavel, Eviatar (2003). *Time Maps: Collective Memory and the Social Shape of the Past.* Chicago: University of Chicago.

Zuckerman, Arthur J. (1972) *A Jewish Princedom in Feudal France, 768–900.* New York: Columbia University Press.

Index